school law.
cases and concepts

Third edition

MICHAEL W. LA MORTE
University of Georgia

Prentice Hall, Englewood Cliffs, New Jersey 07632

Library of Congress Cataloging-in-Publication Data

La Morte, Michael W.
  School law : cases and concepts / Michael W. La Morte.—3rd ed.
    p.   cm.
  Includes index.
  ISBN 0-13-793704-0
  1. Educational law and legislation—United States—Cases.
I. Title.
KF4118.L25 1990
344.73'07—dc20
[347.3047]
                                          89-32832
                                             CIP

Editorial/production supervision: Madelaine Cooke
Cover design: Edsal Enterprises
Manufacturing buyer: Peter Havens

KF
4118
.L25
1990

Printed in the United States of America

10 9 8 7 6 5 4 3 2 1

ISBN 0-13-793704-0

Prentice-Hall International (UK) Limited, *London*
Prentice-Hall of Australia Pty. Limited, *Sidney*
Prentice-Hall Canada Inc., *Toronto*
Prentice-Hall Hispanoamericana, S.A., *Mexico*
Prentice-Hall of India Private Limited, *New Delhi*
Prentice-Hall of Japan, Inc., *Tokyo*
Simon & Schuster Asia Pte. Ltd., *Singapore*
Editora Prentice-Hall do Brasil, Ltda., *Rio de Janeiro*

contents

Table of Cases xi

Preface xvii

A Note to Users of This Text xxi

**1 EDUCATIONAL GOVERNANCE: SOURCES
OF LAW AND THE COURTS**　　　　　　　　　　　　**1**

Introduction 1
I. Sources of Law 3
   A. *Federal Level* *3*
      1. Constitution and Amendments 4
         a. Historical Perspective 4
         b. Due Process and Equal Protection 6
            (1) Due Process 6
            (2) Equal Protection 9
      2. Statutes 10
      3. Case Law 11
      4. Executive Orders and Attorney General Opinions 12
   B. *State Level* *12*
      1. State Constitutions 12
      2. State Statutes 13
      3. Case Law 13
      4. State Board of Education, Chief State School Officer, and State
         Department of Education 14
      5. Attorney General Opinions 14
   C. *Local Level* *15*
II. The American Judicial System 15
   A. *State Court Systems* *16*
   B. *Federal Court System* *17*

    1. District Courts   17
    2. Courts of Appeals   17
    3. Supreme Court   19

2   SCHOOLS AND THE STATE   21

Introduction   21
  I. Compulsory Attendance   22
    A. *Satisified by Parochial, Private, or Home School Attendance*   22
      Pierce v. *Society of Sisters*   22
      Notes and Questions   25
    B. *Regulation of Nonpublic Schools*   27
    C. *Home Instruction*   28
    D. *Admission Issues*   29
 II. Religion in the Schools   30
    A. *School-Sponsored Prayer and Bible Reading*   30
      1. Recitation of a State Prayer   31
        Engel v. *Vitale*   31
      2. Prayer and Bible Reading   36
        School District of Abington Township v. *Schempp* and *Murray*
        v. *Curlett*   36
      3. Silent Prayer, Meditation, and Voluntary Prayer   40
        Wallace v. *Jaffree*   40
        Notes and Questions   47
    B. *The Teaching of Evolution*   50
      Edwards v. *Aguillard*   51
      Notes   55
    C. *Textbooks*   56
    D. *Distribution of Religious Literature*   57
    E. *Released and Shared Time and Religious Instruction*   57
III. Use of Facilities   59
    Country Hills Christian Church v. *Unified School District
    No. 512*   60
    Notes and Questions   63
IV. Aid to Nonpublic Schools   65
 V. School Fees   68
    Hartzell v. *Connell*   68
    Notes and Questions   71
VI. Immunization   72
    Brown v. *Stone*   73
    Notes   75

3 STUDENTS AND THE LAW 76

Introduction 76
- I. Freedom of Expression 77
  - A. The Tinker Doctrine 77
    - Tinker v. Des Moines Independent Community School District 77
    - Notes 85
  - B. Limiting the Tinker Doctrine 86
    - 1. Nonpolitical Speech 86
      - Bethel School District No. 403 v. Fraser 86
      - Notes 91
    - 2. School-Sponsored Expressive Activities 92
      - Hazelwood School District v. Kuhlmeier 92
      - Notes and Questions 97
  - C. Participation in Patriotic Exercises 99
    - Lipp v. Morris 100
    - Notes and Questions 101
- III. Suspension, Expulsion, Disciplinary Transfer 102
  - A. Suspension 102
    - Goss v. Lopez 102
    - Notes and Questions 111
  - B. Expulsion 112
    - Gonzalez v. McEuen 112
    - Notes and Questions 115
  - C. Disciplinary Transfer 116
- III. Corporal Punishment 116
  - Ingraham v. Wright 117
  - Notes and Questions 121
- IV. Search of Students and Lockers 123
  - A. Student Search 124
    - New Jersey v. T.L.O. 124
    - Notes and Questions 130
  - B. Intrusive Search 131
    - Bellnier v. Lund 131
    - Notes and Questions 133
  - C. Locker Search 134
- V. Dress and Grooming 135
  - A. Dress 135
    - Bannister v. Paradis 135
    - Notes and Questions 139
  - B. Grooming 139
    - Davenport v. Randolph County Board of Education 140
    - Notes and Questions 141
- VI. Pregnancy, Parenthood, Marriage 142

VII. Education of Handicapped Students   143
  A. Defining the Limits of a "Free Appropriate Education"   145
     Board of Education of the Hendrick Hudson
     Central School District v. Rowley   145
     Notes   152
  B. Communicable Disease as a Handicap   154
     Thomas v. Atascadero Unified School District   155
     Notes   159
VIII. Participation in Extracurricular Activities   160
  A. Legal Status of Extracurricular Activities   160
     Braesch v. DePasquale   160
     Notes and Questions   165
  B. Athletics   166
     1. Married Students   167
        Beeson v. Kiowa County School District RE-1   167
        Notes and Questions   169
     2. Female Participation   169
        Leffel v. Wisconsin Interscholastic Association   170
        Notes   175
     3. Participation of Handicapped Students   176
        Kampmeier v. Nyquist   176
        Notes and Questions   177
IX. School Punishment for Out-of-School Offenses   177

4 TEACHERS AND THE LAW 182

Introduction   182
  I. Nonrenewal and Dismissal   183
     Board of Regents of State Colleges v. Roth   183
     Notes and Questions   188
 II. Freedom of Expression   189
  A. Tenured Teacher's Public Expression   191
     Pickering v. Board of Education   191
     Notes   195
  B. Nontenured Teacher's Freedom of Expression   197
     Mt. Healthy City School District Board of Education v. Doyle   197
     Notes   201
  C. Use of School-System Mail   201
     Perry Education Association v. Perry Local Educators' Association   201
     Notes   206
 III. Academic Freedom   207

A.   Appropriate Materials   207
    Fowler v. Board of Education of Lincoln County   207
    Notes and Questions   213
B.   Political Speakers   213
    Wilson v. Chancellor   213
    Notes and Questions   219
IV.   Drug Testing   219
V.   Dress   220
East Hartford Education Association v. Board of Education of Town of East Hartford   220
Notes and Questions   224
VI.   Teacher as Exemplar   225
A.   Homosexual Teacher   226
    Gaylord v. Tacoma School District No. 10   226
    Notes and Questions   234
B.   Adulterous Teacher   236
    Erb v. Iowa State Board of Public Instruction   236
    Notes and Questions   240
C.   Criminal Activities   241
    Gillett v. Unified School District No. 276   241
    Note   246
D.   Impropriety with Students   246
    Barcheski v. Board of Education of Grand Rapids Public Schools   246
    Note   250
VII.   Employment Discrimination   251
A.   Racial Discrimination   252
B.   Sex Discrimination   254
    Marshall v. Kirkland   254
    Notes   258
C.   Pregnancy   259
    Ponton v. Newport News School Board   260
    Notes and Questions   264
D.   Religious Discrimination   265
E.   Age Discrimination   266
    Geller v. Markham   267
    Notes and Question   273
F.   Discrimination against the Handicapped   273
VIII.   Teacher Bargaining   275
A.   Dismissal of Striking Teachers   276
    Hortonville Joint School District No. 1 v. Hortonville Education Association   276
B.   Compulsory Union Dues   281
    Abood v. Detroit Board of Education   281
    Note   285

IX. Political Activities 285

5 SCHOOL DESEGREGATION   288

Introduction 288
I. Historical Perspective 289
  A. *Separate but Equal Doctrine* *289*
    Plessy v. *Ferguson* 289
    Notes and Questions 298
  B. *De Jure Public School Segregation*
    Unconstitutional (Brown I) *298*
    Brown v. *Board of Education of Topeka* 299
    Notes and Questions 303
  C. *Implementation (Brown II)* *303*
    Brown v. Board of Education of Topeka 304
    Notes and Questions 306
II. Desegration in the South 306
  A. *Freedom of Choice* *307*
    Green v. *County School Board of New Kent County* 307
    Notes and Questions 312
  B. *Defining the Scope of the Duty to Eliminate the Dual School System* *312*
    Swann v. *Charlotte-Mecklenburg Board of Education* 312
    Notes and Questions 323
III. Desegregation in Nonsouthern States 323
  A. *Nonsouthern Segregation* *324*
    Keyes v. *School District No. 1* 324
    Notes and Questions 336
  B. *Interdistrict Integration* *337*
    Milliken v. *Bradley* 337
    Notes and Questions 347
IV. Litigation after *Milliken* 348
  A. *Release from Court Order* *348*
  B. *Effect of Public Housing* *350*

6 SCHOOL FINANCE REFORM   351

Introduction 351
I. Early Decisions 353
II. Fiscal Neutrality 353
III. *Rodriguez* *354*
  San Antonio Independent School District v. *Rodriguez* 354
  Notes and Questions 369

IV. Post-*Rodriguez* Litigation 369
     Horton v. *Meskill* 372
     Notes and Questions 376
     Listing of Cases 377

7 EDUCATOR AND SCHOOL DISTRICT LIABILITY   381

Introduction 381
  I. School District Immunity 382
      A. *Liability under State Law* *382*
      B. *Liability under Federal Law* *383*
          Wood v. *Strickland* 383
          Notes and Questions 389
          Carey v. *Piphus* 390
 II. Educator Liability 394
      A. *Intentional Torts* *394*
      B. *Negligence* *394*
          1. Duty of Care 395
          2. Standard of Care 395
          3. Proximate Cause 396
          4. Actual Loss or Injury 396
      C. *Defenses for Negligence* *396*
III. Duties of Supervision 397
      A. *Before and after School* *397*
      B. *During School Hours* *398*
      C. *Off-Campus Activities* *400*
 IV. Parental Consent 400
  V. Malpractice 401
 VI. Insurance 401
      Questions 401

APPENDIX A   ANALYZING A COURT DECISION   404

**APPENDIX B   AN INTRODUCTION TO RESEARCH
                IN SCHOOL LAW**   407

**APPENDIX C   THE CONSTITUTION OF THE UNITED
                STATES OF AMERICA—EDITED**   418

APPENDIX D   STATUTORY MATERIAL   425

Title VII of the Civil Rights Act of 1964—P.L. 88-352 425

Pregnancy Discrimination Act of 1978—P.L. 95-555   427

Age Discrimination in Employment Act of 1967—P.L. 90-202   428

Age Discrimination in Employment Act Amendements of 1978—P.L. 95-256   429

Age Discrimination in Employment Act Amendments of 1986—P.L. 99-592   430

Title IX of the Education Amendments of 1972—P.L. 92-318   430

Section 504 of the Rehabilitation Act of 1973—P.L. 93-112   431

Family Educational Rights and Privacy Act of 1974—P.L. 93-380   432

Equal Access Act of 1984—P.L. 98-377   434

Civil Rights–42 U.S.C. § 1981–1983   436

Glossary   437

Index   441

table of cases*

A.W. v. Northwest R-1 School District
Abbott v. Burke
Abood v. Detroit Board of Education
Acanfora v. Board of Education of Montgomery County
Aguilar v. Felton
Albach v. Olde
Alexander v. Holmes County Board of Education
Ambach v. Norwick
Anable v. Ford
Andrews v. Drew Municipal Separate School District
Ansonia Board of Education v. Philbrook
Armour v. Nix
Austin Independent School District v. United States
Avery v. Homewood City Board of Education

B.M. v. Montana
Bailey v. Truby
Bangor Baptist Church v. Maine
Bannister v. Paradis
Barbier v. Connolly
Barcheski v. Board of Education of Grand Rapids Public Schools
Bartell v. Palos Verdes Peninsula School District
Beeson v. Kiowa County School District RE-1
Bell v. Board of Education, Akron Public Schools
Bell v. U-32 Board of Education
Bellnier v. Lund
Bennett v. Livermore School District
Bensalem School District v. Pennsylvania

Bethel School District No. 403 v. Fraser
Bishop v. Colaw
Blackman v. Brown
Blaine v. Board of Education, Haysville Unified School District No. 261
Blase v. Illinois
Blessing v. Mason County Board of Education
Board of Education, Island Trees Union Free School District No. 26 v. Pico
Board of Education, Levittown Union Free School District v. Nyquist
Board of Education of City School District of Cincinnati v. Walter
Board of Education of Hendrick Hudson Central School District v. Rowley
Board of Education of Long Beach Unified School District v. Jack M.
Board of Regents of State Colleges v. Roth
Bob Jones University v. United States
Bonner v. City of Prichard
Boothbay v. Longley
Bowers v. Hardwick
Braesch v. DePasquale
Brands v. Sheldon Community School
Breen v. Kahl
Breese v. Smith
Breitling v. Solenberger
Brosnan v. Livonia Public Schools
Broward County School Board v. Ruiz
Brown v. Bathke
Brown v. Board of Education of Topeka (I)
Brown v. Board of Education of Topeka (II)
Brown v. Board of Education of Topeka (III)
Brown v. Stone
Buckel v. Prentice
Burlington School Committee v. Department of Education of Massachusetts

* Edited cases are indicated by italics.

xi

Burruss v. Wilkerson

Burton v. Cascade School District Union High School No. 5

Buse v. Smith

Caldwell v. Cannady

Calendra v. State College Area School District

California Federal Savings and Loan Association v. Guerra

Campbell v. Board of Education of Town of New Milford

Cape v. Tennessee Secondary School Athletic Association

Cardiff v. Bismarck Public School District

Carey v. Piphus

Cary v. Board of Education of Adams-Arapahoe School District 28-J

Chalk v. United States District Court

Chamberlin v. Dade County Board of Public Instruction

Chicago Teachers Union Local No. 1 v. Hudson

Christensen v. Graham

Citizens Concerned for Separation of Church and State v. City and County of Denver

Clark v. Huntsville City Board of Education

Clark v. Shoreline School District No. 412

Clements v. Board of Trustees of the Sheridan County School District No. 2

Cleveland Board of Education v. La Fleur

Cochran v. Chidester School District

Collins v. Chandler Unified School District

Columbus Board of Education v. Penick

Committee for Public Education and Religious Liberty v. Nyquist

Committee for Public Education and Religious Liberty v. Regan

Connecticut State Federation of Teachers v. Board of Education Members

Connick v. Myers

Cooper v. Aaron

Cooper v. Eugene School District No. 4J

Council for Better Schools v. Wilkerson

Country Hills Christian Church v. Unified School District No. 512

Cox v. Dardanelle Public School District

Crockett v. Sorenson

Dailey v. Los Angeles Unified School District

Dale v. Board of Education, Lemmon Independent School District

Dallam v. Cumberland Valley School District

Danson v. Casey

Davenport v. Randolph County Board of Education

Day v. South Park Independent School District

Dayton Board of Education v. Brinkman

Dibortolo v. Metropolitan School District of Washington Township

Dickens v. Johnson County Board of Education

Dickey v. Robinson

Dike v. School Board of Orange County

diLeo v. Greenfield

District 27 Community School Board v. Board of Education of the City of New York

Doe v. Renfrow

Donohue v. Copiague Union Free School District

Dorsey v. Bale

Dowell v. Board of Education of Oklahoma City Public Schools

Drake v. Covington County Board of Education

Dupree v. Alma School District No. 30

Duro v. District Attorney, Second Judicial District of North Carolina

East Hartford Education Association v. Board of Education of Town of East Hartford

East Jackson Public Schools v. Michigan

Ector County Independent School District v. Hopkins

Edgewood Independent School District v. Kirby

Edwards v. Aguillard

Engel v. Vitale

Erb v. Iowa State Board of Public Instruction

Estate of Thornton v. Caldor, Inc.

Everson v. Board of Education of Township of Ewing

Fair School Finance Council of Oklahoma v. Oklahoma

Farrington v. Tokushige

Ferrell v. Dallas Independent School District

Firefighters Local Union No. 1784 v. Stotts

Fisher v. Snyder
Florey v. Sioux Falls School District 49-5
Ford v. Manuel
Fowler v. Board of Education of Lincoln County
Fowler v. Williamson
Freeman v. Flake

Garcia v. Miera
Garnett v. Trenton School District
Gaylord v. Tacoma School District No. 10
Geller v. Markham
General Electric Company v. Gilbert
Georgia Association of Retarded Citizens v. McDaniel
Gillett v. Unified School District No. 276
Gish v. Board of Education of the Borough of Paramus
Givhan v. Western Line Consolidated School District
Goetz v. Ansell
Gong Lum v. Rice
Gonzales v. McEuen
Goodwin v. Cross County School District No. 7
Gosney v. Sonora Independent School District
Goss v. Lopez
Graham v. Central Community School District of Decatur County
Grand Rapids School District v. Ball
Green v. County School Board of New Kent County
Griffin v. County School Board of Prince Edward County
Grigg v. Virginia
Grove City College v. Bell
Gutierrez v. School District R-1

Hall v. Board of School Commissioners of Mobile County
Hall v. Shelby County Board of Education
Hampton v. Orleans Parish School Board
Harlow v. Fitzgerald
Harrah Independent School District v. Martin
Hartzell v. Connell
Hazelwood School District v. Kuhlmeier
Heard v. Payne
Helena Elementary School District No. 1 v. Montana

Hennessy v. Webb
Hernandez v. Hanson
Honig v. Doe
Hornbeck v. Somerset County Board of Education
Horton v. Goose Creek Independent School District
Horton v. Meskill
Hortonville Joint School District No. 1 v. Hortonville Education Association
Hoyem v. Manhatten Beach City School District
Hunter v. Board of Education of Montgomery County

In re Grossman
Independent School District No. 8 of Seiling v. Swanson
Ingraham v. Wright
Irving Independent School District v. Tatro

Jackson v. Dorrier
Jager v. Douglas County School District
James v. Board of Education of Central School District No. 1
Jefferson v. Ysleta Independent School District
Jefferson County School District R-1 v. Justus
Jenkins v. State of Missouri
Jepsen v. Florida Board of Regents
Jesseman v. New Hampshire
Johnson v. Ouachita Parish Police Jury
Johnson v. Transportation Agency, Santa Clara
Jones v. Latexo Independent School District
Jordan v. School District of City of Erie

Kampmeier v. Nyquist
Kansas v. Stein
Kardmas v. Dickinson Public Schools
Katzman v. Cumberland Valley School District
Kelley v. Metropolitan County Board of Education of Nashville and Davidson County
Keyes v. School District No. 1
Kimble v. Worth County R-III Board of Education
King v. Saddleback Junior College District
Knights of the Ku Klux Klan v. East Baton Rouge Parish School Board

Knowles v. Kansas
Kohl v. Woodhaven Learning Center
Kraus v. Board of Education of the City of Jennings
Kukor v. Grover

Labrosse v. Saint Bernard Parish School Board
Lamb v. Panhandle Community Unit School District No. 2
Lanner v. Wimmer
Larry P. v. Riles
Leffel v. Wisconsin Interscholastic Athletic Association
Lemon v. Kurtzman
Levitt v. Committee for Public Education and Religious Liberty
Lipp v. Morris
Livingston School Board v. Louisiana State Board of Education
Louisiana v. Mora
Lujan v. Colorado State Board of Education
Lynch v. Donnelly

M.M. v. Anker
Madera v. Board of Education of the City of New York
Maine v. Thiboutot
Malnak v. Yogi
Marbury v. Madison
Mark A. v. Grant Wood Area Education Agency
Marsh v. Chambers
Marshall v. Kirkland
Martinez v. School Board of Hillsborough County
Massie v. Henry
Matter of McMillan
May v. Evansville-Vanderburgh School Corporation
Mazanec v. North Judson-San Pierre School Corporation
McClung v. Board of Education of City of Washington C. H.
McCollum v. Board of Education of School District No. 71
McConnell v. Anderson
McDaniel v. Thomas
McInnis v. Ogilvie
McInnis v. Shapiro
McLean Independent School District v. Andrews

McNaughton v. Circleville Board of Education
Meek v. Pittenger
Meltzer v. Board of Public Instruction of Orange County
Members of the Jamestown School Committee v. Schmidt
Memphis American Federation of Teachers v. Board of Education of Memphis City Schools
Mercer v. Board of Trustees, North Forest Independent School District
Milliken v. Bradley
Milliken v. Green
Mills v. Board of Education of the District of Columbia
Missouri ex rel. Gaines v. Canada
Monell v. Department of Social Services of City of New York
Monnier v. Todd County Independent School District
Monroe v. Pape
Montana v. Board of Trustees of School District No. 1
Moore v. Knowles
Morgan v. Nucci
Morrison v. State Board of Education
Mozert v. Hawkins County Board of Education
Mt. Healthy City School District Board of Education v. Doyle
Mueller v. Allen
Muka v. Sturgis
Murray v. Curlett

National Gay Task Force v. Board of Education of Oklahoma City
National Socialist White People's Party v. Ringers
Nebraska v. Faith Baptist Church
Neuhaus v. Federico
New Braunfels Independent School District v. Armke
New Jersey v. Massa
New Jersey v. T.L.O.
New Life Baptist Church Academy v. Town of East Long Meadow
New Mexico State Board of Education v. Stoudt
New York State Association for Retarded Children v. Carey

Newport News Shipbuilding and Dry Dock Company v. Equal Employment Opportunity Commission
North Dakota v. Rivinius
North Dakota v. Shaver
North Haven Board of Education v. Bell
Northshore School District No. 417 v. Kinnear

Odenheim v. Carlstadt-East Rutherford Regional School District
Ohio v. Schmidt
Ohio Civil Rights Commission v. Dayton Christian Schools
Olesen v. Board of Education
Olsen v. Oregon
Oster v. Kneip
Owen v. City of Independence

Palmer v. Board of Education of the City of Chicago
Parents Association of P.S. 16 v. Quinones
Patchogue-Medford Congress of Teachers v. Board of Education of Patchogue-Medford Union Free School District
Patsy v. Board of Regents of Florida
Pauley v. Bailey
Pauley v. Kelly
Paulson v. Minidoka County School District No. 331
Pegram v. Nelson
Pennsylvania Association for Retarded Children v. Pennsylvania
Perry v. Sindermann
Perry Education Association v. Perry Local Educators' Association
Peter W. v. San Francisco Unified School District
Peterson v. Board of Education of School District No. 1
Pickering v. Board of Education of Township High School District 205
Pierce v. Society of Sisters
Plessy v. Ferguson
Plyler v. Doe
Police Department of the City of Chicago v. Mosley
Ponton v. Newport News School Board
Public Funds for Public Schools of New Jersey v. Byrne

R.R. v. Board of Education of the Shore Regional High School District
Raleigh v. Independent School District No. 625
Resnick v. East Brunswick Township Board of Education
Richard v. St. Landry Parish School Board
Richards v. Thurston
Riddick v. School Board of City of Norfolk
Ring v. Grand Forks School District No. 1
Roberts v. Van Buren Public Schools
Robinson v. Cahill (I)
Romans v. Crenshaw
Ross v. Springfield School District No. 19
Rowland v. Mad River School District
Rucker v. Colonial School District
Rupp v. Bryant
Russo v. Central School District No. 1

S. v. Board of Education, San Francisco Unified School District
Salazer v. Honig
Salinas v. School District of Kansas City
San Antonio Independent School District v. Rodriguez
San Diego Committee Against Registration and the Draft v. Governing Board of Grossmont Union High School District
Scarnato v. Parker
Schaill v. Tippecanoe School Corporation
Schmerber v. California
School Board of Nassau County v. Arline
School Board of Palm Beach County v. State Board of Education of Florida
School District of Abington Township v. Schempp
Seattle School District No. 1 of King County v. Washington
Serrano v. Priest
Shofstall v. Hollins
Sloan v. Lemon
Smith v. Board of School Commissioners of Mobile County
Smith v. West Virginia State Board of Education
Snyder v. Charlotte Public School District
Spring Branch Independent School District v. Stamos
Stanton v. Brunswick School Department
State ex rel. Woodahl v. Straub
Stein v. Plainwell Community Schools

Stoddard v. School District No. 1
Stone v. Graham
Sullivan v. Meade Independent School District No. 101
Swann v. Charlotte-Mecklenburg Board of Education
Sweatt v. Painter
Sweezy v. New Hampshire

Taborn v. Hammonds
Tasby v. Estes
Texas v. Project Principle
Thomas v. Atascadero Unified School District
Thomas v. Engelking
Tibbs v. Board of Education of the Township of Franklin
Tinker v. Des Moines Independent Community School District
Titus v. Lindberg
Trent v. Perritt
Truelove v. Wilson
Tudor v. Board of Education of Borough of Rutherford
Tyler v. Hot Springs School District No. 6

United States v. Board of Education of Jackson County
United States v. LULAC
United States v. Overton

United States v. South Carolina
United States v. Yonkers Board of Education
Upshur v. Love

Van Dusartz v. Hatfield

Wallace v. Jaffree
Warren v. National Association of Secondary School Principals
Washakie County School District No. 1 v. Herschler
Webb v. McCullough
Webby v. Dukakis
West Virginia State Board of Education v. Barnette
Wiley v. Franklin
Williams v. Board of Education for Marianna School District
Willoughby v. Lehrbass
Wilson v. Chancellor
Wimberly v. Labor and Industrial Relations Commission of Missouri
Wisconsin v. Yoder
Wolman v. Walter
Wood v. Strickland
Wygant v. Jackson Board of Education

Zamora v. Pomeroy
Zorach v. Clauson
Zweifel v. Joint District No. 1

preface

Public school educators are well aware that courts, over the last several decades, have played a significant role in establishing educational policy. Decisions in such areas as school desegregation, prayer and Bible reading, public school financing, student rights, and personnel issues attest to the extent and magnitude of judicial influence. Foremost among the many reasons for the increased court involvement has been the perception, especially of those holding minority views, that the judiciary was a receptive and efficacious branch of government. Although this contention is no longer as strongly held as it once was, the judiciary continues to be viewed as an institution willing to address issues other branches of government refuse to address or are reluctant even to recognize.

Over the years, judicial activity has produced a sizable body of school law with which educators should be familiar if they wish to conduct themselves in a legally defensible manner. Those educators who "fly by the seat of their pants" or who act on the basis of what they think the law "should be" may be in difficulty if sufficient thought is not given to the legal implications and ramifications of their policies or conduct. Consequently, this text provides introductory material for those educators and lay persons interested in K-12 educational issues who have little or no knowledge of, or background in, school law. This would include such groups as teachers, school administrators, school board members, preservice teachers, and public school students and their families.

It would be difficult for a one-volume work to cover all of the significant topics in school law. Therefore, this text attempts to address important issues in school law with an emphasis on those having an impact at the school-building level. Additionally, material is presented to enable the reader to better understand the sources of law under which educational policy is developed and carried out and a brief description of the dual judicial system. Also included are several appendices containing sections on how to analyze a court decision, how to research school law issues, an edited federal constitution, and edited statutory material. A glossary is included to provide the definitions of commonly used legal terminology.

Chapter 1 offers sufficient background to facilitate comprehension of succeeding chapters. Included in this chapter is a discussion of topics of underlying importance with which educators may be unfamiliar: the legal significance of the sources of law under which educators operate; federal and state constitutions; federal and state statutes; state school board policy; attorney general's opinions; local school board policy and local school policy; the significance of the Fourteenth Amendment's Due Process and Equal Protection provisions as a basis for many school lawsuits; the importance of case law in establishing educational policy; and the organization of the American dual court system.

Chapter 2 examines the extent of the state's and local school system's authority when individuals disagree with educational policy. A reading of the court decisions in this chapter reveals the judiciary's attempt to establish a balance between the legitimate demands or objections of individuals toward education policy and school authorities' perception of their responsibility to the greater population. School law issues selected to illuminate this area include compulsory school attendance; religion in the schools; use of facilities; aid to nonpublic schools; school fees; and immunization.

This writer has found that issues pertaining to students and teachers are of particular interest to school law students; therefore, Chapters 3 and 4, which address these topics, comprise a major portion of the text. Chapter 3 presents material pertinent to student interests, such as freedom of expression; suspension, disciplinary transfer, expulsion; corporal punishment; search; dress and grooming; pregnancy, parenthood, and marriage; education of handicapped students; participation in extracurricular activities; and school punishment for out-of-school offenses. Chapter 4 examines such teacher-related issues as nonrenewal and dismissal; freedom of expression; academic freedom; drug testing; dress; the teacher as an exemplar; employment discrimination based on race, sex, pregnancy, religion, and age; teacher bargaining; and political activities of teachers.

Chapters 5 and 6 provide a historical legal perspective to the issues of school desegregation and the legal attacks on the adequacy of state school finance plans. Although a 1954 United States Supreme Court decision held de jure public school segregation to be unconstitutional, racial segregation in the schools—the subject of Chapter 5—continues to be an issue in many school systems across the country. Chapter 6 examines the issue of wealth disparity within a state as a factor in challenging a state's school-financing plan. This issue emerged as a legal one in the early 1970s and continues to be an issue in many states. A knowledge of the complexities of school finance is not necessary for an understanding of the material in this chapter.

Chapter 7 addresses the extent, if any, of educator and school district liability for damages as a result of their official action or inaction. Since the law in this area varies considerably among the states, emphasis is given to such general concepts as duty and standard of care, school district immunity, duties of supervision, and malpractice. Tort law is a highly specialized branch of law that is exceedingly complicated; therefore, this chapter makes the reader aware of the potential of liability for damages resulting from improper behavior.

Appendices provide additional information enabling the reader to gain a broader perspective. Appendices A and B are designed to be primers for the reader who wishes to become more adept at analyzing court decisions or engaging in school-related legal research. Appendix B is designed to provide rudimentary legal-research methodology and information on primary and secondary legal resources available to those interested in legal research. Appendix C contains sections of the United States Constitution and amendments that are most relevant for educators. Appendix D contains edited federal statutes having significance for educators. A glossary of often-used legal terminology is included for the reader's convenience in better understanding the edited court decisions.

Edited verbatim decisions constitute a substantial portion of this book. Such decisions provide a rich source of information, enabling a reader to gain an insight and understanding of school law that cannot be obtained through secondary analysis. The reading of a judge's or justice's written opinion—majority, concurring, or dissenting—provides valuable philosophical underpinnings for a thorough understanding of judicial rationale. It also enables the reader to relate a court's legal rationale to a specific factual context. Emphasis is on substantive school law issues. Deleted from the edited cases is material not related to the issue being examined, material pertaining to technical legal matters, and procedural legal issues that are of primary interest to attorneys.

Inclusion of a particular decision was based on several factors. These included selecting the case decided by the highest level court that had addressed the specific school law issue under consideration, thereby providing the widest applicability; the case that best represented the majority of cases in areas where the law was not well settled; or the case that best illustrated the historic evolvement of the case law under consideration.

Notes and questions follow many of the edited decisions. The notes are designed to provide helpful information to the reader, such as background material; additional citations for those interested in pursuing further the issue under consideration; the extent to which the law is well settled; or other views if the law is not well settled. Provocative questions are included to illuminate the topic and foster discussion.

This book has not been written with the intention of expressing opinions for or against views espoused by school administrators, teachers, or students, nor to contend that the judiciary is a meddlesome institution thwarting the efforts of educators. Rather, the book's pupose is to provide those who are involved in public education with a rudimentary knowledge base for making educationally sound decisions within the legal framework. Having such knowledge may reduce the tendency to act on the basis of what the law should be rather than what it is. In that sense, this book stresses the descriptive, not the prescriptive.

The author assumes that public school students learn best about law and order through its observance by knowledgeable teachers, school administrators, and school board members. And since an important aspect of public school education is the inculcation in students of the notion that we are a "nation of laws and not of men," educators must be familiar with the school law to abide by it. This is of considerable concern to the author because of his experience as a youth under Adolph Hitler in Nazi Germany. It was observed that one strategy a dictator such as Hitler used to strengthen and solidify his power was the systematic breakdown of law in Germany. As the law was increasingly disregarded, the power of the Nazis increased, and the country became a "nation of men and not of laws."

In acknowledgment, students in my school law classes over the years deserve a special word of thanks not only for their scintillating and penetrating questions but also for sharing with me those school law topics they deemed important as they carried out their school-related responsibilities. Over the years, several students—Robert Meadows, Betty Hull, Jeffrey Williams, Lauren Anderson, and Pat McCollum—have made valuable contributions, and they have my gratitude. Neil McIntyre deserves special recognition for his assistance with this edition. He not only checked sources for accuracy and was persistent in dealing with administrative details, but proved himself to be an intellectually stimulating student of school law. Of course, any failure of omission or commission in this book is the sole responsibility of the author.

A book such as this does not serve as a substitute for competent legal advice should it be needed; however, in addition to a knowledge of school law, an understanding of the material in this book should help to foster a more fruitful exchange with an attorney when that is necessary.

Finally, it was a delight to have the opportunity of again revising this text, as the examination of school law issues continues to be, for me, an exciting and rewarding enterprise.

a note to users of this text

This textbook borrows from the teaching traditions of the legal community. It is a "casebook" not unlike those routinely used in the preparation of lawyers in law schools. Such texts are collections of actual court opinions, in which instructional material and exposition are minimized and through which students are expected on their own to induce legal principles. Casebook authors—who must also be considered to be editors if one is to understand the essence of a casebook—select, edit, and arrange judicial opinions so as to facilitate extracting what the author considers to be important points of law. Brief written comments and questions assist in this process. Accordingly, this author intends the presentation of cases herein not as supplementary illustrations of the textual material but rather as the book's primary raw material.

A major advantage ascribed to discovering the law from casebooks is the opportunity to learn both legal rationale and reasoning. To this end, students encounter noteworthy examples of judicial decision making and engaging, themselves, in such reasoning. Although a knowledge of specific information is essential, understanding legal rationale and learning to engage in legal reasoning are more important, in this author's view, than acquiring an encyclopedic knowledge of specific laws. The author submits that educators must be able to do more than merely recite laws affecting schools, and readers looking for a comprehensive treatment of school law in this text will be frustrated. Few factual patterns encountered by the practicing educator will match perfectly an explicit legal rule. Having a broad understanding of legal precedent combined with staying abreast of school law developments will provide the educator on the firing line with a background to deal with the host of novel situations which may be faced.

This text may be used with a Socratic method of teaching. When employing this teaching strategy, the instructor assigns a group of cases to be read and analyzed, and in class he or she calls individually on students orally to "brief" the cases (see Analyzing a Court Decision—Appendix A). The instructor attempts through questioning to draw from students relevant legal principles; in this process students are challenged to the limits of their abilities to make increasingly fine observations and distinctions; and criticism of the student's recitation is provided. Initially, this individual questioning may not always be pleasant for students, but they soon learn that casual readings of cases for their main ideas are insufficient; instead, cases must be read slowly, deliberately, and repeatedly. The technique demands thorough preparation from both instructor and student. This method prepares students well for written examinations consisting of hypothetical, complex fact patterns, which students are required to analyze in accordance with applicable law.

This author has for some time successfully employed this demanding method in his school law classes. He has found that analyzing case law does indeed cause students to restructure their thinking on the law. Additionally, the promise of having to recite in class motivates most students to superb performance which unquestionably enhances learning. Inducing students to think "on their feet" and to perform under pressure seems to be highly appropriate in the preparation of educational leaders. Whether or not other instructors choose to complement this casebook with the Socratic method, it is hoped that the cases speak to at least the rudiments of an enormous, diffuse body of law and that the book will challenge readers to further study.

Finally, for those instructors who have access to a law library, a class visit is highly recommended. Such a visit has a number of advantages. It not only provides an opportunity to discuss and locate legal material (see An Introduction to Research in School Law—Appendix B), but it also lessens the common perception that a law library is a foreboding place where only lawyers are welcome. Introducing students in this manner to the various reporter systems, *Index to Legal Periodicals,* law reviews, state materials, *Shepard's Citations,* "slip" opinions, and *United States Law Week* has always been a well-received class activity.

educational governance: sources of law and the courts

Introduction

Governance in America is based on the notion that we are "a nation of laws and not of men." Consequently, those involved in making and enforcing public school policy should ensure that their actions are lawful. Educational policy may not be enforced arbitrarily or capriciously but must be based on such appropriate legal authority as federal or state constitutional or statutory provisions, state board of education or state department of education regulations, case law, or local school board policy.

Several forces are operating, however, that at times make it difficult for those who administer public schools to function in a lawful manner. These forces include a federal system of government composed of several levels and corresponding branches that bear on the educational enterprise, changing and sometimes conflicting laws or policies, and a climate of uncertainty regarding case law due to the frequent involvement of the judiciary in establishing educational policy.

Under the federal system, the three levels of government—federal, state, and local—all have a voice in educational matters, although not necessarily in unison. Difficulties develop, since some areas of educational governance overlap considerably in responsibility among the three levels of government and their corresponding branches. These difficulties are exacerbated not only by the unclear delineation of authority but also by the uncertainty of determining which authority is supreme when irreconcilable conflicts exist.

Although education is not specifically mentioned in the federal Constitution, the federal government has had an historic involvement in it. Programs under various federal laws pertaining to education in recent years have made up approximately 6 percent of the total amount of money expended for public elementary and secondary education. Perhaps of greater importance is the pervasive and significant force of the federal judiciary in influencing educational policy. Controversial education issues such as racial segregation in schools, financing of schools, due process for both students and teachers, the role of religion in the schools, and the extent to which students and teachers may engage in freedom of expression have all been addressed by the federal judiciary.

State government has plenary power over public education, and this power is carried out by constitutional and statutory provisions, executive acts, state board of education policies, and actions of chief state school officers. The roles of governmental participants vary among the state governments. The extent of state authority over local school systems is also not uniform; however, it is generally considered to be directly proportional to the state's financial contribution to public education.

The degree of authority that local school systems have over educational matters depends on a state's constitutional and statutory provisions. These local powers may be delegated or implied. Although it is the prevailing belief that public schools are controlled locally, many students of educational governance suggest that a so-called myth of local control may be operating. They argue that in many instances the state has more meaningful power over education policy than the local school system does.

Since each level of government is inextricably intertwined in public educational governance, problems often arise for building-level educators—for instance, when one level or branch of government does not agree with policies or decisions made by another level or branch. Misunderstanding on the part of educators may also exist regarding the legitimate role of each of the levels of governance. Examples of these conflicts abound: a local school system not wishing to desegregate but forced to by a federal court order; "wealthy" local school systems barred, as a result of a state supreme court decision, from appreciably supplementing the state-financed program; and local school systems having to accept an amount of disruption by students wishing to express themselves on political, social or economic matters, protected by a United States Supreme Court decision.

The difficulty of attempting to administer schools in a lawful manner is compounded when educators, unfamiliar with the nuances of the legal system, perceive seeming inconsistencies and occasionally acrimonious disagreement among judges in certain court decisions. Such a situation occurs when a decision is changed one or more times as an educational issue winds its way through the appellate process. Occasionally, this process reveals sharp philosophical differences among judges. The lack of consistency in court decisions regarding certain issues is also troubling to some educators. They often find it difficult to understand why an educational practice has court approval in one state or area of federal jurisdiction and not in another. The legitimacy of a federal court overruling a state court's decision is also not always completely understood, especially when such a ruling increases the difficulty of administering schools because of strong local, state, or regional disagreement with such a ruling.

School administrators often view themselves as working in a climate of uncertainty as to the legality of their administrative decisions. This may be due to an insufficient knowledge of constitutional law as it pertains to educational matters or an inadequate knowledge of recent court decisions. Relying on what is perceived as sound educational practice in making administrative decisions is helpful, but it is not always a guarantee that the practice will avoid conflict with case law.

One remedy for ensuring lawful administrative conduct and reducing conflict and misunderstanding among educators is a systematic study of the sources of law under which educators operate. Such a study follows and is designed to illuminate the legitimate role of the various levels of government and their component branches. Although sources of law may be examined in various ways, a particularly fruitful method is to analyze those sources that spring from each level of government.

I. Sources of Law

A. Federal Level

At the federal level, the Constitution and its amendments, statutes, rules and regulations of administrative agencies, case law, presidential executive orders, and attorney general's opinions all constitute sources of law under which educators operate.

1. Constitution and Amendments

Although the federal Constitution does not contain the word education, constitutional interpretation by the judiciary has had unquestionable impact on educational policymaking. Particularly significant is the judiciary's interpretation of the Fourteenth Amendment to the Constitution. A brief examination of this amendment may be helpful, on the basis both of its historical origins and of its requirements for due process and equal protection of the law as they pertain to educational matters.

a. Historical Perspective Prior to the adoption of the Fourteenth Amendment in 1868, Americans, under the federal system of government, had a particular kind of dual relationship with state and national governments regarding their civil rights. This came about largely as a result of skepticism, if not an outright distrust, of central government that existed after the Revolutionary War as a consequence of experiences under British rule. To ensure that a central government would not again run roughshod over an individual's civil rights, a Bill of Rights was added to the Constitution shortly after that document was ratified. Protections afforded those early Americans under the Bill of Rights included: freedoms regarding religion, speech, press, peaceable assembly, and petitioning for a redress of grievances; a right to bear arms; protection against unreasonable searches and seizures; guarantee of a grand jury indictment in capital offenses; protection against being subject to double jeopardy or self-incrimination; the right of due process; the right to own property; the right to have a speedy trial by an impartial jury; and protection against excessive bail and cruel and unusual punishments. These protections, however, were those Americans had against their *central* government. They did not automatically have these rights against their state government as a result of the inclusion of the rights in the federal Constitution.

Protection of civil rights against state action was provided by state constitutions, and every state, as it was accepted into the Union, provided for a Bill of Rights similar to that found in the federal Constitution. It should be noted, however, that prior to the adoption of the Fourteenth Amendment, if a state's constitution did not contain a provision for guaranteeing, for instance, freedom of speech or religion, an American did not necessarily have those protections against his or her state. Although state constitutions may have contained language that afforded individuals their civil rights, as a practical matter, state-guaranteed civil rights protections were not always uniformly applied.

In the years prior to the Civil War, another factor influenced the dual relationship Americans had with their state and federal governments. For the most part, Americans, during that time, thought of themselves primarily as citizens of the state within which they resided and citizens of the United States secondarily. An individual considered himself a Virginian or New Yorker first, for instance, and an American citizen second. Although we have no way of knowing with any exactitude, it is entirely conceivable that regional allegiance, too, ran higher than national allegiance on the part of many (the South, before the Civil War, may be a prime example of this).

This dual relationship with state and central governments and the historic primary allegiance to one's state was significantly altered by the adoption of the Fourteenth Amendment to the Constitution in 1868. This amendment provided, in part, that

> All persons born or naturalized in the United States and subject to the jurisdiction thereof, are citizens of the United States and of the State wherein they reside. No State shall make or enforce any law which shall abridge the privileges or immunities of citizens of the United States. Nor shall any State deprive any person of life, liberty or property, without due process of law, nor deny to any person within its jurisdiction the equal protection of the laws.

From a constitutional standpoint, the juxtaposition of the words "are citizens of the United States and of the State wherein they reside" is most revealing, since the United States is mentioned first. The legal significance of this juxtaposition and subsequent language of the amendment have been interpreted as establishing national citizenship as being primary where certain questions dealing with individual rights are concerned.

This amendment, which was intended initially to guarantee rights to newly freed slaves, has also provided protection for the individual from various forms of arbitrary or capricious state action. Since the amendment affords national citizenship primacy regarding constitutional rights, an individual is shielded against state action that may run counter to guarantees he or she has as a citizen of the United States. Under this concept, the state cannot deprive a person of rights he or she has as an American. As a result of United States Supreme Court action, for instance, a state may not condone de jure racially segregated school systems. Neither may students be deprived of their freedoms pertaining to religion by school board policy that allows Bible reading or prayers during normal school hours. These are the kinds of rights individuals have as United States citizens, and no state action, local administrative conduct, or local school board policy may violate them.

Under the Fourteenth Amendment, a state and those operating under its auspices must honor those rights, guaranteed by the Constitution, federal statutes, and case law, that a person has as a result of being an

American. From a constitutional standpoint, these rights must be observed by the state and those operating under the color of the state, and they may not be infringed upon as a result of a state or local election, state or local administrative action, or state court action.

Proponents of a "state's rights theory" for American government have reluctantly accepted certain court decisions based on the Fourteenth Amendment and have adamantly refused to abide by others. Objection to the amendment by such groups is often based on the method used to gain its ratification. Ratification of the amendment was a required step for readmittance to the Union after the Civil War.

b. Due Process and Equal Protection   In addition to establishing the primacy of national citizenship with the protection of certain individual rights, the Fourteenth Amendment also provides for due process and equal protection of the law. These two concepts stem from an ideal of fairness in applying the law, and they are not necessarily mutually exclusive. In cases dealing with educational matters where the Fourteenth Amendment is cited, it is generally alleged that either (or both) due process or equal protection of the law has been denied. Although extremely complex in a legal sense, these concepts may best be understood by keeping in mind that they require government officials, which of course includes educators, to be fair as they conduct governmental business. This necessitates reasonable and noncapricious action, in addition to abiding by statute and case law, on the part of public school officials when dealing with clients or personnel.

[1] Due Process

In the broadest sense, a person has received due process of law under the Fourteenth Amendment when he or she has been treated essentially the same by state action or local government action as another person has under similar circumstances when he or she is subject to deprivation of life, liberty, or property. Under this concept, governmental action may not be unreasonable or capricious, and when clients are not treated alike there must be a sound basis for dissimilar treatment.

Although the line between substance and procedure is often quite hazy, some have drawn a distinction between so-called procedural and substantive due process of law. According to this view, procedural due process, in the larger sense, deals with the question of whether or not a person has been accorded fair and proper treatment or procedure when apprehended or tried in a court. Accused persons must be given twelve jurors, for instance, if everyone else in their circumstances is given twelve jurors. Evidence to be presented against them must have been obtained properly, and their trials must be conducted according to established procedures. Questions dealing with procedural due process in the educational arena have received increasing attention, particularly in the area of suspension and expulsion from school. Substantive due process essentially deals with the question of fair treatment of persons by those acting under the color of the state and also with the question of the fairness and reasonableness of laws, regulations, and policies in the light of our constitutional heritage. The Fifth Amendment also contains a due process clause, and although there are similarities with the Fourteenth Amendment provision, the Fifth Amendment is considered exclusively to be protection against the federal government.

As is the case with many concepts, due process resists definition in the dictionary sense. It is a dynamic rather than a static concept. The definition in each instance depends largely on a combination of the specific facts in a situation, the law governing the situation, the particular time in history in which judgment is being rendered, and the predilections of the individual judge(s) rendering the decision. The Supreme Court, for instance, has never unanimously agreed on a standard for due process. Yet it is the body that renders the ultimate and final decision regarding whether or not due process has been denied. This point, in addition to a discussion of the question of due process, was asserted by Justice Frankfurter in *Sweezy* v. *New Hampshire*, 354 U.S. 234 (1957):

> To be sure, this is a conclusion based on a judicial judgment in balancing two contending principles—the right of the citizen to political privacy, as protected by the Fourteenth Amendment, and the right of the State to self-protection. And striking the balance implies the exercise of judgment. This is the inescapable judicial task in giving substantive content, legally enforced, to the Due Process Clause, and it is a task ultimately committed to this Court. It must not be an exercise of whim or will. It must be an overriding judgment founded on something much deeper and more justifiable than personal preference. As far as it lies within human limitations, it must be an impersonal judgment. It must rest on fundamental presuppositions rooted in history to which widespread acceptance may be fairly attributed. Such a judgment must be arrived at in a spirit of humility when it counters the judgment of the State's highest court. But, in the end, judgment cannot be escaped—the judgment of this Court. (Pp. 266–67)

A basic issue—the balance between an individual's rights and the necessity to protect the larger society—is addressed by courts when deprivation of due process is alleged. Courts must determine whether or not a regulation, policy, law, lower-court decision, or action on the part of someone who had a duty to perform was warranted in either limiting or condoning a person's actions. A review of decisions involving educational matters reveals that courts consider many factors when examining alleged deprivation of due process by school officials. Foremost among these factors is whether, overall, the school official's judgment was educationally sound. Additionally, courts examine whether an official's actions were guided primarily by administrative convenience or represented the spirit of a conformity-minded, arrogant majority when there should have been a willingness on the part of the majority to accept a degree of nondisruptive deviance.

A brief discussion of social contract theory may amplify the genesis of the due process idea. Although the theory was discussed as early as Plato, its more familiar philosophical underpinnings were advanced by political philosophers several centuries ago, notably, Thomas Hobbes (*Leviathan*), John Locke (*Two Treaties of Government*), and Jean Jacques Rousseau (*The Social Contract*). Locke, whose social contract theory is probably the one most familiar in the English-speaking world, attacked the divine right of kings theory. He contended that societies were organized and ruled by the consent of the governed and not by one who had potential for becoming autocratic. Furthermore, he asserted that individuals by their nature had certain rights, which included life, liberty, and property. When by their own volition individuals left the primitive state of nature and agreed to be governed, they made a social contract with government that protected these natural rights. The justification for the state's existence, according to Locke, was based on its ability to protect these rights better than individuals could on their own. The price individuals paid for governmental protection was a relinquishment of the freedom they had in the state of nature. This was a limited type of "freedom," however, since it existed in an environment where there was greater potential for the "law of the jungle" and "might makes right" to prevail.

Many modern-day political theorists agree that the original thoughts of Locke and others regarding the social contract have come to stand for several propositions concerning the individual's relationship to government. These propositions include the notion that government rests on the consent of the governed; persons willingly yielded the freedom they had in the state of nature because they thought the state could offer them certain protections they could not provide for themselves; and although persons relinquished the freedom they had in the state of nature, their entering into a social contract with government included the government's guarantee against an arbitrary, capricious, and unreasonable denial of their rights of life, liberty, and property when they and the government interacted.

These propositions have considerable implications for educators. In accordance with social contract theory, school authorities have not only a legitimate but a mandatory role to play in protecting health and safety and in maintaining order. Students violating legitimate school rules may be subject to appropriate punitive action. Yet school authorities may not act arbitrarily, capriciously, or unreasonably toward individuals when protecting the majority, and due process must be provided when a liberty or property interest is involved.

[2] Equal Protection

Constitutional authorities contend that the Equal Protection Clause was inserted in the Fourteenth Amendment to ensure that blacks would be provided the same civil protections as white Americans. Under this notion, Negroes would not only have their civil rights protected, but they would also have the benefit of applicable laws. Although originally intended to ameliorate the transition from slavery to free status, the equal protection provision has had a dramatic effect in influencing policy in American public education.

From an educational standpoint, the Equal Protection Clause represents the legal basis for prohibiting unreasonable classifications. Although some type of classification is often necessary in laws, rules, or policies, arbitrariness may not play a part. Methods of classifying students in public schools have often been based on such factors as sex, age, intelligence, marital status, parents' residence, race, pregnancy or motherhood, conduct, test scores, and wealth of their community. For these methods of classification to conform with equal protection guarantees, a reasonable relationship must exist between the objective to be accomplished and the type of classification employed. Also, if the state renders a benefit to one person within a class, all within that class must receive the benefit equally; and if one person within a class is deprived of a benefit by the state, all within that class must be deprived equally. This concept was expressed many years ago by the United States Supreme Court in *Barbier* v. *Connolly,* 113 U.S. 27 (1885), when it stated:

> Class legislation, discriminating against some and favoring others, is prohibited, but legislation which, in carrying out a public purpose, is limited in its application, if within the sphere of its operation it affects alike all persons similarly situated, is not within the amendment. (P. 32)

The principal idea inherent in equal protection, as in due process, is the concept of fairness. And as is the case with due process, whether or not equal protection has been granted or denied depends upon a balancing of several elements. These include sociological and psychological factors, sound educational policy, the benefit of a larger good to society as a result of the classification, contemporary customs and mores, and the protection of the individual's rights in the light of these considerations.

Courts have often employed a two-level test for measuring classifications against the Equal Protection Clause. One is a "rational basis" test, which is employed when a "fundamental interest" is not involved. Under this test, there must be a sound reason for the classification, and all those classified alike must be treated as uniformly as possible. Additionally, the burden of proof is on the complainant to demonstrate that a challenged law or policy has no rational basis to achieve a legitimate state objective. By using this test, the United States Supreme Court has commonly exercised restraint in holding legislation in violation of the equal-protection provision of the Fourteenth Amendment.

A strict-scrutiny test is applied when a "fundamental interest" or "suspect classification" is involved. A presumption of constitutional validity disappears when a classification is "suspect." Examples of such classification include race, national origin, alienage, indigency, and illegitimacy. At this time sex is not considered a suspect classification. The strict-scrutiny test was discussed by the United States Supreme Court in *Plyler* v. *Doe*, 457 U.S. 202 (1982). The Court explained that some classifications are more likely than others to reflect deep-seated prejudice rather than legislative rationality in pursuit of some legitimate objective. It also stated that certain groups have historically experienced "political powerlessness" and thus have needed special protection from the majority. In situations where a suspect class or fundamental right is involved, the Court indicated that it is appropriate to enforce the mandate of equal protection by requiring the state to demonstrate that its classification has been precisely tailored to serve a compelling governmental interest. Although the complainant has the burden of proof when the rational-basis test is used, under the strict-scrutiny test the burden of proof is placed upon the state to show that the law or policy in question is necessary to accomplish a compelling state interest.

2. Statutes

Congress has enacted many statutes that provide educators with sources of law. The legal basis for this congressional involvement derives from the so-called General Welfare Clause in Article I of the United States Constitution. Some of the areas the national legislature has dealt with over the years include: vocational education (Vocational Education Act of 1963—P.L. 88–210); building construction and operating expenses for schools affected by federal activities (School Facilities, Areas Affected by Federal Activities—P.L. 81–815 and Educational Agencies, Areas Affected by Federal Activities, Financial Aid—P.L. 81–874); defense (National Defense Education Act of 1958—P.L. 85–864); elementary and secondary education (Elementary and Secondary Education Act of 1965—P.L. 89–10); civil rights (Civil Rights Act of 1964—P.L. 88–352 and its various amendments); protecting information concerning students (Family Educational Rights and Privacy Act of 1974—P.L. 93–380*); sex discrimination (Title IX of the Education Amendments of 1972—P.L. 92–318*); handicapped children (Section 504 of the Rehabilitation Act of 1973—P.L. 93–112* and the Education for all Handicapped Children Act of 1975—P.L. 94–142 as amended by P.L. 98–199); bilingual education (Bilingual Education Act of 1968—Section 701 of P.L. 89–10 and Title VII of E.S.E.A. of 1965 as added by P.L. 90–247 and P.L. 93–380); and pregnancy bias (Pregnancy Discrimination Act of 1978—P.L. 95–555*).

Although local and federal educational agencies may occasionally disagree over the purpose and administration of federal statutes, compliance at the local level with controversial federal legislation has often been attained by the threat of a lawsuit, the lure of federal money, or a threat of a cutoff of federal funds already being received.

3. Case Law

Case law refers to principles of law established by courts. It is largely based on legal precedents declared in earlier court decisions in which there were similar factual situations. It is believed that following precedent affords a greater likelihood that citizens will be treated equally, and it has the added advantage of allowing a degree of predictability in future disputes. Although generally guided by precedent, courts are not bound by it in reaching a decision. A court may decide that the factual situation in the case being decided is not sufficiently similar to the one offering precedent or that the legal or philosophical rationale in the precedent-setting case no longer applies.

Federal courts, especially in the last several decades, have established a sizable body of case law. As a result, federal case law has been an influential, if not dominant, force in educational policymaking in recent years. Federal courts have addressed such issues as racial segregation, questions of equity in state methods for financing education, separation of church and state, due process and equal-protection considerations involving both students and teachers, the extent of freedom of expression for students and teachers, and dress and grooming standards for students and teachers. Precedent established by the federal judiciary in these areas provides educators with a significant source of law. Unfortunately, the case law is not always well settled, and conflicting opinions may occur among the federal district courts and courts of appeals. In this

---

* See Appendix D for material pertaining to this legislation.

event educators must follow the case law established for their particular jurisdiction; however, vigilance must be exercised to ascertain appellate or Supreme Court actions that may reverse or modify existing case law. Consequently, it is vital that educators have a thorough understanding of cases where the law is well settled and be familiar with those relating to areas where it is not.

Although not always clearly understood by educators, a decision of the United States Supreme Court has the force of law and may be altered or modified only by another High Court decision or an amendment to the Constitution.* High Court decisions are not always observed by local school systems. Desegregation decisions and those dealing with Bible reading and recitation of sectarian prayers during school hours are prime examples. Since the Court does not have an enforcement arm, compliance with a decision must often be gained by continued court action, which may include requesting writs of injunction or mandamus.

4. Executive Orders and Attorney General Opinions
The president of the United States may issue an executive order that applies to education. Once issued, it would be a source of law for educators.

The attorney general of the United States may be asked to provide an official opinion pertaining to a constitutional or statutory educational provision or a controversial educational practice. Such an opinion may be thought of as advisory and does not represent as compelling a source of law as case law.

B. State Level

Major state-level sources of law include the state's constitution, statutes, case law, state board of education policy, state department of education directives, rules and regulations of administrative agencies, executive orders, and attorney general opinions. As discussed previously, these state-level sources of law may not deprive individuals of the due process or equal protection of the laws they have as persons under the Fourteenth Amendment.

1. State Constitutions
Most state constitutions contain language committing the state to a responsibility for providing education. Although the constitutional terminology varies, it often takes the form of requiring that the legislature

---

* Article III of the Constitution provides that the Supreme Court has appellate jurisdiction "with such exceptions, and under such regulations as the Congress shall make." Therefore, congressional action could conceivably restrict the Court's jurisdiction.

ensure the establishment and maintenance of a thorough and uniform or efficient system of schools. Such broad language is recognized as the ultimate authority within a state for furnishing education. Constitutional provisions may designate constitutional offices for education officials, such as state superintendent of schools and state board members. Constitutional provisions may also specify the creation of local school systems, method of selection and number of members for local school boards, qualifications and selection of local school superintendents, and authority and possibly limitations for local taxation for school purposes. A review of constitutional provisions pertaining to educational matters among the states reveals a wide range of format, from a few general designations in some states to a large number that are rather specific in other states.

Many states also have due process and/or equal protection of the law requirements similar to those found in the amendments to the federal Constitution. Consequently, state courts are often asked to interpret these in an educational context.

2. State Statutes

State statutes represent a significant source of law for educators. They are often more explicit than state constitutional provisions, and their purpose is to bring a more specific outline to broad constitutional directives or to codify case law. Statutes may regulate governmental functions such as the method of selection, terms, and responsibilities of state-level education officials. They may also stipulate the type of local or regional school systems; the method of selection, responsibilities, and terms of local school officials; and the powers of local education units.

State statutes generally deal with financing of the public schools, tax instruments, and the degree to which these instruments may be employed to raise local revenue. Often teacher-pupil ratios are specified, as are the teaching of certain subjects, minimum and maximum ages for subjection to compulsory education laws, length of school day and year, and rules regarding suspension and expulsion of students.

State statutes may also address areas dealing with personnel, such as tenure, retirement, collective bargaining or professional negotiation, meet-and-confer provisions, and fair dismissal procedures. Details pertaining to teaching certificates may be written into law, although this area is usually covered by state board of education policies.

3. Case Law

State court decisions can greatly aid educators in sensitive areas where there is no policy direction from statute, the constitution, or the state board of education. A decision by one state's highest court does not serve as binding precedent in another state. However, it does provide educators within the state with a significant source of law by enabling them to determine the rationale or philosophy of another state's highest legal body regarding an area of conflict.

For instance, building-level administrators are regularly faced with the dilemma of whether to search a student suspected of drug possession. This problem may be compounded by the absence of authoritative state directives and conflicting case law in other states. Consequently, a decision by a state's highest court on such an issue can aid building-level administrators as they attempt to discharge their duties in providing students with a drug-free environment.

There are notable exceptions, but in general, state courts historically have been reluctant to overturn existing school policies in the absence of clearly unreasonable, capricious, or arbitrary conduct on the part of school officials. Consequently, plaintiffs, when possible, have often opted to have their day in federal court instead of a state court.

4. State Board of Education, Chief State School Officer, and State Department of Education

The specific roles of the state board of education, the chief state school officer, and the state department of education vary considerably among the states; yet these offices collectively and individually provide an important source of law for educators. Functional diversity among these offices in the various states often stems from different constitutional or statutory provisions and the political dynamism of the individuals associated with these offices. The formal relationship among the state board of education, the chief state school officer, and the state department of education is rarely detailed in state legislation. Therefore, in practice, the relationship often depends on the people involved. Occasionally, educators at the local level are not sufficiently familiar with the differences in authority among the three divisions. Consequently, pronouncements from one of these authorities may be viewed mistakenly as agreed-upon policy emanating from the state level.

Although the duties and responsibilities of state boards of education also vary, their primary function is to adopt the necessary policies, rules, and regulations to implement legislation and constitutional requirements. When not in conflict with constitutional decrees, these policies, rules, and regulations have the force of law.

The chief state school officer's role does not have uniformity among the states. This person administers the state department of education, the agency that deals directly with the local school systems. The department is the bureaucratic mechanism through which state policy is transmitted to local systems.

5. Attorney General Opinions

As the state's legal counsel, the attorney general may be asked for an opinion regarding an educational question when a constitutional or statutory provision is not clear or when case law does not serve as a distinct precedent. Such attorney general opinions serve as useful guides for the educator, but they do not represent the same degree of authority as a decision by a state's courts or by a federal court in whose jurisdiction the state lies.

C. Local Level

Sources of law with which educators in a local school system are most familiar are the local school board policies, rules, or regulations and their individual school's rules or regulations. Such local sources of law, among school systems, are widely dissimilar in regard to their length, comprehensiveness, and compliance with federal and/or state constitutional or statutory provisions. In many instances building-level administrators rely on this authority in dealing with such issues as administering corporal punishment, suspending a student, searching a student, censorship of the school newspaper or yearbook, student or teacher refusal to participate in patriotic exercises, use of a school building by members of the community, and dress and grooming standards for both students and teachers.

II. The American Judicial System

A dual judicial system composed of state and federal courts exists in the United States. The federal court system has its basis in the United States Constitution, which may be limited by acts of Congress or rulings of the United States Supreme Court. State court systems have their basis in state constitutional provisions or statutory enactments.

In some instances state and federal courts have concurrent jurisdiction, which presents a unique interplay between the two legal systems. This provides a prospective litigant with a choice in selecting the judicial system in which he or she wishes to initiate court action. Federal courts may be used, however, only if it can be shown that a federal question exists, and they may not interfere with state court proceedings unless a federal question is present, such as an alleged abridgement of a constitutional right.

When concurrent jurisdiction exists, plaintiffs will naturally select the court system perceived to be more sympathetic to their cause of action. In recent years plaintiffs have often viewed the federal judiciary in this light; therefore, an increasing number of cases that heretofore had been brought to state courts have been brought to the federal courts.

Prior to instituting court action, with few exceptions, one must exhaust all local and state administrative remedies before seeking a redress of grievances through court litigation. Failure to exhaust these administrative remedies by the plaintiff may result in a court's refusal to grant standing required for a hearing before the court.

Proceedings in school law often involve suits dealing with questions of due process and equal protection of the law brought in a branch of civil law termed equity law. The regular court system usually administers equity law, as separate courts do not normally exist to deal with it. However, in this type of action there is generally no jury, and the judge(s) is the sole determiner of what constitutes due process or equal protection, subject only to review by a higher court. Equity judgments regarding due process and equal protection are generally made on the basis of many variables, such as a close examination of the particular facts of a case, decisions in previous cases, and possibly the introduction of social science findings. If arbitrary or capricious conduct on the part of a governmental official can be demonstrated, the likelihood increases that either due process or equal protection has been denied. On the other hand, if educationally sound reasons are offered by the educator in attempting to explain the actions or conduct in dispute, the likelihood increases that due process or equal protection has been afforded. Ultimately, however, the judge(s) must determine—given a particular factual situation, present societal mores, actual or possible inconvenience or danger to society, and constitutional and other rights—where the balance lies between providing an individual with his or her constitutional rights and the legitimate demands of the larger society.

A. State Court Systems

Each state has the responsibility of establishing its own judicial system. Although this has resulted in the creation of fifty independent state court systems, certain basic similarities exist among them. Common to most states' judicial systems is a court of original jurisdiction and some sort of appellate structure.

In most instances cases dealing with educational matters are initiated in the state's appropriate court of original jurisdiction. These courts are called circuit courts, district courts, courts of common pleas, or supreme courts (New York only), but in many states they are referred to as superior courts. Most litigation is settled in these courts, and they serve as the sole determiner of the facts in most cases.

Intermediate appellate courts constitute a second level of many state court systems. Approximately half of the states have established intermediate appellate courts, and they are called courts of appeals, appellate divisions or departments of the superior courts, appellate divisions of the supreme court (New York only), or appeals courts. Where present, these appellate-level courts provide a tribunal between the trial court and the state's highest court of last resort. Unlike courts of original jurisdiction, state appellate courts do not engage in factual inquiries; rather these courts determine questions of law. Opinions are based on a written record provided by the court of original jurisdiction.

A state's highest-level court is generally called the supreme court; however, it may be called the court of appeals, supreme judicial court, or the supreme court of appeals. Most state supreme courts rarely have original jurisdiction except under specific conditions mandated by state law. Their basic function is to review lower-court decisions on appeal. Purely state matters may not be appealed beyond a state's supreme court; however, if a federal question is involved an appeal may be made to the United States Supreme Court.

B. Federal Court System

By constitutional design, the federal judiciary was established as a separate and independent branch of the United States government. Subsequent federal legislation has provided for a federal judicial system, which presently includes district courts, courts of appeals, and the United States Supreme Court. A litigant must raise a federal question to have standing in a federal court. When dealing with educational issues this may be accomplished by alleging violation of a federal statute, such as 42 U.S.C. § 1983, or of amendments to the Constitution, such as the Fourteenth, First, Fourth, or Fifth.

1. District Courts

The district court, of which there are over ninety, is the court of original jurisdiction in the federal judicial system. Each state has at least one district court, and many states have between two and four districts. A district may be divided into divisions, and cases may be heard in different locations within those divisions.

2. Courts of Appeals

Courts of appeals represent the intermediate appellate level of the federal court system. Their primary function is to review appeals from district courts within the circuit, and decisions by a court of appeals are binding on the lower federal courts in the circuit. A decision by one court of appeals may stand as a persuasive decision for other courts of appeals, but it does not stand as binding authority. Courts of appeals base their decisions on the trial court's proceedings and any briefs filed by concerned parties. A case may be remanded to a lower court for further proceedings when the appellate court finds that the facts presented in the written record are insufficient to render a decision. The nation is

UNITED STATES COURTS OF APPEALS and UNITED STATES DISTRICT COURTS

Since October 1, 1981, Alabama, Florida, and Georgia, formerly in the Fifth Circuit, have comprised the Eleventh Circuit. See Fifth Circuit Court of Appeals Reorganization Act of 1980, P.L. 96-452.

LEGEND
- Circuit boundaries
- State boundaries
- District boundaries

divided into twelve federal judicial circuits, comprising eleven geographic regions and a twelfth circuit encompassing the District of Columbia (see map on page 18).

3. Supreme Court

The Supreme Court is the highest-level court in the federal judicial system, and there is no appeal from a decision rendered by this court. When ruling on the constitutionality of a federal statute or practices within a state or local subdivision, such a ruling can be overturned only by an amendment to the Constitution or by a subsequent ruling by the Court. Nine justices including one chief justice make up the Court. As with other federal judges, their appointment is for life, and their compensation cannot be reduced during their tenure.

Most cases reach the Supreme Court by means of a writ of certiorari. Under this method an unsuccessful litigant in a lower-court decision petitions the Court to review the case, setting forth reasons why the case should be granted a writ. A case is accepted for review only if four justices vote to grant certiorari. Acceptance for review under this "rule of four" indicates that at least four members of the Court consider the case to have sufficient merit to be considered by the entire Court. Denial of certiorari leaves the decision of the lower court undisturbed but does not have the force of a written decision.

The Court's term begins on the first Monday in October and usually lasts for nine months. The number of cases docketed during a term has increased significantly. More than 5,000 cases have been docketed in recent years, while 2,313 cases were docketed in 1960 and 1,460 in 1945. Although the Court decides between 200 and 250 cases in a term, formal written opinions are rendered in approximately half of these decisions.

Court decisions dealing with educational matters have had a significant impact on educational policy in the last several decades. Many difficult decisions have had to be made by the Court because other branches or levels of government were unable to agree or were unwilling to make them. This has prompted some observers to suggest that the United States Supreme Court may have become the modern-day American oracle.

Some educators have doubts about the authority under which the Supreme Court determines questions of constitutionality. Although this right of judicial review is not explicitly provided for in the United States Constitution, many scholars agree that the framers of the Constitution expected the Court to assume this function. This notion was addressed by Alexander Hamilton in *Federalist Paper Number 78*, in which he asserted:

. . . the courts were designed to be an intermediate body between the people and the legislature . . . to keep the latter within the limits assigned to their authority. The interpretation of the laws is the proper and peculiar province of the courts. . . . It therefore belongs to them to ascertain its meaning, as well as the meaning of any particular act proceeding from the legislative body. . . .

The Court's role as the final authority on interpreting the Constitution was established in its landmark decision, *Marbury* v. *Madison,* 1 Cranch 137 (1803), and it has continued to engage in judicial review since that time.

schools
and the state

Introduction

Public education is a governmental enterprise that receives enormous resources from the citizenry and with which most persons have direct contact for fairly extended periods of time. Consequently, since we live in a democratic society that allows for the close scrutiny of such public institutions, honest differences often arise concerning public school policies. This chapter's purpose is to examine the extent of state and local authority when individuals disagree with educational policy involving such issues as compulsory attendance, religion in the schools, use of facilities, aid to nonpublic schools, school fees, and immunization. The thread woven throughout many of the court decisions dealing with these issues is the attempt by the courts to establish a balance between the legitimate demands or objections of individuals toward educational policy and school authorities' perception of their responsibility to the greater population.

I. Compulsory Attendance

A. Satisfied by Parochial, Private, or Home School Attendance

Every state has some form of compulsory education law. These laws generally provide that children between certain ages must attend a public, private, or home school, and failure to comply may be a criminal violation. Central to the legal disputes pertaining to compulsory attendance laws is the balancing of the state's interest in ensuring that students receive an appropriate education and the rights of parents to decide when and where their child attends school.

Pierce v. *Society of Sisters,* a landmark United States Supreme Court decision, affirmed the doctrine of compulsory school attendance. It also established the role of parochial and private schools in satisfying the state's demand that children receive schooling.

Pierce v. Society of Sisters

Supreme Court of the United States, 1925
268 U.S. 510

MR. JUSTICE McREYNOLDS delivered the opinion of the Court.

These appeals are from decrees, based upon undenied allegations, which granted preliminary orders restraining appellants from threatening or attempting to enforce the Compulsory Education Act adopted November 7, 1922, under the initiative provision of her Constitution by the voters of Oregon. * * *

The challenged Act, effective September 1, 1926, requires every parent, guardian or other person having control or charge or custody of a child between eight and sixteen years to send him "to a public school for the period of time a public school shall be held during the current year" in the district where the child resides; and failure to do so is declared a misdemeanor. * * * The manifest purpose is to compel general attendance at public schools by normal children, between eight and sixteen, who have not completed the eighth grade. And without doubt enforcement of the statute would seriously impair, perhaps destroy, the profitable features of appellees' business and greatly diminish the value of their property.

Appellee, the Society of Sisters, is an Oregon corporation, organized in 1880, with power to care for orphans, educate and instruct the youth, establish and maintain academies or schools, and acquire necessary real and personal property. It has long devoted its property and effort to the secular and religious education and care of children, and has acquired the valuable good will of many parents and guardians. It conducts interdependent primary and high schools and junior colleges, and maintains orphanages for the custody and control of children between eight and sixteen. In its primary schools many children between those ages are taught the subjects usually pursued in Oregon public schools during the first eight years. Systematic religious instruction and moral training according to the tenets of the Roman Catholic Church are also regularly provided. All courses of study, both temporal and religious, contemplate continuity of training under the appellee's charge; the primary schools are essential to the system and the most profitable. It owns valuable buildings, especially constructed and equipped for school purposes. The business is remunerative—the annual income from primary schools exceeds thirty thousand dollars—and the successful conduct of this requires long time contracts with teachers and parents. The Compulsory Education Act of 1922 has already caused the withdrawal from its schools of children who would otherwise continue, and their income has steadily declined. The appellants, public officers, have proclaimed their purpose strictly to enforce the statute.

After setting out the above facts the Society's bill alleges that the enactment conflicts with the right of parents to choose schools where their children will receive appropriate mental and religious training, the right of the child to influence the parents' choice of a school, the right of schools and teachers therein to engage in a useful business or profession, and is accordingly repugnant to the Constitution and void. And, further, that unless enforcement of the measure is enjoined the corporation's business and property will suffer irreparable injury.

Appellee, Hill Military Academy, is a private corporation organized in 1908 under the laws of Oregon, engaged in owning, operating and conducting for profit an elementary, college preparatory and military training school for boys between the ages of five and twenty-one years. * * * It owns considerable real and personal property, some useful only for school purposes. The business and incident good will are very valuable. In order to conduct its affairs long time contracts must be made for supplies, equipment, teachers and pupils. Appellants, law officers of the State and County, have publicly announced that the Act of November 7, 1922, is valid and have declared their intention to enforce it. By reason of the statute and threat of enforcement appellee's business is being destroyed and its property depreciated; parents and guardians are refusing to make contracts for the future instruction of their sons, and some are being withdrawn.

The Academy's bill states the foregoing facts and then alleges that the challenged Act contravenes the corporation's rights guaranteed by the Fourteenth Amendment and that unless appellants are restrained from proclaiming its validity and threatening to enforce it irreparable injury will result. The prayer is for an appropriate injunction.

No answer was interposed in either cause, and after proper notices they were heard by three judges * * * on motions for preliminary injunctions upon the specifically alleged facts. The court ruled that the Fourteenth Amendment guaranteed appellees against the deprivation of their property without due process of law consequent upon the unlawful interference by appellants with the free choice of patrons, present and prospective. It declared the right to conduct schools was property and that parents and guardians, as part of their liberty, might direct the education of children by selecting reputable teachers and places. Also, that these schools were not unfit or harmful to the public, and that enforcement of the challenged statute would unlawfully deprive them of patronage and thereby destroy their owners' business and property. Finally, that the threats to enforce the Act would continue to cause irreparable injury; and the suits were not premature.

No question is raised concerning the power of the State reasonably to regulate all schools, to inspect, supervise and examine them, their teachers and pupils; to require that all children of proper age attend some school, that teachers shall be of good moral character and patriotic disposition, that certain studies plainly essential to good citizenship must be taught, and that nothing be taught which is manifestly inimical to the public welfare.

The inevitable practical result of enforcing the Act under consideration would be destruction of appellees' primary schools, and perhaps all other private primary schools for normal children within the State of Oregon. These parties are engaged in a kind of undertaking not inherently harmful, but long regarded as useful and meritorious. Certainly there is nothing in the present records to indicate that they have failed to discharge their obligations to patrons, students or the State. * * *

* * * [We] think it entirely plain that the Act of 1922 unreasonably interferes with the liberty of parents and guardians to direct the up-bringing and education of children under their control. As often here-tofore pointed out, rights guaranteed by the Constitution may not be abridged by legislation which has no reasonable relation to some purpose within the competency of the State. The fundamental theory of liberty upon which all governments in this Union repose excludes any general power of the State to standardize its children by forcing them to accept instruction from public teachers only. The child is not the mere creature of the State; those who nurture him and direct his destiny have the right, coupled with the high duty, to recognize and prepare him for additional obligations.

* * *

Generally it is entirely true, as urged by counsel, that no person in any business has such an interest in possible customers as to enable him to restrain exercise of proper power of the State upon the ground that he will be deprived of patronage. But the injunctions here sought are not against the exercise of any *proper* power. Plaintiffs asked protection against arbitrary, unreasonable and unlawful interference with their patrons and the consequent distribution of their business and property. Their interest is clear and immediate. * * *

The suits were not premature. The injury to appellees was present and very real, not a mere possibility in the remote future. If no relief had been possible prior to the effective date of the Act, the injury would have become irreparable. Prevention of impending injury by unlawful action is a well recognized function of courts of equity.

The decrees below are

Affirmed.

Notes and Questions

Does the Court's decision in **Pierce** reveal a bias in favor of the individual parent to have access to a pluralistic educational system by not allowing the state to have a monopoly over education?

The challenged Oregon law in **Pierce** had been promoted primarily by members of the Ku Klux Klan and the Oregon Scottish Rite Masons. Their actions were evidence of a xenophobic response on the part of some Americans after World War I to ensure that children would be properly socialized in the tenets of Americanism. The strong feelings against many foreigners and Catholics in particular at that time prompted a leading klansman to state: "Somehow these mongrel hordes must be Americanized; failing that, deportation is the only remedy." An attempt was made to picture Catholics as members of an organization that conducted its worship services in a foreign language, was controlled by a foreigner called a Pope, and practiced secret rituals.

An Amish group contested Wisconsin's compulsory attendance law, which required attendance at a public or private school until age sixteen. The Amish did not want their children to attend either a public or private high school after the eighth grade, because they considered such schools to be "worldly." A Supreme Court decision upheld the Amish position on several grounds. The Court contended that enforcing the state law would gravely endanger, if not destroy, the free exercise of Amish religious beliefs. Additionally, the Court's decision was influenced not only by the group's nearly three hundred years of existence but also by the perception that, although perhaps unconventional, the Amish had evidenced a highly successful social unit characterized by members who were productive, law abiding, and unwilling to accept welfare in any of its usual modern forms. See *Wisconsin* v. *Yoder*, 406 U.S. 205 (1972). Would the Court's rationale prevail if the group contesting a compulsory attendance law were the Ku Klux Klan rather than the Amish? Should students have a voice in this issue? Justice Douglas's opinion in *Yoder*, in which he dissents in part, suggests that students should have such a voice.

A Pentecostal parent who objected to sending his children to public schools was not upheld. The court ruled that the state's interest in compulsory attendance overrides the parent's interest in avoiding exposure to the unisex movement, secular humanism, and medical care. See *Duro* v. *District Attorney, Second Judicial District of North Carolina*, 712 F.2d 96 (4th Cir. 1983), *cert. denied*, 465 U.S. 1006 (1984). Parents were also not upheld when they refused to send their children to public school because those schools did not teach Indian heritage and culture. See *Matter of McMillan*, 30 N.C. App. 235, 226 S.E.2d 693 (1976).

The Supreme Court decision in **Pierce** had immediate applicability only to the contested Oregon Compulsory Education Act and the issues arising from its attempted implementation. It did not automatically affect similar laws in other states. Individual state legislative action would be necessary to revoke similar laws in those states, and the absence of such legislative action would require a law suit to gain compliance with the **Pierce** rationale. Given the **Pierce** precedent, such a suit would undoubtedly be successful.

Some school districts have instituted policies under which a student is denied academic credit when a specified number of "unexcused" absences are incurred during a quarter or semester. Under these policies, unexcused absences may include tardies, truancies, suspension days, and other absences that school policy deems to be illegitimate. Such a policy was held to be invalid in *Gutierrez* v. *School District R-1*, 41 Colo. App. 411, 585 P.2d 935 (1978), because it was inconsistent with applicable statutory provisions. Other courts have held similarly to *Gutierrez*. See *Blackman* v. *Brown*, 100 Misc.2d 566, 419 N.Y.S.2d 796 (1978) and *Katzman* v. *Cumberland Valley School District*, 479 A.2d 671 (Pa. Commw. Ct. 1984). However, academic sanctions for unexcused absences were upheld in *Williams* v. *Board of Education for Marianna School District*, 274 Ark. 538, 626 S.W.2d 361 (1982) and *Campbell* v. *Board of Education of Town of New Milford*, 193 Conn. 93, 475 A.2d 289 (1984). Several courts have made a distinction between unexcused absences based on truancy and those resulting from disciplinary action. See *Dorsey* v. *Bale*, 521 S.W.2d 76 (Ky. 1975), and *Jones* v. *Latexo Independent School District*, 499

F. Supp. 223 (Tex. 1980), in which academic sanctions resulting from suspensions were not upheld. In *New Braunfels Independent School District v. Armke*, 658 S.W.2d 330 (Tex. App. 1983), however, a school's use of academic sanctions for disciplinary purposes was upheld.

In the absence of statutory or case law prohibition, school systems having such policies should ensure that accurate attendance records are maintained, that the policy does not adversely have a disproportionate impact on any discrete group of students, such as minorities or the economically disadvantaged, and that exceptions to the policy are not made disproportionately, favoring a discrete group.

What are the provisions of the compulsory attendance law in your state?

B. Regulation of Nonpublic Schools

Once *Pierce* established the doctrine that private school attendance could satisfy a state's compulsory attendance requirements, the question arose as to the extent to which a state could regulate the private schools within its jurisdiction. The United States Supreme Court addressed this issue, one year after its *Pierce* decision, in *Farrington v. Tokushige*, 273 U.S. 284 (1926).

Farrington resulted from a state attempt to Americanize students: in this case Hawaii's attempt to regulate the predominately-Japanese foreign language schools on the islands. The contested regulations required teachers in these schools to possess "ideals of democracy," knowledge of American history, and fluency in English. Additionally they restricted hours of operation, established entrance requirements, and prescribed textbooks. These regulations, the Court held, served no demonstrable public interest, but instead amounted to a deliberate plan of strict governmental control, infringing on the rights of both parents and school owners.

Both *Pierce* and *Farrington,* therefore, reflect a philosophy that parents should have freedom of choice in the education of their children. Moreover, in sanctioning what many people feared was subversive, these decisions affirm a faith in the sustaining power of American tolerance.

Regulation of private schools varies among the states. Some states require that the quality of education provided by the private school be essentially equivalent to that provided in the public schools. This may include a requirement for certified teachers and certain course offerings. Other states merely have regulations dealing primarily with health, safety, and sanitation. Since attendance at a private school satisfies a state's compulsory attendance law, it is a legitimate state function to require attendance information from private schools.

State regulation of religious private schools has received court attention in recent years. These schools generally allege that their First Amendment religious freedom is being restricted. Courts have tended to reject these challenges to minimal instructional programs and requirements that teachers have baccalaureate degrees. See *Nebraska* v. *Faith Baptist Church*, 207 Neb. 802, 301 N.W.2d 571 (1981), *appeal dismissed*, 454 U.S. 803 (1981), *Bangor Baptist Church* v. *Maine*, 549 F. Supp. 1208 (Me. 1982), *North Dakota* v. *Shaver*, 294 N.W.2d 883 (N.D. 1981) and *North Dakota* v. *Rivinius*, 328 N.W.2d 220 (N.D. 1982), *cert. denied*, 460 U.S. 1070 (1983). Also see *New Life Baptist Church Academy* v. *Town of East Long Meadow*, 666 F. Supp. 293 (Mass. 1987), in which the court interpreted a Massachusetts law requiring a local school committee to approve a private school when the committee was satisfied that the school's instruction in certain identified subjects was equal in thoroughness, efficiency, and progress to that of the public schools in the same town. In its opinion, the court ruled that the state in fulfilling its obligation should employ the least restrictive means to ensure that there would not be an excessive entanglement with religion. The court cited the use of standardized tests as an example of a less-restricted means.

What is the status of private school regulation in your state? In addition to reviewing court decisions, you may wish to consult your state constitution, statutes, state school board policies, and attorney general opinions.

C. Home Instruction

Parents dissatisfied with both public and private schools frequently elect to instruct their children at home. Although some states do not have statutory provisions pertaining specifically to home instruction, those states that do often require the home program to be essentially "equivalent" to that offered in the public schools. Several courts have held that the absence of social contact tends to vitiate a home-instruction program. Some states require that the parent(s) providing the home instruction must be a qualified teacher.

When challenged by local school authorities and law enforcement officials, parents engaged in home instruction are generally brought to trial in a criminal action for failure to comply with a state's compulsory education law. Although there are exceptions, in most states the burden of demonstrating that the home instruction is substantially "equivalent" to that offered in the public schools is on the parents. See *New Jersey* v. *Massa*, 95 N.J. Super. 382, 231 A.2d 252 (1967), in which the court held that equivalent education elsewhere than at school requires only a showing of academic equivalence.

A Virginia court upheld the state's compulsory attendance law, which required home school instructors to be "tutors or teachers" but did not require similar qualifications for private school instructors. See *Grigg* v. *Virginia*, 224 Va. 356, 297 S.E.2d 799 (1982). Also see *Mazanec* v. *North Judson–San Pierre School Corporation*, 798 F.2d 230 (7th Cir. 1987), and *Ohio* v. *Schmidt*, 29 Ohio St. 3d 32, 505 N.E.2d 627 (1987), *cert. denied*, 484 U.S. 942 (1987), in which objections on religious grounds to verifying compliance with attendance laws pertaining to home instruction were not upheld.

Does your state or local system have any provisions concerning home instruction for those unwilling to attend either public or private schools?

D. Admission Issues

Compulsory-attendance laws often state a minimum age at which formal education must begin. Disputes may arise when a child's birthday is a few days or perhaps weeks after a designated date or when parents believe their child is emotionally and intellectually ready to begin school at an earlier age.

This issue was addressed by the West Virginia Supreme Court of Appeals. Although a state statute required, as a prerequisite to school admittance, that students attain the age of five on or before September 1, the court found that an intellectually mature child, whose birthday fell on September 3, should have been admitted to school. The court reasoned that it was the state legislature's intent that school boards adopt flexible policies—consistent with resources at their disposal—to ease the burden of such unfortunate situations. See *Blessing* v. *Mason County Board of Education*, 341 S.E.2d 407 (W. Va. 1985). In the absence of state statutes or constitutional provisions establishing the age for entrance to school, local boards of education have an implied authority to establish them. See *Zweifel* v. *Joint District No. 1*, 76 Wis.2d 648, 251 N.W.2d 822 (1977).

Parents who have changed their state of residence may also question restrictions prohibiting a child who has completed kindergarten in one state from enrolling in first grade in another state.

The United States Supreme Court addressed the issue of public school admission of illegal aliens in *Plyler* v. *Doe*, 457 U.S. 202 (1981). The Court held that funding for the education of these children could not be withheld from local school districts, nor could local school districts deny enrollment to children not legally admitted to the country. This decision emphasized both the importance of public education in maintaining basic civic institutions and the lasting impact of educational deprivation on the life of a child.

Does your state or local school system have any provisions concerning a minimum age for school entry? If so, is there a provision for early admission or transfer from other states?

II. Religion in the Schools

Although the United States Supreme Court and lower federal court decisions have been consistent in declaring Bible reading for sectarian purposes and prayer in the public schools during normal school hours to be unconstitutional, this issue and others dealing with religious activities at public schools remain highly charged and emotional ones. Consequently, these issues have provided a persistent stream of litigation focusing on church-state relations.

In an effort to ensure a separation of church and state, the framers of the Constitution included the following language in the First Amendment: "Congress shall make no law respecting an establishment of religion, or prohibiting the free exercise thereof." On the basis of these words courts must determine the constitutionality of such questions as prayer and Bible reading in the public schools during normal school hours, baccalaureate services, Bible study or other religious clubs, dissemination of Gideon Bibles or other religious tracts, or observance of religious holidays.

Courts have not erected an unassailably high wall between the church and the state that would absolutely restrict governmental involvement with religion. Rather, a review of court decisions dealing with these issues reveals that the thread woven throughout the decisions is the attempt by courts to determine the height of the wall, given a particular factual situation.

A. School-Sponsored Prayer and Bible Reading

Two United States Supreme Court decisions in the early 1960s dramatically established the case law pertaining to prayer and Bible reading in the public schools. In *Engel* v. *Vitale* the Court, with one dissent, held that recitation of a prayer composed by the New York State Board of Regents, which was to be said in the presence of a teacher at the beginning of school each day, was unconstitutional and in violation of the establishment clause.

In *School District of Abington Township* v. *Schempp,* a lengthy decision of 117 pages, which included a majority opinion, three concurring opinions, and one dissent, the Court held that reading the Bible for sectarian purposes and reciting the Lord's Prayer in public schools during normal hours were unconstitutional. However, the Court asserted that the Bible could be read as literature in an appropriate class and that the history of religion or comparative religion could be taught.

Prayer in some public schools did not stop as a result of these decisions. The issue has remained a highly controversial one that has been inter-jected into local, state, and national political debate. Although litigation involving the issue continued uninterrupted in the lower courts, the United States Supreme Court did not directly address the issue again until *Wallace v. Jaffree* in 1985. In discussing the issue of prayer in the public schools the six-to-three decision in *Jaffree* held that the setting aside of classroom time for school-sponsored silent prayer was uncon-stitutional.

1. Recitation of a State Prayer

Engel v. Vitale

Supreme Court of the United States, 1962
370 U.S. 421

MR. JUSTICE BLACK delivered the opinion of the Court.

The respondent Board of Education of Union Free School District No. 9, New Hyde Park, New York, acting in its official capacity under state law, directed the School District's principal to cause the following prayer to be said aloud by each class in the presence of a teacher at the beginning of each school day:

"Almighty God, we acknowledge our dependence upon Thee, and we beg Thy blessings upon us, our parents, our teachers and our Country."

This daily procedure was adopted on the recommendation of the State Board of Regents, a governmental agency created by the State Consti-tution to which the New York Legislature has granted broad supervisory, executive, and legislative powers over the State's public school system. These state officials composed the prayer which they recommended and published as part of their "Statement on Moral and Spiritual Training in the Schools," saying: "We believe that this Statement will be subscribed to by all men and women of good will, and we call upon all of them to aid in giving life to our program."

Shortly after the practice of reciting the Regents' prayer was adopted by the School District, the parents of ten pupils brought this action in a New York State Court insisting that use of this official prayer in the public schools was contrary to the beliefs, religions, or religious practices of both themselves and their children. Among other things, these parents challenged the constitutionality of both the state law authorizing the School District to direct the use of prayer in public schools and the School District's regulation ordering the recitation of this particular prayer on the ground that these actions of official governmental agencies violate that part of the First Amendment of the Federal Constitution which commands that "Congress shall make no law respecting an establishment of religion"—a command which was "made applicable to the State of New York by the Fourteenth Amendment of the said Constitution." The New York Court of Appeals * * * sustained an order of the lower state courts which had upheld the power of New York to use the Regents' prayer as a part of the daily procedures of its public schools so long as the schools did not compel any pupil to join in the prayer over his or her parents' objection. We granted certiorari to review this important decision involving the rights protected by the First and Fourteenth Amendments.

We think that by using its public school system to encourage recitation of the Regents' prayer, the State of New York has adopted a practice wholly inconsistent with the Establishment Clause. There can, of course, be no doubt that New York's program of daily classroom invocation of God's blessings as prescribed in the Regents' prayer is a religious activity. It is a solemn avowal of divine faith and supplication for the blessings of the Almighty. The nature of such a prayer has always been religious, none of the respondents has denied this and the trial court expressly so found. * * *

The petitioners contend among other things that the state laws requiring or permitting use of the Regents' prayer must be struck down as a violation of the Establishment Clause because that prayer was composed by government officials as a part of a governmental program to further religious beliefs. For this reason, petitioners argue, the State's use of the Regents' prayer in its public school system breaches the constitutional wall of separation between Church and State. We agree with that contention since we think that the constitutional prohibition against laws respecting an establishment of religion must at least mean that in this country it is no part of the business of government to compose official prayers for any group of the American people to recite as a part of a religious program carried on by government.

It is a matter of history that this very practice of establishing governmentally composed prayers for religious services was one of the reasons which caused many of our early colonists to leave England and seek religious freedom in America. The Book of Common Prayer, which was created under governmental direction and which was approved by Acts of Parliament in 1548 and 1549, set out in minute detail the accepted form and content of prayer and other religious ceremonies to be used in the established, tax-supported Church of England. The controversies over the Book and what should be its content repeatedly threatened to disrupt the peace of that country as the accepted forms of prayer in the established church changed with the views of the particular ruler that happened to be in control at the time. Powerful groups representing some of the varying religious views of the people struggled among themselves to impress their particular views upon the Government and obtain amendments of the Book more suitable to their respective notions of how religious services should be conducted in order that the official religious establishment would advance their particular beliefs. Other groups, lacking the necessary political power to influence the Government on the matter, decided to leave England and its established church and seek freedom in America from England's governmentally ordained and supported religion.

It is an unfortunate fact of history that when some of the very groups which had most strenuously opposed the established Church of England found themselves sufficiently in control of colonial governments in this country to write their own prayers into law, they passed laws making their own religion the official religion of their respective colonies. Indeed, as late as the time of the Revolutionary War, there were established churches in at least eight of the thirteen former colonies and established religions in at least four of the other five. But the successful Revolution against English political domination was shortly followed by intense opposition to the practice of establishing religion by law. * * *

By the time of the adoption of the Constitution, our history shows that there was a widespread awareness among many Americans of the dangers of a union of Church and State. These people knew, some of them from bitter personal experience, that one of the greatest dangers to the freedom of the individual to worship in his own way lay in the Government's placing its official stamp of approval upon one particular kind of prayer or one particular form of religious services. They knew the anguish, hardship and bitter strife that could come when zealous religious groups struggled with one another to obtain the Government's stamp of approval from each King, Queen, or Protector that came to temporary power. The Constitution was intended to avert a part of this danger by leaving the government of this country in the hands of the people rather than in the hands of any monarch. But this safeguard was not enough. Our Founders were no more willing to let the content of their prayers and their privilege of praying whenever they pleased be influenced by the ballot box than they were to let these vital matters of personal conscience depend upon the succession of monarchs. The First Amendment was added to the Constitution to stand as a guarantee that neither the power nor the prestige of the Federal Government would be used to control, support or influence the kinds of prayer the American people can say—that the people's religions must not be subjected to the pressures of government for change each time a new political administration is elected to office. Under that Amendment's prohibition against governmental establishment of religion, as reinforced by the provisions of the Fourteenth Amendment, government in this country, be it state or federal, is without power to prescribe by law any particular form of prayer which is to be used as an official prayer in carrying on any program of governmentally sponsored religious activity.

There can be no doubt that New York's state prayer program officially establishes the religious beliefs embodied in the Regents' prayer. The respondents' argument to the contrary, which is largely based upon the contention that the Regents' prayer is "non-denominational" and the fact that the program, as modified and approved by state courts, does not require all pupils to recite the prayer but permits those who wish to do so to remain silent or be excused from the room, ignores the essential nature of the program's constitutional defects. Neither the fact that the prayer may be denominationally neutral nor the fact that its observance on the part of the students is voluntary can serve to free it from the limitations of the Establishment Clause, as it might from the Free Exercise Clause, of the First Amendment, both of which are operative against the States by virtue of the Fourteenth Amendment. Although these two clauses may in certain instances overlap, they forbid two quite different kinds of governmental encroachment upon religious freedom. The Establishment Clause, unlike the Free Exercise Clause, does not depend upon any showing of direct governmental compulsion and is violated by the enactment of laws which establish an official religion whether those laws operate directly to coerce nonobserving individuals or not. This is not to say, of course, that laws officially prescribing a particular form of religious worship do not involve coercion of such individuals. When the power, prestige and financial support of the government is placed behind a particular religious belief, the indirect coercive pressure upon religious minorities to conform to the prevailing officially approved religion is plain. But the purposes underlying the Establishment Clause go much further than that. Its first and most immediate purpose rested on the belief that a union of government and religion tends to destroy government and to degrade religion. The history of governmentally established religion, both in England and in this country, showed that whenever government had allied itself with one particular form of religion, the inevitable result had been that it had incurred the hatred, disrespect and even contempt of those who held contrary beliefs. That same history showed that many people had lost their respect for any religion that had relied upon the support of government to spread its faith. The Establishment Clause thus stands as an expression of principle on the part of the Founders of our Constitution that religion is too personal, too sacred, too holy, to permit its "unhallowed perversion" by a civil magistrate. Another purpose of the Establishment Clause rested upon an awareness of the historical fact that governmentally established religions and religious persecutions go hand in hand. The Founders knew that only a few years after the Book of Common Prayer became the only accepted form of religious services in the established Church of England, an Act of Uniformity was passed to compel all the Englishmen to attend those services and to make it a criminal offense to conduct or attend religious gatherings of any kind— a law which was consistently flouted by dissenting religious groups in England and which contributed to widespread persecutions of people like John Bunyan who persisted in holding "unlawful [religious] meetings . . . to the great disturbance and distraction of the good subjects of this kingdom. . . ." And they knew that similar persecutions had received the sanction of law in several of the colonies in this country soon after the establishment of official religions in those colonies. It was in large part to get completely away from this sort of systematic religious persecution that the Founders brought into being our Nation, our Constitution, and our Bill of Rights with its prohibition against any governmental establishment of religion. The New York laws officially prescribing the Regents' prayer are inconsistent both with the purposes of the Establishment Clause and with the Establishment Clause itself.

It has been argued that to apply the Constitution in such a way as to prohibit state laws respecting an establishment of religious services in public schools is to indicate a hostility toward religion or toward prayer. Nothing, of course, could be more wrong. The history of man is inseparable from the history of religion. And perhaps it is not too much to say that since the beginning of that history many people have devoutly believed that "More things are wrought with prayer than this world dreams of." It was doubtless largely due to men who believed this that there grew up a sentiment that caused men to leave the cross-currents of officially established state religions and religious persecution in Europe and come to this country filled with the hope that they could find a place in which they could pray when they pleased to the God of their faith in the language they chose. And there were men of this same faith in the power of prayer who led the fight for adoption of our Constitution and also for our Bill of Rights with the very guarantees of religious freedom that forbid the sort of governmental activity which New York has attempted here. These men knew that the First Amendment, which tried to put an end to governmental control of religion and of prayer, was not written to destroy either. They knew rather that it was written to quiet well-justified fears which nearly all of them felt arising out of an awareness that governments of the past had shackled men's tongues to make them speak only the religious thoughts that government wanted them to speak and to pray only to the God that government wanted them to pray to. It is neither sacrilegious nor antireligious to say that each separate government in this country should stay out of the business of writing or sanctioning official prayers and leave that purely religious function to the people themselves and to those the people choose to look to for religious guidance.

It is true that New York's establishment of its Regents' prayer as an officially approved religious doctrine of that State does not amount to a total establishment of one particular religious sect to the exclusion of all others—that, indeed, the government endorsement of that prayer seems relatively insignificant when compared to the governmental encroachments upon religion which were commonplace 200 years ago. To those who may subscribe to the view that because the Regents' official prayer is so brief and general there can be no danger to religious freedom in its governmental establishment, however, it may be appropriate to say in the words of James Madison, the author of the First Amendment:

"[I]t is proper to take alarm at the first experiment on our liberties. . . . Who does not see that the same authority which can establish Christianity, in exclusion of all other Religions, may establish with the same ease any particular sect of Christians, in exclusion of all other Sects? That the same authority which can force a citizen to contribute three pence only of his property for the support of any one establishment, may force him to conform to any other establishment in all cases whatsoever?"

The judgment of the Court of Appeals of New York is reversed and the cause remanded for further proceedings not inconsistent with this opinion.

Reversed and remanded.

2. Prayer and Bible Reading

School District of Abington Township v. Schempp
Murray v. Curlett

Supreme Court of the United States, 1963
374 U.S. 203

MR. JUSTICE CLARK delivered the opinion of the Court.
* * * These companion cases present the issues in the context of state action requiring that schools begin each day with readings from

the Bible. While raising the basic questions under slightly different factual situations, the cases permit of joint treatment. In light of the history of the First Amendment and of our cases interpreting and applying its requirements, we hold that the practices at issue and the laws requiring them are unconstitutional under the Establishment Clause, as applied to the States through the Fourteenth Amendment.

* * * The Commonwealth of Pennsylvania by law * * * requires that "At least ten verses from the Holy Bible shall be read, without comment, at the opening of each public school on each school day. Any child shall be excluded from such Bible reading, or attending such Bible reading, upon the written request of his parent or guardian." The Schempp family, husband and wife and two of their three children, brought suit to enjoin enforcement of the statute * * *. A three-judge statutory District Court for the Eastern District of Pennsylvania held that the statute is violative of the Establishment Clause of the First Amendment as applied to the States by the Due Process Clause of the Fourteenth Amendment and directed that appropriate injuctive relief issue. * * *

The apelleess Edward Lewis Schempp, his wife Sidney, and their children, Roger and Donna, are of the Unitarian faith and are members of the Unitarian Church in Germantown, Philadelphia, Pennsylvania, where they * * * regularly attend religious services. * * *

On each school day at the Abington Senior High School between 8:15 and 8:30 a.m., while the pupils are attending their home rooms or advisory sections, opening exercises are conducted pursuant to the statute. The exercises are broadcast into each room in the school building through an intercommunications system and are conducted under the supervision of a teacher by students attending the school's radio and television workshop. Selected students from this course gather each morning in the school's workshop studio for the exercises, which include readings by one of the students of 10 verses of the Holy Bible, broadcast to each room in the building. This is followed by the recitation of the Lord's Prayer, likewise over the intercommunications system, but also by the students in the various classrooms, who are asked to stand and join in repeating the prayer in unison. The exercises are closed with the flag salute and such pertinent announcements as are of interest to the students. Participation in the opening exercises, as directed by the statute, is voluntary. The student reading the verses from the Bible may select the passages and read from any version he chooses, although the only copies furnished by the school are the King James version, copies of which are circulated to each teacher by the school district. During the period in which the exercises have been conducted the King James, the Douay and the Revised Standard versions of the Bible have been used, as well as the Jewish Holy Scriptures. There are no prefatory statements, no questions asked or solicited, no comments or explanations made and no interpretations given at or during the exercises. The students and parents are advised that the student may absent himself from the classroom or, should he elect to remain, not participate in the exercises.

* * *

At the first trial Edward Schempp and the children testified as to specific religious doctrines purveyed by a literal reading of the Bible "which are contrary to the religious beliefs which they held and to their familial teaching." * * * The children testified that all of the doctrines to which they referred were read to them at various times as part of the exercises. Edward Schempp testified at the second trial that he had considered having Roger and Donna excused from attendance at the exercise but decided against it for several reasons, including his belief that the children's relationships with their teachers and classmates would be adversely affected.

* * *

In 1905 the Board of School Commissioners of Baltimore City adopted a rule * * *. The rule provided for the holding of opening exercises in the schools of the city, consisting primarily of the "reading, without comment, of a chapter in the Holy Bible and/or the use of the Lord's Prayer." The petitioners, Mrs. Madalyn Murray and her son, William J. Murray III, are both professed atheists. Following unsuccessful attempts to have the respondent school board rescind the rule, this suit was filed for mandamus to compel its recission and cancellation. It was alleged that William was a student in a public school of the city and Mrs. Murray, his mother, was a taxpayer therein; that it was the practice under the rule to have a reading on each school morning from the King James version of the Bible; that at petitioners' insistence the rule was amended to permit children to be excused from the exercise on request of the parent and that William had been excused pursuant thereto; that nevertheless the rule as amended was in violation of the petitioners' rights to "freedom of religion under the First and Fourteenth Amendments" and in violation of "the principle of separation between church and state, contained therein. . . ." The petition particularized the petitioners' atheistic beliefs and stated that the rule, as practiced, violated their rights

"in that it threatens their religious liberty by placing a premium on belief as against non-belief and subjects their freedom of conscience to the rule of the majority; it pronounces belief in God as the source of all moral and spiritual values, equating these values with religious values, and thereby renders sinister, alien and suspect the beliefs and ideals of your Petitioners, promoting doubt and question of their morality, good citizenship and good faith."

* * * The Maryland Court of Appeals affirmed, the majority of four justices holding the exercise not in violation of the First and Fourteenth Amendments, with three justices dissenting. * * *

* * *

The wholesome "neutrality" of which this Court's cases speak * * * stems from a recognition of the teachings of history that powerful sects or groups might bring about a fusion of governmental and religious functions or a concert of dependency of one upon the other to the end that official support of the State or Federal Government would be placed behind the tenets of one or of all orthodoxies. This the Establishment Clause prohibits. And a further reason for neutrality is found in the Free Exercise Clause, which recognizes the value of religious training, teaching and observance and, more particularly, the right of every person to freely choose his own course with reference thereto, free of any compulsion from the state. This the Free Exercise Clause guarantees. Thus, as we have seen, the two clauses may overlap. As we have indicated, the Establishment Clause has been directly considered by this Court eight times in the past score of years and, with only one Justice dissenting on the point, it has consistently held that the clause withdrew all legislative power respecting religious belief or the expression thereof. The test may be stated as follows: what are the purpose and the primary effect of the enactment? If either is the advancement or inhibition of religion then the enactment exceeds the scope of legislative power as circumscribed by the Constitution. That is to say that to withstand the strictures of the Establishment Clause there must be a secular legislative purpose and a primary effect that neither advances nor inhibits religion. * * *

Applying the Establishment Clause principles to the cases at bar we find that the States are requiring the selection and reading at the opening of the school day of verses from the Holy Bible and the recitation of the Lord's Prayer by the students in unison. These exercises are prescribed as part of the curricular activities of students who are required by law to attend school. They are held in the school buildings under the supervision and with the participation of teachers employed in those schools. * * * The trial court * * * has found that such an opening exercise is a religious ceremony and was intended by the State to be so. We agree with the trial court's finding as to the religious character of the exercises. Given that finding, the exercises and the law requiring them are in violation of the Establishment Clause.

* * *

It is insisted that unless these religious exercises are permitted a "religion of secularism" is established in the schools. We agree of course that the State may not establish a "religion of secularism" in the sense of affirmatively opposing or showing hostility to religion, thus "preferring those who believe in no religion over those who do believe." * * * We do not agree, however, that this decision in any sense has that effect. In addition, it might well be said that one's education is not complete without a study of comparative religion or the history of religion and its relationship to the advancement of civilization. It certainly may be said that the Bible is worthy of study for its literary and historic qualities. Nothing we have said here indicates that such study of the Bible or of religion, when presented objectively as part of a secular program of education, may not be effected consistently with the First Amendment. But the exercises here do not fall into those categories. They are religious exercises, required by the States in violation of the command of the First Amendment that the Government maintain strict neutrality, neither aiding nor opposing religion.

* * *

The place of religion in our society is an exalted one, achieved through a long tradition of reliance on the home, the church and the inviolable citadel of the individual heart and mind. We have come to recognize through bitter experience that it is not within the power of government to invade that citadel, whether its purpose or effect be to aid or oppose, to advance or retard. In the relationship between man and religion, the State is firmly committed to a position of neutrality. Though the application of that rule requires interpretation of a delicate sort, the rule itself is clearly and concisely stated in the words of the First Amendment.
* * *

3. Silent Prayer, Meditation, and Voluntary Prayer

Wallace v. Jaffree

Supreme Court of the United States, 1985
472 U.S. 38

JUSTICE STEVENS delivered the opinion of the Court.
At an early stage of this litigation, the constitutionality of three Alabama statutes was questioned: (1) § 16–1–20, enacted in 1978, which

authorized a one-minute period of silence in all public schools "for meditation," (2) § 16-1-20.1, enacted in 1981, which authorized a period of silence "for meditation or voluntary prayer," and (3) § 16-1-20.2, enacted in 1982, which authorized teachers to lead "willing students" in a prescribed prayer to "Almighty God . . . the Creator and Supreme Judge of the world."

* * *

The Court of Appeals agreed with the District Court's initial interpretation of the purpose of both § 16-1-20.1 and § 16-1-20.2, and held them both unconstitutional. We have already affirmed the Court of Appeals' holding with respect to § 16-1-20.2. Moreover, appellees have not questioned the holding that § 16-1-20 is valid. Thus, the narrow question for decision is whether § 16-1-20.1, which authorizes a period of silence for "meditation or voluntary prayer," is a law respecting the establishment of religion within the meaning of the First Amendment.

* * *

Appellee Ishmael Jaffree is a resident of Mobile County, Alabama. On May 28, 1982, he filed a complaint on behalf of three of his minor children; two of them were second-grade students and the third was then in kindergarten. The complaint named members of the Mobile County School Board, various school officials, and the minor plaintiffs' three teachers as defendants. The complaint alleged that the appellees brought the action "seeking principally a declaratory judgment and an injunction restraining the Defendants and each of them from maintaining or allowing the maintenance of regular religious prayer services or other forms of religious observances in the Mobile County Public Schools in violation of the First Amendment as made applicable to states by the Fourteenth Amendment to the United States Constitution." The complaint further alleged that two of the children had been subjected to various acts of religious indoctrination "from the beginning of the school year in September, 1981"; that the defendant teachers had "on a daily basis" led their classes in saying certain prayers in unison; that the minor children were exposed to ostracism from their peer group class members if they did not participate, and that Ishmael Jaffree had repeatedly but unsuccessfully requested that the devotional services be stopped. * * *

* * *

In its lengthy conclusions of law, the District Court viewed a number of opinions of this Court interpreting the Establishment Clause of the First Amendment, and then embarked on a fresh examination of the question whether the First Amendment imposes any barrier to the establishment of an official religion by the State of Alabama. After reviewing at length what it perceived to be newly discovered historical evidence, the District Court concluded that "the establishment clause of the first amendment to the United States Constitution does not prohibit the state from establishing a religion." In a separate opinion, the District Court dismissed appellees' challenge to the three Alabama statutes because of a failure to state any claim for which relief could be granted. The court's dismissal of this challenge was also based on its conclusion that the Establishment Clause did not bar the States from establishing a religion.

The Court of Appeals consolidated the two cases; not surprisingly, it reversed. The Court of Appeals noted that this Court had considered and had rejected the historical arguments that the District Court found persuasive, and that the District Court had misapplied the doctrine of *stare decisis.* The Court of Appeals then held that the teachers' religious activities violated the Establishment Clause of the First Amendment. With respect to § 16–1–20.1 and § 16–1–20.2, the Court of Appeals stated that "both statutes advance and encourage religious activities." The Court of Appeals then quoted with approval the District Court's finding that § 16–1–20.1, and § 16–1–20.2, were efforts "to encourage a religious activity. Even though these statutes are permissive in form, it is nevertheless state involvement respecting an establishment of religion." Thus, the Court of Appeals concluded that both statutes were "specifically the type which the Supreme Court addressed in *Engel* [v. *Vitale,* 370 U.S. 421 (1962)]." * * *

* * *

Our unanimous affirmance of the Court of Appeals' judgment concerning § 16–1–20.2 makes it unnecessary to comment at length on the District Court's remarkable conclusion that the Federal Constitution imposes no obstacle to Alabama's establishment of a state religion. Before analyzing the precise issue that is presented to us, it is nevertheless appropriate to recall how firmly embedded in our constitutional jurisprudence is the proposition that the several States have no greater power to restrain the individual freedoms protected by the First Amendment than does the Congress of the United States.

* * *

Just as the right to speak and the right to refrain from speaking are complementary components of a broader concept of individual freedom of mind, so also the individual's freedom to choose his own creed is the counterpart of his right to refrain from accepting the creed established by the majority. At one time it was thought that this right merely proscribed the preference of one Christian sect over another, but would not require equal respect for the conscience of the infidel, the atheist, or the adherent of a non-Christian faith such as Mohammedism or Judaism. But when the underlying principle has been examined in the crucible of litigation, the Court has unambiguously concluded that the individual freedom of conscience protected by the First Amendment embraces the right to select any religious faith or none at all. This conclusion derives support not only from the interest in respecting the individual's freedom of conscience, but also from the conviction that religious beliefs worthy of respect are the product of free and voluntary choice by the faithful, and from recognition of the fact that the political interest in forestalling intolerance extends beyond intolerance among Christian sects—or even intolerance among "religions"—to encompass intolerance of the disbeliever and the uncertain. * * *

* * *

The legislative intent to return prayer to the public schools is, of course, quite different from merely protecting every student's right to engage in voluntary prayer during an appropriate moment of silence during the school day. The 1978 statute already protected that right, containing nothing that prevented any student from engaging in voluntary prayer during a silent minute of meditation. Appellants have not identified any secular purpose that was not fully served by § 16-1-20 before the enactment of § 16-1-20.1. Thus, only two conclusions are consistent with the text of § 16-1-20.1: (1) the statute was enacted to convey a message of State endorsement and promotion of prayer; or (2) the statute was enacted for no purpose. No one suggests that the statute was nothing but a meaningless or irrational act.

We must, therefore, conclude that the Alabama Legislature intended to change existing law and that it was motivated by the same purposes that the Governor's Answer to the Second Amended Complaint expressly admitted; that the statement inserted in the legislative history revealed; and that Senator Holmes' testimony frankly described. The Legislature enacted § 16-1-20.1 despite the existence of § 16-1-20 for the sole purpose of expressing the State's endorsement of prayer activities for one minute at the beginning of each school day. The addition of "or voluntary prayer" indicates that the State intended to characterize prayer as a favored practice. Such an endorsement is not consistent with the established principle that the Government must pursue a course of complete neutrality toward religion.

The importance of that principle does not permit us to treat this as an inconsequential case involving nothing more than a few words of symbolic speech on behalf of the political majority. For whenever the State itself speaks on a religious subject, one of the questions that we must ask is "whether the Government intends to convey a message of endorsement or disapproval of religion." The well-supported concurrent findings of the District Court and the Court of Appeals—that § 16-1-20.1 was intended to convey a message of State-approval of prayer activities in the public schools—make it unnecessary, and indeed inappropriate, to evaluate the practical significance of the addition of the words "or voluntary prayer" to the statute. Keeping in mind, as we must, "both the fundamental place held by the Establishment Clause in our constitutional scheme and the myriad, subtle ways in which Establishment Clause values can be eroded," we conclude that § 16-1-20.1 violates the First Amendment.

The judgment of the Court of Appeals is affirmed.

It is so ordered.

* * *

JUSTICE O'CONNOR, concurring in the judgment

* * *

It once appeared that the Court had developed a workable standard by which to identify impermissible government establishments of religion. See *Lemon* v. *Kurtzman,* 403 U.S. 602 (1971). Under the now familiar *Lemon* test, statutes must have both a secular legislative purpose and a principal or primary effect that neither advances nor inhibits religion, and in addition they must not foster excessive government entanglement with religion. * * * Despite its initial promise, the *Lemon* test has proven problematic. The required inquiry into "entanglement" has been modified and questioned, * * * and in one case we have upheld state action against an Establishment Clause challenge without applying the *Lemon* test at all. *Marsh* v. *Chambers,* 463 U.S. 783 (1983). * * *

JUSTICE REHNQUIST today suggests that we abandon *Lemon* entirely, and in the process limit the reach of the Establishment Clause to state discrimination between sects and government designation of a particular church as a "state" or "national" one. * * *

Perhaps because I am new to the struggle, I am not ready to abandon all aspects of the *Lemon* test. I do believe, however, that the standards announced in *Lemon* should be reexamined and refined in order to make them more useful in achieving the underlying purpose of the First Amendment. We must strive to do more than erect a constitutional "signpost," * * *, to be followed or ignored in a particular case as our predilections may dictate. Instead, our goal should be "to frame a principle for constitutional adjudication that is not only grounded in the history and language of the first amendment, but one that is also capable of consistent application to the relevant problems." * * * Last Term, I proposed a refinement of the *Lemon* test with this goal in mind. *Lynch* v. *Donnelly*, 465 U.S., at _____ (concurring opinion).

The *Lynch* concurrence suggested that the religious liberty protected by the Establishment Clause is infringed when the government makes adherence to religion relevant to a person's standing in the political community. Direct government action endorsing religion or a particular religious practice is invalid under this approach because it "sends a message to nonadherents that they are outsiders, not full members of the political community, and an accompanying message to adherents that they are insiders, favored members of the political community." * * * Under this view, *Lemon's* inquiry as to the purpose and effect of a statute requires courts to examine whether government's purpose is to endorse religion and whether the statute actually conveys a message of endorsement.

The endorsement test is useful because of the analytic content it gives to the *Lemon*-mandated inquiry into legislative purpose and effect: In this country, church and state must necessarily operate within the same community. Because of this coexistence, it is inevitable that the secular interests of Government and the religious interests of various sects and their adherents will frequently intersect, conflict, and combine. A statute that ostensibly promotes a secular interest often has an incidental or even a primary effect of helping or hindering a sectarian belief. Chaos would ensue if every such statute were invalid under the Establishment Clause. For example, the State could not criminalize murder for fear that it would thereby promote the Biblical command against such killing. The task for the Court is to sort out those statutes and government practices whose purpose and effect go against the grain of religious liberty protected by the First Amendment.

The endorsement test does not preclude government from acknowledging religion or from taking religion into account in making law and policy. It does preclude government from conveying or attempting to convey a message that religion or a particular religious belief is favored or preferred. Such an endorsement infringes the religious liberty of the non-adherent, for "[w]hen the power, prestige and financial support of government is placed behind a particular religious belief, the indirect coercive pressure upon religious minorities to conform to the prevailing officially approved religion is plain." * * * At issue today is whether state moment of silence statutes in general, and Alabama's moment of silence statute in particular, embody an impermissible endorsement of prayer in public schools.

Twenty-five states permit or require public school teachers to have students observe a moment of silence in their classrooms.[1] A few statutes provide that the moment of silence is for the purpose of meditation alone. * * * The typical statute, however, calls for a moment of silence at the beginning of the school day during which students may meditate, pray, or reflect on activities of the day.

* * *

By mandating a moment of silence, a State does not necessarily endorse any activity that might occur during the period. * * * Even if a statute specifies that a student may choose to pray silently during a quiet moment, the State has not thereby encouraged prayer over other specified alternatives. Nonetheless, it is also possible that a moment of silence statute, either as drafted or as actually implemented, could effectively favor the child who prays over the child who does not. For example, the message of endorsement would seem inescapable if the teacher exhorts children to use the designated time to pray. Similarly, the face of the statute or its legislative history may clearly establish that it seeks to encourage or promote voluntary prayer over other alternatives, rather than merely provide a quiet moment that may be dedicated to prayer by those so inclined. The crucial question is whether the State has conveyed or attempted to convey the message that children should use the moment of silence for prayer. This question cannot be answered in the abstract, but instead requires courts to examine the history, language, and administration of a particular statute to determine whether it operates as an endorsement of religion. * * *

* * *

[1] See Ala. Code §§ 16-1-20, 16-1-20.1 (Supp. 1984); Ariz. Rev. Stat. Ann. § 15-522 (1984); Ark. Stat. Ann. § 80-1607.1 (1980); Conn. Gen Stat. § 10-16a (1983); Del. Code Ann., tit. 14, § 4101 (1981) (as interpreted in Del. Op. Atty. Gen. 79-1011 (1979); Fla. Stat. § 233.062 (1983); Ga. Code Ann. § 20-2-1050 (1982); Ill. Rev. Stat., ch 122, ¶771 (1983); Ind. Code § 20-10.1-7-11 (1982); Kan. Stat. Ann § 72.5308a (1980); La. Rev. Stat. Ann § 17:2115(A) (West 1982); Me. Rev. Stat. Ann., tit. 20-A, § 4805 (1983); Md. Educ. Code Ann. § 7-104 (1985); Mass. Gen. Laws Ann., ch. 71, § 1A (1982); Mich. Comp. Laws Ann. § 380.1565 (Supp. 1984-1985); N.J. Stat. Ann. § 18A:36-4 (West Supp. 1984-1985); N.M. Stat. Ann. § 22-5-4.1 (1981); N.Y. Educ. Law § 3029-a (McKinney 1981); N.D. Cent. Code § 15-47-30.1 (1981); Ohio Rev. Code Ann. §3313.60.1 (1980); Pa. Stat. Ann., tit. 24, § 15.1516.1 (Purdon Supp. 1984-1985); R.I. Gen. Laws § 16-12-3.1 (1981); Tenn. Code Ann. § 49-6-1004 (1983); Va. Code § 22.1-203 (1980); W. Va. Const., Art. III, § 15-a.

The Court does not hold that the Establishment Clause is so hostile to religion that it precludes the State from affording schoolchildren an opportunity for voluntary silent prayer. To the contrary, the moment of silence statutes of many States should satisfy the Establishment Clause standard we have here applied. The Court holds only that Alabama has intentionally crossed the line between creating a quiet moment during which those so inclined may pray, and affirmatively endorsing the particular religious practice of prayer. This line may be a fine one, but our precedents and the principles of religious liberty require that we draw it. In my view, the judgment of the Court of Appeals must be affirmed.

* * *

Notes and Questions

Sandra Day O'Connor, who wrote a concurring opinion in *Jaffree,* is the first woman Supreme Court justice. Prior to her appointment by President Reagan in 1981, she was an assistant attorney general and a legislator in Arizona.

Although the Court struck down the practice of school-sponsored silent prayer, which was authorized in sixteen states at the time of the decision, a careful reading of the decision suggests that allowing for a moment of silence, which was authorized in nine states, may be constitutional. According to Justice O'Connor, the crucial question regarding a moment of silence is "whether the state has conveyed or attempted to convey the message that children should use the moment of silence for prayer."

Is the issue of non-school-sponsored silent prayer really a nonissue since students cannot be prevented from silently praying during the course of a school day?

Suppose every child in a public school classroom voted to begin each class with a prayer and Bible reading. Would this lift any constitutional infirmity?

Prayer issues dealing with governmental agencies other than public schools have also appeared before the judiciary. See *Marsh* v. *Chambers,* 463 U.S. 783 (1983), which upheld the Nebraska legislative practice of opening the day with prayer.

North Dakota's Ten Commandments Law, which required the display of a placard containing the Ten Commandments of the Christian and Jewish religions in a conspicuous place in every classroom, was held to violate the Establishment Clause of the First Amendment. See *Ring* v. *Grand Forks School District No. 1,* 483 F. Supp. 272 (N.D. 1980). Although a state law that required the posting of the Ten Commandments in public classrooms was upheld by a tie vote of the Kentucky Supreme Court, *Stone* v. *Graham*, 599 S.W.2d 157 (Ky. 1980), this provision was struck down by a five-to-four decision of the United States Supreme Court in 449 U.S. 1104 (1981).

Some states provide penalties for noncompliance with statutory provisions prohibiting Bible reading or prayer. In Arizona, a "teacher . . . who conducts . . . any religious exercises in school is guilty of unprofessional conduct and his certificate shall be revoked." In Alaska and Nevada school funds may be withheld if noncompliance with statutory provisions exists.

May the singing of Christmas carols with religious significance be prohibited as part of a school program? See *Muka* v. *Sturgis*, 53 App. Div.2d 716, 383 N.Y.S.2d 933 (1976), which upheld such a prohibition. But see *Citizens Concerned for Separation of Church and State* v. *City and County of Denver*, 508 F. Supp. 823 (Colo. 1981), upholding a city's observance of a holiday with religious music, and *Florey* v. *Sioux Falls School District 49-5*, 619 F.2d 1311 (8th Cir. 1980), *cert. denied*, 449 U.S. 987 (1980), which upheld the presentation of holiday assemblies that contained religious art, literature, and music, as long as such materials were not presented in an attempt to advance or inhibit religion. The decision held that

> Only holidays with both religious and secular bases may be observed; music, art, literature and drama may be included in the curriculum only if presented in a prudent and objective manner and only as part of the cultural and religious heritage of the holiday; and religious symbols may be used only as a teaching aid or resource and only if they are displayed as part of the cultural and religious heritage of the holiday and are temporary in nature. Since all programs and materials authorized by the rules must deal with the secular or cultural basis or heritage of the holidays and since the materials must be presented in a prudent and objective manner and symbols used as a teaching aid, the advancement of a "secular program of education," and not of religion, is the primary effect of the rules. (P. 1317)

However, this court stated that a kindergarten program that was primarily religious in content was unconstitutional.

In reference to holiday displays, the United States Supreme Court upheld in a five-to-four decision a forty-year practice of having a nativity scene in a park owned by a nonprofit organization. See *Lynch* v. *Donnelly*, 465 U.S. 668 (1984).

May public schools conduct baccalaureate services? *Chamberlin* v. *Dade County Board of Public Instruction*, 377 U.S. 402 (1964) and 171 So.2d 535 (Fla. 1965), and *Goodwin* v. *Cross County School District No. 7*, 394

F. Supp. 417 (Ark. 1973), address this question but do not provide a definitive answer. Decisions allowing school-sponsored baccalaureate services generally stress the voluntary nature of such services. Would the same reasoning hold for prayers offered at an athletic contest?

May invocations and benedictions be offered at a public school graduation exercise? Although it upheld the practice, a federal appellate court declared that the language used should remain within the "standards for ceremonial prayer" and not "employ the language of Christian theology and prayer." Such a religious exercise, the court asserted, only passes constitutional muster if it does not symbolically place the state's seal of approval on one religious view. See *Stein* v. *Plainwell Community Schools*, 822 F.2d 1406 (6th Cir. 1987). However, the practice was not upheld in *Bennett* v. *Livermore School District*, 193 Cal. App. 3d 1012, 238 Cal. Rptr. 819 (1987). The California court held that commencement invocations violate the Establishment Clause because the primary purpose of prayer is religious and the effect of the practice is governmental approval of religion. A similar ruling was rendered in *Graham* v. *Central Community School District of Decatur County*, 608 F. Supp. 531 (Iowa 1985).

Permitting prayers at student assemblies, even when attendance is voluntary, violates the prohibition against governmental establishment of religion according to *Collins* v. *Chandler Unified School District*, 644 F.2d 759 (9th Cir. 1981), *cert. denied*, 454 U.S. 863 (1981). The practice of permitting religious invocations before high school football games has also been held to be unconstitutional. See *Jager* v. *Douglas County School District*, 862 F.2d 824 (11th Cir. 1989), *cert. denied*, __U.S. __ (1989).

Many public schools have Bible or other religious study groups that meet on school grounds before, during, or after school. In some instances they have been recognized as official student-body organizations and have often advertised their activities on bulletin boards or through the school newspaper. Occasionally, such groups meet during an "activity period." Meetings such as these have been the subject of much litigation, and prior to the passage of the Equal Access Act, P.L. 98–377, in 1984,* several courts had held against permitting them. Federal appeals courts for the Second, Fifth, Tenth, and Eleventh Circuits had prohibited such religious meetings, and opinion in the Third Circuit was divided.

Under the Equal Access Act it is unlawful for a public secondary school which receives federal financial assistance and has created a limited open forum to deny recognition of student-initiated groups on the basis of the religious, political, or philosophical content of the speech at meetings. Although faculty may be present, they may not participate, and outsiders may not control or regularly attend group meetings. The

---

* See Appendix D for a partial text of this act.

law declares that a limited open forum has been created when one or more noncurricular student groups are allowed to meet on school premises during noninstructional time. A limited open forum is not created when the clubs are curriculum oriented.

Passage of the Equal Access Act has not eliminated difficulties, as evidenced by the several suits that have been brought. In one instance a school's refusal to allow a group to meet on campus during noninstructional time to discuss the Bible and its application to student issues and to offer prayer was upheld. The court stated that the club did not fall under the Equal Access Act's provisions since (1) the club's activities could be viewed as part of the curriculum or closely related thereto, (2) the club's inception was not initiated by students, and (3) faculty directed and supervised the club. Additionally, the court held that the state's constitution was much stricter than the federal constitution regarding separation of church and state, and thus, the school's decision was justified under the state constitution. The opinion cited language in the act which stated that schools should not be placed in the position "to sanction meetings that are otherwise unlawful." See *Garnett* v. *Trenton School District*, 675 F. Supp. 1268 (Wash. 1987).

Does your state or local school system have provisions for school-sponsored Bible reading or prayer, silent prayer, meditation, voluntary prayer, observance of religious holidays, or religious study groups? Will noncompliance with statutory provisions prohibiting Bible reading or prayer result in any penalties in your state?

B. The Teaching of Evolution

The famous "Scopes monkey trial" in 1925 focused the nation's attention on the teaching of evolution in the public schools. Although John Scopes was found guilty of teaching evolution, his conviction was overturned on a technicality and the issue remained relatively dormant until the 1970s. At that time, forces opposed to the teaching of evolution developed a new strategy, which sought to establish that the Biblical account of creation is a respectable scientific theory and thus deserves public classroom time for its teaching. Although debated in several legislatures, creationism, as this theory became known, was enacted into law in Arkansas and Louisiana. These statutes were quickly challenged on the basis of their constitutionality. In **Edwards v. Aquillard,** a seven-to-two decision, the United States Supreme Court declared the practice as violative of the First Amendment's prohibition against establishment of religion.

Edwards v. Aguillard

Supreme Court of the United States, 1987
482 U.S. 578

JUSTICE BRENNAN delivered the opinion of the Court.

The question for decision is whether Louisiana's "Balanced Treatment for Creation-Science and Evolution-Science in Public School Instruction" Act (Creationism Act), La. Rev. Stat. Ann. §§ 17:286.1–17:286.7 is facially invalid as violative of the Establishment Clause of the First Amendment.

The Creationism Act forbids the teaching of the theory of evolution in public schools unless accompanied by instruction in "creation science." No school is required to teach evolution or creation science. If either is taught, however, the other must also be taught. The theories of evolution and creation science are statutorily defined as "the scientific evidences for [creation or evolution] and inferences from those scientific evidences."

* * *

It is clear from the legislative history that the purpose of the legislative sponsor, Senator Bill Keith, was to narrow the science curriculum. During the legislative hearings, Senator Keith stated: "My preference would be that neither [creationism nor evolution] be taught." Such a ban on teaching does not promote—indeed, it undermines—the provision of a comprehensive scientific education.

It is equally clear that requiring schools to teach creation science with evolution does not advance academic freedom. The Act does not grant teachers a flexibility that they did not already possess to supplant the present science curriculum with the presentation of theories, besides evolution, about the origin of life. Indeed, the Court of Appeals' found that no law prohibited Louisiana public schoolteachers from teaching any scientific theory. * * * As the president of the Louisiana Science Teachers Association testified, "[a]ny scientific concept that's based on established fact can be included in our curriculum already, and no legislation allowing this is necessary." The Act provides Louisiana schoolteachers with no new authority. Thus the stated purpose is not furthered by it.

* * *

Furthermore, the goal of basic "fairness" is hardly furthered by the Act's discriminatory preference for the teaching of creation science and against the teaching of evolution. While requiring that curriculum guides

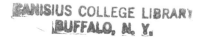

be developed for creation science, the Act says nothing of comparable guides for evolution. * * * Similarly, research services are supplied for creation science but not for evolution. Only "creation scientists" can serve on the panel that supplies the resource services. The Act forbids school boards to discriminate against anyone who "chooses to be a creation-scientist" or to teach "creationism," but fails to protect those who choose to teach evolution or any other non-creation science theory, or who refuse to teach creation science.

If the Louisiana legislature's purpose was solely to maximize the comprehensiveness and effectiveness of science instruction, it would have encouraged the teaching of all scientific theories about the origins of humankind. But under the Act's requirements, teachers who were once free to teach any and all facets of this subject are now unable to do so. Moreover, the Act fails even to ensure that creation science will be taught, but instead requires the teaching of this theory only when the theory of evolution is taught. Thus we agree with the Court of Appeals' conclusion that the Act does not serve to protect academic freedom, but has the distinctly different purpose of discrediting "evolution by counterbalancing its teaching at every turn with the teaching of creation science. . . ."

*   *   *

As in *Stone* and *Abington*, we need not be blind in this case to the legislature's preeminent religious purpose in enacting this statute. There is a historic and contemporaneous link between the teachings of certain religious denominations and the teaching of evolution. It was this link that concerned the Court in *Epperson* v. *Arkansas*, * * * which also involved a facial challenge to a statute regulating the teaching of evolution. In that case, the Court reviewed an Arkansas statute that made it unlawful for an instructor to teach evolution or to use a textbook that referred to this scientific theory. Although the Arkansas anti-evolution law did not explicitly state its predominate religious purpose, the Court could not ignore that "[t]he statute was a product of the upsurge of 'fundamentalist' religious fervor" that has long viewed this particular scientific theory as contradicting the literal interpretation of the Bible. After reviewing the history of anti-evolution statutes, the Court determined that "there can be no doubt that the motivation for the [Arkansas] law was the same [as other antievolution statutes]: to suppress the teaching of a theory which, it was thought, 'denied' the divine creation of man." The Court found that there can be no legitimate state interest in protecting particular religions from scientific views "distasteful to them," and concluded "that the First Amendment does

not permit the State to require that teaching and learning must be tailored to the principles or prohibitions of any religious sect or dogma"
* * *

These same historic and contemporaneous antagonisms between the teachings of certain religious denominations and the teaching of evolution are present in this case. The preeminent purpose of the Louisiana legislature was clearly to advance the religious viewpoint that a supernatural being created humankind. The term "creation science" was defined as embracing this particular religious doctrine by those responsible for the passage of the Creationism Act. Senator Keith's leading expert on creation science, Edward Boudreaux, testified at the legislative hearings that the theory of creation science included belief in the existence of a supernatural creator. * * * Senator Keith also cited testimony from other experts to support the creation-science view that "a creator [was] responsible for the universe and everything in it." The legislative history therefore reveals that the term "creation science," as contemplated by the legislature that adopted this Act, embodies the religious belief that a supernatural creator was responsible for the creation of humankind.

Furthermore, it is not happenstance that the legislature required the teaching of a theory that coincided with this religious view. The legislative history documents that the Act's primary purpose was to change the science curriculum of public schools in order to provide persuasive advantage to a particular religious doctrine that rejects the factual basis of evolution in its entirety. The sponsor of the Creationism Act, Senator Keith, explained during the legislative hearings that his disdain for the theory of evolution resulted from the support that evolution supplied to views contrary to his own religious beliefs. According to Senator Keith, the theory of evolution was consonant with the "cardinal principle[s] of religious humanism, secular humanism, theological liberalism, aetheistism [sic]." * * * The state senator repeatedly stated that scientific evidence supporting his religious views should be included in the public school curriculum to redress the fact that the theory of evolution incidentally coincided with what he characterized as religious beliefs antithetical to his own. The legislation therefore sought to alter the science curriculum to reflect endorsement of a religious view that is antagonistic to the theory of evolution.

In this case, the purpose of the Creationism Act was to restructure the science curriculum to conform with a particular religious viewpoint. Out of many possible science subjects taught in the public schools, the legislature chose to affect the teaching of the one scientific theory that historically has been opposed by certain religious sects.

* * *

We do not imply that a legislature could never require that scientific critiques of prevailing scientific theories be taught. Indeed, the Court acknowledged in *Stone* that its decision forbidding the posting of the Ten Commandments did not mean that no use could ever be made of the Ten Commandments, or that the Ten Commandments played an exclusively religious role in the history of Western Civilization. In a similar way, teaching a variety of scientific theories about the origins of humankind to schoolchildren might be validly done with the clear secular intent of enhancing the effectiveness of science instruction. But because the primary purpose of the Creationism Act is to endorse a particular religious doctrine, the Act furthers religion in violation of the Establishment Clause.

*   *   *

The Louisiana Creationism Act advances a religious doctrine by requiring either the banishment of the theory of evolution from public school classrooms or the presentation of a religious viewpoint that rejects evolution in its entirety. The Act violates the Establishment Clause of the First Amendment because it seeks to employ the symbolic and financial support of government to achieve a religious purpose. The judgment of the Court of Appeals therefore is

Affirmed.

*   *   *

JUSTICE SCALIA, with whom THE CHIEF JUSTICE joins, dissenting.

Even if I agreed with the questionable premise that legislation can be invalidated under the Establishment Clause on the basis of its motivation alone, without regard to its effects, I would still find no justification for today's decision. The Louisiana legislators who passed the "Balanced Treatment for Creation-Science and Evolution-Science Act," *   *   * each of whom had sworn to support the Constitution, were well aware of the potential Establishment Clause problems and considered that aspect of the legislation with great care. After seven hearings and several months of study, resulting in substantial revision of the original proposal, they approved the Act overwhelmingly and specifically articulated the secular purpose they meant it to serve. Although the record contains abundant evidence of the sincerity of that purpose (the only issue pertinent to this case), the Court today holds, essentially on the basis of "its visceral knowledge regarding what *must* have motivated the legislators," *   *   * that the members of the Louisiana Legislature knowingly violated their oaths and then lied about it. I dissent. Had requirements of the Balanced Treatment Act that are not apparent on its face been clarified by an interpretation of the Louisiana Supreme Court, or by the manner of its implementation, the Act might well be found unconstitutional; but the question of its constitutionality cannot rightly be disposed of on the gallop, by impugning the motives of its supporters.

* * *

* * * Even if one concedes, for the sake of argument, that a majority of the Louisiana Legislature voted for the Balanced Treatment Act partly in order to foster (rather than merely eliminate discrimination against) Christian fundamentalist beliefs, our cases establish that that alone would not suffice to invalidate the Act, so long as there was a genuine secular purpose as well.

* * *

The people of Louisiana, including those who are Christian fundamentalists, are quite entitled, as a secular matter, to have whatever scientific evidence there may be against evolution presented in their schools, just as Mr. Scopes was entitled to present whatever scientific evidence there was for it. Perhaps what the Louisiana Legislature has done is unconstitutional because there *is* no such evidence, and the scheme they have established will amount to no more than a presentation of the Book of Genesis.

* * *

Because I believe that the Balanced Treatment Act had a secular purpose, which is all the first component of the *Lemon* test requires, I would reverse the judgment of the Court of Appeals and remand for further consideration.

* * *

Notes

Chief Justice William H. Rehnquist, who joined in the **Aguillard** dissent, was appointed by President Ronald Reagan in 1986 to become the sixteenth Chief Justice of the Supreme Court. He had been an associate justice since 1972. Before his tenure on the Court, Chief Justice Rehnquist was a law clerk for Justice Robert Jackson in Jackson's private practice and an assistant attorney general in the Justice Department.

Justice William Brennan, who wrote the majority opinion in **Aguillard,** was appointed to the Court by President Dwight D. Eisenhower in 1956. He had been an associate justice of the New Jersey Supreme Court. Justice Antonin Scalia, who wrote the dissenting opinion, was appointed by President Ronald Reagan in 1986 to replace Justice Rehnquist when he was elevated to the Chief Justiceship. Justice Scalia came to the Court from the federal appellate court in the District of Columbia.

A state supreme court upheld the nonrenewal of a teacher who devoted excessive time to creationism and religion in his biology class and who failed to cover basic biology principles. The school board had established guidelines that allowed the teacher a specified amount of time to teach the theories of evolution or creation. See *Dale* v. *Board of Education, Lemmon Independent School District,* 316 N.W.2d 108 (N.D. 1982).

C. Textbooks

Parents may object to the use of certain textbooks on the grounds that the books advance secular humanism and inhibit theistic religion. In one instance parents charged that history, social studies, and home economics books promoted secular humanism by excluding facts about religion and by failing to present a Biblically based or divine framework for decision making. The Eleventh United States Circuit Court of Appeals did not uphold the parents' contentions and declared:

> Examination of the contents of these textbooks, including the passages pointed out by Appellees as particularly offensive, in the context of the books as a whole and the undisputedly nonreligious purpose sought to be achieved by their use, reveals that the message conveyed is not one of endorsement of secular humanism or any religion. Rather, the message conveyed is one of a governmental attempt to instill in Alabama public school children such values as independent thought, tolerance of diverse views, self-respect, maturity, self-reliance and logical decision-making. This is an entirely appropriate secular effect. Indeed, one of the major objectives of public education is the "inculcat[ion of] fundamental values necessary to the maintenance of a democratic political system." * * *
> Nor do these textbooks evidence an attitude antagonistic to theistic belief. The message conveyed by these textbooks with regard to theistic religion is one of neutrality: the textbooks neither endorse theistic religion as a system of belief, nor discredit it. Indeed, many of the books specifically acknowledge that religion is one source of moral values and none preclude that possibility. (P. 692)

See *Smith* v. *Board of School Commissioners of Mobile County,* 827 F.2d 684 (11th Cir. 1987).

In another instance a parent objected to the use of the Holt, Rinehart and Winston basic reading series and specifically to a story about mental telepathy. The parent wanted an alternative reading program. In rejecting this petition, the Sixth United States Circuit Court of Appeals stated:

> The divisiveness and disruption caused by the opt-out remedy would be magnified if the schools had to grant other exemptions. Although the District Court found that no other objections to the Hawkins County public school curriculum have been raised and that Hawkins County is homogeneous from a religious perspective, this case would create a precedent for persons from other religions to request exemptions from core subjects because of religious objections. If the school district were required to accommodate exceptions and permit other students to opt-out of the reading program and other core courses with materials others found objectionable, this would result in a public school system impossible to administer. (Pp. 1072–73)

See *Mozert* v. *Hawkins County Board of Education*, 827 F.2d 1058 (6th Cir. 1987), *cert. denied*, 484 U.S. 1066 (1988).

D. Distribution of Religious Literature

Distribution in the public schools of Bibles and other religious literature has been a much litigated issue. In one of the earliest decisions, *Tudor* v. *Board of Education of Borough of Rutherford*, 100 A.2d 857 (N.J. 1953), distribution of Gideon Bibles was prohibited. However, a policy that allowed all religions to distribute their literature has been upheld. In this instance, although literature could not be distributed by going from classroom to classroom or by walking up and down aisles, it could be distributed at a designated place. See *Meltzer* v. *Board of Public Instruction of Orange County*, 577 F.2d 311 (5th Cir. 1978). Another court did not uphold the distribution of sectarian literature such as leaflets advertising religious activities. See *Hernandez* v. *Hanson*, 430 F. Supp. 1154 (Neb. 1977).

E. Released and Shared Time and Religious Instruction

Two significant United States Supreme Court decisions have addressed the questions of releasing public school students during normal school hours and thereby enabling them to receive religious instruction. In one of the decisions, *McCollum* v. *Board of Education of School District No. 71*, 333 U.S. 203 (1948), the Court invalidated a plan under which separate Protestant, Catholic, and Jewish religious classes were taught in the public school buildings. The Court contended that the use of tax-supported property for religious instruction, the close cooperation between school authorities and religious officials, and the use of the state's compulsory-education system all tended to promote religious education, and, therefore, violated the First Amendment. In another decision, *Zorach v. Clauson*, 343 U.S. 306 (1952), the Court upheld a plan whereby students were released during public school hours to attend religious instruction classes off the school premises. The Court stated:

> The government must be neutral when it comes to competition between sects. It may not thrust any sect on any person. It may not make a religious observance compulsory. It may not coerce anyone to attend church, to observe a religious holiday, or to take religious instruction. But it can close its doors or suspend its operations as to those who want to repair to their religious sanctuary for worship or instruction. No more than that is undertaken here. (P. 314)

A plan under which Hasidic Jewish girls would be taught on public school premises was held to be unconstitutional. Under the plan the girls would be taught only by women who spoke Yiddish and only in an area designated for their exclusive use. See *Parents Association of P.S. 16* v. *Quinones*, 803 F.2d 1235 (2d Cir. 1986).

A federal district court, in *Lanner* v. *Wimmer*, 463 F. Supp. 867 (Utah 1978), has held that academic credit could not be given in a released-time seminary program for courses in the Old Testament and New Testament. The Tenth Circuit Court of Appeals modified this decision in 662 F.2d 1349 (10th Cir. 1981). The court ruled that the process of gathering attendance slips and the necessity of judging whether the courses were mainly denominational violated the First Amendment. The court held that neither the released-time program itself nor the granting of credit toward participation in extracurricular activities offended the Establishment and Free Exercise Clauses.

Several cases have addressed the issue of shared time. In one case a public school would not enroll a parochial school student in a band course at the public school. The public school had a policy of allowing attendance in its schools only by fulltime students. See *Snyder* v. *Charlotte Public School District*, 421 Mich. 517, 365 N.W.2d 151 (1984), in which the Michigan Supreme Court ruled that public schools must open "non-essential elective courses" such as band, art, and advanced mathematics to private school students.

A shared-time and a community-education program conducted by public school teachers within participating non-public school facilities were struck down by the United States Supreme Court in *Grand Rapids School District* v. *Ball*, 473 U.S. 373 (1985). In this case public school teachers taught remedial math and reading, art, music, and physical education in parochial schools during the school day. Public school teachers also taught gymnastics, home economics, Spanish, and drama after school.

Is it permissible for a public school system to offer Bible study courses? See *Wiley* v. *Franklin*, 474 F. Supp. 525 (Tenn. 1979), which held that such courses could not be offered unless they were (1) secular in nature, intent, and purpose; (2) neither advancing nor inhibiting religion; and (3) offered in a manner that avoided excessive entanglement between government and religion. See *Crockett* v. *Sorenson*, 568 F. Supp. 1422 (Va. 1983) for a similar view. A course entitled Science of Creative Intelligence—Transcendental Meditation, which involved religious activity, was held to constitute establishment of religion proscribed by the First Amendment. See *Malnak* v. *Yogi*, 592 F.2d 197 (3rd Cir. 1979).

III. Use of Facilities

Another issue that often arises at the local school level has to do with the extent, if any, that school buildings may be used during noninstructional hours. In most instances the local school board has either implied or specific authority to promulgate reasonable rules for the use of school buildings when they are not being used for school purposes or when their use does not interfere with normal school operations. Controversies often arise when the use of school facilities is requested by a group whose purpose or speaker may be offensive to some in the community, that represents certain religious organizations, or that is primarily interested in using the facility for commercial gain.

A general rule that has evolved concerning the use of school facilities suggests that if facilities are to be leased to one type of group, they must be available to all within the group. However, such use may be denied if (1) the user fails or refuses to abide by reasonable rules and regulations pertaining to the use, (2) there is a demonstrated danger of violence or disruption associated with meetings of this particular group, or (3) the meeting violates a local ordinance or either state or federal constitutional provisions or law. It should be noted that in the absence of a state statute mandating their use, local systems are not obligated to make school buildings available for public activities.

Those denied use of a school facility often allege that their right of freedom of expression has been denied. The United States Supreme Court addressed this notion in *Police Department of the City of Chicago* v. *Mosley*, 408 U.S. 92 (1972), when it stated:

> Necessarily, then, under the Equal Protection Clause, not to mention the First Amendment itself, government may not grant the use of a forum to

people whose views it finds acceptable, but deny use to those wishing to express less favored or more controversial views. And it may not select which issues are worth discussing or debating in public facilities. There is an "equality of status in the field of ideas," and government must afford all points of view an equal opportunity to be heard. Once a forum is opened up to assembly or speaking by some groups, government may not prohibit others from assembling or speaking on the basis of what they intend to say. Selective exclusions from a public forum may not be based on content alone, and may not be justified by reference to content alone. (P. 96)

Country Hills Christian Church v. Unified School District No. 512

United States District Court, District of Kansas, 1983
560 F. Supp. 1207

SAFFELS, District Judge.

* * *

Defendants have made available their school buildings and facilities to non-school community organizations at a reasonable rent. Groups as diverse as the Democratic Party and the Y.M.C.A. make use of defendants' buildings. Community groups use these buildings for singing songs, cooking group suppers, staging theatrical productions, playing basketball and airing their political and moral views. For example, the court heard testimony about the Voice of Reason meeting at night on December 7, 1982, at Indian Hills Junior High School, at which meeting school prayer, sex education and abortion were discussed.

The traditional public forum is a park or a public street. The First Amendment, through the Fourteenth, prohibits a state from abridging or denying use of a street or park for purposes of assembly, communication and discussion of public questions. * * * Use of the streets or parks may be subject to reasonable time, place and manner restrictions * * *, but only to the extent necessary to avoid a threat to public safety, peace or order. * * *

Streets and parks are not the only public places subject to the protection of the First Amendment. A public library may be a public forum, and, in some cases, a local government must allow its library to be used as a stage for political expression. * * * A railroad station is a public forum * * *, and a municipal bus terminal is a public forum * * *, while a city-owned bus is not. * * * A municipally-owned theater is a public forum. * * * Even a privately-owned shopping center can be a public forum. * * *

A public school is a public forum for its students and teachers. * * * If it is opened to the school district community for meetings and discussions during non-school hours, then it becomes a public forum for the community. * * *

Defendants, by and through their Policies Nos. 2000 and 2020, have created a public forum for the exercise of First Amendment rights. The forum is open to "recognized community groups." The dedication of school district facilities as a public forum for community groups makes the school buildings virtually the same, in concept, as streets and parks as far as the First Amendment is concerned.

This does not mean, however, that school buildings cannot be regulated to a greater degree than parks and streets. The nature of the school building, its function in the community and the activities normally conducted there, dictate that reasonable regulations of time, place and manner of use by community organizations may be imposed. * * * Defendants allege that if the court allows the Country Hills Christian Church to use Mill Creek Elementary School on Easter Sunday, the floodgates will be opened and the court must also order them to allow into their buildings snake cults, groups that practice animal sacrifices, groups that wear odd clothes, and groups that smoke and use fire in their worship services.

That is a bridge the court does not have to cross at this time. From the evidence, the court finds that plaintiffs conduct worship services of a more tame variety. Nevertheless, if defendants find that the handling of poisonous reptiles, fire and smoke, or the use of alcoholic beverages in a religious service conducted in a school building are activities which should be regulated, the First Amendment should pose no obstacle so long as the regulations are reasonable.

Religious worship and discussion are "forms of speech and association protected by the First Amendment." * * *

Once a forum is opened to assembly or speaking by some groups, a school district may not prohibit other groups from assembling or speaking on the basis of what they intend to say. Selective exclusions from a public forum may not be based on content alone, and may not be justified by reference to content. * * * The First Amendment prohibits excluding groups from a public forum based on the content of the group's intended speech even where the government was not required to create the forum in the first place. * * *

Defendants review requests to use School District facilities to determine whether or not each group will be engaging in religious worship. If the group is deemed to be making a request to use the School District facilities for a non-religious use, then the group's request is granted. If defendants determine the group will make religious use of the building, permission is denied. Plaintiffs fall into the latter group. Defendants have denied plaintiffs access to a public forum solely because of the content of plaintiff's proposed speech. This is a violation of the First Amendment. * * *

Defendants' primary function, that of educating children, does not exempt them from the provisions of the First Amendment. The First Amendment extends to public schools * * *, and unconstitutional exclusion of those who wish to use school buildings cannot be rationalized by reference to the school setting. "School desks and blackboards, like trees [in a park] or street lights [on a street], are but the trappings of the forum; what imports is the meeting of minds and not the meeting place." * * *

Defendants argue that children are impressionable and easily confused. They argue that children who attend Sunday school in the same building as their public school classes will come to feel that the School District endorses their church. Defendants argue that a child who attends Sunday school at a church may feel that the School District disapproves of his church because another sect is permitted to rent the child's school building during non-school hours. Defendants further argue that children will acquire an irreconcilable conflict between an apparently school-district-approved sect and their family's religion and church. This may or may not be true. There is no evidence in the record to support these contentions. Dr. Cormack, School District Psychologist, testified that he believed these contentions to be true, but he admitted that no empirical evidence existed in support of his theories and that no studies had been done to verify them. The court finds his testimony to be speculative and declines to give it any weight. * * *

* * *

The Establishment Clause requires the School District to be neutral in its relations with groups of religious believers, but does not require the School District to be an adversary to religious groups. The court finds the School District may not close their doors to groups who wish to rent School District facilities for purposes of religious worship during non-school hours, and that the Establishment Clause provides no defense to this action.

* * *

The present policy presents an unacceptable degree of entanglement with religion by the School District because of enforcement of its policy of exclusion of religious worship. The School District must determine in every questionable case what words and conduct constitute religious use or religious worship. Of course, this is "an impossible task in an age where many and various beliefs meet the constitutional definition of religion." * * * An open access policy would eliminate the need for the School District to determine what uses are religious and what uses are not religious.

"Entanglement" refers not only to the day-to-day interaction between government and religion; it also refers to the effect of government policies toward religion. In the end, the test for entanglement is one of degree. The question is whether or not government policy calls for "official or continuing surveillance" or excessive government involvement in religious organizations. * * *

"Entanglement" refers to either a governmentally-established religion or governmental interference with religion. Avoiding excessive entanglement does not require "perfect or absolute separation" of church and state * * *: there is "room for play in the joints productive of a benevolent neutrality which will permit religious exercise to exist without sponsorship" by the government. * * * A school district does not engage in excessive entanglement if it maintains a "kind of benevolent neutrality toward churches and religious exercise generally." * * * An open access policy would, at most foster such a benevolent neutrality, but would not subject defendants to an unconstitutional level of entanglement.

The court concludes that by allowing their facilities to be used during non-school hours by non-school community groups, defendants have created a public forum. Having created a public forum, defendants cannot exclude plaintiffs from the forum because of the religious content of plaintiff's intended speech unless such exclusion is justified under applicable constitutional case law. Defendants have not and cannot justify their policy of exclusion. The Establishment Clause does not justify excluding plaintiffs' religious services from School District buildings, and there is no evidence either that children will be harmed or that defendants risk placing an imprimatur of approval on religious sects which rent School District facilities.

Notes and Questions

In upholding the use of school property for religious services during nonschool hours, the New Jersey Supreme Court contended that a rental schedule should include the actual costs of utilities and administrative and janitorial services. Five years was considered "approaching the outer bounds of reasonable time and nearing the point of prohibited entanglement." See *Resnick* v. *East Brunswick Township Board of Education*, 77

N.J. 88, 389 A.2d 944 (1978). However, a school district's policy of renting its elementary school buildings for use immediately before and after regular school hours was held to be unconstitutional. In its holding a federal district court contended that such a practice creates an appearance of official support for religious instruction and that it benefits from students' compliance with compulsory attendance law. See *Ford* v. *Manuel*, 629 F. Supp. 771 (Ohio 1985).

In addressing the issue of conditioning the off-time use of public school facilities on the political or ideological views of the applicant, on its membership policies, or on its attendance restrictions, a federal appellate court declared that the school system was not responsible for the views expressed or for the composition of the group that expressed them. The court also stated that "merely permitting the occasional and temporary use of state facilities by racially discriminatory groups along with all others does not constitute significant state involvement in their practices." See *Knights of the Ku Klux Klan* v. *East Baton Rouge Parish School Board*, 578 F.2d 1122 (5th Cir. 1978). Also see *National Socialist White People's Party* v. *Ringers*, 473 F.2d 1010 (4th Cir. 1973).

Although a school board delegated authority over most permit applications to its building-level administrators, it retained the authority to consider, with advice of counsel, the applications of religious groups for non-social or non-recreational meetings. In upholding this practice a federal appellate court contended that the school board's need to assess the complex issues concerning the Establishment Clause was sufficient justification for the minor inconvenience caused by the policy. See *Salinas* v. *School District of Kansas City*, 751 F.2d 288 (8th Cir. 1984).

California has a statute establishing a "civic center" at "each and every public school building and grounds within the state." Although the local board may adopt reasonable rules and regulations pertaining to the statute, community groups may use the facilities without charge to discuss subjects that "appertain to the educational, political, economic, artistic, and moral interests of the citizens."

Local businesspeople are often concerned that allowing the use of school facilities, which have been constructed at public expense, is a form of competition against them. This view was not upheld in *Hall* v. *Shelby County Board of Education*, 472 S.W.2d 489 (Ky. 1971), where a local civic group organized and charged admission to musical programs. All profits were used for civic activities.

Assume a local school board had a policy of allowing school facilities to be used by local groups. Would the school board be on sound constitutional footing if they barred any of the following local groups: a gay liberation league? a group wishing to legalize the use of marijuana, cocaine, or heroin? American Nazis? Save the Whales? Impeach the

President Committee? Committee to recall local school board members? Devil worshippers? Nudists? Communists? What is the basis for your response in each of these instances?

Does your state have legislation pertaining to the use of public school facilities when they are not being used by the school system? Does your public school system have policies regulating the use of facilities?

IV. Aid to Nonpublic Schools

Approximately 10 percent of American students attend nonpublic schools. About 70 percent of those students are enrolled in Catholic schools, and approximately 15 percent of nonpublic school students attend non-church-related schools. Legislatures in several states having large numbers of nonpublic school students have passed measures which have attempted to financially assist the nonpublic school sector. Since these measures have raised serious questions pertaining to the proper separation of church and state under the First Amendment, their constitutionality has been examined by the United States Supreme Court.

As discussed previously, three tests have been developed by the Court to determine whether or not the Establishment Clause of the First Amendment has been violated. By employing these tests, the Court has attempted to determine whether or not a challenged statute (1) has a clearly secular purpose, (2) has a principal or primary effect that neither advances nor inhibits religion, and (3) does not foster an excessive government entanglement with religion.

In *Lemon* v. *Kurtzman*, 403 U.S. 602 (1971) the Court struck down both an attempt by the Rhode Island legislature to provide a 15 percent salary supplement to be paid to those teachers dealing with secular subjects in nonpublic schools and a Pennsylvania statute that provided financial support to nonpublic elementary and secondary schools by way of reimbursement for the cost of teachers' salaries, textbooks, and instructional materials in specified secular subjects. The Court held that the "cumulative impact of the entire relationship arising under the statutes in each state involves excessive entanglement between government and religion." Furthermore, the Court reasoned that these state programs had a divisive political potential that would be a threat to the normal political process. Since candidates would be forced to declare their position on amounts of money to be expended in such programs, political division along religious lines would develop. The Court contended that this was a principal evil that the First Amendment was intended to protect against.

A New York statute was struck down by the Court in *Levitt* v. *Committee for Public Education and Religious Liberty*, 413 U.S. 472 (1973). Under this statute nonpublic schools would have been reimbursed for expenses incurred in administering, grading, compiling, and reporting test results; maintaining pupil attendance and health records; recording qualifications and characteristics of personnel; and preparing and submitting various reports to the state. The Court ruled that such aid would have the primary purpose or effect of advancing religion or religious education and that it would lead to excessive entanglement between church and state. However, in *Committee for Public Education and Religious Liberty* v. *Regan*, 442 U.S. 928 (1980), a five-to-four opinion, the Court upheld a revised version of the law that had been declared unconstitutional in *Levitt*. The revised law allowed the state to reimburse private schools, including sectarian schools, for the expenses connected with keeping official attendance and other records, for administering three state tests, and for grading two of the tests.

Another New York law was invalidated, in *Committee for Public Education and Religious Liberty* v. *Nyquist*, 413 U.S. 756 (1973), which provided for the maintenance and repair of nonpublic school facilities, tuition reimbursement for parents of nonpublic school students, and tax relief for those not qualifying for tuition reimbursement. And a Pennsylvania law providing for parent reimbursement for nonpublic school students was also invalidated in *Sloan* v. *Lemon*, 413 U.S. 825 (1973). The majority opinion declared that there was no constitutionally significant difference between Pennsylvania's tuition-grant scheme and New York's tuition-reimbursement program, which was held violative of the establishment clause in *Nyquist*.

In *Meek* v. *Pittenger*, 421 U.S. 349 (1975), the Court was asked to rule on a Pennsylvania statute that provided for auxiliary services for exceptional, remedial, or educationally disadvantaged nonpublic school students; for lending instructional materials and equipment to nonpublic schools; and for lending textbooks to nonpublic school students. The Court invalidated all but the textbook-loan provision of the Pennsylvania law. It held that the act had the unconstitutional primary effect of advancing religion because of the predominantly religious character of the benefiting schools. Additionally, the Court stated that the act provided excessive opportunities for political fragmentation and division along religious lines. Expanding on this theme, the Court declared:

> This potential for political entanglement, together with the administrative entanglement which would be necessary to ensure that auxiliary-services personnel remain strictly neutral and nonideological when functioning in church-related schools . . . violates the constitutional prohibition against laws "respecting an establishment of religion." (P. 372)

In another decision, *Wolman* v. *Walter,* 433 U.S. 229 (1977), the Court addressed the constitutionality of an Ohio statute that had attempted to conform to the *Meek* ruling. The decision, which revealed wide disagreement among the justices, held that the provisions providing nonpublic students with books, standardized testing and scoring, diagnostic services, and therapeutic and remedial services were constitutional. However, provisions relating to instructional materials and equipment and field trip services were held to be unconstitutional.

In a five-to-four decision, *Mueller* v. *Allen,* 463 U.S. 388 (1983), the Court upheld a Minnesota law permitting taxpayers to claim a deduction from gross income on their state income tax returns for expenses incurred for "tuition, textbooks and transportation" not exceeding $500 for dependents in grades K–6 and $700 for dependents in grades 7–12. A distinction between this decision and the Court's 1973 *Nyquist* ruling appears to be that *Nyquist* rejected a tax *credit* for parents whose children attended nonpublic school, while *Mueller* allowed a tax *deduction* for all parents, including those whose children attended public schools. The tax deduction, the *Mueller* majority reasoned, was simply part of the state's tax law permitting deductions for a number of things. The dissenters argued that the difference between a tax credit and a deduction was "a distinction without a difference," and that 90 percent of private school students were in sectarian schools. However, a New Jersey statute was held to be unconstitutional that provided taxpayers with a $1,000 tax deduction for each child attending nonpublic schools. See *Public Funds for Public Schools of New Jersey* v. *Byrne,* 590 F.2d 514 (3rd Cir. 1979), *aff'd,* 442 U.S. 907 (1979).

The United States Supreme Court, in a five-to-four decision, upheld the constitutionality of providing transportation to parochial school students in *Everson* v. *Board of Education of Township of Ewing,* 330 U.S. 1 (1947). More than thirty years later, a Rhode Island statute providing for the busing of students to nonpublic schools was held not to violate state or federal constitutional provisions. See *Members of the Jamestown School Committee* v. *Schmidt,* 405 A.2d 16 (R.I. 1979).

Under the Internal Revenue Code, tax exemptions may be granted to "corporations . . . organized and operated exclusively for religious, charitable . . . or educational purposes." A private religious university was devoted to the teaching and propagation of fundamentalist religious beliefs, which included that God intends segregation of the races and that scripture forbids interracial dating and marriage. Students were expelled if they did not follow these prohibitions. The Internal Revenue Service, upheld by the Supreme Court, withdrew the college's tax-exempt status, having determined that the racial policy was not "charitable" as required by the Code. See *Bob Jones University* v. *United States*, 461 U.S. 574 (1983).

The Court struck down the use of federal education funds under Chapter I (formerly Title I of the Elementary and Secondary Education Act) to pay public school teachers who taught in programs aimed at helping low-income, educationally deprived students in parochial schools. See *Aguilar* v. *Felton*, 473 U.S. 402 (1985).

Does your state have any provisions for aid to nonpublic schools?

V. School Fees

Disputes often arise in regard to the charging of fees by public school systems for supplies, materials, extracurricular activities, transportation to school and texts. Whether or not fees may be legitimately charged depends upon statutory provisions or the interpretation of a state's constitution. Although decisions in several states have denied the charging of fees for textbooks and/or supplies, decisions in other states have taken an opposite view.

The California Supreme Court considered the issue of charging fees for extracurricular activities in *Hartzell* v. *Connell.*

Hartzell v. Connell

Supreme Court of California, 1984
35 Cal.3d 899, 679 P.2d 35, 201 Cal. Rptr. 601

BIRD, Chief Justice.

May a public high school district charge fees for educational programs simply because they have been denominated "extracurricular"?

The Santa Barbara High School District (District) offers a wide variety of extracurricular activities, ranging from cheerleading to madrigal singing, and from archery to football. Many of these activities are of relatively recent origin. For example, in 1956, Santa Barbara High School fielded six athletic teams while today there are thirty-eight.

Prior to the 1980–1981 school year, any student could participate in these activities free of charge. The programs were financed by a combination of District contributions (mostly state aid and local tax revenues), ticket sales, and fundraising activities conducted by the constituent high schools.

In the spring of 1980, the District school board (Board) decided to cut its budget by $1.1 million. This decision reflected a drop in revenues due to the combined effects of inflation, declining enrollment, and the adoption of Proposition 13. Among the items to be reduced was the District's contribution to the high school extracurricular programs.

The Board considered two plans for adapting the programs to fit its reduced budget. The first plan called for a major cut in interscholastic athletic competition, including the reduction of the high school program from over 30 teams to only 8 and the elimination of interscholastic competition at the ninth grade level. Under this plan, the surviving programs were to remain open to all students free of charge.

The second plan provided for a less extensive cut in athletic competition—elimination of the ninth grade program only. To make up the difference, it proposed to raise money by charging students fees for participation in dramatic productions, musical performances, and athletic competition.

The Board chose the second option. Under the plan finally adopted, students are required to pay $25 for *each* athletic team in which they wish to participate, and $25 per category for any or all activities in *each* of the following four categories: (1) dramatic productions (e.g., plays, dance performances and musicals); (2) vocal music groups (e.g., choir and madrigal groups); (3) instrumental groups (e.g., orchestra, marching band, and related groups such as the drill team and flag twirlers); and (4) cheerleading groups.

* * *

In an attempt to ensure that the fees would not prevent any students from participating, the District has implemented a fee-waiver program. Upon showing a financial need, a student may obtain a "scholarship" to participate without paying the fee. The standard of need is similar to that of the free lunch program.

The fee-waiver policy has been supplemented with an outreach program. Teachers and coaches are asked to inform their principals of any students who, though expected to participate in an activity, do not do so. These students are then interviewed by the principal to determine whether the fee prevented them from participating.

* * *

The trial court rejected all of the plaintiffs' claims, primarily on the ground that none of the activities covered by the fee program are "integral" to credit courses.

The California Constitution requires the Legislature to "provide for a system of common schools by which a *free school* shall be kept up and supported in each district. . . ." (Cal. Const., art. IX, § 5, emphasis added.) This provision entitles "the youth of the State . . . to be educated at the public expense." * * *

Plaintiffs assert that the imposition of fees for educational extracurricular activities violates the free school guarantee. They are correct.

* * *

Accordingly, this court holds that all educational activities—curricular or "extracurricular"—offered to students by school districts fall within the free school guarantee of article IX, section 5. Since it is not disputed that the programs involved in this case are "educational" in character, they fall within that guarantee.

Defendants argue, however, that the fee-waiver policy for needy students satisfies the requirement of the free school guarantee. They suggest that the right "to be educated at the public expense" * * * amounts merely to a right *not to be financially prevented* from enjoying educational opportunities. This argument contradicts the plain language of the Constitution.

In guaranteeing "free" public schools, article IX, section 5 fixes the precise extent of the financial burden which may be imposed on the right to an education—none. * * * A school which conditions a student's participation in educational activities upon the payment of a fee clearly is *not* a "free school."

The free school guarantee reflects the people's judgment that a child's public education is too important to be left to the budgetary circumstances and decisions of individual families. It makes no distinction between needy and nonneedy families. Individual families, needy or not, may value education more or less depending upon conflicting budget priorities. * * *

The free school guarantee lifts budgetary decisions concerning public education out of the individual family setting and requires that such decisions be made by the community as a whole. Once the community has decided that a particular educational program is important enough to be offered by its public schools, a student's participation in that program cannot be made to depend upon his or her family's decision to pay a fee or buy a toaster.

Nor may a student's participation be conditioned upon application for a special waiver. The stigma that results from recording some students as needy was recognized early in the struggle for free schools. * * *

Finally, defendants warn that, if the fees are invalidated, many school districts may be forced to drop some extracurricular activities. They argue that invalidation would—in the name of the free school guarantee—produce the anomalous result of reducing the number of educational opportunities available to students.

This court recognizes that, due to legal limitations on taxation and spending * * *, school districts do indeed operate under difficult financial constraints. However, financial hardship is no defense to a violation of the free school guarantee. * * *

Perhaps, in the view of some, public education could be more efficiently financed by peddling it on the open market. Under the California Constitution, however, access to public education is a right enjoyed by all—not a commodity for sale. Educational opportunities must be provided to all students without regard to their families' ability or willingness to pay fees or request special waivers. This fundamental feature of public education is not contingent upon the inevitably fluctuating financial health of local school districts. A solution to those financial difficulties must be found elsewhere—for example, through the political process.

In conclusion, this court holds that the imposition of fees for educational activities offered by public high school districts violates the free school guarantee. The constitutional defect in such fees can neither be corrected by providing waivers to indigent students, nor justified by pleading financial hardship.

Plaintiffs also argue that the fee requirement violates title 5, section 350 of the California Administrative Code (hereafter title 5, section 350). That section provides: "A pupil enrolled in a school shall not be required to pay *any* fee, deposit, or other charge not specifically authorized by law." * * *

* * *

In conclusion, the imposition of fees as a precondition for participation in educational programs offered by public high schools on a non-credit basis violates the free school guarantee of the California Constitution and the prohibition against school fees contained in title 5, section 350 of the California Administrative Code.

The judgment is reversed.

* * *

Notes and Questions

A short survey of states' constitutional provisions and case law concerning the issue of school fees is discussed in *Cardiff* v. *Bismarck Public School District*, 263 N.W.2d 105 (N.D. 1978). May a student's transcript be withheld for failure to pay school fees? See *Paulson* v. *Minidoka County*

School District No. 331, 93 Idaho 469, 463 P.2d 935 (1970), where the court stated that "free common schools" were not being provided when access to official reports of students' records depended upon payment of a $25 unconstitutional school fee. May a transcript of grades be withheld for failure to pay a legitimate fee?

Incidental fees for attendance at athletic or literary events and the use of the library have generally been upheld even when there is a constitutional requirement for providing free public schools. What determines whether or not a school may charge an "incidental" fee but not other fees?

A United States Supreme Court decision upheld a North Dakota statute that allowed local school boards to assess fees for transporting pupils to school. Inasmuch as the policy caused education to be more expensive for some citizens than for others, plaintiffs contended that the statute offended the Equal Protection Clause of the United States Constitution. In rejecting that contention, the Court declined on two counts to subject the statute to "strict scrutiny." First, it reaffirmed its position that education is not a "fundamental" constitutional right. Second, it held that laws impacting disproportionately on the poor do not, on that account, invoke such scrutiny. Moreover, the Court declared, a state's choosing to offer a service does not impose upon the state a constitutional obligation to offer it free of charge. See *Kardmas* v. *Dickinson Public Schools,* 487 U.S. _____ (1988).

A California statute allowing school districts to assess fees for children who ride school buses was held to be violative of the state constitution's equal protection clause. The California court held that such a law was counter to the guarantee of free schools, and it failed to meet the state's strict-scrutiny test. See *Salazer* v. *Honig,* 200 Cal. App. 3d 1541, 246 Cal. Rptr. 837 (1988).

Does your state constitution or statutory law address the issue of school fees? What is the practice or policy regarding fees in your school system?

VI. Immunization

State statutes authorizing or requiring vaccination or immunization as a condition of school attendance have been upheld in every instance where they have been challenged. Such statutes often contain an exemption for those who are members of religious organizations that do not permit inoculation or that rely on spiritual means or prayer for healing.

Brown v. Stone

Supreme Court of Mississippi, 1980
378 So. 2d 218, *cert. denied.*
449 U.S. 887 (1980)

SMITH, Presiding Justice, for the Court.

This is an appeal by Charles H. Brown, father and next friend of Chad Allan Brown, a six-year-old boy, from a decree of the Chancery Court of Chickasaw County sustaining a demurrer filed to his bill which sought an injunction to compel the Board of Trustees of the Houston Municipal Separate School District to admit his son as a student without compliance with the immunization requirements of Mississippi Code Annotated section 41–23–37 (1972 Supp.) This statute provides (among other things):

> Except as provided hereinafter, it shall be unlawful for any child to attend any school, kindergarten or similar type of facility intended for the instruction of children (hereinafter called "schools"), either public or private, unless they shall first have been vaccinated against those diseases specified by the State Health Officer.
>
> A certificate of exemption from vaccination for medical reasons may be offered on behalf of a child by a duly licensed physician and may be accepted by the local health officer when, in his opinion, such exemption will not cause undue risk to the community. A certificate of religious exemption may be offered on behalf of a child by an officer of a church of a recognized denomination. This certificate shall certify that parents or guardians of the child are bona fide members of a recognized denomination whose religious teachings require reliance on prayer or spiritual means of healing.

There was filed with the bill the following certificate, signed by a minister of the Church of Christ:

> Be it known that the church of Christ as a religious body does not teach against the use of medecines, [sic] immunizations or vaccinations as prescribed by a duly [sic] physician. However, Dr. Charles Brown, our local chiropractor, who is a member of the North Jackson Street Church of Christ in Houston, Mississippi does have strong convictions against the use of any kind of medications and we respect his views.
>
> /s/ *Charles E. Bland*
> Charles E. Bland
> Minister

* * *

If the religious exemption from immunizations is to be granted only to members of certain recognized sects or denominations whose doctrines forbit it, and, as contended by appellants, to individuals whose private or personal religious beliefs will not allow them to permit immunization of their children, to this extent the highly desirable and paramount public purpose of the Act, that is, the protection of school children generally comprising the school community, is defeated.

* * *

It is a matter of common knowledge that prior to the development of protection against smallpox by vaccination, the disease, on occasion, ran rampant and caused great suffering and sickness throughout the world. According to the great weight of authority, it is within the police power of the State to require that school children be vaccinated against smallpox, and that such requirement does not violate the constitutional rights of anyone, on religious grounds or otherwise. In fact, this principle is so firmly settled that no extensive discussion is required.

* * *

After a thoughtful consideration of the facts and the arguments advanced by the appellants, we have concluded that the statute in question, requiring immunization against certain crippling and deadly diseases particularly dangerous to children before they may be admitted to school, serves an overriding and compelling public interest, and that such interest extends to the exclusion of a child until such immunization has been effected, not only as a protection of that child but as a protection of the large number of other children comprising the school community and with whom he will be daily in close contact in the school room. The relationship of parent and child is one in which the law concerns itself more with parental duties than with parental rights. The relationship carries with it a duty resting upon the parent to provide the child with food, clothing and shelter and to protect the child from preventable exposure to danger, disease and immorality. It must not be forgotten that a child is indeed himself an individual, although under certain disabilities until majority, with rights in his own person which must be respected and may be enforced. Where its safety, morals and health are involved, it becomes a legitimate concern of the state.

The protection of the great body of school children attending the public schools of Mississippi against the horrors of crippling and death resulting from poliomyelitis or smallpox or from one of the other diseases against which means of immunization are known and have long been practiced successfully, demand that children who have not been immunized should be excluded from the school community until immunization has been accomplished. That is the obvious overriding and compelling public purpose of Senate Bill No. 2650. To the extent that it may conflict with the religious beliefs of a parent, however sincerely entertained, the interests of the school children must prevail. Senate Bill No. 2650 is a reasonable and constitutional exercise of the police power of the state insofar as it provides for the immunization of children before they are permitted to enter school.

The exception, which would provide for the exemption of children of parents whose religious beliefs conflict with the immunization requirements, would discriminate against the great majority of children whose parents have no such religious convictions. To give it effect would result in a violation of the Fourteenth Amendment to the United States Constitution which provides that no state shall make any laws denying to any person within its jurisdiction the equal protection of the laws, in that it would require the great body of school children to be vaccinated and at the same time expose them to the hazard of associating in school with children exempted under the religious exemption who had not been immunized as required by the statute.

* * *

We have no difficulty here in deciding that the statute is "complete in itself" without the provision for religious exemption and that it serves a compelling state interest in the protection of school children. Therefore, we hold that the provision providing an exception from the operation of the statute because of religious belief is in violation of the Fourteenth Amendment to the United States Constitution and therefore is void. * * *

We find that all of the other provisions of the statute are valid and constitutional and embody a reasonable exercise of the police power of the state.

The decree appealed from will, therefore, be affirmed.

Affirmed.

* * *

Notes

Exemption may not be provided for students receiving a note of medical exemption from a chiropractor. See *Heard* v. *Payne*, 281 Ark. 485, 665 S.W.2d 865 (1984).

A school rule requiring a tetanus shot as a condition of playing on a baseball team was upheld. A Pennsylvania court held that a school district's compelling interest to immunize did not infringe on a boy's religious practice. See *Calendra* v. *State College Area School District*, 99 Pa. Commw. 223, 512 A.2d 809 (1986).

students
and the law

Introduction

Countless interactions between students and school officials occur in the public schools, and inevitably, some students or their parents become displeased either with a school official's actions or with school policy. The vast majority of such disputes are not litigable, however, unless school authorities have violated a student's constitutional rights or have defied applicable federal or state statutes.

Prior to the 1970s courts usually upheld school authorities who demonstrated no more than that their actions were reasonable. Public schools were perceived as enjoying parental prerogatives, and it was uncertain whether constitutional rights extended to students. However, in a 1969 landmark decision, the United States Supreme Court declared that students do not "shed their constitutional rights to freedom of speech or expression at the schoolhouse gate." Subsequently, in 1975 the high court held that public school students possess liberty and property interests in their education, and therefore, that constitutional principles of due process apply to school officials' treatment of students. Several important federal statutes emerged in the early-1970s, further expanding the scope of student rights. As a result of these changes in students' legal status, a period ensued during which students often were successful in challenging school policies and procedures and in which many school officials perceived an erosion of their authority.

In the mid-1980s, however, a shift became evident in the courts' tendency to uphold students. In particular, several Supreme Court decisions since then clearly have increased the authority of public school officials regarding students' freedom of expression and several other areas of conflict.

In addition to discussing students' rights to free expression, this chapter addresses issues associated with suspension, expulsion, and involuntary disciplinary transfer from school; corporal punishment; search of students and their lockers; dress and grooming; pregnancy, parenthood, and marriage; handicapped students; participation in extracurricular activities; and school punishment for out-of-school offenses.

An examination of court decisions in these areas reveals that courts often must balance students' constitutional rights against the duty of public school officials to maintain an appropriate environment for learning and safety. A deceptively simple administrative practice emerges which reduces legal confrontations and also facilitates school operations; namely, school officials should ensure the adoption of policies that are legally and educationally sound, that are clearly written, and that are adequately communicated to students.

I. Freedom of Expression

A. The *Tinker* Doctrine

Students were not recognized as having the First Amendment right of freedom of speech in 1969 when the United States Supreme Court addressed the question in *Tinker v. Des Moines Independent Community School District.* Although the decision did not address the question of "pure speech"—the issue before the Court involved the wearing of armbands by students—the Court's decision in Tinker provided the public school community with a clear message that a student has the right of political freedom of expression.

Tinker v. Des Moines Independent Community School District
Supreme Court of the United States, 1969
393 U.S. 503

MR. JUSTICE FORTAS delivered the opinion of the Court.

Petitioner John F. Tinker, 15 years old, and petitioner Christopher Eckhardt, 16 years old, attended high schools in Des Moines, Iowa.

Petitioner Mary Beth Tinker, John's sister, was a 13-year-old student in junior high school.

In December 1965, a group of adults and students in Des Moines held a meeting at the Eckhardt home. The group determined to publicize their objections to the hostilities in Vietnam and their support for a truce by wearing black armbands during the holiday season and by fasting on December 16 and New Year's Eve. Petitioners and their parents had previously engaged in similar activities, and they decided to participate in the program.

The principals of the Des Moines schools became aware of the plan to wear armbands. On December 14, 1965, they met and adopted a policy that any student wearing an armband to school would be asked to remove it, and if he refused he would be suspended until he returned without the armband. Petitioners were aware of the regulation that the school authorities adopted.

On December 16, Mary Beth and Christopher wore black armbands to their schools. John Tinker wore his armband the next day. They were all sent home and suspended from school until they would come back without their armbands. They did not return to school until after the planned period for wearing armbands had expired—that is, until after New Year's Day.

This complaint was filed in the United States District Court by petitioners, through their fathers, under § 1983 of Title 42 of the United States Code. It prayed for an injunction restraining the respondent school officials and the respondent members of the board of directors of the school district from disciplining the petitioners, and it sought nominal damages. After an evidentiary hearing the District Court dismissed the complaint. It upheld the constitutionality of the school authorities' action on the ground that it was reasonable in order to prevent disturbance of school discipline. * * * The court referred to but expressly declined to follow the Fifth Circuit's holding in a similar case that the wearing of symbols like the armbands cannot be prohibited unless it "materially and substantially interfere[s] with the requirements of appropriate discipline in the operation of the school." * * *

On appeal, the Court of Appeals for the Eighth Circuit considered the case *en banc.* The court was equally divided, and the District Court's decision was accordingly affirmed, without opinion. * * * We granted certiorari. * * *

The District Court recognized that the wearing of an armband for the purpose of expressing certain views is the type of symbolic act that is within the Free Speech Clause of the First Amendment. * * * As we shall discuss, the wearing of armbands in the circumstances of this case was entirely divorced from actually or potentially disruptive conduct by those participating in it. It was closely akin to "pure speech" which, we have repeatedly held, is entitled to comprehensive protection under the First Amendment. * * *

First Amendment rights, applied in light of the special characteristics of the school environment, are available to teachers and students. It can hardly be argued that either students or teachers shed their constitutional rights to freedom of speech or expression at the schoolhouse gate. This has been the unmistakable holding of this Court for almost 50 years. * * *

* * * On the other hand, the Court has repeatedly emphasized the need for affirming the comprehensive authority of the States and of school officials, consistent with fundamental constitutional safeguards, to prescribe and control conduct in the schools. * * * Our problem lies in the area where students in the exercise of First Amendment rights collide with the rules of the school authorities.

The problem posed by the present case does not relate to regulation of the length of skirts or the type of clothing, to hair style, or deportment. * * * It does not concern agressive, disruptive action or even group demonstrations. Our problem involves direct, primary First Amendment rights akin to "pure speech."

The school officials banned and sought to punish petitioners for a silent, passive expression of opinion, unaccompanied by any disorder or disturbance on the part of petitioners. There is no evidence whatever of petitioners' interference, actual or nascent, with the schools' work or of collision with the rights of other students to be secure and to be let alone. Accordingly, this case does not concern speech or action that intrudes upon the work of the schools or the rights of other students.

Only a few of the 18,000 students in the school system wore the black armbands. Only five students were suspended for wearing them. There is no indication that the work of the schools or any class was disrupted. Outside the classrooms, a few students made hostile remarks to the children wearing armbands, but there were no threats or acts of violence on school premises.

The District Court concluded that the action of the school authorities was reasonable because it was based upon their fear of a disturbance from the wearing of the armbands. But, in our system, undifferentiated fear or apprehension of disturbance is not enough to overcome the right of freedom of expression. Any departure from absolute regimentation may cause trouble. Any variation from the majority's opinion may inspire fear. Any word spoken, in class, in the lunchroom, or on the campus, that deviates from the views of another person may start an argument or cause a disturbance. But our Constitution says we must take this risk, * * * ; and our history says that it is this sort of hazardous freedom—

this kind of openness—that is the basis of our national strength and of the independence and vigor of Americans who grow up and live in this relatively permissive, often disputatious, society.

In order for the State in the person of school officials to justify prohibition of a particular expression of opinion, it must be able to show that its action was caused by something more than a mere desire to avoid the discomfort and unpleasantness that always accompany an unpopular viewpoint. Certainly where there is no finding and no showing that engaging in the forbidden conduct would "materially and substantially interfere with the requirements of appropriate discipline in the operation of the school," the prohibition cannot be sustained. * * *

In the present case, the District Court made no such finding, and our independent examination of the record fails to yield evidence that the school authorities had reason to anticipate that the wearing of the armbands would substantially interfere with the work of the school or impinge upon the rights of other students. Even an official memorandum prepared after the suspension that listed the reasons for the ban on wearing the armbands made no reference to the anticipation of such disruption.

On the contrary, the action of the school authorities appears to have been based upon an urgent wish to avoid the controversy which might result from the expression, even by the silent symbol of armbands, of opposition to this Nation's part in the conflagration in Vietnam. It is revealing, in this respect, that the meeting at which the school principals decided to issue the contested regulation was called in response to a student's statement to the journalism teacher in one of the schools that he wanted to write an article on Vietnam and have it published in the school paper. (The student was dissuaded.)

It is also relevant that the school authorities did not purport to prohibit the wearing of all symbols of political or controversial significance. The record shows that students in some of the schools wore buttons relating to national political campaigns and some even wore the Iron Cross, traditionally a symbol of Nazism. The order prohibiting the wearing of armbands did not extend to these. Instead, a particular symbol—black armbands worn to exhibit opposition to this Nation's involvement in Vietnam—was singled out for prohibition. Clearly, the prohibition of expression of one particular opinion, at least without evidence that it is necessary to avoid material and substantial interference with school-work or discipline, is not constitutionally permissible.

In our system, state-operated schools may not be enclaves of totalitarianism. School officials do not possess absolute authority over their students. Students in school as well as out of school are "persons" under our Constitution. They are possessed of fundamental rights which the

State must respect, just as they themselves must respect their obligations to the State. In our system, students may not be regarded as closed-circuit recipients of only that which the State chooses to communicate. They may not be confined to the expression of those sentiments that are officially approved. In the absence of a specific showing of constitutionally valid reasons to regulate their speech, students are entitled to freedom of expression of their views. * * *

* * *

* * * The principal use to which the schools are dedicated is to accommodate students during prescribed hours for the purpose of certain types of activities. Among those activities is personal intercommunication among the students. This is not only an inevitable part of the process of attending school; it is also an important part of the educational process. A student's rights, therefore, do not embrace merely the classroom hours. When he is in the cafeteria, or on the playing field, or on the campus during the authorized hours, he may express his opinions, even on controversial subjects like the conflict in Vietnam, if he does so without "materially and substantially interfer[ing] with the requirements of appropriate discipline in the operation of the school" and without colliding with the rights of others. * * * But conduct by the student, in class or out of it, which for any reason—whether it stems from time, place, or type of behavior—materially disrupts classwork or involves substantial disorder or invasion of the rights of others is, of course, not immunized by the constitutional guarantee of freedom of speech. * * *

Under our constitution, free speech is not a right that is given only to be so circumscribed that it exists in principle but not in fact. Freedom of expression would not truly exist if the right could be exercised only in an area that a benevolent government has provided as a safe haven for crackpots. The Constitution says that Congress (and the States) may not abridge the right to free speech. This provision means what it says. We properly read it to permit reasonable regulation of speech-connected activities in carefully restricted circumstances. But we do not confine the permissible exercise of First Amendment rights to a telephone booth or the four corners of a pamphlet, or to supervised and ordained discussion in a school classroom.

If a regulation were adopted by school officials forbidding discussion of the Vietnam conflict, or the expression by any student of opposition to it anywhere on school property except as part of a prescribed classroom exercise, it would be obvious that the regulation would violate the constitutional rights of students, at least if it could not be justified by a showing that the students' activities would materially and substantially disrupt the work and discipline of the school. * * * In the circumstances of the present case, the prohibition of the silent passive "witness of the armbands," as one of the children called it, is no less offensive to the Constitution's guarantees.

As we have discussed, the record does not demonstrate any facts which might reasonably have led school authorities to forecast substantial disruption of or material interference with school activities, and no disturbances or disorders on the school premises in fact occurred. These petitioners merely went about their ordained rounds in school. Their deviation consisted only in wearing on their sleeve a band of black cloth, not more than two inches wide. They wore it to exhibit their disapproval of the Vietnam hostilities and their advocacy of a truce, to make their views known, and, by their example, to influence others to adopt them. They neither interrupted school activities nor sought to intrude in the school affairs or the lives of others. They caused discussion outside of the classrooms, but no interference with work and no disorder. In the circumstances, our Constitution does not permit officials of the State to deny their form of expression.

We express no opinion as to the form of relief which should be granted, this being a matter for the lower courts to determine. We reverse and remand for further proceedings consistent with this opinion.

Reversed and remanded.

* * *

MR. JUSTICE BLACK, dissenting.

The Court's holding in this case ushers in what I deem to be an entirely new era in which the power to control pupils by the elected "officials of state supported public schools . . ." in the United States is in ultimate effect transferred to the Supreme Court. * * *

* * *

Assuming that the Court is correct in holding that the conduct of wearing armbands for the purpose of conveying political ideas is protected by the First Amendment * * * , the crucial remaining questions are whether students and teachers may use the schools at their whim as a platform for the exercise of free speech—"symbolic" or "pure"—and whether the courts will allocate to themselves the function of deciding how the pupils' school day will be spent. While I have always believed that under the First and Fourteenth Amendments neither the State nor the Federal Government has any authority to regulate or censor the content of speech, I have never believed that any person has a right to give speeches or engage in demonstrations where he pleases and when he pleases. * * *

While the record does not show that any of these armband students shouted, used profane language, or were violent in any manner, detailed testimony by some of them shows their armbands caused comments, warnings by other students, the poking of fun at them, and a warning by an older football player that other, nonprotesting students had better let them alone. There is also evidence that a teacher of mathematics had his lesson period practically "wrecked" chiefly by disputes with Mary Beth Tinker, who wore her armband for her "demonstration." Even a casual reading of the record shows that this armband did divert students' minds from their regular lessons, and that talk, comments, etc., made John Tinker "self-conscious" in attending school with his armband. While the absence of obscene remarks or boisterous and loud disorder perhaps justified the Court's statement that the few armband students did not actually "disrupt" the classwork, I think the record overwhelmingly shows that the armbands did exactly what the elected school officials and principals foresaw they would, that is, took the students' minds off their classwork and diverted them to thoughts about the highly emotional subject of the Vietnam war. And I repeat that if the time has come when pupils of state-supported schools, kindergartens, grammar schools, or high schools, can defy and flout orders of school officials to keep their minds on their own schoolwork, it is the beginning of a new revolutionary era of permissiveness in this country fostered by the judiciary. The next logical step, it appears to me, would be to hold unconstitutional laws that bar pupils under 21 or 18 from voting, or from being elected members of the boards of education.

* * *

* * * But even if the record were silent as to protests against the Vietnam war distracting students from their assigned class work, members of this Court, like all other citizens, know, without being told, that the disputes over the wisdom of the Vietnam war have disrupted and divided this country as few other issues ever have. Of course students, like other people, cannot concentrate on lesser issues when black armbands are being ostentatiously displayed in their presence to call attention to the wounded and dead of the war, some of the wounded and the dead being their friends and neighbors. It was, of course, to distract the attention of other students that some students insisted up to the very point of their own suspension from school that they were determined to sit in school with their symbolic armbands.

Change has been said to be truly the law of life but sometimes the old and the tried and true are worth holding. The schools of this Nation have undoubtedly contributed to giving us tranquility and to making us a more law-abiding people. Uncontrolled and uncontrollable liberty is an enemy to domestic peace. We cannot close our eyes to the fact that some of the country's greatest problems are crimes committed by the youth, too many of school age. School discipline, like parental discipline, is an integral and important part of training our children to be good citizens—to be better citizens. Here a very small number of students have crisply and summarily refused to obey a school order designed to give pupils who want to learn the opportunity to do so. One does not need to be a prophet or the son of a prophet to know that after the Court's holding today some students in Iowa schools and indeed in all schools will be ready, able, and willing to defy their teachers on practically all orders. This is the more unfortunate for the schools since groups of students all over the land are already running loose, conducting break-ins, sit-ins, lie-ins, and smash-ins. Many of these student groups, as is all too familiar to all who read the newspapers and watch the television news programs, have already engaged in rioting, property seizures, and destruction. They have picketed schools to force students not to cross their picket lines and have too often violently attacked earnest but frightened students who wanted an education that the pickets did not want them to get. Students engaged in such activities are apparently confident that they know far more about how to operate public school systems than do their parents, teachers, and elected school officials. It is no answer to say that the particular students here have not yet reached such high points in their demands to attend classes in order to exercise their political pressures. Turned loose with lawsuits for damages and injunctions against their teachers as they are here, it is nothing but wishful thinking to imagine that young, immature students will not soon believe it is their right to control the schools rather that the right of the States that collect the taxes to hire the teachers for the benefit of the pupils. This case, therefore, wholly without constitutional reasons in my judgment, subjects all the public schools in the country to the whims and caprices of their loudest-mouthed, but maybe not their brightest, students. I, for one, am not fully persuaded that school pupils are wise enough, even with this Court's expert help from Washington, to run the 23,390 public school systems in our 50 States. I wish, therefore, wholly to disclaim any purpose on my part to hold that the Federal Constitution compels the teachers, parents, and elected school officials to surrender control of the American public school system to public school students. I dissent.

Notes

It should be kept in mind that the freedom of expression protected in *Tinker* pertains to social, political, and economic issues. Insolence or disrespect on the part of students is not protected, nor is screaming or cursing at teachers in a classroom or at school administrators.

Tinker was filed as a legal action under § 1983 of Title 42 of the United States Code. This section of the Civil Rights Act has been increasingly employed as a legal basis for bringing a suit involving students or teachers. See Chapter 7, page 436 for a brief discussion of this act.

According to *Tinker*, "undifferentiated fear or apprehension of disturbance is not enough to overcome the right to freedom of expression," and school authorities must accept "mere disturbance" when students exercise their First Amendment rights. Only when students engage in conduct that would "*materially* and *substantially* interfere with the requirements of appropriate discipline in the operation of the school" (emphasis added) may authorities prohibit the conduct. Unfortunately, the Court did not provide a test that school authorities could employ to determine whether actual disruption or merely a forecast of "substantial disruption" was necessary before they could prohibit conduct where freedom of expression was at issue. Further complicating the picture for school administrators was the failure by the Court to provide sufficient guidance concerning the meaning of a forecast of "substantial disruption."

There is little doubt that school officials may enforce reasonable rules to ensure the orderly operation of the school. However, *Tinker* proclaimed that when freedom of expression is involved, school officials may not restrict this freedom because the viewpoint expressed displeases an official or has the potential to bring about a degree of disruption. Part of the desired political socialization of students is that they learn that a government official—a school authority in this instance—may not restrict freedom of expression merely because it may be annoying or somewhat disruptive. Although some school officials may feel uncomfortable with such a doctrine, its rationale is based on the notion that if students are to become full participants in a free and democratic society, they must thoroughly understand that they are free to express themselves on any social, political, or economic issue without undue restraint or reprisal from government. The Court's contention was that the school is the proper place for a student to come to this understanding through the observance of freedom of expression in the school environment rather than through lectures or through policies that imply that freedom of expression is conferred at a specific age or upon graduation from high school.

Students attending private schools do not have the First Amendment protections provided by the *Tinker* decision, nor do such students necessarily have civil rights guaranteed by other amendments through the Fourteenth Amendment. Such rights are available to public school students because the public school operates under the "color of the State"; however, private school activity is not considered "state action." A substantial linkage between a private school and the state or federal government would have to be present for a private school to be considered acting under the "color of the state." As a result, private school students do not have many of the rights afforded public school students discussed in the succeeding sections of this chapter. Disagreements over "student rights" in a private school setting are generally resolved by applying contract law to the agreement governing the student's attendance.

B. Limiting the *Tinker* Doctrine

Active and lively litigation after *Tinker* addressed such issues as the wearing of buttons or other symbols, the use of obscenity and "fighting words," censorship of student publications, and distribution of "underground" newspapers. Frequently, this litigation did little to dispel fears that the *Tinker* court had bestowed upon students unbridled license to behave as they pleased. Several federal courts, relying on the *Tinker* decision, upheld forms of student expression that many parents and school authorities considered inappropriate. However, Supreme Court decisions in the late 1980s undoubtedly have tended to limit what many observers heretofore thought the *Tinker* decision allowed.

1. Nonpolitical Speech

Bethel School District No. 403 v. Fraser

Supreme Court of the United States, 1986
478 U.S. 675

CHIEF JUSTICE BURGER delivered the opinion of the Court.

We granted certiorari to decide whether the First Amendment prevents a school district from disciplining a high school student for giving a lewd speech at a school assembly.

On April 26, 1983, respondent Matthew N. Fraser, a student at Bethel High School in Bethel, Washington, delivered a speech nominating a fellow student for student elective office. Approximately 600 high school students, many of whom were 14-year-olds, attended the assembly. Students were required to attend the assembly or to report to the study hall. The assembly was part of a school-sponsored educational program in self-government. Students who elected not to attend the assembly were required to report to study hall. During the entire speech, Fraser referred to his candidate in terms of an elaborate, graphic, and explicit sexual metaphor.

Two of Fraser's teachers, with whom he discussed the contents of his speech in advance, informed him that the speech was "inappropriate and that he probably should not deliver it," * * * and that his delivery of the speech might have "severe consequences." * * *

During Fraser's delivery of the speech, a school counselor observed the reaction of students to the speech. Some students hooted and yelled; some by gestures graphically simulated the sexual activities pointedly alluded to in respondent's speech. Other students appeared to be bewildered and embarrassed by the speech. One teacher reported that on the day following the speech, she found it necessary to forgo a portion of the scheduled class lesson in order to discuss the speech with the class.

A Bethel High School disciplinary rule prohibiting the use of obscene language in the school provides:

> "Conduct which materially and substantially interferes with the educational process is prohibited, including the use of obscene, profane language or gestures."

The morning after the assembly, the Assistant Principal called Fraser into her office and notified him that the school considered his speech to have been a violation of this rule. Fraser was presented with copies of five letters submitted by teachers, describing his conduct at the assembly; he was given a chance to explain his conduct, and he admitted to having given the speech described and that he deliberately used sexual innuendo in the speech. Fraser was then informed that he would be suspended for three days, and that his name would be removed from the list of candidates for graduation speaker at the school's commencement exercises.

Fraser sought review of this disciplinary action through the School District's grievance procedures. The hearing officer determined that the speech given by respondent was "indecent, lewd, and offensive to the modesty and decency of many of the students and faculty in attendance at the assembly." The examiner determined that the speech fell within the ordinary meaning of "obscene," as used in the disruptive-conduct rule, and affirmed the discipline in its entirety. Fraser served two days of his suspension, and was allowed to return to school on the third day.

Respondent, by his father as guardian *ad litem*, then brought this action in the United States District Court for the Western District of Washington. Respondent alleged a violation of his First Amendment right to freedom of speech and sought both injunctive relief and monetary damages under 42 U.S.C. § 1983. The District Court held that the school's sanctions violated respondent's right to freedom of speech under the First Amendment to the United States Constitution, that the school's disruptive-conduct rule is unconstitutionally vague and overbroad, and that the removal of respondent's name from the graduation speaker's list violated the Due Process Clause of the Fourteenth Amendment because the disciplinary rule makes no mention of such removal as a possible sanction. The District Court awarded respondent $278 in damages, $12,750 in litigation costs and attorney's fees, and enjoined the School District from preventing respondent from speaking at the commencement ceremonies. Respondent, who had been elected graduation speaker by a write-in vote of his classmates, delivered a speech at the commencement ceremonies on June 8, 1983.

The Court of Appeals for the Ninth Circuit affirmed the judgment of the District Court, * * * holding that respondent's speech was indistinguishable from the protest armband in *Tinker* v. *Des Moines Independent Community School Dist.*, 393 U.S. 503 (1969). The court explicitly rejected the School District's argument that the speech, unlike the passive conduct of wearing a black armband, had a disruptive effect on the educational process. The Court of Appeals also rejected the School District's argument that it had an interest in protecting an essentially captive audience of minors from lewd and indecent language in a setting sponsored by the school, reasoning that the school board's "unbridled discretion" to determine what discourse is "decent" would "increase the risk of cementing white, middle-class standards for determining what is acceptable and proper speech and behavior in our public schools." * * * Finally, the Court of Appeals rejected the School District's argument that, incident to its responsibility for the school curriculum, it had the power to control the language used to express ideas during a school-sponsored activity.

We granted certiorari * * * . We reverse.

This Court acknowledged in *Tinker* v. *Des Moines Independent Community School Dist.* * * * that students do not "shed their constitutional rights to freedom of speech or expression at the schoolhouse gate." * * * The Court of Appeals read that case as precluding any discipline of Fraser for indecent speech and lewd conduct in the school assembly. That court appears to have proceeded on the theory that the use of lewd and obscene speech in order to make what the speaker considered to be a point in a nominating speech for a fellow student was essentially the same as the wearing of an armband in *Tinker* as a form of protest or the expression of a political position.

The marked distinction between the political "message" of the armbands in *Tinker* and the sexual content of respondent's speech in this case seems to have been given little weight by the Court of Appeals. In upholding the students' right to engage in a nondisruptive, passive expression of a political viewpoint in *Tinker*, this Court was careful to note that the case did "not concern speech or action that intrudes upon the work of the schools or the rights of other students." * * *

It is against this background that we turn to consider the level of First Amendment protection accorded to Fraser's utterances and actions before an official high school assembly attended by 600 students.

The role and purpose of the American public school system was well described by two historians, saying "public education must prepare pupils for citizenship in the Republic. . . . It must inculcate the habits and manners of civility as values in themselves conducive to happiness and as indispensable to the practice of self-government in the community and the nation." * * *

These fundamental values of "habits and manners of civility" essential to a democratic society must, of course, include tolerance of divergent political and religious views, even when the views expressed may be unpopular. But these "fundamental values" must also take into account consideration of the sensibilities of others, and, in the case of a school, the sensibilities of fellow students. The undoubted freedom to advocate unpopular and controversial views in schools and classrooms must be balanced against the society's countervailing interest in teaching students the boundaries of socially appropriate behaviour. Even the most heated political discourse in a democratic society requires consideration for the personal sensibilities of the other participants and audiences.

* * *

Surely it is a highly appropriate function of public school education to prohibit the use of vulgar and offensive terms in public discourse. Indeed, the "fundamental values necessary to the maintenance of a democratic political system" disfavor the use of terms of debate highly offensive or highly threatening to others. Nothing in the Constitution prohibits the states from insisting that certain modes of expression are inappropriate and subject to sanctions. The inculcation of these values is truly the "work of the schools." * * * The determination of what manner of speech in the classroom or in school assembly is inappropriate properly rests with the school board.

The process of educating our youth for citizenship in public schools is not confined to books, the curriculum, and the civics class; schools must teach by example the shared values of a civilized social order. Consciously or otherwise, teachers—and indeed the older students—demonstrate the appropriate form of civil discourse and political expression by their conduct and deportment in and out of class. Inescapably, like parents, they are role models. The schools, as instruments of the state, may determine that the essential lessons of civil, mature conduct cannot be conveyed in a school that tolerates lewd, indecent, or offensive speech and conduct such as that indulged in by this confused boy.

The pervasive sexual innuendo in Fraser's speech was plainly offensive to both teachers and students—indeed to any mature person. By glorifying male sexuality, and in its verbal content, the speech was acutely insulting to teenage girl students. * * * The speech could well be seriously damaging to its less mature audience, many of whom were only 14 years old and on the threshold of awareness of human sexuality. Some students were reported as bewildered by the speech and the reaction of mimicry it provoked.

* * *

We hold that petitioner School District acted entirely within its permissible authority in imposing sanctions upon Fraser in response to his offensively lewd and indecent speech. Unlike the sanctions imposed on the students wearing armbands in *Tinker,* the penalties imposed in this case were unrelated to any political viewpoint. The First Amendment does not prevent the school officials from determining that to permit a vulgar and lewd speech such as respondent's would undermine the school's basic educational mission. A high school assembly or classroom is no place for a sexually explicit monologue directed towards an unsuspecting audience of teenage students. Accordingly, it was perfectly appropriate for the school to disassociate itself to make the point to the pupils that vulgar speech and lewd conduct is wholly inconsistent with the "fundamental values" of public school education. * * *

* * *

Respondent contends that the circumstances of his suspension violated due process because he had no way of knowing that the delivery of the speech in question would subject him to disciplinary sanctions. * * * Two days' suspension from school does not rise to the level of a penal sanction calling for the full panoply of procedural due process protections applicable to a criminal prosecution. * * * The school disciplinary rule proscribing "obscene" language and the prespeech admonitions of teachers gave adequate warning to Fraser that his lewd speech could subject him to sanctions.

The judgment of the Court of Appeals for the Ninth Circuit is

Reversed.

JUSTICE BRENNAN, concurring in the judgment.
Respondent gave the following speech at a high school assembly in support of a candidate for student government office:

> I know a man who is firm—he's firm in his pants, he's firm in his shirt, his character is firm—but most . . . of all, his belief in you, the students of Bethel, is firm.
>
> Jeff Kuhlman is a man who takes his point and pounds it in. If necessary, he'll take an issue and nail it to the wall. He doesn't attack things in spurts—he drives hard, pushing and pushing until finally—he succeeds.
>
> Jeff is a man who will go to the very end—even the climax, for each and every one of you.
>
> So vote for Jeff for A. S. B. vice-president—he'll never come between you and the best our high school can be.

The Court, referring to these remarks as "obscene," "vulgar," "lewd," and "offensively lewd," concludes that school officials properly punished respondent for uttering the speech. Having read the full text of respondent's remarks, I find it difficult to believe that it is the same speech the Court describes. To my mind, the most that can be said about respondent's speech—and all that need be said—is that in light of the discretion school officials have to teach high school students how to conduct civil and effective public discourse, and to prevent disruption of school educational activities, it was not unconstitutional for school officials to conclude, under the circumstances of this case, that respondent's remarks exceeded permissible limits. Thus, while I concur in the Court's judgment, I write separately to express my understanding of the breadth of the Court's holding.

Notes

Chief Justice Warren E. Burger, who wrote the majority opinion in *Fraser,* was nominated by President Nixon in 1969. Prior to his nomination, he was a judge on the United States Circuit of Appeals for the District of Columbia since 1956. Chief Justice Burger retired from the Court in 1986.

In *Fraser* the Court made it clear that *Tinker* was not to be read as recognizing that student rights are coextensive with those of adults. It is important to note that Mr. Fraser's speech made by an adult in public almost certainly would have enjoyed constitutional protection. *Fraser,* however, disclosed the Court's conviction that public schools have an important role in imparting respect for civility of public discourse. The holding also revealed the majority's view that judging the appropriateness of student speech ought to be left to school officials rather than to federal judges.

A policy prohibiting the wearing or display of any gang symbol, any act or speech showing gang affiliation, and any conduct in furtherance of gang activity was upheld by a federal district court. The court related that in this instance the wearing of earrings by males generally connoted gang membership and did not have First Amendment protection. An equal protection argument was rejected by the court's stating "while girls may be gang members they symbolize their affiliation in other ways—ways that are prohibited by school policy." See *Olesen* v. *Board of Education*, 676 F. Supp. 820 (Ill. 1987).

2. School-Sponsored Expressive Activities

Another widely litigated freedom-of-expression issue concerned school authorities' control over school-sponsored expressive activities such as student publications. Although several federal appellate courts had addressed the issue, prior to 1988 the United States Supreme Court had not. The result was a complex, confusing body of case law.

In many jurisdictions school newspapers were considered to be "public forums," immune from attempts to regulate the viewpoints expressed therein. Student writing that was sexually suggestive, that advocated drug use, or that was potentially libelous seemingly enjoyed constitutional protection. Thus many school authorities saw their only options as either allowing the publication of such material or ceasing altogether to publish student newspapers. Against this background the United States Supreme Court's decision in *Hazelwood School District* v. *Kuhlmeier,* which addressed a school principal's censorship of student news articles, has enormous significance.

Hazelwood School District v. Kuhlmeier

Supreme Court of the United States, 1988
484 U.S. 260

JUSTICE WHITE delivered the opinion of the Court.

This case concerns the extent to which educators may exercise editorial control over the contents of a high school newspaper produced as part of the school's journalism curriculum.

* * *

Spectrum was written and edited by the Journalism II class at Hazelwood

East. The newspaper was published every three weeks or so during the 1982–1983 school year. More than 4,500 copies of the newspaper were distributed during that year to students, school personnel, and members of the community.

The Board of Education allocated funds from its annual budget for the printing of *Spectrum.* These funds were supplemented by proceeds from sales of the newspaper. The printing expenses during the 1982–1983 school year totaled $4,668.50; revenue from sales was $1,166.84. The other costs associated with the newspaper—such as supplies, textbooks, and a portion of the journalism teacher's salary—were borne entirely by the Board.

* * *

We deal first with the question whether *Spectrum* may appropriately be characterized as a forum for public expression. The public schools do not possess all of the attributes of streets, parks, and other traditional public forums that "time out of mind, have been used for purposes of assembly, communicating thoughts between citizens, and discussing public questions." * * * Hence, school facilities may be deemed to be public forums only if school authorities have "by policy or by practice" opened those facilities "for indiscriminate use by the general public" * * * or by some segment of the public, such as student organizations. * * * If the facilities have instead been reserved for other intended purposes, "communicative or otherwise," then no public forum has been created, and school officials may impose reasonable restrictions on the speech of students, teachers, and other members of the school community. * * * "The government does not create a public forum by inaction or by permitting limited discourse, but only by intentionally opening a nontraditional forum for public discourse."

The policy of school officials toward *Spectrum* was reflected in Hazelwood School Board Policy 348.51 and the Hazelwood East Curriculum Guide. Board Policy 348.51 provided that "[s]chool sponsored publications are developed within the adopted curriculum and its educational implications in regular classroom activities." * * * The Hazelwood East Curriculum Guide described the Journalism II course as a "laboratory situation in which the students publish the school newspaper applying skills they have learned in Journalism I." * * * The lessons that were to be learned from the Journalism II course, according to the Curriculum Guide, included development of journalistic skills under deadline pressure, "the legal, moral, and ethical restrictions imposed upon journalists within the school community," and "responsibility and acceptance of criticism for articles of opinion."* * * Journalism II was taught by a faculty member during regular class hours. Students received grades and academic credit for their performance in the course.

School officials did not deviate in practice from their policy that production of *Spectrum* was to be part of the educational curriculum and a "regular classroom activit[y]." The District Court found that Robert Stergos, the journalism teacher during most of the 1982–1983 school year, "both had the authority to exercise and in fact exercised a great deal of control over *Spectrum.*" * * * For example, Stergos selected the editors of the newspaper, scheduled publication dates, decided the number of pages for each issue, assigned story ideas to class members, advised students on the development of their stories, reviewed the use of quotations, edited stories, selected and edited the letters to the editor, and dealt with the printing company. Many of these decisions were made without consultation with the Journalism II students.

*   *   *

* * * Board Policy 348.51, which stated in part that "[s]chool sponsored student publications will not restrict free expression or diverse viewpoints within the rules of responsible journalism," also stated that such publications were "developed within the adopted curriculum and its educational implications." One might reasonably infer from the full text of Policy 348.51 that school officials retained ultimate control over what constituted "responsible journalism" in a school-sponsored newspaper. Although the Statement of Policy published in the September 14, 1982, issue of *Spectrum* declared that "*Spectrum,* as a student-press publication, accepts all rights implied by the First Amendment," this statement, understood in the context of the paper's role in the school's curriculum, suggests at most that the administration will not interfere with the students' exercise of those First Amendment rights that attend the publication of a school-sponsored newspaper. It does not reflect an intent to expand those rights by converting a curricular newspaper into a public forum. Finally, that students were permitted to exercise some authority over the contents of *Spectrum* was fully consistent with the Curriculum Guide objective of teaching the Journalism II students "leadership responsibilities as issue and page editors." A decision to teach leadership skills in the context of a classroom activity hardly implies a decision to relinquish school control over that activity. * * * School officials did not evince either "by policy or by practice" * * * any intent to open the pages of *Spectrum* to "indiscriminate use" by its student reporters and editors, or by the student body generally. Instead, they "reserve[d] the forum for its intended purpos[e]" as a supervised learning experience for journalism students. Accordingly, school officials

were entitled to regulate the contents of *Spectrum* in any reasonable manner. It is this standard, rather than our decision in *Tinker*, that governs this case.

The question whether the First Amendment requires a school to tolerate particular student speech—the question that we addressed in *Tinker*—is different from the question whether the First Amendment requires a school affirmatively to promote particular student speech. The former question addresses educators' ability to silence a student's personal expression that happens to occur on the school premises. The latter question concerns educators' authority over school-sponsored publications, theatrical productions, and other expressive activities that students, parents, and members of the public might reasonably perceive to bear the imprimatur of the school. These activities may fairly be characterized as part of the school curriculum, whether or not they occur in a traditional classroom setting, so long as they are supervised by faculty members and designed to impart particular knowledge or skills to student participants and audiences.

Educators are entitled to exercise greater control over this second form of student expression to assure that participants learn whatever lessons the activity is designed to teach, that readers or listeners are not exposed to material that may be inappropriate for their level of maturity, and that the views of the individual speaker are not erroneously attributed to the school. Hence, a school may in its capacity as publisher of a school newspaper or producer of a school play "disassociate itself" * * * not only from speech that would "substantially interfere with [its] work . . . or impinge upon the rights of other students" * * * but also from speech that is, for example, ungrammatical, poorly written, inadequately researched, biased or prejudiced, vulgar or profane, or unsuitable for immature audiences. A school must be able to set high standards for the student speech that is disseminated under its auspices— standards that may be higher than those demanded by some newspaper publishers or theatrical producers in the "real" world—and may refuse to disseminate student speech that does not meet those standards. In addition, a school must be able to take into account the emotional maturity of the intended audience in determining whether to disseminate student speech on potentially sensitive topics, which might range from the existence of Santa Claus in an elementary school setting to the particulars of teenage sexual activity in a high school setting. A school must also retain the authority to refuse to sponsor student speech that might reasonably be perceived to advocate drug or alcohol use, irresponsible sex, or conduct otherwise inconsistent with "the shared values of a civilized social order" * * * or to associate the school with any position other than neutrality on matters of political controversy. Otherwise, the schools would be unduly constrained from fulfilling their role as "a principal instrument in awakening the child to cultural values, in preparing him for later professional training, and in helping him to adjust normally to his environment." * * *

Accordingly, we conclude that the standard articulated in *Tinker* for determining when a school may punish student expression need not also be the standard for determining when a school may refuse to lend its name and resources to the dissemination of student expression. Instead, we hold that educators do not offend the First Amendment by exercising editorial control over the style and content of student speech in school-sponsored expressive activities so long as their actions are reasonably related to legitimate pedagogical concerns.

This standard is consistent with our oft-expressed view that the education of the Nation's youth is primarily the responsibility of parents, teachers, and state and local school officials, and not of federal judges. * * * It is only when the decision to censor a school-sponsored publication, theatrical production, or other vehicle of student expression has no valid educational purpose that the First Amendment is so "directly and sharply implicate[d]" as to require judicial intervention to protect students' constitutional rights.

We also conclude that Principal Reynolds acted reasonably in requiring the deletion from the May 13 issue of *Spectrum* of the pregnancy article, the divorce article, and the remaining articles that were to appear on the same pages of the newspaper.

The initial paragraph of the pregnancy article declared that "[a]ll names have been changed to keep the identity of these girls a secret." The principal concluded that the students' anonymity was not adequately protected, however, given the other identifying information in the article and the small number of pregnant students at the school. Indeed, a teacher at the school credibly testified that she could positively identify at least one of the girls and possibly all three. It is likely that many students at Hazelwood East would have been at least as successful in identifying the girls. Reynolds therefore could reasonably have feared that the article violated whatever pledge of anonymity had been given to the pregnant students. In addition, he could reasonably have been concerned that the article was not sufficiently sensitive to the privacy interests of the students' boyfriends and parents, who were discussed in the article but who were given no opportunity to consent to its publication or to offer a response. The article did not contain graphic accounts of sexual activity. The girls did comment in the article, however, concerning their sexual histories and their use or nonuse of birth control. It was not unreasonable for the principal to have concluded that such frank talk was inappropriate in a school-sponsored publication distributed to

14-year-old freshmen and presumably taken home to be read by students' even younger brothers and sisters.

The student who was quoted by name in the version of the divorce article seen by Principal Reynolds made comments sharply critical of her father. The principal could reasonably have concluded that an individual publicly identified as an inattentive parent—indeed, as one who chose "playing cards with the guys" over home and family—was entitled to an opportunity to defend himself as a matter of journalistic fairness. These concerns were shared by both of *Spectrum*'s faculty advisers for the 1982–1983 school year, who testified that they would not have allowed the article to be printed without deletion of the student's name.

* * *

In sum, we cannot reject as unreasonable Principal Reynolds' conclusion that neither the pregnancy article nor the divorce article was suitable for publication in *Spectrum*. Reynolds could reasonably have concluded that the students who had written and edited these articles had not sufficiently mastered those portions of the Journalism II curriculum that pertained to the treatment of controversial issues and personal attacks, the need to protect the privacy of individuals whose most intimate concerns are to be revealed in the newspaper, and "the legal, moral, and ethical restrictions imposed upon journalists within [a] school community" that includes adolescent subjects and readers. Finally, we conclude that the principal's decision to delete two pages of *Spectrum*, rather than to delete only the offending articles or to require that they be modified, was reasonable under the circumstances as he understood them. Accordingly, no violation of First Amendment rights occurred.

The judgment of the Court of Appeals for the Eighth Circuit is therefore

Reversed.

Notes and Questions

Justice Byron "Whizzer" White, who wrote the **Kuhlmeier** opinion, brought a unique background to the Supreme Court. He was a Phi Beta Kappa, Rhodes scholar, all-American football star at the University of Colorado, professional football player (leading ground gainer in the National Football League in 1938), member of the Football Hall of Fame, decorated naval officer, Supreme Court clerk, lawyer, and a deputy attorney general. He was the leader of the Citizens for Kennedy in Colorado, and he was appointed to the Court by President Kennedy in 1962.

Courts in the United States look especially skeptically at attempts to censor materials prior to their publication. Was the Supreme Court's upholding of Principal Reynolds significant in this regard?

Will the holding in *Kuhlmeier,* a five-to-three decision, coupled with the seven-to-two decision in *Fraser,* have a chilling effect on related suits being brought before the courts? For example, what effect will the decision have on other "school-sponsored expressive activities" such as plays, yearbooks, program notices, and debates?

It is clear that a majority on the Court perceived a major purpose of public schooling to be the inculcation of society's values as defined by society's elders. Does the Court's articulation of this viewpoint represent a retreat from the educational philosophy expressed in *Tinker,* that a school should be a marketplace of ideas and that the proper socialization for a free people is the early exercise of freedom?

As a consequence of *Fraser* and *Kuhlmeier* it seems likely that school authorities will be less hesitant to prohibit student expression that they heretofore may have thought was protected under the *Tinker* doctrine. Nevertheless, authorities apparently may choose to establish public forums within their schools and, thus, to surrender their discretion to censor student expression. To preserve such discretion they should clearly distinguish curricular activities from activities intended for students' expression of their views. Hazelwood authorities prevailed partly because they retained, "by policy and practice," the curricular identity of *Spectrum,* and consequently they "retained ultimate control over what constituted responsible journalism." Written policies and curriculum coupled with consistent practices bolstered their position and may be considered a model for legally defensible behavior in school administration.

May a school refuse to publish a student's picture in the yearbook because the student was in violation of the grooming code? The Ohio Supreme Court held that a picture of a student whose hair style was in violation of the code could not be excluded from the school yearbook, which was to be distributed after the school year ended. However, the school could refrain from publishing a yearbook. See *McClung v. Board of Education of City of Washington C.H.,* 46 Ohio St. 2d 149, 346 N.E.2d 691 (1976). Also see *Stanton v. Brunswick School Department,* 577 F. Supp. 1560 (Me. 1984), which addressed the appropriateness in a yearbook of a student-selected quotation vividly describing execution by electrocution. The court stated that the school had created a public forum by permitting students to include a quote under their pictures and that matters of taste may not be censored by vague, subjective, or nondiscrete standards.

A federal district court upheld a school board's decision not to produce *Runaways,* a play in which child abuse, rape, murder, and drug abuse were simulated. In its holding the court declared that seventh- through twelfth-grade students were not denied their First Amendment rights and that the school board was within its authority to protect the well-being of its students. See *Bell* v. *U-32 Board of Education,* 630 F. Supp. 939 (Vt. 1986).

School newspapers often accept, and in fact solicit, advertising to defray expenses and to provide students with valuable business experience relating to the operation of a newspaper. A federal appellate court did not uphold a school board's refusal to accept advertising from the San Diego Committee Against Registration and the Draft. The court in this instance reasoned that the school board had created a limited public forum by allowing some members of the public to use its newspapers to engage in speech that combined elements of political and commercial speech. See *San Diego Committee against Registration and the Draft* v. *Governing Board of Grossmont Union High School District,* 790 F.2d 1471 (9th Cir. 1986).

May visitors to a school be barred from distributing literature? See *Peterson* v. *Board of Education of School District No. 1,* 370 F. Supp. 1208 (Neb. 1973), where the court stated:

> . . . I find no fault with the present policy of requiring "all visitors to . . . report to the school at the beginning of their visit." However, the banning of distribution of the newspaper because it may involve visitors, without any showing that the mere having of visitors will disrupt the school or result in danger to other persons on school grounds, is not constitutionally permissible. (P. 1215)

Can parents force school authorities to have students distribute a circular prepared by a parent? A federal appellate court held that a school may refuse to distribute certain materials, since such distribution would create a public forum. See *Buckel* v. *Prentice,* 572 F.2d 141 (6th Cir. 1978).

Does your school system have policies pertaining to school-sponsored expressive activities?

C. Participation in Patriotic Exercises

Students have challenged local policies or state statutes requiring their participation in patriotic exercises. The most common challenge centers on participation in the pledge of allegiance. **Lipp v. Morris** upheld the student's position and follows the rationale of other courts that have addressed this issue.

Lipp v. Morris

United States Court of Appeals, Third Circuit, 1978
579 F.2d 834

PER CURIAM:
This case involves the constitutionality of a New Jersey statute requiring school students to stand at attention during the salute to the flag. The appeal brings before the court two questions: (1) Did the District Judge abuse his discretion in declining to abstain because the New Jersey statute involved here is clear and unambiguous, and (2) Is the statute unconstitutional because it compels an affirmation of belief or punishes protected activity in violation of the First and Fourteenth Amendments of the Constitution of the United States.

* * *

Plaintiff, Deborah Lipp, a 16-year-old, alleged that because the statute directed that she stand during the recitation of the pledge of allegiance to the flag, compelling her to make what she termed a "symbolic gesture," it violated her rights under the First and Fourteenth Amendments. The action was brought under 42 U.S.C. § 1983 (1970). Plaintiff was a student at Mountain Lakes High School, New Jersey. Defendants were Harry Morris, principal of the high school * * *. Plaintiff emphasized that in her belief, the words of the pledge were not true and she stood only because she had been threatened if she did not do so.

Defendant argues first that the district court should have abstained from ruling on the constitutionality of the New Jersey statute to permit a New Jersey court to construe the law and thereby avoid a decision on federal constitutional grounds. The clearest answer to this argument is the statement of the District Judge which we adopt: "I can only do that [abstain] where the statute is open to an alternative construction which would avoid the Constitutional issue. This statute permits no such construction. It's plain, simple, blunt English." * * * Here we hold that the statute is not of an uncertain nature and, therefore, the case does not qualify for application of the abstention doctrine.

Secondly, defendant asserts that being required to stand while others engage in the flag salute ceremony is in no way a violation of the First and Fourteenth Amendments. The attorney general of New Jersey argues that mere standing does not rise to the level of "symbolic speech."

Defendant suggests that standing silently is the same as just remaining seated, and that by the simple act of standing, the plaintiff in no way engages in protected activity.

* * * Deborah Lipp urges that her right to remain silent and not to be forced to stand springs directly from the precise First Amendment right against compelled participation in the flag ceremony recognized in *Barnette*.

Banks and *Goetz* are precisely on point. They interdict the state from requiring a student to engage in what amounts to implicit expression by standing at respectful attention while the flag salute is being administered and being participated in by other students. * * *

In the words of Judge Meanor: "I find this statute to be severable, that is, the portion thereof attacked as unconstitutional may rationally be severed from the remainder of the statute. * * * This mandatory condition upon the student's right not to participate in the flag salute ceremony is an unconstitutional requirement that the student engage in a form of speech and may not be enforced. The unconstitutionality of this severable portion of the statute is declared at this time." We concur.

Accordingly, * * * the judgment of the district court will be affirmed.

Notes and Questions

In an earlier decision, a student's position was upheld in a refusal to stand during the pledge, because he believed "that there [isn't] liberty and justice for all in the United States." The court did not agree that the option of either leaving the room or standing quietly during the pledge ceremony was a viable option. See *Goetz* v. *Ansell*, 477 F.2d 636 (2nd Cir. 1973).

The United States Supreme Court upheld the rights of Jehovah's Witnesses not to participate in the pledging of the flag. See *West Virginia State Board of Education* v. *Barnette*, 319 U.S. 624 (1943). This opinion was rendered while the United States was engaged in World War II, and many observers contend that the decision is a dramatic espousal of the individual's right of freedom of expression. In often quoted sections, the Court stated:

. . . One's right to life, liberty and property, to free speech, a free press, freedom of worship and assembly, and other fundamental rights may not be submitted to vote; they depend on the outcome of no elections. (P. 638)

* * *

If there is any fixed star in our constellation, it is that no official, high or petty, can prescribe what shall be orthodox in politics, nationalism, religion, or other matters of opinion or force citizens to confess by word or act their faith therein. If there are any circumstances which permit an exception, they do not now occur to us. (P. 642)

Georgia has a statutory provision that states:

Each student in the public schools of the State of Georgia shall be afforded the opportunity to recite the Pledge of Allegiance to the flag of the United States of America during each school day. It shall be the duty of each local board of education to establish a policy setting the time and manner for recitation of the Pledge of Allegiance. Said policy shall be established in writing and shall be distributed to each teacher within the school (Ga. Code §20-2-286, 1976).

Does your state have a provision addressing student participation in patriotic exercises? What is your local school system's policy on this issue?

II. Suspension, Expulsion, Disciplinary Transfer

Students may be excluded from school for failure to conform to legitimate rules. A student may be suspended; exclusion from school for ten days or less is the usual practice for minor violations of school rules. Expulsion is an exclusion from school for the remainder of a quarter, for a semester, for an academic year, or permanently and occurs upon repeated or major infractions of school rules or criminal conviction. Court opinions have held that since students have a valuable property interest in school attendance, students must be provided due process prior to their being excluded from school. Careful reading of these opinions reveals that the degree of due process that must be afforded a student varies in direct proportion to the length of the exclusion.

Students may also be transferred, for disciplinary reasons, to another school from the one they are attending. Consequently, courts have had to determine the degree of due process required, if any, prior to such a transfer.

A. Suspension

Goss v. Lopez

Supreme Court of the United States, 1975
419 U.S. 565

MR. JUSTICE WHITE delivered the opinion of the Court.

This appeal by various administrators of the Columbus, Ohio, Public School System (CPSS) challenges the judgment of a three-judge federal court, declaring that appellees—various high school students in the CPSS—were denied due process of law contrary to the command of the Fourteenth Amendment in that they were temporarily suspended from their high schools without a hearing either prior to suspension or within a reasonable time thereafter, and enjoining the administrators to remove all references to such suspensions from the students' records.

Ohio law, Rev. Code Ann. § 3313.64 (1972), provides for free education to all children between the ages of six and 21. Section 3313.66 of the Code empowers the principal of an Ohio public school to suspend a pupil for misconduct for up to 10 days or to expel him. In either case, he must notify the student's parents within 24 hours and state the reasons for his action. A pupil who is expelled, or his parents, may appeal the decision to the Board of Education and in connection therewith shall be permitted to be heard at the board meeting. The Board may reinstate the pupil following the hearing. No similar procedure is provided in § 3313.66 or any other provision of state law for a suspended student. Aside from a regulation tracking the statute, at the time of the imposition of the suspensions in this case the CPSS itself had not issued any written procedure applicable to suspensions. Nor, so far as the record reflects, had any of the individual high schools involved in this case. Each, however, had formally or informally described the conduct for which suspension could be imposed.

The nine named appellees, each of whom alleged that he or she had been suspended from public high school in Columbus for up to 10 days without a hearing pursuant to § 3313.66, filed an action under 42 U.S.C. § 1983 against the Columbus Board of Education and various administrators of the CPSS. The complaint sought a declaration that § 3313.66 was unconstitutional in that it permitted public school administrators to deprive plaintiffs of their rights to an education without a hearing of any kind, in violation of the procedural due process component of the Fourteenth Amendment. It also sought to enjoin the public school officials from issuing future suspensions pursuant to § 3313.66 and to require them to remove references to the past suspensions from the records of the students in question.

The proof below established that the suspensions arose out of a period of widespread student unrest in the CPSS during February and March 1971. Six of the named plaintiffs, Rudolph Sutton, Tyrone Washington, Susan Cooper, Deborah Fox, Clarence Byars, and Bruce Harris, were students at the Marion-Franklin High School and were each suspended for 10 days on account of disruptive or disobedient conduct committed in the presence of the school administrator who ordered the suspension. One of these, Tyrone Washington, was among a group of students demonstrating in the school auditorium while a class was being conducted there. He was ordered by the school principal to leave, refused to do so, and was suspended. Rudolph Sutton, in the presence of the principal, physically attacked a police officer who was attempting to remove Tyrone Washington from the auditorium. He was immediately suspended. The other four Marion-Franklin students were suspended for similar conduct. None was given a hearing to determine the operative facts underlying the suspension, but each, together with his or her parents, was offered the opportunity to attend a conference, subsequent to the effective date of the suspension, to discuss the student's future.

Two named plaintiffs, Dwight Lopez and Betty Crome, were students at the Central High School and McGuffey Junior High School, respectively. The former was suspended in connection with a disturbance in the lunchroom which involved some physical damage to school property. Lopez testified that at least 75 other students were suspended from his school on the same day. He also testified below that he was not a party to the destructive conduct but was instead an innocent bystander. Because no one from the school testified with regard to this incident, there is no evidence in the record indicating the official basis for concluding otherwise. Lopez never had a hearing.

Betty Crome was present at a demonstration at a high school other than the one she was attending. There she was arrested together with others, taken to the police station, and released without being formally charged. Before she went to school on the following day, she was notified that she had been suspended for a 10-day period. Because no one from the school testified with respect to this incident, the record does not disclose how the McGuffey Junior High School principal went about making the decision to suspend Crome, nor does it disclose on what information the decision was based. It is clear from the record that no hearing was ever held.

* * *

On the basis of this evidence, the three-judge court declared that plaintiffs were denied due process of law because they were "suspended without hearing prior to suspension or within a reasonable time thereafter," and that Ohio Rev. Code Ann. § 3313.66 (1972) and regulations issued pursuant thereto were unconstitutional in permitting such suspensions. It was ordered that all references to plaintiffs' suspensions be removed from school files.

Although not imposing upon the Ohio school administrators any particular disciplinary procedures and leaving them "free to adopt regulations providing for fair suspension procedures which are consonant with the educational goals of their schools and reflective of the characteristics of their school and locality," the District Court declared that there were "minimum requirements of notice and a hearing prior to suspension, except in emergency situations." In explication, the court stated that relevant case authority would: (1) permit "[i]mmediate removal of a student whose conduct disrupts the academic atmosphere of the school, endangers fellow students, teachers or school officials, or damages property"; (2) require notice of suspension proceedings to be sent to the student's parents within 24 hours of the decision to conduct them; and (3) require a hearing to be held, with the student present, within 72 hours of his removal. Finally, the court stated that, with respect to the nature of the hearing, the relevant cases required that statements in support of the charge be produced, that the student and others be permitted to make statements in defense or mitigation, and that the school need not permit attendance by counsel.

* * *

Although Ohio may not be constitutionally obligated to establish and maintain a public school system, it has nevertheless done so and has required its children to attend. * * * The authority possessed by the State to prescribe and enforce standards of conduct in its schools although concededly very broad, must be exercised consistently with constitutional safeguards. Among other things, the State is constrained to recognize a student's legitimate entitlement to a public education as a property interest which is protected by the Due Process Clause and which may not be taken away for misconduct without adherence to the minimum procedures required by that Clause.

The Due Process Clause also forbids arbitrary deprivations of liberty. "Where a person's good name, reputation, honor, or integrity is at stake because of what the government is doing to him," the minimal requirements of the Clause must be satisfied. * * * School authorities here suspended appellees from school for periods of up to 10 days based on charges of misconduct. If sustained and recorded, those charges could seriously damage the students' standing with their fellow pupils and their teachers as well as interfere with later opportunities for higher education and employment. It is apparent that the claimed right of the State to determine unilaterally and without process whether that misconduct has occurred immediately collides with the requirements of the Constitution.

Appellants proceed to argue that even if there is a right to a public education protected by the Due Process Clause generally, the Clause comes into play only when the State subjects a student to a "severe detriment or grievous loss." The loss of 10 days, it is said, is neither severe nor grievous and the Due Process Clause is therefore of no relevance. * * * A 10-day suspension from school is not *de minimis* in our view and may not be imposed in complete disregard of the Due Process Clause.

A short suspension is, of course, a far milder deprivation than expulsion. But "education is perhaps the most important function of state and local governments," * * * and the total exclusion from the educational process for more than a trivial period, and certainly if the suspension is for 10 days, is a serious event in the life of the suspended child. Neither the property interest in educational benefits temporarily denied nor the liberty interest in reputation, which is also implicated, is so insubstantial that suspensions may constitutionally be imposed by any procedure the school chooses, no matter how arbitrary.

"Once it is determined that due process applies, the question remains what process is due." * * * We turn to that question, fully realizing as our cases regularly do that the interpretation and application of the Due Process Clause are intensely practical matters and that "[t]he very nature of due process negates any concept of inflexible procedures universally applicable to every imaginable situation."* * *

* * * At the very minimum, therefore, students facing suspension and the consequent interference with a protected property interest must be given *some* kind of notice and afforded *some* kind of hearing. "Parties whose rights are to be affected are entitled to be heard; and in order that they may enjoy that right they must first be notified."* * *

It also appears from our cases that the timing and content of the notice and the nature of the hearing will depend on appropriate accommodation of the competing interests involved. * * * The student's interest is to avoid unfair or mistaken exclusion from the educational process, with all of its unfortunate consequences. The Due Process Clause will not shield him from suspensions properly imposed, but it disserves both his interest and the interest of the State if his suspension is in fact unwarranted. The concern would be mostly academic if the disciplinary process were a totally accurate, unerring process, never mistaken and never unfair. Unfortunately, that is not the case, and no one suggests that it is. Disciplinarians, although proceeding in utmost good faith, frequently act on the reports and advice of others; and the controlling facts and the nature of the conduct under challenge are often disputed. The risk of error is not all trivial, and it should be guarded against if that may be done without prohibitive cost or interference with the educational process.

The difficulty is that our schools are vast and complex. Some modicum of discipline and order is essential if the educational function is to be performed. Events calling for discipline are frequent occurrences and sometimes require immediate, effective action. Suspension is considered not only to be a necessary tool to maintain order but a valuable educational device. The prospect of imposing elaborate hearing requirements in every suspension case is viewed with great concern, and many school authorities may well prefer the untrammeled power to act unilaterally, unhampered by rules about notice and hearing. But it would be a strange disciplinary system in an educational institution if no communication was sought by the disciplinarian with the student in an effort to inform him of his dereliction and to let him tell his side of the story in order to make sure that an injustice is not done. "[F]airness can rarely be obtained by secret, one-sided determination of the facts decisive of rights. . . ." "Secrecy is not congenial to truth-seeking and self-righteousness gives too slender an assurance of rightness. No better instrument has been devised for arriving at truth than to give a person in jeopardy of serious loss notice of the case against him and opportunity to meet it." * * *

We do not believe that school authorities must be totally free from notice and hearing requirements if their schools are to operate with acceptable efficiency. Students facing temporary suspension have interests qualifying for protection of the Due Process Clause, and due process requires, in connection with a suspension of 10 days or less, that the student be given oral or written notice of the charges against him and, if he denies them, an explanation of the evidence the authorities have and an opportunity to present his side of the story. The Clause requires at least these rudimentary precautions against unfair or mistaken findings of misconduct and arbitrary exclusion from school.

There need be no delay between the time "notice" is given and the time of the hearing. In the great majority of cases the disciplinarian may informally discuss the alleged misconduct with the student minutes after it has occurred. We hold only that, in being given an opportunity to explain his version of the facts at this discussion, the student first be told what he is accused of doing and what the basis of the accusation is. Lower courts which have addressed the question of the nature of the procedures required in short suspension cases have reached the same conclusion. * * * Since the hearing may occur almost immediately following the misconduct, it follows that as a general rule notice and hearing should precede removal of the student from school. We agree with the District Court, however, that there are recurring situations in which prior notice and hearing cannot be insisted upon. Students whose presence poses a continuing danger to persons or property or an ongoing threat of disrupting the academic process may be immediately removed from school. In such cases, the necessary notice and rudimentary hearing should follow as soon as practicable, as the District Court indicated.

In holding as we do, we do not believe that we have imposed procedures on school disciplinarians which are inappropriate in a classroom setting.

Instead we have imposed requirements which are, if anything, less than a fair-minded school principal would impose upon himself in order to avoid unfair suspensions. Indeed, according to the testimony of the principal of Marion-Franklin High School, that school had an informal procedure, remarkably similar to that which we now require, applicable to suspension generally but which was not followed in this case. * * *

We stop short of construing the Due Process Clause to require, countrywide, that hearings in connection with short suspensions must afford the student the opportunity to secure counsel, to confront and cross-examine witnesses supporting the charge, or to call his own witnesses to verify his version of the incident. Brief disciplinary suspensions are almost countless. To impose in each such case even truncated trial-type procedures might well overwhelm administrative facilities in many places and, by diverting resources, cost more than it would save in educational effectiveness. Moreover, further formalizing the suspension process and escalating its formality and adversary nature may not only make it too costly as a regular disciplinary tool but also destroy its effectiveness as part of the teaching process.

On the other hand, requiring effective notice and informal hearing permitting the student to give his version of the events will provide a meaningful hedge against erroneous action. At least the disciplinarian will be alerted to the existence of disputes about facts and arguments about cause and effect. He may then determine himself to summon the accuser, permit cross-examination, and allow the student to present his own witnesses. In more difficult cases, he may permit counsel. In any event, his discretion will be more informed and we think the risk of error substantially reduced.

* * *

We should also make it clear that we have addressed ourselves solely to the short suspension, not exceeding 10 days. Longer suspensions or expulsions for the remainder of the school term, or permanently, may require more formal procedures. Nor do we put aside the possibility that in unusual situations, although involving only a short suspension, something more than the rudimentary procedures will be required.

The District Court found each of the suspensions involved here to have occurred without a hearing, either before or after the suspension, and that each suspension was therefore invalid and the statute unconstitutional insofar as it permits such suspensions without notice or hearing. Accordingly, the judgement is

Affirmed.

MR. JUSTICE POWELL, with whom THE CHIEF JUSTICE, MR. JUSTICE BLACKMUN, and MR. JUSTICE REHNQUIST join, dissenting.

The Court today invalidates an Ohio statute that permits student suspensions from school without a hearing "for not more than ten days." The decision unnecessarily opens avenues for judicial intervention in the operation of our public schools that may affect adversely the quality of education. The Court holds for the first time that the federal courts, rather than educational officials and state legislatures, have the authority to determine the rules applicable to routine classroom discipline of children and teenagers in the public schools. It justifies this unprecedented intrusion into the process of elementary and secondary education by identifying a new constitutional right: the right of a student not to be suspended for as much as a single day without notice and a due process hearing either before or promptly following the suspension.

The Court's decision rests on the premise that, under Ohio law, education is a property interest protected by the Fourteenth Amendment's Due Process Clause and therefore that any suspension requires notice and a hearing. In my view, a student's interest in education is not infringed by a suspension within the limited period prescribed by Ohio law. Moreover, to the extent that there may be some arguable infringement, it is too speculative, transitory, and insubstantial to justify imposition of a *constitutional* rule.

* * *

One of the more disturbing aspects of today's decision is its indiscriminate reliance upon the judiciary, and the adversary process, as the means of resolving many of the most routine problems arising in the classroom. In mandating due process procedures the Court misapprehends the reality of the normal teacher-pupil relationship. There is an ongoing relationship, one in which the teacher must occupy many roles— educator, adviser, friend, and, at times, parent-substitute. It is rarely adversary in nature except with respect to the chronically disruptive or insubordinate pupil whom the teacher must be free to discipline without frustrating formalities.

The Ohio statute, providing as it does for due notice both to parents and the Board, is compatible with the teacher-pupil relationship and the informal resolution of mistaken disciplinary action. We have relied for generations upon the experience, good faith and dedication of those who staff our public schools, and the nonadversary means of airing grievances that always have been available to pupils and their parents. One would have thought before today's opinion that this informal method of resolving differences was more compatible with the interests of all concerned than resort to any constitutionalized procedure, however blandly it may be defined by the Court.

*   *   *

It hardly need be said that if a student, as a result of a day's suspension, suffers "a blow" to his "self esteem," "feels powerless," views "teachers with resentment," or feels "stigmatized by his teachers," identical psychological harms will flow from many other routine and necessary school decisions. The student who is given a failing grade, who is not promoted, who is excluded from certain extracurricular activities, who is assigned to a school reserved for children of less than average ability, or who is placed in the "vocational" rather than the "college preparatory" track, is unlikely to suffer any less psychological injury than if he were suspended for a day for a relatively minor infraction.

If, as seems apparent, the Court will now require due process procedures whenever such routine school decisions are challenged, the impact upon public education will be serious indeed. The discretion and judgment of federal courts across the land often will be substituted for that of the 50 state legislatures, the 14,000 school boards, and the 2,000,000 teachers who heretofore have been responsible for the administration of the American public school system. If the Court perceives a rational and analytically sound distinction between the discretionary decision by school authorities to suspend a pupil for a brief period, and the types of discretionary school decisions described above, it would be prudent to articulate it in today's opinion. Otherwise, the federal courts should prepare themselves for a vast new role in society.

Not so long ago, state deprivations of the most significant forms of state largesse were not thought to require due process protection on the ground that the deprivation resulted only in the loss of a state-provided "benefit." * * * In recent years the Court, wisely in my view, has rejected the "wooden distinction between 'rights' and 'privileges,' " * * * and looked instead to the significance of the state-created or state-enforced right and to the substantiality of the alleged deprivation. Today's opinion appears to abandon this reasonable approach by holding in effect that government infringement of any interest to which a person is entitled, no matter what the interest or how inconsequential the infringement, requires *constitutional* protection. As it is difficult to think of any less consequential infringement than suspension of a junior high school student for a single day, it is equally difficult to perceive any principled limit to the new reach of procedural due process.

Notes and Questions

Goss, a five-to-four decision, reveals a sharp division among the Court's justices. Does such a division make *Goss* any less the supreme law of the land? Is the due process requirement established in *Goss* educationally sound? Would seriatim ten-day suspensions for the same offense violate the rationale established in *Goss?*

A high school senior who admitted to drinking on a school outing was suspended for three days at the end of the academic year, and consequently he missed a final examination and failed to make the required grade point for graduation. His parents contended that the punishment amounted to more than a suspension. However, although seeming to sympathize with the student, a federal appellate court did not agree that he was entitled to the same degree of due process as that for an expulsion. A meeting with the principal and an opportunity for the parents to present a "mitigative argument" to the principal met the due process requirement. The court stated that "it is not the role of the federal courts to set aside the decisions of school administrators which the court may view as lacking a basis in wisdom or compassion." See *Lamb* v. *Panhandle Community Unit School District No. 2,* 826 F.2d 526 (7th Cir. 1987).

The use of a so-called timeout box, a device temporarily to isolate unruly students, has been upheld in *Dickens* v. *Johnson County Board of Education,* 661 F. Supp. 155 (Tenn. 1987). In this instance the "box" had three sides enclosing a desk at which the student could see the teacher and hear the class but could not see other pupils. He was allowed to go to the rest room and to attend scheduled activities such as lunch, physical education, and specialty classes. It was alleged that he had spent as long as four and one-half hours on six consecutive days in the "box." In explaining that the student's due process property interest had not been violated, the court stated:

> Of course, students are entitled to hearings before they are expelled or suspended since these actions totally excluded them from the educational process. But teachers should be free to impose minor forms of classroom discipline, such as admonishing students, requiring special assignments, restricting activities, and denying certain privileges, without being subjected to the strictures of due process scrutiny. (P. 157)

And the court further stated:

> It appears that judicious use of behavioral modification techniques such as "timeout" should be favored over expulsion in disciplining disruptive students. This is not to say that educators may arbitrarily cage students in a corner of the classroom for an indeterminate length of time. Nevertheless, the Court finds the defendants' use of timeout in this case was not unduly harsh or grossly disproportionate. (P. 158)

Does your state have a statutory provision pertaining to suspension? What are your local school system's rules regarding suspension?

B. Expulsion

Gonzales v. McEuen

United States District Court, Central District of California, 1977
435 F. Supp. 460

TAKASUGI, District Judge.
Eleven high school students, by their next friends, have brought this action under the Civil Rights Act, 42 U.S.C. § 1983, and the Due Process Clause of the Fourteenth Amendment to the Constitution of the United States. The case stems from the suspension and expulsion of the named plaintiffs from Oxnard Union High School following a period of student unrest on campus during October 14–15, 1976. The plaintiffs were charged with having committed certain acts which, it was alleged, led to a riot at Oxnard High School.

* * *

Plaintiffs' strongest and most serious challenge is to the impartiality of the Board. They contend that they were denied their right to an impartial hearing before an independent fact-finder. The basis for this claim is, first, overfamiliarity of the Board with the case; second, the multiple role played by defendants' counsel; and third, the involvement of the Superintendent of the District, Mr. McEuen, with the Board of Trustees during the hearings.

No one doubts that a student charged with misconduct has a right to an impartial tribunal * * * . There is doubt, however, as to what this means. Various situations have been identified in which experience teaches that the probability of actual bias on the part of the judge or decisionmaker is too high to be constitutionally tolerable. Bias is presumed to exist, for example, in cases in which the adjudicator has a pecuniary interest in the outcome; * * * or in which he has been the target of personal attack or criticism from the person before him. * * * The decision maker may also have such prior involvement with the case as to acquire a disqualifying bias. * * * The question before the Court is not whether the Board was actually biased, but whether, under the circumstances, there existed probability that the decisionmaker would be tempted to decide the issues with partiality to one party or the other. It is with this view that the plaintiffs' claims must be considered.

Much has been made of "The Red Book" which, it is claimed, contained information about the academic and disciplinary records of plaintiffs. It is alleged that the Board had access to this material from twenty to thirty days before the expulsion hearings. Depositions submitted to the court show that the members of the Board met with school officials prior to the hearings. Plaintiffs contend that this prior involvement by the Board deprived plaintiffs of the opportunity for a fair hearing. The court rejects this contention. Exposure to evidence presented in a nonadversary investigative procedure is insufficient in itself to impugn the fairness of the Board members at a later adversary hearing. * * * Nor is a limited combination of investigatory and adjudicatory functions in an administrative body necessarily unfair, absent a showing of other circumstances such as malice or personal interest in the outcome. * * * A school board would be amiss in its duties if it did not make some inquiry to know what was going on in the district for which it is responsible. Some familiarity with the facts of the case gained by an agency in the performance of its statutory role does not disqualify a decisionmaker. * * *

Turning now to the issue of the multiple roles performed by defendents' counsel, the court notes that the board members are defendants in this pending related action and may thereby become subject to personal liability.

It is undisputed that attorneys for the District who prosecuted the charges against the plaintiffs in the expulsion proceedings, also represent the Board members in this action. Plaintiffs claim that the attorneys acted in dual roles at the expulsion hearing: as prosecutors for the Administration and as legal advisors to the Board. Counsel for defendants admit that they advised the Board prior to the hearings with respect to its obligations regarding these expulsions, but they deny that they advised the Board during the proceedings themselves.

A reading of the transcripts reveals how difficult it was to separate the two roles. Special mention should be made of the fact that the Board enjoys no legal expertise and must rely heavily upon its counsel. This places defendants' attorneys in a position of intolerable prominence and influence.

It is the opinion of this court that the confidential relationship between the attorneys for the District and the members of the Board, reinforced by the advisory role played by the attorneys for the Board, created an unacceptable risk of bias. Bearing in mind also that the Board members are subject to personal liability in this action, the court concludes that bias can be presumed to exist.

Superintendent McEuen sat with the Board members during the expulsion hearings; he acted as Secretary of the Board on at least one occasion. By statute, Mr. McEuen is the chief advisor to the Board. The fact remains, however, that he is also the chief of the "prosecution" team, to wit, the District.

It is clear from the record that at least on one occasion, at the joint hearing of plaintiffs, Flores, Chavez and Rodriguez, Superintendent McEuen was present with the Board for approximately forty-five minutes during its deliberations on the issue of expelling these plaintiffs. The plaintiffs contend that their due process rights were violated by the involvement of Mr. McEuen with the Board. This court agrees.

Defendants' counsel maintain that Mr. McEuen did not participate in the deliberations and did no more, perhaps, than serve cookies and coffee to the Board members. Whether he did or did not participate, his presence to some extent might operate as an inhibiting restraint upon the freedom of action and expression of the Board. Defendants argue that there is no evidence that Mr. McEuen influenced or biased the Board. Proof of subjective reasoning processes are incapable of corroboration or disproval. Plaintiffs should not be forced to rely upon the memory or sense of fairness of Superintendent McEuen or the Board as to what occurred there. Perhaps Mr. McEuen's physical presence in deliberation becomes more offensive because of the pre-hearing comments which showed something less than impartiality.

The court concludes that the process utilized by the Board was fundamentally unfair. This raises a presumption of bias. In view of the alternatives for the selection of an impartial hearing body under California Education Code Section 10608, it would have been more reasonable to provide procedures that insured not only that justice was done, but also that it appeared to have been done.

* * *

Plaintiffs Barrington and Munden were expelled at a meeting of the Board on November 10, 1976. Neither Barrington nor Munden was present; neither was represented by either parent or counsel.

On October 29, 1976, letters had been sent to the parents advising them that the principal was recommending expulsion of the students. The letters contained a specific statement of the charges: in the case of Barrington, that he was involved in a riot at school at which time he had threatened physical violence against a teacher; in the case of Munden, that he was involved in a fight with another student, Wayne Berry. The letters contained no notice to the student or parent of the student's right to be present at the hearing, to be represented by counsel, and to present evidence. This was a clear violation of § 10608 of the California Education Code. The letters to the parents stated, "If you feel that the school does not have just cause for this recommendation, you may want to attend this meeting to present your reasons why [the students] should not be expelled."

* * *

Goss clearly anticipates that where the student is faced with the severe penalty of expulsion he shall have the right to be represented by and through counsel, to present evidence on his own behalf, and to confront and cross-examine adverse witnesses.

* * *

Notice to be adequate must communicate to the recipient the nature of the proceeding. In an expulsion hearing, the notice given to the student must include a statement not only of the specific charge, but also the basic rights to be afforded the student: to be represented by counsel, to present evidence, and to confront and cross-examine adverse witnesses. Section 10608 of the California Education Code provides, *inter alia,* for notice to the student and the parent of the specific charge, of the right to be represented by counsel, and of the right to present evidence. Federal due process requires no less.

Defendants next argue that even if the notice was defective, the court must still determine whether the plaintiffs were given a fair and impartial hearing. Defendants misapprehend the meaning of notice. It is not "fair" if the student does not know, and is not told, that he has certain rights which he may exercise at the hearing.

* * *

The court holds that the notice given to plaintiffs Barrington and Munden was defective in that it did not adequately inform them of their constitutional rights. It follows that their expulsions were improper.

* * *

Notes and Questions

According to *Gonzales,* a notice of expulsion hearing, to be adequate, must communicate the nature of the proceedings to the recipient. Such a notice must also include a statement of the specific charges and basic rights available to the student, such as the right to be represented by counsel, to present evidence, and to confront and cross-examine adverse witnesses. Several decisions prior to *Gonzales* did not require notice of the right to be represented by counsel.

May a school superintendent participate, merely by being present at the expulsion deliberations, according to *Gonzales?*

The question of whether the same attorney may advise the school board and present the superintendent's case at a hearing is discussed in *Breitling* v. *Solenberger,* 585 F. Supp. 289 (Va. 1984). The federal district court in this instance held that this dual role did not violate due process requirements.

A school district's policy of expelling students for possession of marijuana on school grounds was upheld. The court stated that "[t]he policy of the Board as clearly set forth in its Code of Conduct is not arbitrary or capricious, but is a commendable effort in dealing with a serious, destructive problem." See *Rucker* v. *Colonial School District,* 517 A.2d 703 (Del. Super. Ct. 1986). However, an expulsion was not upheld in a case dealing with possession of marijuana off the school grounds. In this instance, the authority to expel was limited by statute to possession of marijuana on school grounds or on school buses. See *Labrosse* v. *Saint Bernard Parish School Board,* 483 So. 2d 1253 (La. Ct. App. 1986).

Does your state have a statutory provision pertaining to expulsion? What are your local school system's rules or policies regarding expulsion?

C. Disciplinary Transfer

Transfer to a so-called alternative school, designed to meet the needs of disruptive students, is not considered to be the equivalent of an expulsion. Appropriate due process in such an instance includes: (1) written notice to both the student and his parents; (2) an opportunity for a meeting among school authorities, parents, and the student, at which the situation may be discussed; and (3) a meeting at which evidence may be presented and witnesses examined. See *Jordan* v. *School District of City of Erie,* 583 F.2d 91 (3d Cir. 1978), and *Zamora* v. *Pomeroy,* 639 F.2d 662 (10th Cir. 1981). A lawyer need not be present at such a conference. See *Madera* v. *Board of Education of the City of New York,* 386 F.2d 778 (2d Cir. 1967).

III. Corporal Punishment

Corporal punishment may be defined as the use of such physical contact as striking, paddling, or spanking of a student by an educator. Although widely used, it is a controversial practice that has received much debate.

Proponents view it as a necessary and educationally sound disciplinary measure. Those opposed view the practice as archaic, cruel, and inhuman and an unjustifiable act on the part of the state.

The issue had been repeatedly litigated until the United States Supreme Court upheld the practice in *Ingraham* v. *Wright.* In its opinion the Court addressed two major issues: whether or not the administration of corporal punishment represented cruel and unusual punishment in. violation of the Eighth Amendment; and whether or not prior notice. and an opportunity to be heard were required.

Ingraham v. Wright
Supreme Court of the United States, 1977
430 U.S. 651

MR. JUSTICE POWELL delivered the opinion of the Court.

This case presents questions concerning the use of corporal punishment in public schools: First, whether the paddling of students as a means of maintaining school discipline constitutes cruel and unusual punishment in violation of the Eighth Amendment; and, second, to the extent that paddling is constitutionally permissible, whether the Due Process Clause of the Fourteenth Amendment requires prior notice and an opportunity to be heard.

* * *

Petitioners' evidence may be summarized briefly. In the 1970–1971 school year many of the 237 schools in Dade County used corporal punishment as a means of maintaining discipline pursuant to Florida legislation and a local school board regulation. The statute then in effect authorized limited corporal punishment by negative inference, proscribing punishment which was "degrading or unduly severe" or which was inflicted without prior consultation with the principal or the teacher in charge of the school. * * * The regulation * * * contained explicit directions and limitations. The authorized punishment consisted of paddling the recalcitrant student on the buttocks with a flat wooden paddle measuring less than two feet long, three to four inches wide, and about one-half inch thick. The normal punishment was limited to one to five "licks" or blows with the paddle and resulted in no apparent physical injury to the student. School authorities viewed corporal punishment as a less drastic means of discipline than suspension or expulsion. Contrary to the procedural requirements of the statute and regulation, teachers often paddled students on their own authority without first consulting the principal.

* * * Because he was slow to respond to his teacher's instructions, Ingraham was subjected to more than 20 licks with a paddle while being held over a table in the principal's office. The paddling was so severe that he suffered a hematoma requiring medical attention and keeping him out of school for several days. Andrews was paddled several times for minor infractions. On two occasions he was struck on his arms, once depriving him of the full use of his arm for a week.

* * *

The use of corporal punishment in this country as a means of disciplining schoolchildren dates back to the colonial period. It has survived the transformation of primary and secondary education from the colonials' reliance on optional private arrangements to our present system of compulsory education and dependence on public schools. Despite the general abandonment of corporal punishment as a means of punishing criminal offenders, the practice continues to play a role in the public education of schoolchildren in most parts of the country. Professional and public opinion is sharply divided on the practice, and has been for more than a century. Yet we can discern no trend toward its elimination.

At common law a single principle has governed the use of corporal punishment since before the American Revolution: Teachers may impose reasonable but not excessive force to discipline a child. * * * The basic doctrine has not changed. The prevalent rule in this country today privileges such force as a teacher or administrator "reasonably believes to be necessary for [the child's] proper control, training, or education." * * * To the extent that the force is excessive or unreasonable, the educator in virtually all States is subject to possible civil and criminal liability.

Although the early cases viewed the authority of the teacher as deriving from the parents, the concept of parental delegation has been replaced by the view—more consonant with compulsory education laws—that the State itself may impose such corporal punishment as is reasonably necessary "for the proper education of the child and for the maintenance of group discipline." * * * All of the circumstances are to be taken into account in determining whether the punishment is reasonable in a particular case. Among the most important considerations are the seriousness of the offense, the attitude and past behavior of the child, the nature and severity of the punishment, the age and strength of the child, and the availability of less severe but equally effective means of discipline. * * *

Of the 23 States that have addressed the problem through legislation, 21 have authorized the moderate use of corporal punishment in public schools. Of these States only a few have elaborated on the common-law test of reasonableness, typically providing for approval or notification of the child's parents, or for infliction of punishment only by the principal or in the presence of an adult witness. Only two States, Massachusetts and New Jersey, have prohibited all corporal punishment in their public schools. Where the legislatures have not acted, the state courts have uniformly preserved the common-law rule permitting teachers to use reasonable force in disciplining children in their charge.

Against this background of historical and contemporary approval of reasonable corporal punishment, we turn to the constitutional questions before us.

The Eighth Amendment provides: Excessive bail shall not be required, nor excessive fines imposed, nor cruel and unusual punishments inflicted." Bail, fines, and punishment traditionally have been associated with the criminal process, and by subjecting the three to parallel limitations the text of the Amendment suggests an intention to limit the power of those entrusted with the criminal-law function of government. An examination of the history of the Amendment and the decisions of this Court construing the proscription against cruel and unusual punishment confirms that it was designed to protect those convicted of crimes. We adhere to this long-standing limitation and hold that the Eighth Amendment does not apply to the paddling of children as a means of maintaining discipline in public schools.

* * *

"[T]he question remains what process is due." * * * Were it not for the common-law privilege permitting teachers to inflict reasonable corporal punishment on children in their care, and the availability of the traditional remedies for abuse, the case for requiring advance procedural safeguards would be strong indeed. But here we deal with a punishment—paddling—within that tradition, and the question is whether the common-law remedies are adequate to afford due process. * * * Whether in this case the common-law remedies for excessive corporal punishment constitute due process of law must turn on an analysis of the competing interests at stake, viewed against the background of "history, reason, [and] the past course of decisions." The analysis requires consideration of three distinct factors: "First, the private interest that will be affected . . . ; second, the risk of an erroneous deprivation of such interest . . . and the probable value, if any, of additional or substitute procedural safeguards; and finally, the [state] interest, including the function involved and the fiscal and administrative burdens that the additional or substitute procedural requirement would entail." * * *

* * *

Florida has continued to recognize, and indeed has strengthened by statute, the common-law right of a child not to be subjected to excessive corporal punishment in school. Under Florida law the teacher and principal of the school decide in the first instance whether corporal punishment is reasonably necessary under the circumstances in order to discipline a child who has misbehaved. But they must exercise prudence and restraint. For Florida has preserved the traditional judicial proceedings for determining whether the punishment was justified. If the punishment inflicted is later found to have been excessive—not reasonably believed at the time to be necessary for the child's discipline or training—the school authorities inflicting it may be held liable in damages to the child and, if malice is shown, they may be subject to criminal penalties.

*   *   *

It still may be argued, of course, that the child's liberty interest would be better protected if the common-law remedies were supplemented by the administrative safeguards of prior notice and a hearing. We have found frequently that some kind of prior hearing is necessary to guard against arbitrary impositions on interests protected by the Fourteenth Amendment. * * * But where the State has preserved what "has always been the law of the land," * * * the case for administrative safeguards is significantly less compelling.

*   *   *

But even if the need for advance procedural safeguards were clear, the question would remain whether the incremental benefit could justify the cost. Acceptance of petitioners' claims would work a transformation in the law governing corporal punishment in Florida and most other States. Given the impracticability of formulating a rule of procedural due process that varies with the severity of the particular imposition, the prior hearing petitioners seek would have to precede any paddling, however moderate or trivial.

Such a universal constitutional requirement would significantly burden the use of corporal punishment as a disciplinary measure. Hearings—even informal hearings—require time, personnel, and a diversion of attention from normal school pursuits. School authorities may well choose to abandon corporal punishment rather than incur the burdens of complying with the procedural requirements. Teachers, properly concerned with maintaining authority in the classroom, may well prefer to rely on other disciplinary measures—which they may view as less effective—rather than confront the possible disruption that prior notice and a hearing may entail. Paradoxically, such an alteration of disciplinary policy is most likely to occur in the ordinary case where the contemplated punishment is well within the common-law privilege.

Elimination or curtailment of corporal punishment would be welcomed by many as a societal advance. But when such a policy choice may result from this Court's determination of an asserted right to due process, rather than from the normal processes of community debate and legislative action, the societal costs cannot be dismissed as insubstantial. We are reviewing here a legislative judgment, rooted in history and reaffirmed in the laws of many States, that corporal punishment serves important educational interests. This judgment must be viewed in light of the disciplinary problems commonplace in the schools. * * *

* * * In view of the low incidence of abuse, the openness of our schools, and the common-law safeguards that already exist, the risk of error that may result in violation of a schoolchild's substantive rights can only be regarded as minimal. Imposing additional administrative safeguards as a constitutional requirement might reduce that risk marginally, but would also entail a significant intrusion into an area of primary educational responsibility. We conclude that the Due Process Clause does not require notice and a hearing prior to the imposition of corporal punishment in the public schools, as that practice is authorized and limited by the common law.

Petitioners cannot prevail on either of the theories before us in this case. The Eighth Amendment's prohibition against cruel and unusual punishment is inapplicable to school paddlings, and the Fourteenth Amendment's requirement of procedural due process is satisfied by Florida's preservation of common-law constraints and remedies. We therefore agree with the Court of Appeals that petitioners' evidence affords no basis for injunctive relief, and that petitioners cannot recover damages on the basis of any Eighth Amendment or procedural due process violation.

Affirmed.

Notes and Questions

Ingraham was a five-to-four decision. Chief Justice Burger and Justices Powell, Stewart, Blackmun, and Rehnquist composed the majority.

Justice Powell, who wrote the *Ingraham* decision, brought a background of public school experience to the Court. He was chairman of the Richmond, Virginia, School Board during the time public schools were being desegregated in the 1950s, and he headed the Virginia State Board of Education. Although a Democrat, he was nominated to the Court by President Nixon and took office in 1972. He retired in 1987 and was replaced by Justice Anthony Kennedy in 1988. Justice Kennedy came to the Court from the Ninth Circuit Court of Appeals.

According to *Ingraham,* in the absence of legislation to the contrary, teachers may inflict corporal punishment. Several states do not allow the practice of corporal punishment. State legislatures have prohibited the practice in California, Massachusetts, Nebraska, New Jersey, Vermont, and Wyoming. State boards of education have banned the practice in Hawaii, New Hampshire, and New York. All local school boards in Rhode Island have done likewise. In Maine regulations forbid corporal punishment, and the legislature has defeated its reinstatement.

Is it possible to reconcile the majority opinion in *Ingraham* with the majority opinion in *Goss?*

Does the *Ingraham* decision cite empirical data that establish the effectiveness of corporal punishment? Are such data necessary to support the Court's ruling?

A decision discussing the doctrine of *in loco parentis* concluded that the application of corporal punishment to public school children by means of a paddle, whip, stick, or other mechanical devices could not be permitted under this doctrine; however, the doctrine did not prohibit spanking by hand, physically seizing and removing unruly students from a classroom, or using physical force to restrain students from fighting or engaging in destructive or illegal acts. See *Smith* v. *West Virginia State Board of Education*, 295 S.E.2d 680 (W. Va. 1982).

The Court's decision in *Ingraham* did not put the issue to rest. A federal appellate court has held that excessive force used for corporal punishment is a violation of substantive due process. The court stated:

> Although *Ingraham* makes clear that ordinary corporal punishment violates no substantive due process rights of school children, by acknowledging that corporal punishment implicates a fundamental liberty interest protected by the due process clause, we believe that, at some degree of excessiveness or cruelty, the meting out of such punishment violates the substantive due process rights of the pupil. (P. 654)

Additionally, the court revealed that three categories of corporal punishment exist.

> Punishments that do not exceed the traditional common law standard of reasonableness are not actionable; punishments that exceed the common law standard without adequate state remedies violate procedural due process

rights; and finally, punishments that are so grossly excessive as to be shocking to the conscience violate substantive due process rights, without regard to the adequacy of state remedies. (P. 656)

See *Garcia* v. *Miera*, 817 F.2d 650 (10th Cir. 1987), *cert. denied*, 485 U.S. 959 (1988).

Tying a child to a chair for a full day and part of the next, which was alleged to be an instructional technique, was also held to be a violation of substantive due process. See *Jefferson* v. *Ysleta Independent School District*, 817 F.2d 303 (5th Cir. 1987). In both *Garcia* and *Jefferson*, the courts ruled that a claim for damages had arisen under 42 U.S.C. § 1983.

Are you familiar with the statutory provisions, if any, in your state pertaining to corporal punishment? Are practices in your school system regarding the administration of corporal punishment in conformance with state and local provisions? Are there statutory provisions designed to protect teachers and administrators from suits resulting from their administration of corporal punishment?

IV. Search of Students and Lockers

The desire to have the Fourth Amendment included in the Bill of Rights grew out of British practices prior to the Revolutionary War. Early Americans wanted assurance that their homes would not be invaded without just cause. Many held that without this protection, government authorities could intimidate the citizenry by pursuing "fishing expeditions" such as conducting searches of homes of politically nonconforming citizens until something incriminating was found. With this fear in mind, the Fourth Amendment was included in the Bill of Rights, to protect the individual from possible harassment by an unresponsive government. Originally, the protection of the Fourth Amendment applied only to the federal government, as was the case with the other first eight amendments of the Constitution; however, as a result of decisions involving the Fourteenth Amendment, this protection for the individual is now also available against the state.

School officials may be placed in the position of searching a student because they have a reasonable suspicion that the student has stolen an article or money or has something illegal in his or her possession, such as drugs. Courts faced with such questions have had to balance an individual student's right to the Fourth Amendment's protection from unreasonable search against the duty of school officials to provide all students with a safe and secure school environment. Several factors have complicated the courts' attempt to grapple with the issue of student searches. Foremost among these has been the contention that protection under the Fourth Amendment applies only when a government official acting under the color of the state conducts the search. Therefore, courts have had to determine whether or not a school official could be considered to be a state official whose actions were indeed state action. Another question is the degree of suspicion a school official must have before a search may be conducted. Police must have probable cause to search someone. This is a higher standard than reasonable cause, which has been required by those courts upholding searches by school officials. Also, courts have made a distinction when a search involves any indignities toward students such as a mass or strip search. Such searches, according to several courts, require a standard higher than reasonable cause and, depending on the severity of the intrusion on the student, may require probable cause.

The majority of state courts that have addressed the issue have held that school officials require only reasonable cause to search a student. The United States Supreme Court decision in *New Jersey* v. *T.L.O.* agreed with this notion. *Bellnier* v. *Lund,* a district court decision, discusses the issue of so-called strip searches.

A. Student Search

New Jersey v. T.L.O.

Supreme Court of the United States, 1985
469 U.S. 325

JUSTICE WHITE delivered the opinion of the Court.

We granted certiorari in this case to examine the appropriateness of the exclusionary rule as a remedy for searches carried out in violation of the Fourth Amendment by public school authorities. Our consideration of the proper application of the Fourth Amendment to the public schools, however, has led us to conclude that the search that gave rise to the case now before us did not violate the Fourth Amendment. Accordingly, we here address only the questions of the proper standard for assessing the legality of searches conducted by public school officials and the application of that standard to the facts of this case.

On March 7, 1980, a teacher at Piscataway High School in Middlesex County, N.J., discovered two girls smoking in a lavatory. One of the two girls was the respondent T.L.O., who at that time was a 14-year-old high school freshman. Because smoking in the lavatory was a violation of a school rule, the teacher took the two girls to the Principal's office, where they met with Assistant Vice Principal Theodore Choplick. In response to questioning by Mr. Choplick, T.L.O.'s companion admitted that she had violated the rule. T.L.O., however, denied that she had been smoking in the lavatory and claimed that she did not smoke at all.

Mr. Choplick asked T.L.O. to come into his private office and demanded to see her purse. Opening the purse, he found a pack of cigarettes, which he removed from the purse and held before T.L.O. as he accused her of having lied to him. As he reached into the purse for the cigarettes, Mr. Choplick also noticed a package of cigarette rolling papers. In his experience, possession of rolling papers by high school students was closely associated with the use of marihuana. Suspecting that a closer examination of the purse might yield further evidence of drug use, Mr. Choplick proceeded to search the purse thoroughly. The search revealed a small amount of marihuana, a pipe, a number of empty plastic bags, a substantial quantity of money in one-dollar bills, an index card that appeared to be a list of students who owed T.L.O. money, and two letters that implicated T.L.O. in marihuana dealing.

Mr. Choplick notified T.L.O.'s mother and the police, and turned the evidence of drug dealing over to the police. At the request of the police, T.L.O.'s mother took her daughter to police headquarters, where T.L.O. confessed that she had been selling marihuana at the high school. On the basis of the confession and the evidence seized by Mr. Choplick, the State brought delinquency charges against T.L.O. in the Juvenile and Domestic Relations Court of Middlesex County. Contending that Mr. Choplick's search of her purse violated the Fourth Amendment, T.L.O. moved to suppress the evidence found in her purse as well as her confession, which, she argued, was tainted by the allegedly unlawful search.

* * *

In determining whether the search at issue in this case violated the Fourth Amendment, we are faced initially with the question whether that Amendment's prohibition on unreasonable searches and seizures applies to searches conducted by public school officials. We hold that it does.

It is now beyond dispute that "the Federal Constitution, by virtue of the Fourteenth Amendment, prohibits unreasonable searches and seizures by state officers." * * * Equally indisputable is the proposition that the Fourteenth Amendment protects the rights of students against encroachment by public school officials:

"The Fourteenth Amendment, as now applied to the States, protects the citizen against the State itself and all of its creatures—Boards of Education not excepted. These have, of course, delicate, and highly discretionary functions, but none that they may not perform within the limits of the Bill of Rights. That they are educating the young for citizenship is reason for scrupulous protection of Constitutional freedoms of the individual, if we are not to strangle the free mind at its source and teach youth to discount important principles of our government as mere platitudes." *West Virginia State Board of Education* v. *Barnette*, 319 U.S. 624, 637 (1943).

These two propositions—that the Fourth Amendment applies to the States through the Fourteenth Amendment, and that the actions of public school officials are subject to the limits placed on state action by the Fourteenth Amendment—might appear sufficient to answer the suggestion that the Fourth Amendment does not proscribe unreasonable searches by school officials. On reargument, however, the State of New Jersey has argued that the history of the Fourth Amendment indicates that the Amendment was intended to regulate only searches and seizures carried out by law enforcement officers; accordingly, although public school officials are concededly state agents for purposes of the Fourteenth Amendment, the Fourth Amendment creates no rights enforceable against them.

It may well be true that the evil toward which the Fourth Amendment was primarily directed was the resurrection of the pre-Revolutionary practice of using general warrants or "writs of assistance" to authorize searches for contraband by officers of the Crown. * * * But this Court has never limited the Amendment's prohibition on unreasonable searches and seizures to operations conducted by the police. Rather, the Court has long spoken of the Fourth Amendment's strictures as restraints imposed upon "governmental action"—that is, "upon the activities of sovereign authority." * * * Accordingly, we have held the Fourth Amendment applicable to the activities of civil as well as criminal authorities: building inspectors, * * * and even firemen entering privately owned premises to battle a fire, * * * are all subject to the restraints imposed by the Fourth Amendment. As we observed * * * [t]he basic purpose of this Amendment, as recognized in countless decisions of this Court, is to safeguard the privacy and security of individuals against arbitrary invasions by governmental officials."

* * *

Notwithstanding the general applicability of the Fourth Amendment to the activities of civil authorities, a few courts have concluded that school officials are exempt from the dictates of the Fourth Amendment by virtue of the special nature of their authority over schoolchildren.

* * * Teachers and school administrators, it is said, act *in loco parentis* in their dealings with students: their authority is that of the parent, not the State, and is therefore not subject to the limits of the Fourth Amendment.

Such reasoning is in tension with contemporary reality and the teachings of this Court. * * * Today's public school officials do not merely exercise authority voluntarily conferred on them by individual parents; rather, they act in furtherance of publicly mandated educational and disciplinary policies. * * * In carrying out searches and other disciplinary functions pursuant to such policies, school officials act as representatives of the State, not merely as surrogates for the parents, and they cannot claim the parents' immunity from the strictures of the Fourth Amendment.

* * *

Although this Court may take notice of the difficulty of maintaining discipline in the public schools today, the situation is not so dire that students in the schools may claim no legitimate expectations of privacy. We have recently recognized that the need to maintain order in a prison is such that prisoners retain no legitimate expectations of privacy in their cells, but it goes almost without saying that "[t]he prisoner and the schoolchild stand in wholly different circumstances, separated by the harsh facts of criminal conviction and incarceration." * * * We are not yet ready to hold that the schools and the prisons need be equated for purposes of the Fourth Amendment.

Nor does the State's suggestion that children have no legitimate need to bring personal property into the schools seem well anchored in reality. Students at a minimum must bring to school not only the supplies needed for their studies, but also keys, money, and the necessaries of personal hygiene and grooming. In addition, students may carry on their persons or in purses or wallets such nondisruptive yet highly personal items as photographs, letters, and diaries. Finally, students may have perfectly legitimate reasons to carry with them articles of property needed in connection with extracurricular or recreational activities. In short, schoolchildren may find it necessary to carry with them a variety of legitimate, noncontraband items, and there is no reason to conclude that they have necessarily waived all rights to privacy in such items merely by bringing them onto school grounds.

Against the child's interest in privacy must be set the substantial interest of teachers and administrators in maintaining discipline in the classroom and on school grounds. Maintaining order in the classroom has never been easy, but in recent years, school disorder has often taken particularly ugly forms: drug use and violent crime in the schools have become major social problems. * * * Even in schools that have been spared the most severe disciplinary problems, the preservation of order and a proper educational environment requires close supervision of schoolchildren, as well as the enforcement of rules against conduct that would be perfectly permissible if undertaken by an adult. "Events calling for discipline are frequent occurrences and sometimes require immediate, effective action." * * * Accordingly, we have recognized that maintaining security and order in the schools requires a certain degree of flexibility in school disciplinary procedures, and we have respected the value of preserving the informality of the student-teacher relationship. * * *

How, then, should we strike the balance between the schoolchild's legitimate expectations of privacy and the school's equally legitimate need to maintain an environment in which learning can take place? It is evident that the school setting requires some easing of the restrictions to which searches by public authorities are ordinarily subject. The warrant requirement, in particular, is unsuited to the school environment: requiring a teacher to obtain a warrant before searching a child suspected of an infraction of school rules (or of the criminal law) would unduly interfere with the maintenance of the swift and informal disciplinary procedures needed in the schools. Just as we have in other cases dispensed with the warrant requirement when "the burden of obtaining a warrant is likely to frustrate the governmental purpose behind the search," * * * we hold today that school officials need not obtain a warrant before searching a student who is under their authority.

The school setting also requires some modification of the level of suspicion of illicit activity needed to justify a search. Ordinarily, a search—even one that may permissibly be carried out without a warrant—must be based upon "probable cause" to believe that a violation of the law has occurred. * * * However, "probable cause" is not an irreducible requirement of a valid search. The fundamental command of the Fourth Amendment is that searches and seizures be reasonable, and although "both the concept of probable cause and the requirement of a warrant bear on the reasonableness of a search, . . . in certain limited circumstances neither is required." * * * Thus, we have in a number of cases recognized the legality of searches and seizures based on suspicions that, although "reasonable," do not rise to the level of probable cause. * * * Where a careful balancing of governmental and private interests suggests that the public interest is best served by a Fourth Amendment standard of reasonableness that stops short of probable cause, we have not hesitated to adopt such a standard.

We join the majority of courts that have examined this issue in concluding that the accommodation of the privacy interests of schoolchildren with the substantial need of teachers and administrators for freedom to maintain order in the schools does not require strict adherence to the requirement that searches be based on probable cause to beleive that the subject of the search has violated or is violating the law. Rather, the legality of a search of a student should depend simply on the reasonableness, under all the circumstances, of the search. Determining the reasonableness of any search involves a twofold inquiry: first, one must consider "whether the . . . action was justified at its inception"; * * * second, one must determine whether the search as actually conducted "was reasonably related in scope to the circumstances which justified the interference in the first place." Under ordinary circumstances, a search of a student by a teacher or other school official will be "justified at its inception" when there are reasonable grounds for suspecting that the search will turn up evidence that the student has violated or is violating either the law or the rules of the school. Such a search will be permissible in its scope when the measures adopted are reasonably related to the objectives of the search and not excessively intrusive in light of the age and sex of the student and the nature of the infraction.

This standard will, we trust, neither unduly burden the efforts of school authorities to maintain order in their schools nor authorize unrestrained intrusions upon the privacy of schoolchildren. By focusing attention on the question of reasonableness, the standard will spare teachers and school administrators the necessity of schooling themselves in the niceties of probable cause and permit them to regulate their conduct according to the dictates of reason and common sense. At the same time, the reasonableness standard should ensure that the interests of students will be invaded no more than is necessary to achieve the legitimate end of preserving order in the schools.

There remains the question of the legality of the search in this case.

* * *

* * * It cannot be said that Mr. Choplick acted unreasonably when he examined T.L.O.'s purse to see if it contained cigarettes.

Our conclusion that Mr. Choplick's decision to open T.L.O.'s purse was reasonable brings us to the question of the further search for marihuana once the pack of cigarettes was located. The suspicion upon which the search for marihuana was founded was provided when Mr. Choplick observed a package of rolling papers in the purse as he removed the pack of cigarettes. Although T.L.O. does not dispute the reasonableness of Mr. Choplick's belief that the rolling papers indicated the presence of marihuana, she does contend that the scope of the search Mr. Choplick conducted exceeded permissible bounds when he seized and read certain letters that implicated T.L.O. in drug dealing. This argument, too, is unpersuasive. The discovery of the rolling papers concededly gave rise to a reasonable suspicion that T.L.O. was carrying marihuana as well as cigarettes in her purse. This suspicion justified further exploration of T.L.O.'s purse, which turned up more evidence of drug-related activities: a pipe, a number of plastic bags of the type commonly used to store marihuana, a small quantity of marihuana, and a fairly substantial amount of money. Under these circumstances, it was not unreasonable to extend the search to a separate zippered compartment of the purse; and when a search of that compartment revealed an index card containing a list of "people who owe me money" as well as two letters, the inference that T.L.O. was involved in marihuana trafficking was substantial enough to justify Mr. Choplick in examining the letters to determine whether they contained any further evidence. In short, we cannot conclude that the search for marihuana was unreasonable in any respect.

Because the search resulting in the discovery of the evidence of marihuana dealing by T.L.O. was reasonable, the New Jersey Supreme Court's decision to exclude that evidence from T.L.O.'s juvenile delinquency proceedings on Fourth Amendment grounds was erroneous. Accordingly, the judgment of the Supreme Court of New Jersey is

Reversed.

Notes and Questions

A federal appellate court addressed the issue of a school official's search of a student's hotel room during a "spring break" trip, 5000 miles from home. Citing **T.L.O.**, the court held that the search required extraordinary justification, owing to the fact that the student had paid for the room and that the incident occurred in less than a fully educational context. Nevertheless, the court found such a justification since school officials were charged with supervisory duties in an environment requiring unusual vigilance. Relying also on the doctrine of *in loco parentis,* the court stated that many parents would be reluctant to allow their children on such trips if school officials did not have sufficient authority to supervise. See *Webb* v. *McCullough,* 828 F.2d 1151 (6th Cir. 1987).

Prior to the Court's decision in **T.L.O.** virtually all state and federal courts had held that school officials only required reasonable cause to search a student. *Louisiana* v. *Mora,* 330 So. 2d 900 (La. 1976), *cert. denied,* 429 U.S. 1004 (1976), represents a minority viewpoint. In that decision, the Louisiana Supreme Court held that school officials are government agents, that a warrantless search is in violation of the Fourth Amendment, and that evidence obtained in such a manner was not admissible in the subsequent criminal proceeding.

May a school official search a car in the school parking lot when there is a reasonable suspicion that the car contains drugs? firearms or other weapons? liquor?

B. Intrusive Search

Bellnier v. Lund

United States District Court, Northern District of New York, 1977
438 F. Supp. 47

MUNSON, District Judge.

This is an action whereby the plaintiff children, through their parents *comme* next friends, seek redress for an allegedly unlawful strip search claimed to have been conducted or condoned by defendants, all of whom are employed by the Auburn Enlarged City School District in one capacity or another. Plaintiffs seek legal, injunctive, and declaratory relief in their action, which is maintained under 42 U.S.C. §§ 1983 and 1985, as well as the Fourth, Ninth and Fourteenth Amendments of the United States Constitution. * * *

On the morning of December 6, 1974, plaintiffs and their classmates, members of the fifth grade class at Auburn's Lincoln Elementary School, arrived at the classroom in their usual fashion. Each of the students entered the classroom and placed his outer garment in a coatroom located wholly within, and accessible only from, the classroom itself. The teacher of the class, defendant Reardon, stood at or near the classroom door during this time while the student teacher, defendant Olson, remained inside the classroom. Once inside the room, no student left prior to the alleged search now the subject of this action.

Sometime that morning, and prior to the commencement of class, plaintiff Leonti complained to defendant Olson that he was missing $3.00 from his coat pocket. Plaintiff Leonti stated that he was sure that he had $4.00 when he arrived at school, showing defendant Reardon the four raffle ticket stubs indicating sales proceeds in the amount of $4.00, only $1.00 of which remained in Leonti's pocket.

An appeal by defendant Reardon to the class regarding knowledge of the missing money proved fruitless. Being aware of prior complaints from class members of missing money, lunches, and other items, and knowing that no one had left the classroom that morning, defendant Reardon commenced a search of the class, with the aid of fellow teachers and school officials, all of whom are named as defendants herein.

The outer garments hanging in the coatroom were searched initially. The students were then asked to empty their pockets and remove their shoes. A search of those items failed to reveal the missing money. The class members were then taken to their respective restrooms, the girls to the girls' room by defendants Olson and Butcher, and the boys to the boys' room by defendants Reardon, Parker, and Lund. The students were there ordered to strip down to their undergarments, and their clothes were searched. When the strip searches proved futile, the students were returned to the classroom. There, a search was conducted of their desks, books, and once again of their coats.

The entire search lasted approximately two hours, with the strip searches taking about fifteen minutes. The missing money was never located.

*　*　*

In finding that the Fourth Amendment does apply in this case, this Court does not mean to imply that a showing of probable cause is necessary in order to uphold the search as reasonable. In analyzing the search to determine reasonableness, the Court must weigh the danger of the conduct, evidence of which is sought, against the students' right of privacy and the need to protect them from the humiliation and psychological harms associated with such a search. *　*　* In doing so the Court must take into account the special duties and responsibilities imposed upon school officials to provide a safe atmosphere for a student to develop, the attendant limited powers which the school officials possess *in loco parentis* to effectuate the maintenance of proper discipline. *　*　*

This Court holds that, while there need not be a showing of probable cause in a case such as this, there must be demonstrated the existence of some articulable facts which together provided reasonable grounds to search the students, and that the search must have been in furtherance of a legitimate purpose with respect to which school officials are empowered to act, such as the maintenance of discipline or the detection and punishment of misconduct. *　*　* In making such an analysis, some factors which warrant consideration are: (1) the child's age; 2) the child's history and record in school; 3) the seriousness and prevalence of the problem to which the search is directed; and 4) the exigency requiring an immediate warrantless search. *　*　*

On balance, the facts of this case mitigate against the validity of the search in issue. It is entirely possible that there was reasonable suspicion, and even probable cause, based upon the facts, to believe that *someone* in the classroom had possession of the stolen money. There were no facts, however, which allowed the officials to particularize with respect to which students might possess the money, something which has time and again, with exceptions not relevant to this case, been found to be necessary to a reasonable search under the Fourth Amendment. * * * For this reason, the search must be held to have been invalid under the Fourth Amendment, there being no reasonable suspicion to believe that each student searched possessed contraband or evidence of a crime.

The Court is not unmindful of the dilemma which confronts school officials in a situation such as this. However, in view of the relatively slight danger of the conduct involved (as opposed to drug possession, for example), the extent of the search, and the age of the students involved, this Court cannot in good conscience say that the search undertaken was reasonable. * * *

* * *

Notes and Questions

In another decision dealing with a strip search, a federal appellate court, *M.M.* v. *Anker,* 607 F.2d 588 (2d Cir. 1979), contended that

. . . teachers have a unique relationship to their students, both in administering discipline as part of their educational function, and in protecting the well-being of all children in their care and custody. Accordingly, these interests justify greater flexibility when applying the Fourth Amendment in a school setting. . . .
We are also of the view that as the intrusiveness of the search intensifies, the standard of Fourth Amendment "reasonableness" approaches probable cause, even in the school context. . . . Thus, when a teacher conducts a highly intrusive invasion such as the strip search in this case, it is reasonable to require that probable cause be present . . . (P. 589).

May school officials conduct a schoolwide search for drugs by using drug-detecting dogs and then engage in a strip search of suspected students? A federal appellate court has held that sniffing by a dog was not a search and therefore not protected by the Fourth Amendment; requesting students to empty their pockets and purses did not violate the Fourth Amendment; but conducting a nude search of a student as a result of the dog's alert was unreasonable. In entitling the student to damages, the court contended that a nude search was not only unconstitutional, but also contrary to common decency. See *Doe* v. *Renfrow*, 635 F.2d 582 (7th Cir. 1980), *cert. denied*, 451 U.S. 1022 (1981).

The Fifth Circuit Court of Appeals rejected the *Doe* rationale concerning the use of trained "sniffer" dogs and held that it was a search within the purview of the Fourth Amendment. This court contended that the intrusion in dignity that accompanies canine sniffing of students "cannot be justified by the need to prevent abuse of drugs and alcohol when there is not individualized suspicion." Canine sniffing of lockers and cars was not considered a search since they are unattended and in public view. See *Horton* v. *Goose Creek Independent School District*, 690 F.2d 470 (5th Cir. 1982), *cert. denied*, 463 U.S. 1207 (1983).

Some school officials have used drug testing as a condition for either school attendance or interscholastic participation or as a basis for disciplining students. In addressing the issue, a federal district court struck down the use of a urinalysis test for marijuana. It found that the test was capable only of evidencing marijuana use at an indefinite past time but not of proving possession or use during school. Additionally, the court held that since urinalysis involves disrobing in an observer's presence, it is comparable to a nude search. See *Anable* v. *Ford*, 663 F. Supp. 149 (Ark. 1987). Also see *Odenheim* v. *Carlstadt-East Rutherford Regional School District*, 211 N.J. Super. Ct. Ch. Div. 54, 510 A.2d 709 (1985), for a similar ruling. However, a urinalysis program applying only to students participating in interscholastic sports was upheld. Under the program, students testing positively were suspended only from sports participation for certain periods of time; no disciplinary or academic sanctions were imposed. Athletes were randomly selected; a school official stood outside the rest room stall during the urine sampling; and a positive follow-up test was required before sanctions were imposed. See *Schaill* v. *Tippecanoe School Corporation*, 679 F. Supp. 833 (Ind. 1988).

C. Locker Search

Courts have tended to allow school officials to search a student's locker without a warrant and without the student's permission. The court's reasoning is often that schools retain ultimate control over lockers and act *in loco parentis*. This issue was addressed two decades ago in *Kansas* v. *Stein*, 203 Kan. 638, 456 P.2d 1, *cert. denied*, 397 U.S. 947 (1970), which discussed the public nature of student lockers. The court held that school authorities must protect both the school's educational functions and the students' welfare and may, therefore, inspect lockers to prevent their illicit use.

Courts have continued to uphold locker searches by school authorities. Courts usually apply a standard that declares students to have legitimate expectations of privacy in their lockers. However, the expectation is not absolute and must be balanced against the school's need to maintain order and discipline.

V. Dress and Grooming

There were many challenges to dress and grooming regulations during the 1970s. Students and their parents often questioned rules, particularly those pertaining to grooming, which they believed to be unfair or anachronistic. In their suits parents commonly alleged that they, not schools, were responsible for the appearance of their children. They contended that school authorities were warranted in imposing only those standards necessary for health, safety, or an educationally sound program. School authorities, on the other hand, usually contended that they possessed the discretion to determine which policies aided in maintaining order and discipline.

Despite the controversy surrounding the issue and the judiciary's frequent involvement, the Supreme Court has not ruled on a dress-and-grooming case. The resulting variety of holdings among jurisdictions sometimes hindered school officials in determining applicable law. Nevertheless, the markedly reduced level of suits in recent years suggests not only that some of the issues of the 1970s have dissipated but also that adequate school policies have been crafted and that school officials have learned to deal appropriately with these issues when they arise.

A. Dress

Courts, to date, have not been consistent in their decisions pertaining to dress. Generally, dress codes have been upheld that prohibited immodest or suggestive clothing, dress that would create a disturbance or distraction, and clothing that was unsanitary or created a health hazard.

Since there was no showing that the wearing of blue jeans inhibited or tended to inhibit the educational process, a New Hampshire federal court, in *Bannister v. Paradis*, invalidated the prohibition against wearing jeans.

Bannister v. Paradis

United States District Court, District of New Hampshire, 1970
316 F. Supp. 185

BOWNES, District Judge.

*   *   *

Prior to hearing, the parties entered into a stipulation of facts as follows. Kevin Bannister is twelve years old and is a student in the sixth grade of the Pittsfield High School which runs from the fifth through the twelfth grades, and is a public school. The present version of the dress code was adopted unanimously by the School Board on April 27, 1970, and the only section of the dress code in issue is the section * * * referring to dungarees. The plaintiff, however, does not agree that the dress code is constitutional as to its other provisions. Kevin was sent home for violation of the dress code because he was wearing blue jeans. At no time was force used to require Kevin to leave school.

At the outset, the Court has had some difficulty defining the word "dungarees." The principal of the school defined "dungarees" as working clothes made of a coarse cotton blue fabric. The Chairman of the School Board defined "dungarees" as a denim fabric pant used for work with color of no significance. Webster's *Third International Dictionary* defines "dungarees" as heavy cotton work clothes usually made of blue dungaree. For purposes of this case, the Court finds that blue jeans and dungarees are synonymous and that Kevin Bannister deliberately violated the school dress code on at least two occasions by wearing blue jeans to school. These violations were with the full knowledge and consent, if not the actual urging, of Kevin's parents. At the time the violations occurred, the blue jeans were neat and clean, as was all of Kevin's ensemble.

There was no evidence that the wearing of dungarees of any color had ever caused any disturbance at the school or given rise to any disciplinary problems. Kevin's wearing of blue jeans did not cause any disturbance and there was no disciplinary problem involved except the one involving Kevin himself. It can be fairly concluded that wearing clean blue jeans does not constitute a danger to the health or safety of other pupils and that wearing them does not disrupt the other pupils.

The principal of the school, Mr. Paradis, who has had a total of seven years' experience in teaching and school administration, testified that discipline is essential to the educational process, and that proper dress is part of a good educational climate. It was his opinion that if students wear working or play clothes to school, it leads to a relaxed attitude and such an attitude detracts from discipline and a proper educational climate. Mr. Paradis stated further that students with patches on their clothes and students with dirty clothes, regardless of the type of clothing, should be sent home. The Court notes there that there is nothing in the dress code specifically stating that clothes should be neat and clean. The dress code, as to the boys, is directed primarily to specific prohibitions and does not promulgate any positive standards to follow. On cross-examination, the principal stated: "I apply the dress code as I see it. We don't define the term dungarees as to what it is."

The Chairman of the School Board, E. Windsor Burbank, testified that it was his opinion, and the opinion of the School Board, that the relaxed atmosphere induced by wearing work or play clothes to school does not fit into the atmosphere of discipline and learning. This opinion was based on the Chairman's assertion that California students had poor academic records and that this was due to the sloppy and casual attire worn by them to school. The Chairman is a full time pilot for TWA Airlines and his knowledge of the type of school dress worn by students in California was based on his observations at the times that his airplane schedule took him to various sections of California. The Chairman did not explain the basis for his assertion that California high school students have poor academic records.

Prior to the adoption of a revised dress code in 1970, the Student Council had recommended that the prohibition against dungarees be eliminated. The School Board did not accede to this request, but no reasons were given for its refusal.

* * *

There was no suggestion that the wearing of blue jeans, clean or otherwise, in any way constitutes a right of expression. The First Amendment, therefore, does not apply and is not an issue.

Certainly, the prohibition against the wearing of blue jeans or dungarees cannot by any stretch of the imagination touch the right of privacy * * *.

If it were not for the case of Richards v. Thurston, 424 F.2d 1281 (1st Cir. 1970), the Court might be tempted to dispose of this matter on the ground that there was no deprivation of any constitutional rights. The language and reasoning of that case, however, convinces us that a person's right to wear clothes of his own choosing provided that, in the case of a schoolboy, they are neat and clean, is a constitutional right protected and guaranteed by the Fourteenth Amendment. Judge Coffin, in writing the opinion, * * * stated:

> No right is held more sacred, or is more carefully guarded, by the common law, than the right of every individual to the possession and control of his own person, free from all restraint or interference of others, unless by clear and unquestionable authority of law.

Surely, the commodious concept of liberty invoked by Judge Coffin, embracing freedoms great and small, is large enough to include within its embrace the right to wear clean blue jeans to school unless there is an outweighing state interest justifying their exclusion. * * *

Since we have determined that a personal liberty is involved, and that the plaintiff has stated a claim under 42 U.S.C. § 1983, we now consider the second question, and that is whether or not the regulations against the wearing of dungarees is justified under these circumstances. Going again to Richards v. Thurston, *supra,* for our guidelines, we take into account the nature of the liberty asserted, the context in which it is asserted, and the extent to which the intrusion on the liberty is confined to the legitimate public interest to be served.

On the scale of values of constitutional liberties, the right to wear clean blue jeans to school is not very high. There was no suggestion by the plaintiff that he could not afford pants other than blue jeans, although there was testimony by another parent that she had sent her son to school at the end of the year in blue jeans because she could not afford to buy him a pair of dress pants.

On the other hand, there was no showing that the wearing of dungarees in any way inhibited or tended to inhibit the education process. The Court is, of course, mindful of the testimony of the principal and the Chairman of the School Board that wearing work clothes or play clothes is subversive of the educational process because students tend to become lax and indifferent. The Court confesses, however, that it has considerable difficulty accepting this proposition. There was no expert testimony to this effect with the exception of that of Mr. Paradis. While the Court realizes that Mr. Burbank's experience on the School Board of eight years' standing does give him certain credentials, it does not qualify him as an expert in the field of education and teaching. There was no evidence as to how many other school boards in the state followed a similar dress code nor, with the exception of Mr. Burbank's rather casual observations of the California school system, was there any testimony as to the type of dress worn by other pupils in any other schools.

* * *

We realize that a school can, and must, for its own preservation exclude persons who are unsanitary, obscenely or scantily clad. Good hygiene and the health of the other pupils require that dirty clothes of any nature, whether they be dress clothes or dungarees, should be prohibited. Nor does the Court see anything unconstitutional in a school board prohibiting scantily clad students because it is obvious that the lack of proper covering, particularly with female students, might tend to distract other pupils and be disruptive of the educational process and school discipline.

While the Court recognizes that school boards do have power to adopt reasonable restrictions on dress as part of its educational policy and as an educational device, the school board's power must be limited to that required by its function of administering public education. The observation in *Westley* v. *Rossi, supra,* is pertinent.

> The standards of appearance and dress of last year are not those of today nor will they be those of tomorrow. Regulation of conduct by school authorities must bear a reasonable basis to the ordinary conduct of the school curriculum or to carrying out the responsibility of the school. (305 F. Supp. 714)

The Court rules that the defendants have not justified the intrusion on the personal liberty of Kevin Bannister, small as that intrusion may be, and that the prohibition against wearing dungarees is unconstitutional and invalid. The School Board and the principal of the Pittsfield High School are permanently enjoined from enforcing that portion of the dress code which prohibits boys from wearing dungarees. * * *

So ordered.

Notes and Questions

A dress regulation requiring proper attire to participate in a graduation ceremony was upheld. The court maintained that receiving a diploma at a commencement program was not a property right under state law, and the student was entitled to receive his diploma separately after the program. See *Fowler* v. *Williamson,* 39 N.C. App. 715, 251 S.E.2d 889 (1979).

Some observers suggest that at one time in our history, schools, especially when serving a homogeneous community, were accepted as a socializing agency that was the arbiter of "proper" dress. If this is an accurate assessment, what factors have contributed to the demise of such a role for the school?

Does your school system have dress regulations?

B. Grooming

Court decisions dealing with grooming issues have not been consistent. Judicial views range from upholding the right of males to wear "long" hair, on the basis that this right is protected by the federal Constitution, to declaring the question an unworthy one for federal court attention. Since the constitutional rights pertaining to male grooming are apparently determined geographically, depending upon the state or the federal circuit involved, it would be prudent, in the absence of a definitive statement by the United States Supreme Court, for educators to apprise themselves of appropriate federal decisions and state appellate opinions.

Davenport v. Randolph County Board of Education

United States Court of Appeals, Eleventh Circuit, 1984
730 F.2d 1395

KRAVITCH, Circuit Judge:

The plaintiffs. Jonathan Davenport and Micky Lazar O'Neal, are high school students who brought suit to challenge the "clean shaven" policy of defendant Ronald Watters, coach of the football and basketball teams at Randolph County High School (RCHS). Defendant Watters suspended Davenport from the RCHS basketball team in December 1981 for refusing to shave and barred both plaintiffs from participating on the football team for the 1982 season because of their refusal to abide by his grooming policy.

Defendant Watters' grooming policy prohibited team members from having beards, wearing mustaches extending beyond the corners of their mouths, or growing sideburns below the ear lobes. The plaintiffs' fathers approved of their sons' decisions not to abide by the coach's policy because they had suffered skin problems when shaving as youths and thus did not want their sons to shave. Defendant Randolph County School Board first considered the issue in March 1982 and recommended that coaches not require a minor to shave if the parents objected. At a later meeting, however, the Board reversed its position and endorsed Coach Watters' "clean shaven" policy. Plaintiffs proceeded to institute this suit pursuant to 42 U.S.C. § 1983 and the fourteenth amendment, requesting declaratory judgment and issuance of an injunction to prevent the defendants from refusing to allow the plaintiffs to participate in athletics at RCHS.

The plaintiffs contend that the "clean shaven" policy is unconstitutional because it is arbitrary and unreasonable to require fourteen and fifteen year-old adolescents to shave in order to participate in high school athletics. This court has previously ruled that in the high school environment there is "a per se rule that [grooming regulations] are constitutionally valid." *Karr* v. *Schmidt*, 460 F.2d 609, 617 (5th Cir. 1972) (en banc);* see also, *Stevenson* v. *Board of Education of Wheeler County, Georgia*, 426 F.2d 1154 (5th Cir.), *cert. denied*, 400 U.S. 957. * * *

---

* The Eleventh Circuit, in the en banc decision *Bonner* v. *City of Prichard*, 661 F.2d 1206, 1209 (11th Cir. 1981), adopted as precedent decisions of the former Fifth Circuit rendered prior to October 1, 1981.

(1970) ("clean shaven" policy not irrational). The rule announced in *Karr* is founded on the premise that grooming regulations are a "reasonable means of furthering the school board's undeniable interest in teaching hygiene, instilling discipline, asserting authority, and compelling uniformity." * * *

This case falls squarely within the holdings of *Karr* and *Stevenson*. The district court found that the policy was "adopted to accomplish the legitimate objective of presenting the school in the light deemed most favorable to the school by the students and coaches at the school." The court further found, and the plaintiffs do not disagree, that there was no evidence that the policy was racially motivated.

The plaintiffs attempt to distinguish the above cases primarily on the ground that their objections to the grooming code are based on a concern that shaving will cause them skin problems. The plaintiffs' fathers testified that they had suffered such problems as youths, and the district court recognized that blacks are prone to such medical problems. No evidence, however, was presented to the court or the school board that the plaintiffs themselves would be likely to suffer from such problems, and defendant Watters testified that he would not enforce the policy if it would have injurious results. Without such medical evidence, we find it unnecessary to decide whether enforcement of the "clean shaven" policy in such a context would amount to a constitutional violation outside the holding of *Karr's* per se rule. * * * (per se rule does not apply if grooming policy has arbitrary effect or is discriminatorily enforced).

* * *

Having found that the disputed policy is within the school board's power to regulate grooming and that the plaintiffs have not proven unique circumstances that would render the policy arbitrary or unreasonable, the district court's denial of relief is

Affirmed.

Notes and Questions

Although grooming regulations were a much-litigated issue in the late 1960s and early 1970s, there was a lack of unanimity among federal appellate courts deciding such cases. Federal appellate courts in the Fifth, Sixth, Ninth, and Tenth Circuits either upheld grooming regulations or contended that grooming regulations were unworthy of their attention. See *Ferrell* v. *Dallas Independent School District,* 392 F.2d 697 (5th Cir. 1968), *cert. denied,* 393 U.S. 856 (1968); *Jackson* v. *Dorrier,* 424 F.2d 213 (6th Cir. 1970), *cert. denied,* 400 U.S. 850 (1970); *King* v. *Saddleback Junior College District,* 445 F.2d 932 (9th Cir. 1971); *Freeman* v. *Flake,* 448 F.2d 258 (10th Cir. 1971). In contrast the First, Fourth, Seventh, and Eighth Circuits found regulations limiting the length of hair invalid. See *Richards* v. *Thurston,* 424 F.2d 1281 (1st Cir. 1970); *Massie* v. *Henry,* 455 F.2d 779 (4th Cir. 1972); *Breen* v. *Kahl,* 419 F.2d 1034 (7th Cir. 1969), *cert. denied,* 398 U.S. 937 (1970); *Bishop* v. *Colaw,* 450 F.2d 1069 (8th Cir. 1971). To date the United States Supreme Court has not rendered a substantive decision in school grooming cases, denying certiorari in cases that concerned male students' hair length.

State courts in Oklahoma, Oregon, and Alaska have held that schools do not have the authority to regulate hair styles. See *Independent School District No. 8 of Seiling* v. *Swanson,* 553 P.2d 496 (Okla. 1976); *Neuhaus* v. *Federico,* 12 Or. App. 314, 505 P.2d 939 (1973); and *Breese* v. *Smith,* 501 P.2d 159 (Alaska, 1972). However, Supreme Courts in Missouri and Kansas have not held similarly. See *Kraus* v. *Board of Education of the City of Jennings,* 492 S.W.2d 783 (Mo. 1973) and *Blaine* v. *Board of Education, Haysville Unified School District No. 261,* 210 Kan. 560, 502 P.2d 693 (1972).

Several courts have addressed the issue of hair regulations that apply only to males. See *Mercer* v. *Board of Trustees, North Forest Independent School District,* 538 S.W. 2d 201 (Tex. Civ. App. 1976) and *Trent* v. *Perritt,* 391 F. Supp. 171 (Miss. 1975), which upheld the schools' regulations. Are grooming regulations that apply only to males a form of sex discrimination in education?

How does your school deal with students who wear "spiked" or brightly colored hair? Are your school's policies adequate enough to deal with this issue?

VI. Pregnancy, Parenthood, Marriage

Not too long ago public school policies often excluded students who were married or pregnant or who were parents. The rationale for such policies was that exclusion would serve as a deterrent and thereby discourage students from becoming pregnant or getting married. Such policies, which in practice applied disproportionately to females, were successfully attacked in the courts in recent years. Enactment of Title IX of the Education Amendments of 1972 addressed the issue on the basis of prohibiting sexual discrimination in any educational programs receiving federal funds.* Section 86.40, Marital or Parental Status, of the implementing regulations for Title IX states:

Marital or parental status.

(a) Status generally. A recipient shall not apply any rule concerning a student's actual or potential parental, family, or marital status which treats students differently on the basis of sex.

(b) Pregnancy and related conditions. (1) A recipient shall not discriminate against any student, or exclude any student from its education program or activity, including any class or extracurricular activity, on the basis of such student's pregnancy, childbirth, false pregnancy, termination of pregnancy or recovery therefrom, unless the student requests voluntarily to participate in a separate portion of the program or activity of the recipient.

(2) A recipient may require such a student to obtain the certification of a physician that the student is physically and emotionally able to continue participation in the normal education program or activity so long as such a certification is required of all students for other physical or emotional conditions requiring the attention of a physician.

(3) A recipient which operates a portion of its education program or activity separately for pregnant students, admittance to which is completely voluntary on the part of the student as provided in paragraph (b) (1) of this section shall ensure that the instructional program in the separate program is comparable to that offered to non-pregnant students.

(4) A recipient shall treat pregnancy, childbirth, false pregnancy, termination of pregnancy and recovery therefrom in the same manner and under the same policies as any other temporary disability with respect to any medical or hospital benefit, service, plan or policy which such recipient administers, operates, offers, or participates in with respect to students admitted to the recipient's educational program or activity.

(5) In the case of a recipient which does not maintain a leave policy for its students, or in the case of a student who does not otherwise qualify for leave under such a policy, a recipient shall treat pregnancy, childbirth, false pregnancy, termination of pregnancy and recovery therefrom as a justification for a leave of absence for so long a period of time as is deemed medically necessary by the student's physician, at the conclusion of which the student shall be reinstated to the status which she held when the leave began. 45 C.F.R. § 86.40.

Does your local school system or state have a policy regarding students who are married or pregnant or who are parents?

VII. Education of Handicapped Students

Prior to the 1970s the state of affairs regarding the education of handicapped students may be characterized by the following: a philosophy that placed the burden of educating handicapped children primarily on

* See Appendix D for an edited Title IX of the Education Amendments of 1972.

the family, a notion that the severely handicapped or those not toilet trained were not the responsibility of the public schools, and the resulting exemption of many handicapped children from compulsory-education laws. Nationwide, adequate and uniform services for handicapped public school children were not available. Support among states for such services was uneven and not extensive. A handful of local school systems provided services; however, the offerings rarely included the entire spectrum of services advocated by those working for reform.

A series of court decisions, the passage of state and federal laws, and other governmental involvement beginning in the 1970s dramatically altered the relationship between handicapped students and public schools. Some of the earliest federal legislation included the Elementary and Secondary Education Act of 1965 and Title VI, which was a 1966 amendment to that act. In 1970 Title VI was repealed and replaced by the Education of the Handicapped Act of 1970. The passage of this legislation brought increased national attention to policy issues regarding handicapped students. A Bureau of Education for the Handicapped was created, and, although early legislation did not provide for "mainstreaming" or a free and appropriate education, it established the groundwork for future legislation dealing with those issues.

Several successful court challenges to existing practices also altered the historic relationship between handicapped students and the public schools. Two of these decisions are particularly noteworthy. A federal district court in *Pennsylvania Association for Retarded Children* v. *Pennsylvania*, 343 F. Supp. 279 (Pa. 1972), held that mentally retarded students between the ages of six and twenty-one should be provided with access to a free public education and that handicapped students should be placed in regular classrooms when possible or in special classes when necessary. In *Mills* v. *Board of Education of the District of Columbia*, 348 F. Supp. 866 (D.C. 1972), another federal district court extended this doctrine to all school-age handicapped children, holding that they must be provided with a free and adequate public education.

Subsequent federal law embodied many of the principles enunciated in these court decisions. Section 504 of the Rehabilitation Act of 1973 represented a national commitment to end discrimination in any program receiving federal funds. The Education for All Handicapped Children Act of 1975 (P.L. 94-142) heralded a national policy under which federal funds would subsidize special education in those states meeting qualification requirements. The cornerstone of this act required states to adopt policies that assure all handicapped children a "free appropriate public education."

A. Defining the Limits of a "Free Appropriate Education"

The Education for All Handicapped Children Act imposed strict obligations upon participating states to meet the educational needs of handicapped children. In the years immediately following the act's passage, school districts claiming in court to lack the resources to implement it usually were unable to prevail on the basis of this claim. It seemed to many observers that the act obligated schools to provide, on demand and regardless of cost, optimal educational services to meet any demonstrated educational need. Then, in 1982, the United States Supreme Court delivered a six-to-three decision that addressed the limitations of the act's guarantees.

Board of Education of the Hendrick Hudson Central School District v. Rowley

Supreme Court of the United States, 1982
458 U.S. 176

JUSTICE REHNQUIST delivered the opinion of the Court.

This case represents a question of statutory interpretation. Petitioners contend that the Court of Appeals and the District Court misconstrued the requirements imposed by Congress upon States which receive federal funds under the Education of the Handicapped Act. We agree and reverse the judgment of the Court of Appeals.

The Education of the Handicapped Act (Act), 84 Stat. 175, as amended, 20 U.S.C. § 1401 *et seq.* (1976 ed. and Supp. IV), provides federal money to assist state and local agencies in educating handicapped children, and conditions such funding upon a State's compliance with extensive goals and procedures. The Act represents an ambitious federal effort to promote the education of handicapped children, and was passed in response to Congress' perception that a majority of handicapped children in the United States "were either totally excluded from schools or [were] sitting idly in regular classrooms awaiting the time when they were old enough to 'drop out.' " * * *

* * *

In order to qualify for federal assistance under the Act, a State must demonstrate that it "has in effect a policy that assures all handicapped children the right to a free appropriate public education." * * * That policy must be reflected in a state plan submitted to and approved by the Secretary of Education * * * which describes in detail the goals, programs, and timetables under which the State intends to educate handicapped children within its borders. * * * States receiving money under the Act must provide education to the handicapped by priority, first "to handicapped children who are not receiving an education" and second "to handicapped children . . . with the most severe handicaps who are receiving an inadequate education," * * * and "to the maximum extent appropriate" must educate handicapped children "with children who are not handicapped." * * * The Act broadly defines "handicapped children" to include "mentally retarded, hard of hearing, deaf, speech impaired, visually handicapped, seriously emotionally disturbed, orthopedically impaired, [and] other health impaired children, [and] children with specific learning disabilities." * * *

The "free appropriate public education" required by the Act is tailored to the unique needs of the handicapped child by means of an "individualized educational program" (IEP). * * * The IEP, which is prepared at a meeting between a qualified representative of the local educational agency, the child's teacher, the child's parents or guardian, and, where appropriate, the child, consists of a written document containing

> "(A) a statement of the present levels of educational performance of such child, (B) a statement of annual goals, including short-term instructional objectives, (C) a statement of the specific educational services to be provided to such child, and the extent to which such child will be able to participate in regular educational programs, (D) the projected date for initiation and anticipated duration of such services, and (E) appropriate objective criteria and evaluation procedures and schedules for determining, on at least an annual basis, whether instructional objectives are being achieved." * * *

Local or regional educational agencies must review, and where appropriate revise, each child's IEP at least annually. * * *

In addition to the state plan and the IEP already described, the Act imposes extensive procedural requirements upon States receiving federal funds under its provisions. Parents or guardians of handicapped children must be notified of any proposed change in "the identification, evaluation, or educational placement of the child or the provision of a free appropriate public education to such child," and must be permitted to bring a complaint about "any matter relating to" such evaluation and education. * * * Complaints brought by parents or guardians must be resolved at "an impartial due process hearing," and appeal to the State educational agency must be provided if the initial hearing is held at the local or regional level. * * * Thereafter, "[a]ny party aggrieved by the findings and decision" of the state administrative hearing has "the right to bring a civil action with respect to the complaint . . . in any State court of competent jurisdiction or in a district court of the United States without regard to the amount in controversy." * * *

Thus, although the Act leaves to the States the primary responsibility for developing and executing educational programs for handicapped children, it imposes significant requirements to be followed in the discharge of that responsibility. Compliance is assured by provisions permitting the withholding of federal funds upon determination that a participating state or local agency has failed to satisfy the requirements of the Act, * * * and by the provision for judicial review. At present, all States except New Mexico receive federal funds under the portions of the Act at issue today. * * *

This case arose in connection with the education of Amy Rowley, a deaf student at the Furnace Woods School in the Hendrick Hudson Central School District, Peekskill, N.Y. Amy has minimal residual hearing and is an excellent lip-reader. During the year before she began attending Furnace Woods, a meeting between her parents and school administrators resulted in a decision to place her in a regular kindergarten class in order to determine what supplemental services would be necessary to her education. Several members of the school administration prepared for Amy's arrival by attending a course in sign-language interpretation, and a teletype machine was installed in the principal's office to facilitate communication with her parents who are also deaf. At the end of the trial period it was determined that Amy should remain in the kindergarten class, but that she should be provided with an FM hearing aid which would amplify words spoken into a wireless receiver by the teacher or fellow students during certain classroom activities. Amy successfully completed her kindergarten year.

As required by the Act, an IEP was prepared for Amy during the fall of her first-grade year. The IEP provided that Amy should be educated in a regular classroom at Furnace Woods, should continue to use the FM hearing aid, and should receive instruction from a tutor for the deaf for one hour each day and from a speech therapist for three hours each week. The Rowleys agreed with parts of the IEP but insisted that Amy also be provided a qualified sign-language interpreter in all her academic classes in lieu of the assistance proposed in other parts of the IEP. Such an interpreter had been placed in Amy's kindergarten class for a 2-week experimental period, but the interpreter had reported that Amy did not need his services at that time. The school administrators likewise concluded that Amy did not need such an interpreter in her first-grade classroom. They reached this conclusion after consulting the school district's Committee on the Handicapped, which had received expert evidence from Amy's parents on the importance of a sign-language interpreter, received testimony from Amy's teacher and other persons familiar with her academic and social progress, and visited a class for the deaf.

When their request for an interpreter was denied, the Rowleys demanded and received a hearing before an independent examiner. After receiving evidence from both sides, the examiner agreed with the administrators' determination that an interpreter was not necessary because "Amy was achieving educationally, academically, and socially" without such assistance. * * *

* * *

The District Court found that Amy "is a remarkably well-adjusted child" who interacts and communicates well with her classmates and has "developed an extraordinary rapport" with her teachers. * * * It also found that "she performs better than the average child in her class and is advancing easily from grade to grade," * * * but "that she understands considerably less of what goes on in class than she could if she were not deaf" and thus "is not learning as much, or performing as well academically, as she would without her handicap," * * * This disparity between Amy's achievement and her potential led the court to decide that she was not receiving a "free appropriate public education," which the court defined as "an opportunity to achieve [her] full potential commensurate with the opportunity provided to other children." * * * According to the District Court, such a standard requires that the potential of the handicapped child be measured and compared to his or her performance, and that the resulting differential or 'shortfall' be compared to the shortfall experienced by non-handicapped children." * * * District Court's definition arose from its assumption that the responsibility for "giv[ing] content to the requirement of an 'appropriate education'" had "been left entirely to the [federal] courts and the hearing officers." * * *

* * *

This is the first case in which this Court has been called upon to interpret any provision of the Act. * * *

* * *

According to the definitions contained in the Act, a "free appropriate public education" consists of educational instruction specially designed to meet the unique needs of the handicapped child, supported by such services as are necessary to permit the child "to benefit" from the instruction. Almost as a checklist for adequacy under the Act, the definition also requires that such instruction and services be provided at public expense and under public supervision, meet the State's educational standards, approximate the grade levels used in the State's regular education, and comport with the child's IEP. Thus, if personalized instruction is being provided with sufficient supportive services to permit the child to benefit from the instruction, and the other items on the definitional checklist are satisfied, the child is receiving a "free appropriate public education" as defined by the Act.

Other portions of the statute also shed light upon congressional intent. Congress found that of the roughly eight million handicapped children in the United States at the time of enactment, one million were "excluded entirely from the public school system" and more than half were receiving an inappropriate education. * * * In addition, as mentioned in Part I, the Act requires States to extend educational services first to those children who are receiving no education and second to those children who are receiving an "inadequate education." * * * When these express statutory findings and priorities are read together with the Act's extensive procedural requirements and its definition of "free appropriate public education," the face of the statute evinces a congressional intent to bring previously excluded handicapped children into the public education systems of the States and to require the States to adopt *procedures* which would result in individualized consideration of and instruction for each child.

Noticeably absent from the language of the statute is any substantive standard prescribing the level of education to be accorded handicapped children. Certainly the language of the statute contains no requirement like the one imposed by the lower courts—that States maximize the potential of handicapped children "commensurate with the opportunity provided to other children." * * * That standard was expounded by the District Court without reference to the statutory definitions or even to the legislative history of the Act. Although we find the statutory definition of "free appropriate public education" to be helpful in our interpretation of the Act, there remains the question of whether the legislative history indicates a congressional intent that such education meet some additional substantive standard. * * *

* * *

The educational opportunities provided by our public school systems undoubtedly differ from student to student, depending upon a myriad of factors that might affect a particular student's ability to assimilate information presented in the classroom. The requirement that States provide "equal" educational opportunities would thus seem to present an entirely unworkable standard requiring impossible measurements and comparisons. Similarly, furnishing handicapped children with only such services as are available to nonhandicapped children would in all probability fall short of the statutory requirement of "free appropriate public education"; to require, on the other hand, the furnishing of every special service necessary to maximize each handicapped child's potential is, we think, further than Congress intended to go. Thus to speak in terms of "equal" services in one instance gives less than what is required by the Act and in another instance more. The theme of the Act is "free appropriate public education," a phrase which is too complex to be captured by the word "equal" whether one is speaking of opportunities or services.

*   *   *

The District Court and the Court of Appeals thus erred when they held that the Act requires New York to maximize the potential of each handicapped child commensurate with the opportunity provided nonhandicapped children. Desirable though that goal may be, it is not the standard that Congress imposed upon States which receive funding under the Act. Rather, Congress sought primarily to identify and evaluate handicapped children, and to provide them with access to a free public education.

*   *   *

The determination of when handicapped children are receiving sufficient educational benefits to satisfy the requirements of the Act presents a more difficult problem. The Act requires participating States to educate a wide spectrum of handicapped children, from the marginally hearing-impaired to the profoundly retarded and palsied. It is clear that the benefits obtainable by children at one end of the spectrum will differ dramatically from those obtainable by children at the other end, with infinite variations in between. One child may have little difficulty competing successfully in an academic setting with nonhandicapped children while another child may encounter great difficulty in acquiring even the most basic of self-maintenance skills. We do not attempt today to establish any one test for determining the adequacy of educational benefits conferred upon all children covered by the Act. Because in this case we are presented with a handicapped child who is receiving substantial specialized instruction and related services and who is performing above average in the regular classrooms of a public school system, we confine our analysis to that situation.

The Act requires participating States to educate handicapped children with nonhandicapped children whenever possible. When that "mainstreaming" preference of the Act has been met and a child is being educated in the regular classrooms of a public school system, the system itself monitors the educational progress of the child. Regular examinations are administered, grades are awarded, and yearly advancement to higher grade levels is permitted for those children who attain an adequate knowledge of the course material. The grading and advancement system thus constitutes an important factor in determining educational benefit. Children who graduate from our public school systems are considered by our society to have been "educated" at least to the grade level they have completed, and access to an "education" for handicapped children is precisely what Congress sought to provide in the Act.

When the language of the Act and its legislative history are considered together, the requirements imposed by Congress become tolerably clear. Insofar as a State is required to provide a handicapped child with a "free appropriate public education," we hold that it satisfies this requirement by providing personalized instruction with sufficient support services to permit the child to benefit educationally from that instruction. Such instruction and services must be provided at public expense, must meet the State's educational standards, must approximate the grade levels used in the State's regular education, and must comport with the child's IEP. In addition, the IEP, and therefore the personalized instruction, should be formulated in accordance with the requirements of the Act and, if the child is being educated in the regular classrooms of the public education system, should be reasonably calculated to enable the child to achieve passing marks and advance from grade to grade.

* * *

Applying these principles to the facts of this case, we conclude that the Court of Appeals erred in affirming the decision of the District Court. Neither the District Court nor the Court of Appeals found that petitioners had failed to comply with the procedures of the Act, and the findings of neither court would support a conclusion that Amy's educational program failed to comply with the substantive requirements of the Act. On the contrary, the District Court found that the "evidence firmly establishes that Amy is receiving an 'adequate' education, since she performs better than the average child in her class and is advancing easily from grade to grade." * * * In light of this finding, and of the fact that Amy was receiving personalized instruction and related services calculated by the Furnace Woods school administrators to meet her educational needs, the lower courts should not have concluded that the Act requires the provision of a sign-language interpreter. Accordingly, the decision of the Court of Appeals is reversed, and the case is remanded for further proceedings consistent with this opinion.

So ordered.

Notes

Another decision by the United States Supreme Court raised the issue of whether or not clean intermittent catheterization (CIC) was a "related service" under the Education of the Handicapped Act, (P.L. 91–230, as amended by the Education for All Handicapped Children Act of 1975, P.L. 94–142). In this case the parents of an eight-year-old daughter born with spina bifida requested that CIC be performed during school hours. The Court held that such services should be provided and should not be subject to exclusion as medical services. The Court reasoned that the child could not benefit from special education without such services and that such services were "no less related to the effort to educate than are services that enable a child to reach, enter, or exit a school." See *Irving Independent School District* v. *Tatro,* 468 U.S. 883 (1984).

A federal appellate court has provided guidelines regarding "mainstreaming." In this case a child with Down's syndrome was placed in a state school for the handicapped, despite his parents' desire that he be placed in a regular elementary school. In upholding the school district, the court noted that the Education for All Handicapped Children Act does not absolutely require mainstreaming but rather mandates it "to the maximum extent appropriate." The court concluded that handicapped children are not entitled to the best possible education; instead, a school district considering a handicapped student's placement may weigh the benefits to the child against the costs to the district. In this case the student was so severely handicapped that his interaction with "regular" students would have been limited to observing them. See *A.W.* v. *Northwest R-1 School District,* 813 F.2d 158 (8th Cir. 1987), *cert. denied,* 484 U.S. 847 (1987).

Another federal appellate court held similarly. Parents had requested that their handicapped daughter be educated in a private center in which handicapped and "normal" children were integrated at the classroom level. The public schools offered only a special class within a regular school. The court found that integrating the child at the school level satisfied the Education for All Handicapped Children Act's mainstreaming requirements, notwithstanding that the option was not the best possible. Furthermore, the court declared that the act's mainstreaming provisions do not require schools to respond to a handicapped child's needs by establishing entirely new levels of educational services. See

Mark A. v. *Grant Wood Area Education Agency,* 795 F.2d 52 (8th Cir. 1986), *cert. denied,* 480 U.S. 936 (1987).

Parents may be reimbursed for expenditures for private special education if a school system cannot provide the educational needs for a handicapped child. Often occurring, however, is the question of parents' entitlement to reimbursement when they place their child in a private setting during the review process of a contested individualized educational program (IEP). In addressing this issue the United States Supreme Court ruled that "parents who unilaterally change their child's placement during the pendency of review proceedings, without the consent of state or local school officials, do so at their own financial risk." Consequently parents will be reimbursed only if they ultimately prevail in the proceedings. See *Burlington School Committee* v. *Department of Education of Massachusetts,* 471 U.S. 359 (1985).

The Education for All Handicapped Children Act's guarantee of a free, appropriate education has been interpreted as prohibiting the expulsion of handicapped students when their misbehavior is a manifestation of their handicap. It may be necessary, nevertheless, to change the educational placement of a disruptive or dangerous handicapped student who requires an environment more structured than that stipulated in his current individualized education plan. Problems often arise over the dispensation of such students during the sometimes-lengthy due process that the act requires to precede a change in placement. Although the act apparently allows short-term suspensions of such students, a "stay put" provision states that during the pendency of due process "the child shall remain in the then current educational placement."

Addressing this issue, the United States Supreme Court has strictly construed the "stay put" provision. At issue in *Honig* v. *Doe,* 108 S. Ct. 592 (1988), were the indefinite suspensions, in accordance with California's school regulations, of two disruptive students in a program for the emotionally disabled. Although it affirmed school officials' discretion to suspend such students for ten days, the Court declared that Congress intended to "strip schools of the unilateral authority they had traditionally employed to exclude disabled students, particularly emotionally disturbed students from school." School officials who perceive the need to remove such students pending the outcome of placement proceedings, and who have failed to reach an accord with parents during an initial ten-day suspension, can effect a removal only by seeking injunctive relief in court.

In examining another issue related to the education of handicapped students, the Eleventh Circuit Court of Appeals held that the Georgia policy of refusing to provide more than 180 days of schooling to handicapped children violated P.L. 94–142 and Section 504 of the Rehabilitation Act. The court contended that the law requires an "appropriate education" suited to the individual needs of the students; for some students the 180-day limit may conflict with the requirement. See *Georgia Association of Retarded Citizens* v. *McDaniel,* 716 F.2d 1565, (11th Cir. 1983).

Litigation regarding the handicapped usually is brought to court by parents desiring increased educational services for their children. In a reversal of this pattern, some parents have contested the labeling of their children as handicapped or the placement of their children into special education programs. In one such suit the use of IQ tests for special education placement was litigated in federal appellate court. Alleging the tests in question to be racially biased, complainants demonstrated that the tests resulted in a disproportionate assignment of black students to classes for the educable mentally retarded. The court declared that owing to this proven discriminatory impact, school officials incurred the burden of proving the tests to be an educational necessity. Inasmuch as the tests were not sufficiently validated to meet this burden, the court found them to be in violation of Title VI of the Civil Rights Act as well as the Education for All Handicapped Children Act, which requires tests to be free of racial and cultural bias. See *Larry P.* v. *Riles,* 793 F.2d 969 (9th Cir. 1984).

B. Communicable Disease as a Handicap

A controversial issue in many communities is whether to allow children infected with the AIDS (Acquired Immune Deficiency Syndrome) virus to attend regular public school classes. Many parents fear that their healthy children could contract the dreaded disease through various contacts that occur among children in school: being bitten by an infected student; having mucus, saliva, or tears enter an open sore or wound; or being breathed upon. Constant media portrayals of the disease's ravages and the absence of a cure heighten parents' concern. Statements from such authorities as the Surgeon General of the United States and officials of the Center for Disease Control often fail to persuade them that their fears are groundless.

States and school systems have developed guidelines governing public school attendance of AIDS-infected students. Suits have been brought both by parents whose infected children were barred from regular school programs and by parents who objected to the admission of these students to regular classes. To date, courts have revealed a high degree of sensitivity to students with AIDS and to their being included in the public school mainstream. This view is presented in ***Thomas*** v. ***Atascadero Unified School District.***

Thomas v. Atascadero Unified School District

United States District Court, Central District of California, 1987
662 F. Supp. 376

* * *

Plaintiffs Robin and Judy Thomas are the parents and guardians of Ryan Thomas and bring this action on his behalf. Ryan Thomas is a five year old boy eligible under California law to attend kindergarten in the Atascadero Unified School District.

Defendant Atascadero Unified School District ("School District") is a public entity organized under the laws of the State of California. The School District is a recipient of "federal financial assistance" within the meaning of 29 U.S.C. § 794.

* * *

Acquired Immune Deficiency Syndrome (AIDS) is the clinical manifestation of a dysfunction of the human immune system caused by a recently discovered virus. The AIDS virus has received several names: Human T-Lymphotropic Virus Type III (HTLV-III); Lymphadenopathy-Associated Virus (LAV); AIDS-Associated Retrovirus (ARV); and, most recently, *Human Immunodeficiency Virus* (HIV).

To date, there is no vaccine against or cure for AIDS. A range of symptoms may result from infection with the AIDS virus which have been classified by the Centers for Disease Control ("CDC") into four groups of symptoms: (I) early acute, though transient, signs of the disease; (II) asymptomatic infection; (III) persistent swollen lymph-nodes; and (IV) presence of opportunistic disease and/or rare types of cancer, including one known as Kaposi's Sarcoma.

* * *

Ryan Thomas is infected with the AIDS virus. He became infected with the AIDS virus as an infant as the result of a contaminated blood transfusion received at Oakland's Children's Hospital where he was being treated for complications arising out of his premature birth. He suffers from significant impairment of his major life activities.

Ryan was diagnosed as being infected with the AIDS virus in early 1985. During the first four years of his life, Ryan Thomas had frequent pulmonary and middle ear problems as well as chronic lymphadenopathy. These difficulties are attributable to his infection with the AIDS virus.

For over a year, since the diagnosis that he was infected with the AIDS virus, and since his treatment for this condition began Ryan's medical condition has improved. * * * At this point it is unclear what course his medical condition will take. Both of Ryan's treating physicians, Dr. Fields and Dr. Church, have written to the School District indicating that there is no medical reason why Ryan cannot attend regular kindergarten classes.

The best available medical evidence shows that the AIDS virus is not spread in the air by infected droplets as are the common cold, influenza and tuberculosis. The virus is fragile and is killed by most household disinfectants. The virus is transmitted from one person to another only by infected blood, semen or vaginal fluids (and, possibly, mother's milk). Transmission by either semen or blood accounts for virtually all reported cases.

There are no reported cases of the transmission of the AIDS virus in a school setting. The CDC has stated that "[n]one of the identified cases of HTLV-III/LAV infection in the United States are known to have been transmitted in the school, daycare, or foster-care setting or through casual person-to-person contact."

The overwhelming weight of medical evidence is that the AIDS virus is not transmitted by human bites, even bites that break the skin. Based upon the abundant medical and scientific evidence before the Court, Ryan poses no risk of harm to his classmates and teachers. Any theoretical risk of transmission of the AIDS virus by Ryan in connection with his attendance in regular kindergarten class is so remote that it cannot form the basis for any exclusionary action by the School District.

In May, 1986, the School District adopted a policy concerning the admission of students infected with "communicable diseases" including the "HTLV-III (AIDS)" virus. Pursuant to this policy a Placement Committee was created, including health professionals, parents, school officials and San Luis Obispo County's Public Health Officer, to advise the School Board on the placement of children covered by the Policy.

On August 28, 1986, the Placement Committee met to make a recommendation concerning Ryan's placement. At this meeting the Committee recommended Ryan's admission to kindergarten. This recommendation was accepted by the School Board on September 2, 1986. No other kindergarten student had his placement considered in this manner. The standard procedure in the District is for a child's parents to decide whether a child of kindergarten age will attend regular kindergarten classes.

Ryan attended kindergarten without incident from September 3 to 5, 1986. On September 8, 1986, Ryan was involved in an incident in which another child and Ryan got into a skirmish and Ryan bit the other child's pants leg. No skin was broken.

Defendant Avina instructed Plaintiffs to keep Ryan at home after the incident so that the Placement Committee could reconsider its August 28th recommendation in light of this incident and determine "whether or not Ryan's potential for again biting another student poses any danger to the health of others in the class." On September 12, 1986, the Placement Committee recommended that Ryan be evaluated by a psychologist. This recommendation was accepted by the School Board. No similar action was taken concerning the other child involved in this incident.

In late September, Dr. Marcus Shira, a psychologist employed by the San Luis Obispo County Board of Education, conducted a "psycho-educational study" of Ryan. Dr. Shira prepared a report dated September 30, 1986, in which he concluded that Ryan would behave "aggressively" in a kindergarten setting because his level of social and language skills and maturity was below those of his classmates. Dr. Shira could not predict what form such "aggressive" behavior might take. Specifically, he did not predict that Ryan would "bite again."

Based upon Dr. Shira's study, on October 2, 1986, the Placement Committee recommended that Ryan be kept out of class and in "home tutoring" for the rest of the academic year. The County Public Health Officer, Dr. Rowland, abstained from this decision. On October 6, 1986, the School Board voted to exclude Ryan from his class until January, 1987, and to have Ryan evaluated before the decision to exclude him would be reconsidered.

Ryan suffered injury because of his exclusion from his kindergarten class after September 8, 1986, even though his injuries were not as great as they would have been if he was an older child.

In taking the actions outlined above, the School District acted cautiously and reasonably in attempting to balance all of the interests involved and to address the fear of AIDS which exists within the Atascadero community.

In August of 1985, the Centers for Disease Control of the United States Government (CDC) published information and recommendations concerning the education of children infected with the AIDS virus. Among the CDC's recommendations are the following:

> "Decisions regarding the type of educational and care setting for HTLV-III/LAV-infected children should be based on the behavior, neurologic development, and physical condition of the child and the expected type of interaction with others in that setting. These decisions are best made using the team approach including the child's physician, public health personnel, the child's parent or guardian, and personnel associated with the proposed care or educational setting. In each case, risks and benefits to both the infected child and to others in the setting should be weighed."

"For the infected preschool-aged child and for some neurologically hand-icapped children who lack control of their body secretions or who display behavior, such as biting, and those children who have uncoverable, oozing lesions, a more restricted environment is advisable until more is known about transmission in these settings. Children infected with HTLV-III/LAV should be cared for and educated in settings that minimize exposure of other children to blood or body fluids."

Substantially similar guidelines and recommendations were issued by the American Academy of Pediatrics (AAP) in March of 1986 and the California State Department of Education (SDE) in May of 1986.

The Placement Committee took the recommendations of the CDC into account in its determinations and recommendations regarding Ryan Thomas following the biting incident on September 5, 1986.

Aside from its citation to the recommendations of the CDC, AAP, and SDE, the School District has presented no medical evidence to prove that the AIDS virus can be transmitted by human bites. The information and recommendations published by the CDC, AAP, and SDE cite no such medical evidence and do not, of themselves, prove that transmission by biting is possible.

The Defendant School District is a recipient of federal funds within the meaning of 29 U.S.C. § 794, § 504 of the Federal Rehabilitation Act of 1973.

Ryan Thomas is a "handicapped person" within the meaning of § 504 of the Rehabilitation Act of 1973. * * *

Ryan Thomas is "otherwise qualified" to attend a regular kindergarten class within the meaning of § 504 of the Rehabilitation Act of 1973. Defendants have failed to meet their burden of demonstrating that Ryan is not "otherwise qualified" to attend kindergarten. * * * There is no evidence that Ryan Thomas poses a significant risk of harm to his kindergarten classmates or teachers.

Ryan Thomas has been subjected to different treatment from the treatment received by other kindergarten students in the District and excluded from his kindergarten class because of his "handicap."

Defendants have not complied with the requirements of 45 C.F.R. § 88.4(b). In particular, Defendants have not complied with the re-quirement that "[a] recipient shall place a handicapped person in the regular educational environment created by the recipient unless it is demonstrated by the recipient that the education of the person in the regular environment with the use of supplementary aids and services cannot be achieved satisfactorily."

Based on the foregoing, Plaintiffs are likely to succeed on the merits. Ryan Thomas has suffered irreparable injury because of his exclusion from class. There are serious questions presented by Plaintiff's Motion and the balance of hardships tips in Plaintiff's favor. Plaintiffs are entitled to the issuance of a preliminary injunction. * * *

* * *

Plaintiffs are, awarded the amount of $40,000.00 in attorneys fees and $2,387.50 in costs.

* * *

Notes

A similar decision was rendered in *District 27 Community School Board v. Board of Education of the City of New York*, 130 Misc. 2d 398, 502 N.Y.S.2d 325 (1986). Here the court held that excluding students with AIDS violates not only Section 504 of the Rehabilitation Act but also the Equal Protection Clause of the Fourteenth Amendment. Additionally, the opinion provides a detailed description of AIDS' epidemiology.

An incontinent student classified as trainable mentally handicapped (TMH) and also diagnosed as suffering from AIDS-related complex was excluded from a TMH class. The court in this instance was persuaded by the testimony of several local physicians, one of whom was the student's treating physician, that the student should not be returned to the TMH classroom. See *Martinez* v. *School Board of Hillsborough County*, 675 F. Supp. 1574 (Fla. 1987). In its decision the court noted:

> Decisions regarding the type of educational and care setting for HTLV-III/LAV-infected children should be based on the behavior, neurologic development, and physical condition of the child and the expected type of interaction with others in that setting. These decisions are best made using the team approach including the child's physician, public health personnel, the child's parent or guardian, and personnel associated with the proposed care or educational setting. In each case, risks and benefits to both the infected child and to others in the setting should be weighed. (P. 1581)

Attempting to exclude children from regular school classes due to their infection with a dangerous disease is not a new issue. A federal appellate court held that under the Rehabilitation Act, mentally retarded students thought to be carriers of hepatitis could not be excluded. In this instance school authorities could not demonstrate that the health hazard posed by the children was anything more than a remote possibility, and the court agreed that isolating the carrier children would have detrimental effects. See *New York State Association for Retarded Children* v. *Carey*, 612 F.2d 644 (2nd Cir. 1979). Also see *Kohl* v. *Woodhaven*

Learning Center, 672 F. Supp. 1221 (Mo. 1987) for a similar ruling, which involved a nonprofit corporation receiving federal financial assistance.

VIII. Participation in Extracurricular Activities

Extracurricular activities are usually thought of as those that are normally conducted outside the classroom before or after regular school hours, usually noncredit, generally supervised by school officials, academically nonremedial and of a voluntary nature on the part of the students. They may include activities such as athletics, drama, clubs, band, cheerleading, and debate.

Two basic legal issues have surfaced when policies excluding a student from extracurricular activities are attacked. One of the issues raises the question of the status of extracurricular activities as a protected property interest and the requisite process due, if any. The other issue deals with the equal protection claim that an excluded student is the victim of a school's arbitrary classification scheme.

A. Legal Status of Extracurricular Activities

In following *Goss,* courts have generally held that students have a property interest in the entire educational process. However, courts have not agreed whether or not participation in one aspect of the process, such as extracurricular activities, is a constitutionally protected property interest. If it is held that such a property interest does exist, courts must then decide the extent of due process which must be provided. These issues were examined by the Supreme Court of Nebraska in *Braesch* v. *DePasquale.*

Braesch v. DePasquale

Supreme Court of Nebraska, 1978
200 Neb. 726, 265 N.W.2d 842
cert. denied, 439 U.S. 1068 (1979)

McCOWN, J.

The plaintiffs brought this proceeding in the District Court for Washington County, Nebraska, to enjoin the defendant school officials from enforcing any rules of conduct that would prevent full participation by the plaintiffs in the interscholastic basketball program of the Arlington Public Schools. The District Court granted a permanent injunction enjoining defendants from preventing plaintiffs from full participation in the interscholastic basketball teams of Arlington, Nebraska. The defendants have appealed.

The plaintiffs in this action were all minors under the age of 19 and represented by their respective parents. All five plaintiffs were senior members of either the boys or the girls interscholastic basketball teams of Arlington High School. Rules of conduct for boys and girls basketball teams were distributed at the beginning of the 1976–77 basketball season. Participants in the basketball program were required to sign them and obtain one parent's signature on a copy of the rules. The rule involved here was: "DRINKING, SMOKING OR DRUGS: Do not come out for basketball if you plan on using any of the above. Any use of them will result in the immediate expulsion from the squad." Each of the plaintiffs and one or more of the parents had signed the rule.

On Saturday evening, January 8, 1977, a party was held at the home of one of the plaintiffs. The other plaintiffs, along with other seniors who were not members of the interscholastic basketball teams, attended the party. A few days later, Robert Krempke, the coach of the boys basketball team, overheard conversations at school about the party and learned that a senior boy not on the basketball team had been arrested on the evening of the party on a charge of minor in possession. On January 12, 1977, the coach approached the plaintiff who had been the host for the party and questioned him about the party. The plaintiff host admitted that there had been beer at the party and that he and other members of the basketball team were "involved." After consulting with the school principal, the basketball coach talked with each of the plaintiff members of the boys basketball team. Each admitted being at the party and drinking. The coach told them to leave basketball practice, and told them that he would arrange a meeting with them and their parents, and the principal, the following morning. The following morning, January 13, 1977, Daniel DePasquale, the principal of the high school, and Mr. Krempke, the coach, met with two of the boys involved, and on the next morning with the third. Each boy was accompanied by a parent or adult member of his family. At these brief meetings the coach told the persons present that the rules required expulsion from the basketball team, and the principal supported the coach. The principal testified that at the conclusion of these meetings he considered the boys suspended from the team and told them the decision would be confirmed by mail.

On January 13, 1977, Eloise Hiemke, the girls basketball coach learned about the drinking party from one of the girls involved and from an assistant coach. On the morning of January 14, 1977, the girls coach met with the two girls involved, asked each of them if they had been at the party, and if they had had any alcoholic beverages to drink. Each of the girls admitted she had. The principal and the girls basketball coach met with the girls and their parents on the afternoon of January 14, 1977. The principal and the girls coach advised the girls and their parents that they felt the girls should be expelled from the team, and that an official letter would be mailed to them advising them of the decision and telling them what could be done to appeal the decision. The principal opinion expressed by the parents at the various meetings was that the penalty was too severe.

By letter dated January 18, 1977, the principal notified all the plaintiffs and their parents that each of the plaintiffs had been suspended from the basketball team until January 31, 1977, and then expelled from the team for the remainder of the season. The letter also informed them that they had 5 days in which to give written notice of their desire to appeal to the board of education, and that at the hearing they would each have the right to present their side of the issue, present any documents or statements, and cross-examine witnesses and be represented by counsel. By letters dated January 20, 1977, each of the plaintiffs requested a hearing.

* * *

On January 28, 1977, following a hearing, the District Court granted a temporary injunction enjoining the defendants from preventing the plaintiffs from full participation on the interscholastic basketball teams. Trial on the permanent injunction was later set for and held on February 18, 1977. Following the hearing, the court specifically found that the right to participate in interscholastic basketball activities was "a constitutional right protected by the due process clause of the state and federal constitutions" and that plaintiffs had been deprived of that right without due process. The District Court entered a permanent injunction enjoining defendants from preventing plaintiffs' full participation in the interscholastic basketball teams of Arlington High School. The defendants have appealed.

* * *

There is some disagreement between the parties as to whether participation in high school athletics is a constitutional right or is a privilege not protected by any constitutional principle. * * * [T]he Supreme Court of the United States has abandoned much of the former dichotomy between rights and privileges in constitutional classifications. The Fourteenth Amendment's protection of property extends to benefits which, under state law or practice, a person has a claim or entitlement. * * *

The Supreme Court of the United States has also held that temporary suspension from public school infringes upon property or liberty interests protected by the due process clause of the Fourteenth Amendment. * * *

The State of Nebraska, as a part of its program for public education, has provided athletic opportunities to all public school students. Participation in interscholastic athletics ordinarily has significantly less important constitutional dimensions than does participation in traditional academic education. A student's interest in participation in high school athletics is nevertheless a significant one. * * * In the light of these constitutional principles, the question is whether the due process clause limits the power of the defendants to exclude the plaintiffs from participation in the interscholastic athletic program of Arlington High School.

Assuming that the application of the rule of conduct involved here implicates a property or liberty interest which is protected by the Fourteenth Amendment, the question becomes one of what process was due the plaintiffs under the circumstances of this case. Due process is not a technical fixed concept to be applied in all conditions, but must be flexible. It calls for such procedural protection as may be appropriate to meet the particular situation. In Goss v. Lopez, * * * the Supreme Court held that due process requires that a student facing a temporary *academic* suspension for disciplinary reasons be given oral or written notice of the charges against him, and, if he denies them, an explanation of the evidence the authorities have and an opportunity to explain his side of the story. The Supreme Court required those rudimental precautions against unfair or mistaken findings and arbitrary exclusion from school. Certainly no greater requirements should be imposed for expulsion from interscholastic athletics.

There can be no doubt that each of the plaintiffs here had specific advance notice of the rule of conduct involved, and notice of the date, time, and place of the violation charged. Each of the plaintiffs admitted his or her violation of the rule. Courts that have considered the issue have generally concluded that when the acts which are the basis for disciplinary action are admitted, the requirements of due process are far less stringent, and that due process requirements with respect to the "guilt" finding process have been met by the admissions. * * *

In the case before us the plaintiffs do not dispute that there was a specific rule of conduct for interscholastic basketball participants; that each of them and their parents had actual notice of the rule in advance; and that each of the plaintiffs violated the rule. The plaintiffs' position is simply that the rule was arbitrary and unreasonable or that the penalty was too great.

Rules prohibiting use of alcoholic liquor or drugs by participants in interscholastic athletics are clearly appropriate. * * * [T]his court upheld the right of public schools to make reasonable rules for student conduct, and held that in order to overturn such rules on the ground that they were unreasonable or arbitrary, or that they invade private rights, the evidence of such facts must be clear and satisfactory. This court said: "The wisdom or expediency of a rule adopted by a school board and the motive prompting it are not open to judicial inquiry, where it is within the administrative power of that body." Rules governing the conduct of participants in interscholastic athletics duly and regularly adopted by school authorities ought to be valid and enforceable unless they are clearly arbitrary and unreasonable and serve no legitimate end of educational athletic policy.

The rule involved in this case, even though the penalty of expulsion for the season might be deemed severe by some persons, clearly serves a legitimate rational interest and directly affects the discipline of student athletes. It cannot be said that the prescribed penalty was an arbitrary and unreasonable means to attain the legitimate end of deterrence of the use of alcoholic liquor by student athletes. * * *

Although due process may also contemplate an opportunity to be heard on the question of the penalty to be imposed where the penalty is discretionary rather than prescribed, the opportunity was also provided here. In addition to the informal procedures and meetings, which met all rudimentary requirements of due process, the plaintiffs here were also given the right to appear at a formal hearing with a right to present evidence, cross-examine witnesses, and be represented by counsel. A hearing examiner was appointed and a date set for hearing but the plaintiffs declined to participate in any of the appeals procedures established by the school board. Instead, they commenced this injunction action 1 day after they had requested the appeals procedures offered by defendants, and the temporary injunction was obtained in the District Court 2 days after the date set for the school hearing which plaintiffs had already refused. Under such circumstances courts should be reluctant to interfere prior to completion of prompt and reasonable procedures for obtaining a final order of the school board. A few days suspension from interscholastic athletic competition can hardly be said to constitute such irreparable harm as to justify judicial interference with orderly and prompt school board procedures.

* * *

It is clear in this case that the school board had the power to change or reduce the penalty if it were determined to be arbitrary and unreasonable. The plaintiffs refused to exhaust that remedy or to pursue it to the point of finality at which it might be ripe for judicial review. Where a board of education has provided effective, reasonable, and prompt procedures for notice, hearing, and review of an order of expulsion from participation in interscholastic athletics, and the athlete neglects or refuses to follow or comply with such procedures and exhaust such remedies, such neglect or refusal ordinarily constitutes a waiver of any right to subsequent injunctive relief.

The action of the District Court in granting the injunction here was erroneous and is therefore reversed.

Reversed.

Notes and Questions

Several federal courts have addressed this issue. In *Dallam* v. *Cumberland Valley School District,* 391 F. Supp. 358 (Pa. 1975), the court stated:

> . . . [T]he property interest in education created by the state is participation in the entire process. The myriad activities which combine to form that educational process cannot be dissected to create hundreds of separate property rights, each cognizable under the Constitution. Otherwise, removal from an athletic team, a club or any extracurricular activity, would each require ultimate satisfaction of procedural due process. (P. 361)

In *Pegram* v. *Nelson,* 469 F. Supp. 1134 (N.C. 1979), the court declared:

> Since there is not a property interest in each separate component of the "educational process," denial of the opportunity to participate in merely one of several extracurricular activities would not give rise to a right to due process. However, *total exclusion* from participation in that part of the educational process designated as extracurricular activities for a *lengthy period of time* could, depending upon the particular circumstances, be a sufficient deprivation to implicate due process. (P. 1140)

And in *Albach* v. *Olde,* 531 F.2d 983 (10th Cir. 1976), the court maintained that

> . . . The educational process is a broad and comprehensive concept with a variable and indefinite meaning. It is not limited to classroom attendance but includes innumerable separate components, such as participation in athletic activity and membership in school clubs and social groups, which combine to provide an atmosphere of intellectual and moral advancement. We do not read *Goss* to establish a property interest subject to constitutional protection in each of these separate components. (P. 985)

School authorities were upheld in declaring a champion high school wrestler ineligible for the state wrestling championship. The school board's decision resulted from the wrestler's participation with three other students in having multiple acts of sexual intercourse with a sixteen-year-old female student. In responding to the issue of the loss of a scholarship, the court stated:

> When scholarships are awarded at the discretion of a college coach, and such discretion has not yet been exercised, no property interest in the receipt of a scholarship can exist, and the plaintiff cannot invoke his expectation that he would earn a scholarship at the state tournament in order to claim a property interest in wrestling there. (P. 631)

See *Brands* v. *Sheldon Community School*, 671 F. Supp. 627 (Iowa 1987).

Potential for litigation exists in such individual sports as swimming, track, and possibly tennis. Consider the situation where an athlete refuses to participate in an event designated by the coach. In such a situation the coach's decision is often based on the notion that athletes should be deployed in a manner to gain as many points as possible for the team. The athlete's refusal, however, is based on the concern that following the coach's decision may reduce the athlete's opportunity to excel in his or her specialty, thereby reducing or eliminating the opportunity for an athletic scholarship. Assuming the issue was justiciable, how would a court rule? Does a partial answer to this dilemma lie in determining whether a sport is an "individual" or a "team" sport?

Courts have addressed the issue of academic requirements for participation in extracurricular activities. These requirements, often referred to as "no pass, no play" rules, generally require that a student maintain a passing grade (C or 70%) in all academic classes in order to be eligible to participate in extracurricular activities. Courts have not upheld contentions that such rules violate the Equal Protection Clause of the Fourteenth Amendment. See *Montana* v. *Board of Trustees of School District No. 1*, 726 P.2d 801 (Mont. 1986); *Spring Branch Independent School District* v. *Stamos*, 695 S.W.2d 556 (Tex. 1985); and *Bailey* v. *Truby*, 321 S.E.2d 302 (W. Va. 1984).

What is your school system's policy regarding the restriction of students from participating in extracurricular activities?

B. Athletics

Exclusion or suspension from participation in athletics makes up the vast majority of court cases dealing with extracurricular activities. Rules barring married students, females, and handicapped students from participation in athletics are frequently challenged. Those barred generally allege that they have not received equal protection guaranteed under the Fourteenth Amendment or that the school conduct violates a federal statute.

1. Married Students

Cases dealing with married students barred from participating in athletics have often involved "star" athletes who claim they will be deprived of an opportunity to be considered for athletic scholarships. Those barred have also alleged that such rules infringe upon the fundamental right of marriage. Historically, courts had upheld rules barring married students from participating in athletics. However, beginning in the early 1970s courts have uniformly and consistently invalidated such rules.

Beeson v. Kiowa County School District RE-1

Colorado Court of Appeals, 1977
567 P.2d 801

RULAND, Judge

* * *

Plaintiff was a senior in high school, married, and the mother of a child at the time she initiated this action seeking to enjoin the school board from enforcing its policy so that she could participate on the girl's varsity basketball team. * * *

* * *

The facts pertinent to this review are not disputed. Plaintiff was a "star player" on the girls' varsity basketball team during her freshman year in high school. However, she married the following summer and a child was born to the married couple during her sophomore year. Plaintiff was aware of the policy at the time she married.

Plaintiff did not seek to participate on the varsity team during either her sophomore or junior years. Plaintiff sought, however, to rejoin the team for her senior year, but was precluded by the school policy from doing so. While she was allowed to practice with the team, she was not allowed to participate in interscholastic competition.

Plaintiff testified that by reason of her inability to compete on the varsity team during her senior year, she lost any opportunity for a college athletic scholarship. She expressed the belief that she would have been offered an athletic scholarship based on her previously demonstrated ability and on the fact that her sister had been offered such a scholarship at sometime in the past.

* * *

We first emphasize that the issue on appeal is whether the school board's policy is valid in the context of plaintiff being a married student. Therefore, we do not consider the validity of a policy which would preclude plaintiff from participating in extracurricular activities because she was the mother of a young child, or whether a policy would be valid if it required married women to meet certain requirements in order to assure the board that no injuries would result from an undetected pregnancy. The additional considerations inherent in such policies are irrelevant here because the policy at issue excluded plaintiff from participating in extracurricular activities based solely on the fact that she was married.

According to § 14–12–101, C.R.S. 1973, "[i]t is the declared public policy of this state . . . to promote and foster the marriage relationship. . . ." We are therefore compelled to hold that the creation of a "marriage relationship" is a fundamental right in this jurisdiction. * * *

Nor is this fundamental right vitiated by the fact that plaintiff needed parental consent to enter her marriage. Plaintiff's marriage was entered into in compliance with § 14–2–106, C.R.S. 1973, of the Uniform Marriage Act. That Act has as one of its purposes "to strengthen and preserve the integrity of marriage and to safeguard meaningful family relationships." * * * [T]he General Assembly has obviously determined that this purpose is fulfilled, if as here, parental consent for plaintiff's marriage is first obtained. Hence, it is clear that a board policy which discriminates against those who exercise that right violates the equal protection clause of the Fourteenth Amendment, unless there exists a compelling interest which justifies that discrimination. * * *

* * *

Looking then to the reasons offered by the school board, we conclude that the acknowledged intent to discourage eligible persons from marrying obviously contravenes the declared public policy of this State "to promote and foster the marriage relationship." * * * Illustrative of the inhibiting effect of the policy is evidence in the record indicating that another star basketball player in the same school district who had fathered a child during his senior year remained eligible for interscholastic competition because he did not marry the mother until after his graduation.

This impact of the policy upon the marriage relationship requires us to consider whether the discrimination created by the board's policy is justified by the need to require married students to focus on their basic education and their family responsibilities by excluding them from extracurricular activities. We find no support for the discrimination here. The focus on basic education can be supplied by a board policy which establishes academic requirements for both married and unmarried students to be eligible for extracurricular activities. On the other hand, the fulfillment of family responsibilities may, in many cases, depend upon further education at the college level, and depriving students of the opportunity to earn a college athletic scholarship, or to participate in extracurricular activities to broaden their general background, could close the door to any opportunity to obtain that education. * * *

Finally, we must evaluate the board's contention that married students who participate in extracurricular activities may tend to promote a lack of discipline among the other students and may not be dependable because of their family responsibility. Since the policy has been in effect for approximately 20 years, we understand why no incidents were cited by the board where these problems have arisen. On the other hand, we are unable to perceive why the same policies which govern the discipline and dependability of unmarried students who participate in extracurricular activities would not serve to resolve any such problems. At least we cannot characterize this potential problem, standing alone, as sufficient justification for discrimination against the fundamental right to marry. * * *

Accordingly, the judgment of the district court is reversed and the cause remanded with directions to enter judgment declaring the board's policy invalid as a denial of equal protection under the Fourteenth Amendment.

Notes and Questions

May a divorced student be barred from engaging in extracurricular activities? See *Romans* v. *Crenshaw*, 354 F. Supp. 868 (Tex. 1972), which upheld a divorced student's right to engage in such activities.

Does your state have a statutory provision pertaining to married students participating in extracurricular activities? What are your local school system's rules or policies regarding married students engaging in such activities?

2. Female Participation

Historically, there has been both de facto and de jure segregation of male and female public school students. In some school systems entire schools have been segregated on the basis of sex. More common, however, has been the separation of the sexes in certain classes and in interscholastic athletic participation. A flagrant example has been the routine assignment of girls to home economics classes and boys to "shop" courses. Opportunities for females in athletic competition were limited, and the stereotypic role for a female was often that of cheerleader, flag girl, or pom-pom girl.

Many female students and their parents considered such treatment, especially in the limited opportunity for athletic competition, to be in violation of the equal protection provision of the Fourteenth Amendment and a form of sex discrimination. Many courts have agreed with this contention, and although Title IX addresses this issue, litigation pertaining to female participation in athletic programs has not abated. *Leffel v. Wisconsin Interscholastic Athletic Association* represents an example of the post-Title IX cases brought before the courts.

Leffel v. Wisconsin Interscholastic Athletic Association

United States District Court, Eastern District of Wisconsin, 1978
444 F. Supp. 1117

MYRON L. GORDON, District Judge.

*   *   *

In these actions, the plaintiffs seek a declaration that a provision of the constitution of the Wisconsin Interscholastic Athletic Association (WIAA) which limits coeducational interscholastic activities violates the equal protection clause of the fourteenth amendment to the United States Constitution. They also seek a permanent injunction enjoining its enforcement. *   *   *

The following facts are undisputed. In case no. 75–C–174, the named plaintiffs, female students at De Pere High School, were denied permission to qualify for competition with male students on the high school interscholastic varsity baseball team. The high school offered no separate female team for interscholastic competition. In case no. 73–C–269, the named plaintiffs, female students at Washington High School, were denied permission to qualify for competition with male students on the high school's interscholastic varsity swim team and tennis team. The school sponsored a girls' swim team but no girls' tennis team.

In both cases, the school officials excluded the plaintiffs from trying out for the teams based on the following provision of the WIAA constitution:

"The Board of Control shall prohibit all types of interscholastic activity involving boys and girls competing with or against each other."

The WIAA is a voluntary, unincorporated, nonprofit organization whose purpose is to organize, develop, direct, and control interscholastic athletic programs for students in the public high schools of Wisconsin. Under the organization's constitution, member schools agree to conduct their athletic program according to the constitution, by-laws and rules of eligibility of the organization. Since most of the state's public high schools and junior high schools were members of the organization at the time these actions were commenced, interscholastic competition with most Wisconsin public high schools depended upon compliance with the prohibition on coeducational competition.

During the pendency of these actions, Title IX of the Education Amendments of 1972 * * * (Title IX) was enacted. Title IX prohibits sex discrimination in any educational program receiving federal funds. The regulations promulgated by the Department of Health, Education and Welfare pursuant to 20 U.S.C. § 1682 include specific provisions relating to sex discrimination in athletics. 45 C.F. R. § 86.41(a) generally prohibits separate athletic programs based on sex, but § 86.41(b) permits separate teams for members of each sex where selection for such teams is based on competitive skills or the activity involved is a contact sport. The same section also provides that "where a recipient [educational institution] operates or sponsors a team in a particular sport for members of one sex but operates or sponsors no such team for members of the other sex, and athletic opportunities for members of that sex have previously been limited, members of the excluded sex must be allowed to try out for the team offered unless the sport involved is a contact sport."

After these actions were commenced, and in response to Title IX and the corresponding regulations, the WIAA amended the challenged provision of its constitution to read as follows:

> "The Board of Control shall prohibit all types of interscholastic activity involving boys and girls competing with or against each other *except (a) as prescribed by state and federal law and (b) as determined by Board of Control interpretations of such law.*" (emphasis added)

The defendants argue that their rule is in full compliance with Title IX and its corresponding regulations. Their position is that Title IX encompasses all that is required by federal law, including the equal protection clause of the fourteenth amendment, thereby insulating their rule from constitutional challenge. The defendants urge that a constitutional attack cannot be waged against the WIAA rule until Title IX itself is determined to be unconstitutional.

In my opinion, the defendants' argument is meritless. The enactment of Title IX did not remove the problem of sex discrimination from constitutional concern; congressional enactments cannot preempt provisions of the Constitution. Moreover, Title IX merely created an administrative remedy, subject to judicial review, to enforce the prohibition of sex discrimination in educational programs receiving federal financial assistance. It does not displace the plaintiffs' right to enforce the commands of the fourteenth amendment through an action under 42 U.S.C. § 1983. * * *

Originally, the plaintiffs argued that the WIAA rule was unconstitutional on its face and as applied. The amended rule, however, permits coeducational athletic activity to the extent required by federal law. The claim of facial unconstitutionality is therefore no longer tenable, but the claim of unconstitutional application remains.

In the complaints filed in these cases, the plaintiffs sought a declaration that the WIAA rule "deprives the plaintiffs and the class they represent of their constitutional rights to be free from state establishment and enforcement of sex-based exclusions unrelated to merit" and an injunction enjoining any such rule or practice. The requested declaration was considerably broader than the declaration sought in the present motion.

The plaintiffs now seek summary judgment declaring that the challenged rule, as applied, deprives the plaintiffs and their class of equal protection under any of the following circumstances:

(1) where their school does not provide a girls' team in a particular sport;
(2) where the girls' team in a particular sport at their school does not provide a program comparable to that maintained for boys;
(3) where the level of competition for the boys' team in a particular sport is higher than the level of competition for the corresponding girls' team.

The plaintiffs also seek a permanent injunction enjoining the defendants from enforcing the rule under such circumstances.

From the manner in which the plaintiffs have narrowed their demand for relief, it is apparent that they do not question whether separate teams for boys and girls, with comparable support and funding, are permissible under the fourteenth amendment. Several other courts have dealt with this problem and have approved of the concept of "separate but equal" teams for male and female high school students. * * *

With respect to "noncontact" sports, the defendants do not dispute that the plaintiffs would be denied equal protection of the laws under the first two circumstances listed above. They argue, however, that Title IX permits different treatment of male and female students insofar as "contact" sports are concerned. The defendants disagree that the plaintiffs have a valid constitutional grievance under the third circumstance.

The defendants' argument that Title IX permits different treatment of boys and girls insofar as "contact" sports are concerned must be rejected in view of my determination that in this case the defendants' rule and policies must be measured against the fourteenth amendment, rather than Title IX.

In its present posture, the case is therefore reduced to the following two issues: First, have the defendants violated the equal protection clause by denying female high school students the opportunity to qualify for a position on a boys' varsity interscholastic team engaging in a contact sport where no separate team is provided for girls, or where the separate team provided does not have a comparable program? Secondly, as to both contact and noncontact sports, does the equal protection clause of the fourteenth amendment require that female high school students be permitted to attempt to qualify for a position on a boys' varsity interscholastic team where the boys' team has a higher level of competition than the corresponding girls' team? The second issue will be addressed first.

There is no dispute that the WIAA rule in question and the defendants' application of the rule is an intentional discrimination, i.e., for what they deem to be legitimate purposes, the defendants intentionally treat boy and girl athletes differently. Since an intentional discrimination is involved, the fourteenth amendment's equal protection clause is implicated. * * *

However, there are no allegations in the instant complaints that the defendants have intentionally imposed different levels of competition on boys and girls. Any such differences arise from the abilities of the team members themselves. Thus, the plaintiffs' claim for declaratory and injunctive relief cannot encompass the concept of equal levels of competition.

The governmental objective posited to the defendants is the prevention of injury to female athletes. The defendants argue that "anatomical and physiological differences between boys and girls" and "differences in athletic abilities" justify the prohibition of coeducational teams in contact sports. The defendants offer affidavits to support the proposition that anatomical and physiological differences between boys and girls will leave girls exposed to unreasonable risk of injury if they were to compete with or against boys.

The plaintiffs do not dispute that the defendants' stated objectives are legitimate, but they argue that the correlation between gender and athletic ability is too weak to withstand equal protection scrutiny. Even if the defendants' generalizations are assumed to be true, I nevertheless find that the exclusion of girls from all contact sports in order to protect female high school athletes from an unreasonable risk of injury is not fairly or substantially related to a justifiable governmental objective in the context of the fourteenth amendment.

The defendant advances no governmental objective whatsoever to justify providing boys with the opportunity to participate in varsity interscholastic competition in contact sports while *absolutely* denying the same opportunity to girls. It is doubtful that any such legitimate governmental objective exists. * * * The defendants do not argue that girls will be exposed to an unreasonable risk of injury in a separate girls' athletic program for contact sports; they argue that girls will be exposed to an unreasonable risk of injury if allowed to compete on boys teams. However, coeducational teams are only one possible remedy for the defendants' constitutional violation. The defendants have the other two alternatives of (1) dropping all varsity interscholastic competition, and (2) establishing separate girls' teams for contact sports. * * * As noted previously, the demand for relief of the plaintiffs at bar would be met by the establishment of separate girls' teams with a comparable program; thus, I need not decide whether the concept of separate girls' teams presents a problem of equal protection.

The state public schools are under no constitutional compulsion to provide interscholastic competition in any sport, but once they choose to do so, this educational opportunity must be provided to all on equal terms. * * * Although the plaintiffs do not have a constitutional right to compete on boys' teams in contact or noncontact sports, the defendants may not afford an educational opportunity to boys that is denied to girls.

It should be noted, however, that a denial of equal protection exists only where members of the plaintiff class request and are denied the opportunity to participate in a particular varsity interscholastic sport. * * *

* * *

It is declared that the defendants' exclusion of the plaintiffs and the class they represent from participation in a varsity interscholastic athletic program in a particular sport where such a program is provided for male students violates the equal protection clause of the fourteenth amendment.

The defendants are hereby permanently enjoined from excluding the plaintiffs and the class they represent from participation in a varsity interscholastic athletic program in a particular sport where such a program is provided for male students.

* * *

Notes

Section 86.41, Athletics, of the implementing regulations for Title IX stipulates as follows:

Athletics.

(a) General. No person shall, on the basis of sex, be excluded from participation in, be denied the benefits of, be treated differently from one another or otherwise be discriminated against in any interscholastic, intercollegiate, club or intramural athletics offered by a recipient, and no recipient shall provide any such athletics separately on such basis.

(b) Separate teams. Notwithstanding the requirements of paragraph (a) of this section, a recipient may operate or sponsor separate teams for members of each sex where selection for such teams is based upon competitive skill or the activity involved is a contact sport. However, where a recipient operates or sponsors a team in a particular sport for members of one sex but operates or sponsors no such team for members of the other sex, and athletic opportunities for members of that sex have previously been limited, members of the excluded sex must be allowed to try out for the team offered unless the sport involved is a contact sport. For the purposes of this part, contact sports include boxing, wrestling, rugby, ice hockey, football, basketball, and other sports the purpose or major activity of which involves bodily contact.

(c) Equal opportunity. A recipient which operates or sponsors interscholastic, intercollegiate, club or intramural athletics shall provide equal athletic opportunity for members of both sexes. In determining whether equal opportunities are available the Director will consider, among other factors:

    (1) Whether the selection of sports and levels of competition effectively accommodate the interests and abilities of members of both sexes;
    (2) The provision of equipment and supplies;
    (3) Scheduling of games and practice times;
    (4) Travel and per diem allowance;
    (5) Opportunity to receive coaching and academic tutoring;
    (6) Assignment and compensation of coaches and tutors;
    (7) Provision of locker rooms, practice and competitive facilities;
    (8) Provision of medical and training facilities and services;
    (9) Provision of housing and dining facilities and services;
   (10) Publicity.

Unequal aggregate expenditures for members of each sex or unequal expenditures for male and female teams if a recipient operates or sponsors separate teams will not constitute non-compliance with this section, but the Director may consider the failure to provide necessary funds for teams for one sex in assessing equality of opportunity for members of each sex. (45 C.F.R. § 86.41).*

* * *

Rules for girls' basketball, which require split court play, six rather than five players, and permit only forwards to shoot, are not unconstitutional according to *Cape* v. *Tennessee Secondary School Athletic Association,* 563 F.2d 793 (6th Cir. 1977).

3. Participation of Handicapped Students

A handicapped student's desire to participate in athletics requires the balancing of the student's and the school system's interest. The student may wish to have the most well-rounded school experience possible; yet, the school has the responsibility of protecting the physical well-being of the student. Most significant in these cases is the determination of possible injury to the handicapped student if he or she is allowed to participate in interscholastic athletics.

Kampmeier v. Nyquist

United States Court of Appeals, Second Circuit, 1977
553 F.2d 296

LUMBARD, Circuit Judge:

Two junior high school students, each with vision in only one eye, and their parents, appeal from an order by Judge Burke in the Western District of New York denying their motion for a preliminary injunction against public school authorities in Pittsford and Canandaigua, New York, who have refused to allow the students to participate in contact sports at school. Plaintiffs contend that the school system's prohibition on participation by one-eyed students in contact sports violates section 504 of the Rehabilitation Act of 1973, 29 U.S.C. § 794, and also deprives them of their fourteenth amendment right to equal protection of the law. Having considered the possible irreparable consequences that may flow from whichever decision the court should choose to make, we conclude that the appellants have not made a sufficient factual showing of likely success of the merits to warrant preliminary relief. Accordingly, we affirm the order of the district court.

In their complaint filed on April 14, 1976, plaintiffs alleged the following: Margaret Kampmeier has a congenital cataract in one eye. As of the beginning of her seventh-grade year in 1975, she was one of

* See Appendix D for an edited Title IX of the Education Amendments of 1972.

the best athletes in her class. Her parents have provided her with protective glasses which have industrial quality safety lenses, wire mesh side shields, and extended ear pieces. The Kampmeiers have also announced their willingness to release the school and its employees from liability for any athletics injury to Margaret's good eye. Steven Genecco is a grade ahead of Margaret. He has been virtually blind in one eye since an injury at age six. Prior to the 1975–76 school year, he had been allowed to participate in all school sports. During 1975 he participated in interscholastic basketball and a community association football league as well as the regular school physical education program. On recommendation by a school physician, each child has now been prohibited from participating in any contact sports at school, solely because of lack of vision in one eye.

In response to plaintiffs' motion for a preliminary injunction, the defendants submitted affidavits explaining that under regulations promulgated by the New York State Commissioner of Education, * * * approval from the school medical officer is required before any student may be allowed to participate in interscholastic athletics. Pamphlets distributed to school officials by the Commissioner list blindness in one eye as a disqualifying condition for participation in contact sports, but not noncontact sports. The lists of disqualifications are advisory only: "[t]hese guidelines . . . are only guidelines and are not absolute mandates for the school physician." "Some of the disqualifying conditions listed are subject to evaluation by the responsible physician with respect to anticipated risks, the otherwise athletic fitness of the candidate, special protective preventive measures that might be utilized, and the nature of the supervisory control." * * *

Letters from physicians who had examined the children were submitted. Their opinions were divided.

* * *

As we read § 504, however, exclusion of handicapped children from a school activity is not improper if there exists a substantial justification for the school's policy. Section 504 prohibits only the exclusion of handicapped persons who are "otherwise qualified." Here, the defendants have relief on medical opinion that children with sight in only one eye are not qualified to play in contact sports because of the high risk of eye injury. The plaintiffs have presented little evidence—medical, statistical, or otherwise—which would cast doubt on the substantiality of this rationale. On the record before us, they have not made a clear showing of probable success on the merits.

Both sides have demonstrated the possibility of irreparable injury. On the one hand, athletics play an important part in the life and growth of teenage children, * * * and the plaintiffs are being deprived of the freedom to participate in sports of their choice. On the other hand, public school officials have a parens patriae interest in protecting the well-being of their students; the defendants, relying on medical opinion, are concerned about the risk of injury to a child's one good eye. In view of the host of noncontact sports which remain open to the plaintiffs, we conclude that the balance of hardships does not tip decidely in their favor.

The motion for a preliminary injunction was properly denied.

Judgment affirmed.

Notes and Questions

Two federal laws often serve as the basis for a lawsuit involving handicapped students. Section 504 of the Rehabilitation Act of 1973 is mentioned in **Kampmeier.** The other is the Education for All Handicapped Children Act of 1975—Public Law 94–142.

Title IX has been responsible for increased participation of females in interscholastic athletics. Do you think Section 504 of the Rehabilitation Act of 1973 and Public Law 94–142 will provide an impetus for the increased participation of handicapped students, perhaps by requiring separate teams, in interscholastic athletics?

What is your local school system's policy regarding the participation of handicapped students in athletics?

IX. School Punishment for Out-of-School Offenses

Out-of-school conduct of students may have an impact on the overall well-being of the school. When there is a problem with out-of-school conduct, school authorities must reconcile their control of student conduct necessary for the orderly operation of the school with their obligation to comply with the standards of constitutionality and reasonableness required by the judiciary to ensure that students receive just treatment.

Several court decisions have addressed issues dealing with noncriminal student off-campus activity. In one case it was alleged that two students were assaulted by a group of others while they were all walking home after school. Although the court agreed that school authorities may punish students for out-of-school physical abuse directed at other students, punishment such as expulsion may not be based on unsigned and unidentified statements by student witnesses. See *Tibbs* v. *Board of Education of the Township of Franklin*, 114 N.J. Super. 287, 276 A.2d 165 (1971).

Parking an automobile off campus contrary to school rules was an issue in *McLean Independent School District* v. *Andrews*, 333 S.W.2d 886 (Tex. Civ. App. 1960). A student's suspension for breaking the school rules was upheld, primarily on the basis of promoting the safety of student pedestrians on the streets adjacent to the school during noon recess. The court noted, however, that the rule in question might provide future complications as students parked at more remote distances from the campus.

An Ohio appellate court, in *McNaughton* v. *Circleville Board of Education*, 46 Ohio Misc. 12, 345 N.E.2d 649 (1974), upheld the suspension from school and from participation in athletic activities of students who held an out-of-school initiation and hazing of new members of an officially recognized high school club. The club's advisor had not been notified nor was he present at the initiation, which occurred at the home of one of the offending students. Initiates were struck with belts, forced to eat onions, and required to rub tabasco sauce on the faces of fellow initiates.

Cases have addressed the dismissal of students from school chapters of the National Honor Society owing to their violation of a rule against the use of alcohol. In two such cases, *Warren* v. *National Association of Secondary School Principals*, 375 F. Supp. 1043 (Tex. 1974), and *Ector County Independent School District* v. *Hopkins*, 518 S.W.2d 576 (Tex. Civ. App. 1975), the violative drinking took place off campus. These courts stressed that students facing dismissal from an honor society as a result of their drinking had to be afforded appropriate due process.

Courts have held that public school students' out-of-school criminal conduct may be subject to school disciplinary hearings, although as a practical matter the particular kind of school response will be influenced by the nature and seriousness of the criminal charges. A non-school-related speeding charge, for instance, might be ignored by authorities, while a murder or rape charge would not be.

R.R. v. *Board of Education of the Shore Regional High School District*, 109 N.J. Super. 337, 263 A.2d 180 (1970), addressed the question of whether public school officials can deprive a student of his or her right to attend school because of criminal acts committed off school grounds. In this instance, a fifteen-year-old boy stabbed a girl during an altercation in a neighbor's house after the boy had returned home at the end of a school day. This court concluded that officials do have the right to expel or suspend students for out-of-school activities when it is reasonably necessary either for the transgressing student's physical or emotional safety and well-being or for the safety and well-being of other students, teachers, or public school property. Despite this conclusion, the court ordered the school to readmit the student because of due process violations.

A California court upheld the suspension of students involved in such offenses as kidnapping, rape, assault with a bumper jack, assault resulting in the death of a boy whose head struck a sidewalk curb, carrying a concealed weapon, and disturbing the peace. The California court made no attempt to distinguish between offenses that occurred on campus and those that occurred off campus. See *S.* v. *Board of Education, San Francisco Unified School District*, 20 Cal. App. 3d 83, 97 Cal. Rptr. 422 (1971).

A federal district court in *Caldwell* v. *Cannady*, 340 F. Supp. 835 (Tex. 1972), upheld the reasonableness of a local school board policy mandating the expulsion of any student possessing, using, or selling dangerous or narcotic drugs. In this instance students were disciplined after they were arrested when marijuana was found in their automobile in a series of incidents at night and away from school.

Authority of school officials to discipline a student acquitted of out-of-school reckless driving charges was addressed by the Supreme Court of Wyoming in *Clements* v. *Board of Trustees of the Sheridan County School District No. 2*, 585 P.2d 197 (Wyo. 1978). The student had been charged with reckless driving for purposely impeding the progress of a school bus. The court held that school authorities may discipline pupils for out-of-school conduct having a direct and immediate effect on the discipline or general welfare of the school.

Constitutional questions regarding double jeopardy and self-incrimination have been raised in the cases ruling on the legality of actions taken by public school officials in response to charges of out-of-school criminal violations against students. Courts have consistently held that both school sanctions and judicial sanctions are permitted without violating the Fifth Amendment prohibition against double jeopardy. They maintain that school hearings and criminal proceedings have different purposes, with school responses being civil or remedial while judicial responses are punitive. Although acknowledging that school discipline has punitive effects, the courts contend that its underlying purpose is the protection of the school environment.

Courts have also held that public school students' out-of-school criminal conduct properly may be the subject of school disciplinary hearings without violating Fifth Amendment rights against compulsory self-incrimination. Students may not be required to testify in these proceedings, and if students' rights are infringed upon in the hearings, courts reason, the students may then ask for a judicial review of the proceedings.

Analysis reveals that the judiciary supports the rationale that students may be subject to school discipline, including suspension or expulsion, if their out-of-school conduct threatens the efficient operation of the school. Generally the courts recognize that the authority to make and enforce policies designed to protect the safety and welfare of students is a reasonable and necessary exercise of the power invested in local school boards. Nevertheless, courts will support the use of that authority over out-of-school criminal conduct only when they perceive the conduct as having a direct and substantial impact on the school and its programs.

When the out-of-school conduct has involved physical violence or otherwise threatened the safety or well-being of students, the judiciary has not been concerned with whether the conduct occurred out of school or in school. Decisions indicate that the test of the public school's authority to control student conduct is not the time or place of the conduct, but rather its effect on the morale and efficiency of the school. It may be concluded that the nature and seriousness of the conduct and its potential impact on the public school and its programs are more important than where the conduct occurred.

teachers
and the law

Introduction

In recent years teachers have increasingly employed the courts to remedy treatment by school authorities with whom they disagreed. In many instances personnel practices that had become institutionalized through custom have been challenged as being discriminatory, violative of statutory or constitutional provisions, or unfair. Although teachers have not always been successful in actions brought before the judiciary, their willingness to employ the courts for a redress of grievances has produced a climate in which public school administrators have become more sensitive to the necessity of treating teachers in a legally defensible manner.

This chapter focuses on law relating to nonrenewal and dismissal of teachers; teachers' freedom of expression; academic freedom; drug testing; standards of dress; the teacher as exemplar; employment discrimination; collective bargaining; and the political rights of teachers.

I. Nonrenewal and Dismissal

Over the years the development of state statutory provisions and the existence of a sizable body of case law have provided teachers with safeguards against arbitrary dismissal. Although school administrators have the primary task of evaluating teachers and determining their fitness, this task must be done in accordance with state statutory provisions and in the light of constitutional protections.

According to a United States Supreme Court decision, *Board of Regents of State Colleges* v. *Roth,* a nontenured teacher need not be given reasons for nonrenewal unless the nonrenewal deprived the teacher of a "liberty" interest or if there was a "property" interest in continued employment. Any statement regarding the reason for the nonrenewal could result in the teacher's requesting a due process hearing.

Depending on a state's statutory provisions, dismissal of a tenured teacher or one under a continuing contract must be in conformance with the state law. State provisions usually contain grounds for dismissal such as nonperformance of duty, incompetency, insubordination, conviction of crimes involving moral turpitude, failure to comply with reasonable orders, violation of contract provisions or local rules or regulations, persistent failure or refusal to maintain orderly discipline of students, and revocation of the teaching certificate. Additionally, all of the procedural aspects of the hearing process provided by state statute must be afforded the teacher. These often include the following requirements: proper notice, containing charges and the names and nature of the testimony of witnesses and stating the time and place of the hearing; compulsory process or subpoena requiring the attendance of witnesses and the production of relevant papers and documents; a fair hearing; and an opportunity for appeal.

Board of Regents of State Colleges v. Roth

Supreme Court of the United States, 1972
408 U.S. 564

MR. JUSTICE STEWART delivered the opinion of the Court.

In 1968 the respondent, David Roth, was hired for his first teaching job as assistant professor of political science at Wisconsin State University-Oshkosh. He was hired for a fixed term of one academic year. The notice of his faculty appointment specified that his employment would begin on September 1, 1968, and would end on June 30, 1969. The respondent completed that term. But he was informed that he would not be rehired for the next academic year.

The respondent had no tenure rights to continued employment. Under Wisconsin statutory law a state university teacher can acquire tenure as a "permanent" employee only after four years of year-to-year employment. Having acquired tenure, a teacher is entitled to continued employment "during efficiency and good behavior." A relatively new teacher without tenure, however, is under Wisconsin law entitled to nothing beyond his one-year appointment. There are no statutory or administrative standards defining eligibility for re-employment. State law thus clearly leaves the decision whether to rehire a nontenured teacher for another year to the unfettered discretion of university officials.

The procedural protection afforded a Wisconsin State University teacher before he is separated from the University corresponds to his job security. As a matter of statutory law, a tenured teacher cannot be "discharged except for cause upon written charges" and pursuant to certain procedures. A nontenured teacher, similarly, is protected to some extent *during* his one-year term. Rules promulgated by the Board of Regents provide that a nontenured teacher "dismissed" before the end of the year may have some opportunity for review of the "dismissal." But the Rules provide no real protection for a nontenured teacher who simply is not re-employed for the next year. He must be informed by February 1 "concerning retention or non-retention for the ensuing year." But "no reason for non-retention need be given. No review or appeal is provided in such case."

In conformance with these Rules, the President of Wisconsin State University-Oshkosh informed the respondent before February 1, 1969, that he would not be rehired for the 1969–1970 academic year. He gave the respondent no reason for the decision and no opportunity to challenge it at any sort of hearing.

The respondent then brought this action in Federal District Court alleging that the decision not to rehire him for the next year infringed his Fourteenth Amendment rights. He attacked the decision both in substance and procedure. First, he alleged that the true reason for the decision was to punish him for certain statements critical of the University administration, and that it therefore violated his right to freedom of speech. Second, he alleged that the failure of University officials to give him notice of any reason for nonretention and an opportunity for a hearing violated his right to procedural due process of law.

The District Court granted summary judgment for the respondent on the procedural issue, ordering the University officials to provide him with reasons and a hearing. * * * The Court of Appeals, with one judge dissenting, affirmed this partial summary judgment. * * * We granted certiorari. * * * The only question presented to us at this stage in the case is whether the respondent had a constitutional right to a statement of reasons and a hearing on the University's decision not to rehire him for another year. We hold that he did not.

The requirements of procedural due process apply only to the deprivation of interests encompassed by the Fourteenth Amendment's protection of liberty and property. When protected interests are implicated, the right to some kind of prior hearing is paramount. But the range of interests protected by procedural due process is not infinite.

The District Court decided that procedural due process guarantees apply in this case by assessing and balancing the weights of the particular interests involved. It concluded that the respondent's interest in re-employment at Wisconsin State University-Oshkosh outweighed the University's interest in denying him re-employment summarily. * * * Undeniably, the respondent's re-employment prospects were of major concern to him—concern that we surely cannot say was insignificant. And a weighing process has long been a part of any determination of the *form* of hearing required in particular situations by procedural due process. But, to determine whether due process requirements apply in the first place, we must look not to the "weight" but to the *nature* of the interest at stake. * * * We must look to see if the interest is within the Fourteenth Amendment's protection of liberty and property.

"Liberty" and "property" are broad and majestic terms. They are among the "[g]reat [constitutional] concepts . . . purposely left to gather meaning from experience . . . [T]hey relate to the whole domain of social and economic fact, and the statesmen who founded this Nation knew too well that only a stagnant society remains unchanged." * * * For that reason, the Court has fully and finally rejected the wooden distinction between "rights" and "privileges" that once seemed to govern the applicability of procedural due process rights. The Court has also made clear that the property interests protected by procedural due process extend well beyond actual ownership of real estate, chattels, or money. By the same token, the Court has required due process protection for deprivations of liberty beyond the sort of formal constraints imposed by the criminal process.

Yet, while the Court has eschewed rigid or formalistic limitations on the protection of procedural due process, it has at the same time observed certain boundaries. For the words "liberty" and "property" in the Due Process Clause of the Fourteenth Amendment must be given some meaning.

"While this Court has not attempted to define with exactness the liberty . . . guaranteed [by the Fourteenth Amendment], the term has received much consideration and some of the included things have been definitely stated. Without doubt, it denotes not merely freedom from bodily restraint but also the right of the individual to contract, to engage in any of the common occupations of life, to acquire useful knowledge, to marry, establish a home and bring up children, to worship God according to the dictates of his own conscience, and generally to enjoy those privileges long recognized . . . as essential to the orderly pursuit of happiness by free men." * * * In a Constitution for a free people, there can be no doubt that the meaning of "liberty" must be broad indeed. * * *

There might be cases in which a State refused to reemploy a person under such circumstances that interests in liberty would be implicated. But this is not such a case.

The State, in declining to rehire the respondent, did not make any charge against him that might seriously damage his standing and associations in his community. It did not base the nonrenewal of his contract on a charge, for example, that he had been guilty of dishonesty, or immorality. Had it done so, this would be a different case. For "[w]here a person's good name, reputation, honor, or integrity is at stake because of what the government is doing to him, notice and an opportunity to be heard are essential." * * * In such a case, due process would accord an opportunity to refute the charge before University officials. In the present case, however, there is no suggestion whatever that the respondent's "good name, reputation, honor, or integrity" is at stake.

Similarly, there is no suggestion that the State, in declining to reemploy the respondent, imposed on him a stigma or other disability that foreclosed his freedom to take advantage of other employment opportunities. The State, for example, did not invoke any regulations to bar the respondent from all other public employment in state universities. Had it done so, this, again, would be a different case. * * *

To be sure, the respondent has alleged that the nonrenewal of his contract was based on his exercise of his right to freedom of speech. But this allegation is not now before us. The District Court stayed proceedings on this issue, and the respondent has yet to prove that the decision not to rehire him was, in fact, based on his free speech activities.

Hence, on the record before us, all that clearly appears is that the respondent was not rehired for one year at one university. It stretches the concept too far to suggest that a person is deprived of "liberty" when he simply is not rehired in one job but remains as free as before to seek another. * * *

The Fourteenth Amendment's procedural protection of property is a safeguard of the security of interests that a person has already acquired in specific benefits. These interests—property interests—may take many forms.

Certain attributes of "property" interests protected by procedural due process emerge from these decisions. To have a property interest in a benefit, a person clearly must have more than an abstract need or desire for it. He must have more than a unilateral expectation of it. He must, instead, have a legitimate claim of entitlement to it. It is a purpose of the ancient institution of property to protect those claims upon which people rely in their daily lives, reliance that must not be arbitrarily undermined. It is a purpose of the constitutional right to a hearing to provide an opportunity for a person to vindicate those claims.

Property interests, of course, are not created by the Constitution. Rather, they are created and their dimensions are defined by existing rules or understandings that stem from an independent source such as state law—rules or understandings that secure certain benefits and that support claims of entitlement to those benefits. Thus, the welfare recipients * * * had a claim of entitlement to welfare payments that was grounded in the statute defining eligibility for them. The recipients had not yet shown that they were, in fact, within the statutory terms of eligibility. But we held that they had a right to a hearing at which they might attempt to do so.

Just as the welfare recipients' "property" interest in welfare payments was created and defined by statutory terms, so the respondent's "property" interest in employment at Wisconsin State University-Oshkosh was created and defined by the terms of his appointment. Those terms secured his interest in employment up to June 30, 1969. But the important fact in this case is that they specifically provided that the respondent's employment was to terminate on June 30. They did not provide for contract renewal absent "sufficient cause." Indeed, they made no provision for renewal whatsoever.

Thus, the terms of the respondent's appointment secured absolutely no interest in re-employment for the next year. They supported absolutely no possible claim of entitlement to re-employment. Nor, significantly, was there any state statute or University rule or policy that secured his interest in re-employment or that created any legitimate claim to it. In these circumstances, the respondent surely had an abstract concern in being rehired, but he did not have a *property* interest sufficient to require the University authorities to give him a hearing when they declined to renew his contract of employment.

Our analysis of the respondent's constitutional rights in this case in no way indicates a view that an opportunity for a hearing or a statement of reasons for nonretention would, or would not, be appropriate or wise in public colleges and universities. For it is a written Constitution that we apply. Our role is confined to interpretation of that Constitution.

We must conclude that the summary judgment for the respondent should not have been granted, since the respondent has not shown that he was deprived of liberty or property protected by the Fourteenth Amendment. The judgment of the Court of Appeals, accordingly, is reversed and the case is remanded for further proceedings consistent with this opinion.

It is so ordered.

Notes and Questions

Roth was a five-to-three decision. In his dissent, Justice Douglas argued that:

> . . . Nonrenewal of a teacher's contract is tantamount in effect to a dismissal and the consequences may be enormous. Nonrenewal can be a blemish that turns into a permanent scar and effectively limits any chance the teacher has of being rehired as a teacher, at least in his State.

Do you agree with his assessment?

Another United States Supreme Court decision dealt with an issue that may have significance in states without tenure statutes. In that decision the Court held that if a teacher had de facto tenure—an expectation of continued employment after many years of satisfactory service although a formal tenure system did not exist—a hearing could be requested to challenge grounds for nonretention. See *Perry* v. *Sindermann*, 408 U.S. 593 (1972).

The United States Supreme Court upheld the dismissal of a tenured teacher who refused to comply with a continuing education policy requiring teachers who held only a bachelor's degree to earn at least five semester hours of college credit every three years. See *Harrah Independent School District* v. *Martin*, 440 U.S. 194 (1979).

A nontenured teacher's nonrenewal was not upheld in *Stoddard* v. *School District No. 1*, 590 F.2d 829 (10th Cir. 1979). The teacher in this case was advised in a letter from her principal that her contract would not be renewed because of failure to maintain order in the classroom and lack of dynamics in motivating students. The teacher alleged that in a private conversation the principal informed her that the "real" reasons for nonrenewal were (1) rumors regarding an affair with another resident of her trailer park, (2) her propensity for playing cards and not attending church regularly, and (3) her obesity, which was the "lack of dynamics" referred to in the letter.

A school district's refusal to renew a teacher's contract for violating a policy against outside employment was not upheld because the policy was not uniformly applied. See *Gosney* v. *Sonora Independent School District*, 603 F.2d 522 (5th Cir. 1979). The court declared that the district's no-outside-employment policy was not itself unconstitutional.

The United States Supreme Court has upheld a New York statute forbidding permanent certification as a public school teacher of any person who is not a United States citizen unless that person has manifested an intention to apply for citizenship. See *Ambach* v. *Norwick*, 441 U.S. 68 (1979).

State statutes often contain a catchall phrase such as "for other due and sufficient cause" as a ground for dismissal. The question of overbreadth and vagueness of such a phrase was discussed in *diLeo* v. *Greenfield*, 541 F.2d 949 (2d Cir. 1976), and the court agreed that the phrase was too general.

A probationary teacher may not be dismissed at midyear except for the same reasons that a tenured teacher may be dismissed, such as lack of funding. Dismissal must be according to the procedures applicable to midyear discharge of tenured teachers. See *Taborn* v. *Hammonds*, 83 N.C. App. 461, 350 S.E.2d 880 (1986).

In the private sector federal statutes protect union members, women, minority-group members, and the handicapped from arbitrary dismissal; however, nonunion employees in the private sector generally fall under the common-law "employment at will" legal doctrine, which allows for dismissal without cause. The doctrine is followed in most states; yet recent court actions appear to be eroding the doctrine. There have been successful court challenges when private sector dismissal involved: an employee's refusal to break a law; failure to discharge a long-service worker "fairly" or "in good faith"; improper notice of dissatisfaction; a broken promise of job security; the false advertisement of a "permanent position"; and jury service. A new phrase, "corporate due process," has been coined by those examining this area of law.

Does your state have statutory provisions dealing with nonrenewal and dismissal of teachers? What are your local school system's policies regarding nonrenewal and dismissal?

II. Freedom of Expression

Public school teachers' status regarding their rights of freedom of expression has received considerable court attention in recent years. Prior to this, several historic forces had contributed to the commonly held view that public employees, which included teachers, had a limited right of freedom of expression. The strongest force contributing to this view was that public employment was considered a privilege rather than a right. Although this distinction has been modified, the belief that public employment was a privilege had received considerable credibility, especially since 1892, as the result of Justice Holmes' often-quoted statement, "The petitioner may have a constitutional right to talk politics, but he has no constitutional right to be a policeman." This judicial view, coupled with the notion that the quid pro quo for government employees' increased job security (a result of the ravages of the spoils system), had the effect of allowing the forfeiture of certain constitutional rights. Formal restrictions of government employees' political activities were embodied in the Hatch Act at the federal level. Several states have enacted "little Hatch Acts," and other states have statutory provisions restricting certain activities of state employees and/or teachers. Such legislation, combined with a judicial view that public employment was a privilege and not a right, tended to solidify the long-held contention that government employees, which included teachers, had a limited right of freedom of expression.

A heightened concern with individual rights during the 1960s, combined with a seemingly receptive federal judiciary, resulted in some teachers challenging the position that teachers had a limited right of freedom of expression. Several Supreme Court and lower court decisions have upheld the teachers' contention.

Pickering v. *Board of Education of Township High School District 205,* a Supreme Court decision, established the principle that public school teachers have the First Amendment right of freedom of expression. Pickering was dismissed from his teaching position for writing a letter, published in a newspaper, critical of several of the school board's actions. These included allocation of school funds between educational and athletic programs and the board's and superintendent's methods of informing, or neglecting to inform, the school district's taxpayers of the real reasons why additional tax revenues were being sought for the schools. In attempting to balance the teacher's interest as a citizen in making public comments, against the state's interest in promoting the efficiency of its employees' public services, the court struck the balance on the side of the teacher.

Another Supreme Court decision, *Mt. Healthy City School District Board of Education* v. *Doyle,* involved an untenured teacher who had been in an altercation with a colleague, argued with school cafeteria employees, swore at students, and made obscene gestures to female pupils. He also called a radio station and provided them with a memorandum from the principal relating to teacher dress and appearance.

Doyle alleged that his not being rehired was due to his exercising his First Amendment rights in calling the radio station. The Court, in vacating the lower court's decision, reasoned that the proper test in such a case is whether or not the school board would have rehired the teacher even in "the absence of the protected conduct."

A provision in a collective bargaining agreement granting exclusive access to teacher mailboxes and the interschool mail system to the association that represented the majority of teachers was upheld by a five-to-four decision of the United States Supreme Court in *Perry Education Association* v. *Perry Local Educators' Association.* The Court found that the mail system was not a public forum and that ample alternative channels for communication existed, such as bulletin boards, meeting facilities, and the United States mail.

A. Tenured Teacher's Public Expression

Pickering v. Board of Education of Township High School District 205

Supreme Court of the United States, 1968
391 U.S. 563

MR. JUSTICE MARSHALL delivered the opinion of the Court.

Appellant Marvin L. Pickering, a teacher in Township High School District 205, Will County, Illinois, was dismissed from his position by the appellee Board of Education for sending a letter to a local newspaper in connection with a recently proposed tax increase that was critical of the way in which the Board and the district superintendent of schools had handled past proposals to raise new revenue for the schools. Appellant's dismissal resulted from a determination by the Board, after a full hearing, that the publication of the letter was "detrimental to the efficient operation and administration of the schools of the district" and hence, under the relevant Illinois statute, * * * that "interests of the school require[d] [his dismissal]."

* * *

In February of 1961 the appellee Board of Education asked the voters of the school district to approve a bond issue to raise $4,875,000 to erect two new schools. The proposal was defeated. Then, in December of 1961, the Board submitted another bond proposal to the voters which called for the raising of $5,500,000 to build two new schools. This second proposal passed and the schools were built with the money raised by the bond sales. In May of 1964 a proposed increase in the tax rate to be used for educational purposes was submitted to the voters by the

Board and was defeated. Finally, on September 19, 1964, a second proposal to increase the tax rate was submitted by the Board and was likewise defeated. It was in connection with this last proposal of the School Board that appellant wrote the letter to the editor * * * that resulted in his dismissal.

Prior to the vote on the second tax increase proposal a variety of articles attributed to the District 205 Teachers' Organization appeared in the local paper. These articles urged passage of the tax increase and stated that failure to pass the increase would result in a decline in the quality of education afforded children in the district's schools. A letter from the superintendent of schools making the same point was published in the paper two days before the election and submitted to the voters in mimeographed form the following day. It was in response to the foregoing material, together with the failure of the tax increase to pass, that appellant submitted the letter in question to the editor of the local paper.

The letter constituted, basically, an attack on the School Board's handling of the 1961 bond issue proposals and its subsequent allocation of financial resources between the schools' educational and athletic programs. It also charged the superintendent of schools with attempting to prevent teachers in the district from opposing or criticizing the proposed bond issue.

The Board dismissed Pickering for writing and publishing the letter. Pursuant to Illinois law, the Board was then required to hold a hearing on the dismissal. At the hearing the Board charged that numerous statements in the letter were false and that the publication of the statements unjustifiably impugned the "motives, honesty, integrity, truthfulness, responsibility and competence" of both the Board and the school administration. The Board also charged that the false statements damaged the professional reputations of its members and of the school administrators, would be disruptive of faculty discipline, and would tend to foment "controversy, conflict and dissension" among teachers, administrators, the Board of Education, and the residents of the district. * * *

* * *

To the extent that the Illinois Supreme Court's opinion may be read to suggest that teachers may constitutionally be compelled to relinquish the First Amendment rights they would otherwise enjoy as citizens to comment on matters of public interest in connection with the operation of the public schools in which they work, it proceeds on a premise that has been unequivocally rejected in numerous prior decisions of this

Court. * * * At the same time it cannot be gainsaid that the State has interests as an employer in regulating the speech of its employees that differ significantly from those it possesses in connection with regulation of the speech of the citizenry in general. The problem in any case is to arrive at a balance between the interests of the teacher, as a citizen, in commenting upon matters of public concern and the interest of the state, as an employer, in promoting the efficiency of the public services it performs through its employees.

* * * Because of the enormous variety of fact situations in which critical statements by teachers and other public employees may be thought by their superiors, against whom the statements are directed, to furnish grounds for dismissal, we do not deem it either appropriate or feasible to attempt to lay down a general standard against which all such statements may be judged. However, in the course of evaluating the conflicting claims of First Amendment protection and the need for orderly school administration in the context of this case, we shall indicate some of the general lines along which an analysis of the controlling interests should run.

An examination of the statements in appellant's letter objected to by the Board reveals that they, like the letter as a whole, consist essentially of criticism of the Board's allocation of school funds between educational and athletic programs, and of both the Board's and the superintendent's methods of informing, or preventing the informing of, the district's taxpayers of the real reasons why additional tax revenues were being sought for the schools. The statements are in no way directed towards any person with whom appellant would normally be in contact in the course of his daily work as a teacher. Thus no question of maintaining either discipline by immediate superiors or harmony among coworkers is presented here. Appellant's employment relationships with the Board and, to a somewhat lesser extent, with the superintendent are not the kind of close working relationships for which it can persuasively be claimed that personal loyalty and confidence are necessary to their proper functioning. * * *

We next consider the statements in appellant's letter which we agree to be false. The Board's original charges included allegations that the publication of the letter damaged the professional reputations of the Board and the superintendent and would foment controversy and conflict among the Board, teachers, administrators, and the residents of the district. However, no evidence to support these allegations was introduced at the hearing. So far as the record reveals, Pickering's letter was greeted by everyone but its main target, the Board, with massive apathy and total disbelief. The Board must, therefore, have decided, perhaps by analogy with the law of libel, that the statements were *per se* harmful to the operation of the schools.

However, the only way in which the Board could conclude, absent any evidence of the actual effect of the letter, that the statements contained therein were *per se* detrimental to the interest of the schools was to equate the Board members' own interests with that of the schools. Certainly an accusation that too much money is being spent on athletics by the administrators of the school system * * * cannot reasonably be regarded as *per se* detrimental to the district's schools. Such an accusation reflects rather a difference of opinion between Pickering and the Board as to the preferable manner of operating the school system, a difference of opinion that clearly concerns an issue of general public interest.

In addition, the fact that particular illustrations of the Board's claimed undesirable emphasis on athletic programs are false would not normally have any necessary impact on the actual operation of the schools, beyond its tendency to anger the Board. For example, Pickering's letter was written after the defeat at the polls of the second proposed tax increase. It could, therefore, have had no effect on the ability of the school district to raise necessary revenue, since there was no showing that there was any proposal to increase taxes pending when the letter was written.

More importantly, the question whether a school system requires additional funds is a matter of legitimate public concern on which the judgment of the school administration, including the School Board, cannot, in a society that leaves such questions to popular vote, be taken as conclusive. On such a question free and open debate is vital to informed decision-making by the electorate. Teachers are, as a class, the members of a community most likely to have informed and definite opinions as to how funds allotted to the operation of the schools should be spent. Accordingly, it is essential that they be able to speak out freely on such questions without fear of retaliatory dismissal.

In addition, the amounts expended on athletics which Pickering reported erroneously were matters of public record on which his position as a teacher in the district did not qualify him to speak with any greater authority than any other taxpayer. The Board could easily have rebutted appellant's errors by publishing the accurate figures itself, either via a letter to the same newspaper or otherwise. We are thus not presented with a situation in which a teacher has carelessly made false statements about matters so closely related to the day-to-day operations of the schools that any harmful impact on the public would be difficult to counter because of the teacher's presumed greater access to the real facts. Accordingly, we have no occasion to consider at this time whether under such circumstances a school board could reasonably require that a teacher make substantial efforts to verify the accuracy of his charges before publishing them.

What we do have before us is a case in which a teacher has made erroneous public statements upon issues then currently the subject of public attention, which are critical of his ultimate employer but which are neither shown nor can be presumed to have in any way either impeded the teacher's proper performance of his daily duties in the classroom or to have interfered with the regular operation of the schools generally. In these circumstances we conclude that the interest of the school administration in limiting teachers' opportunities to contribute to public debate is not significantly greater than its interest in limiting a similar contribution by any member of the general public.

* * *

In sum, we hold that, in a case such as this, absent proof of false statements knowingly or recklessly made by him, a teacher's exercise of his right to speak on issues of public importance may not furnish the basis for his dismissal from public employment. * * *

Notes

Justice Thurgood Marshall, who wrote the **Pickering** opinion, became the first black to be named to the Supreme Court. He was appointed by President Johnson in 1967. He had been counsel for the National Association for the Advancement of Colored People and the NAACP Legal Defense and Educational Fund for twenty-five years. During that time he argued many civil rights cases, including the 1954 landmark public school desegregation case, and he "won" twenty-nine out of the thirty-two cases in which he appeared before the Court.

Reminiscent of **Tinker,** a teacher's dismissal for refusing to remove a black armband worn in class to protest against the Vietnam War was invalidated. See *James* v. *Board of Education of Central School District No. 1,* 461 F.2d 566 (2d Cir. 1972), *cert. denied,* 409 U.S. 1042 (1972).

Although the case did not involve educators, the United States Supreme Court, in a 5–4 decision, did not extend the **Pickering** rationale to a questionnaire circulated within a district attorney's office. In this case an assistant district attorney was transferred to different job responsibilities. In protest she circulated among her co-workers a questionnaire related primarily to the transfer policy. In approving her termination, the Court contended that protecting the circulation of the questionnaire would "require a public office to be run as a roundtable for employee complaints over internal office affairs" and that normal office functioning would be endangered. Additionally, the Court asserted: "When employee expression cannot be fairly considered as relating to any matter of political, social, or other concern to the community, government officials should enjoy wide latitude in managing their offices, without intrusive oversight by the judiciary in the name of the First Amendment." However, the majority reiterated the following caveat from **Pickering:** "Because of the enormous variety of fact situations in which critical statements by . . . public employees may be thought by their superiors . . . to furnish grounds for dismissal, we do not deem it either appropriate or feasible to lay down a general standard against which all such statements may be judged." See *Connick* v. *Myers,* 461 U.S. 138 (1983).

Subsequent decisions have discussed a two-step process to determine whether a teacher's speech enjoys First Amendment protection. First, the disputed speech must address a matter of public concern. Second, the interests of the teacher must be balanced against the interests of the state as employer in rendering a public service through its employees. The second determination, known as the *"Pickering* balance," may be based on: (1) the need for harmony in the office or work place; (2) the need for a close working relationship between the speaker and co-workers and whether the speech in question undermines that relationship; (3) the time, place, and manner of the speech; (4) the context in which a dispute arises; (5) the degree of public interest in the speech; and (6) whether the speech impedes the employee's ability to perform his or her duties. See *Roberts* v. *Van Buren Public Schools,* 773 F.2d 949 (8th Cir. 1985), *Cox* v. *Dardanelle Public School District,* 790 F.2d 668 (8th Cir. 1986), and *Day* v. *South Park Independent School District,* 768 F.2d 696 (5th Cir. 1985), *cert. denied,* 474 U.S. 1101 (1986).

A teacher's dismissal based on her privately expressed complaints and opinions to her principal was addressed in *Givhan* v. *Western Line Consolidated School District,* 439 U.S. 410 (1979). Here the Court announced that teachers do not forfeit their protection against governmental abridgement of freedom of speech if they decide to express their views privately rather than publicly.

Pickering would not apply to private school teachers because a private school does not operate under the "color of the state." Nor would private school teachers necessarily have civil rights protections available to public school teachers. Rights of private school teachers would be governed by their individual contracts with their school and the degree to which a linkage existed between a private school and the state or federal government.

B. Nontenured Teacher's Freedom of Expression

Mt. Healthy City School District Board of Education v. Doyle

Supreme Court of the United States, 1977
429 U.S. 274

MR. JUSTICE REHNQUIST delivered the opinion of the Court.

Respondent Doyle sued petitioner Mt. Healthy Board of Education in the United States District Court for the Southern District of Ohio. Doyle claimed that the Board's refusal to renew his contract in 1971 violated his rights under the First and Fourteenth Amendments to the United States Constitution. After a bench trial the District Court held that Doyle was entitled to reinstatement with backpay. The Court of Appeals for the Sixth Circuit affirmed the judgment. * * *

* * *

Doyle was first employed by the Board in 1966. He worked under one-year contracts for the first three years, and under a two-year contract from 1969 to 1971. In 1969 he was elected president of the Teachers' Association, in which position he worked to expand the subjects of direct negotiation between the Association and the Board of Education. During Doyle's one-year term as president of the Association, and during the succeeding year when he served on its executive committee there was apparently some tension in relations between the Board and the Association.

Beginning early in 1970, Doyle was involved in several incidents not directly connected with his role in the Teachers' Association. In one instance, he engaged in an argument with another teacher which culminated in the other teacher's slapping him. Doyle subsequently refused to accept an apology and insisted upon some punishment for the other teacher. His persistence in the matter resulted in the suspension of both teachers for one day, which was followed by a walk-out by a number of other teachers, which in turn resulted in the lifting of the suspensions.

On other occasions, Doyle got into an argument with employees of the school cafeteria over the amount of spaghetti which had been served him; referred to students in connection with a disciplinary complaint, as "sons of bitches"; and made an obscene gesture to two girls in connection with their failure to obey commands made in his capacity as cafeteria supervisor. Chronologically the last in the series of incidents which respondent was involved in during his employment by the Board was a telephone call by him to a local radio station. It was the Board's consideration of this incident which the court below found to be a violation of the First and Fourteenth Amendments.

In February 1971, the principal circulated to various teachers a memorandum relating to teacher dress and appearance, which was apparently prompted by the view of some in the administration that there was a relationship between teacher appearance and public support for bond issues. Doyle's response to the receipt of the memorandum—on a subject which he apparently understood was to be settled by joint teacher-administration action—was to convey the substance of the memorandum to a disc jockey at WSAI, a Cincinnati radio station, who promptly announced the adoption of the dress code as a news item. Doyle subsequently apologized to the principal, conceding that he should have made some prior communication of his criticism to the school administration.

Approximately one month later the superintendent made his customary annual recommendations to the Board as to the rehiring of nontenured teachers. He recommended that Doyle not be rehired. The same recommendation was made with respect to nine other teachers in the district, and in all instances, including Doyle's, the recommendation was adopted by the Board. Shortly after being notified of this decision, respondent requested a statement of reasons for the Board's actions. He received a statement citing "a notable lack of tact in handling professional matters which leaves much doubt as to your sincerity in establishing good school relationships." That general statement was followed by references to the radio station incident and to the obscene-gesture incident.

The District Court found that all of these incidents had in fact occurred. It concluded that respondent Doyle's telephone call to the radio station was "clearly protected by the First Amendment," and that because it had played a "substantial part" in the decision of the Board not to renew Doyle's employment, he was entitled to reinstatement with backpay. * * * The District Court did not expressly state what test it was applying in determining that the incident in question involved conduct protected by the First Amendment, but simply held that the communication to the radio station was such conduct. The Court of Appeals affirmed in a brief *per curiam* opinion. * * *

Doyle's claims under the First and Fourteenth Amendments are not defeated by the fact that he did not have tenure. Even though he could have been discharged for no reason whatever, and had no constitutional right to a hearing prior to the decision not to rehire him, * * * he may nonetheless establish a claim to reinstatement if the decision not to rehire him was made by reason of his exercise of constitutionally protected First Amendment freedoms. * * *

That question of whether speech of a government employee is constitutionally protected expression necessarily entails striking "a balance between the interests of the teacher, as a citizen, in commenting upon matters of public concern and the interest of the State, as an employer, in promoting the efficiency of the public services it performs through its employees." *Pickering* v. *Board of Education,* 391 U.S. 563, 568 (1968). There is no suggestion by the Board that Doyle violated any established policy, or that its reaction to his communication to the radio station was anything more than an ad hoc response to Doyle's action in making the memorandum public. We therefore accept the District Court's finding that the communication was protected by the First and Fourteenth Amendments. We are not, however, entirely in agreement with that court's manner of reasoning from this finding to the conclusion that Doyle is entitled to reinstatement with backpay.

The District Court made the following "conclusions" on this aspect of the case:

"1) If a non-permissible reason, e.g., exercise of First Amendment rights, played a substantial part in the decision not to renew—even in the face of other permissible grounds—the decision may not stand (citations omitted).

"2) A non-permissible reason did play a substantial part. That is clear from the letter of the Superintendent immediately following the Board's decision, which stated two reasons—the one, the conversation with the radio station clearly protected by the First Amendment. A court may not engage in any limitation of First Amendment rights based on 'tact'—that is not to say that the "tactfulness" is irrelevant to other issues in this case."

* * *

At the same time, though, it stated that

"[i]n fact, as this Court sees it and finds, both the Board and the Super-intendent were faced with a situation in which there did exist in fact reason . . . independent of any First Amendment rights or exercise thereof, to not extend tenure." * * *

Since respondent Doyle had no tenure, and there was therefore not even a state-law requirement of "cause" or "reason" before a decision could be made not to renew his employment, it is not clear what the District Court meant by this latter statement. Clearly the Board legally *could* have dismissed respondent had the radio station incident never come to its attention. One plausible meaning of the court's statement is that the Board and the Superintendent not only could, but in fact *would* have reached that decision had not the constitutionally protected incident of the telephone call to the radio station occurred. We are thus brought to the issue whether, even if that were the case, the fact that the protected conduct played a "substantial part" in the actual decision not to renew would necessarily amount to a constitutional violation justifying remedial action. We think that it would not.

A rule of causation which focuses solely on whether protected conduct played a part, "substantial" or otherwise, in a decision not to rehire, could place an employee in a better position as a result of the exercise of constitutionally protected conduct than he would have occupied had he done nothing. The difficulty with the rule enunciated by the District Court is that it would require reinstatement in cases where a dramatic and perhaps abrasive incident is inevitably on the minds of those responsible for the decision to rehire, and does indeed play a part in that decision—even if the same decision would have been reached had the incident not occurred. The constitutional principle at stake is sufficiently vindicated if such an employee is placed in no worse a position than if he had not engaged in the conduct. A borderline or marginal candidate should not have the employment question resolved against him because of constitutionally protected conduct. But that same candidate ought not to be able, by engaging in such conduct, to prevent his employer from assessing his performance record and reaching a decision not to rehire on the basis of that record, simply because the protected conduct makes the employer more certain of the correctness of its decision.

This is especially true where, as the District Court observed was the case here, the current decision to rehire will accord "tenure." The long-term consequences of an award of tenure are of great moment both to the employee and to the employer. They are too significant for us to hold that the Board in this case would be precluded, because it considered constitutionally protected conduct in deciding not to rehire Doyle, from attempting to prove to a trier of fact that quite apart from such conduct Doyle's record was such that he would not have been rehired in any event.

* * *

Initially, in this case, the burden was properly placed upon respondent to show that his conduct was constitutionally protected, and that this conduct was a "substantial factor"—or, to put it in other words, that it was a "motivating factor" in the Board's decision not to rehire him. Respondent having carried that burden, however, the District Court should have gone on to determine whether the Board had shown by a preponderance of the evidence that it would have reached the same decision as to respondent's reemployment even in the absence of the protected conduct.

We cannot tell from the District Court opinion and conclusions, nor from the opinion of the Court of Appeals affirming the judgment of the District Court, what conclusions those courts would have reached had they applied this test. The judgment of the Court of Appeals is therefore vacated, and the case remanded for further proceedings consistent with this opinion.

So ordered.

Notes

The Court's opinion in **Doyle** reaffirms the doctrine that nontenured teachers have First Amendment rights, and they may establish a claim to reinstatement if the reason for not being rehired was in violation of these rights. However, as the Court stresses, engaging in constitutionally protected conduct may not prevent an employer from dismissing a teacher on the basis of his or her total performance record.

A probationary teacher may not be terminated solely for refusing to participate in a flag-salute ceremony. The teacher stood silently at attention during daily classroom recitation of the pledge of allegiance, in which school regulations required her to participate. See *Russo v. Central School District No. 1*, 469 F.2d 623 (2d Cir. 1972), *cert. denied*, 411 U.S. 932 (1973). However, see *Palmer v. Board of Education of the City of Chicago*, 603 F.2d 1271 (7th Cir. 1979), *cert. denied*, 444 U.S. 1026 (1980), which upheld the discharge of a teacher who, based on her Jehovah's Witness faith, refused to lead her kindergarten students in patriotic exercises and failed to comply with certain aspects of the curriculum. In upholding the discharge, the court distinguished between the freedom to believe in certain religious tenets and following an appropriate curriculum.

C. Use of School-System Mail

Perry Education Association v. Perry Local Educators' Association

Supreme Court of the United States, 1983
460 U.S. 37

JUSTICE WHITE delivered the opinion of the Court.

Perry Education Association is the duly elected exclusive bargaining representative for the teachers of the Metropolitan School District of Perry Township, Ind. A collective-bargaining agreement with the Board of Education provided that Perry Education Association, but no other union, would have access to the interschool mail system and teacher mailboxes in the Perry Township schools. The issue in this case is whether the denial of similar access to the Perry Local Educators'

Association, a rival teacher group, violates the First and Fourteenth Amendments.

The Metropolitan School District of Perry Township, Inc., operates a public school system of 13 separate schools. Each school building contains a set of mailboxes for the teachers. Interschool delivery by school employees permits messages to be delivered rapidly to teachers in the District. The primary function of this internal mail system is to transmit official messages among the teachers and between the teachers and the school administration. In addition, teachers use the system to send personal messages and individual school building principals have allowed delivery of messages from various private organizations.

Prior to 1977, both the Perry Education Association (PEA) and the Perry Local Educators' Association (PLEA) represented teachers in the School District and apparently had equal access to the interschool mail system. In 1977, PLEA challenged PEA's status as *de facto* bargaining representative for the Perry Township teachers by filing an election petition with the Indiana Education Employment Relations Board (Board). PEA won the election and was certified as the exclusive representative, as provided by Indiana law. * * *

The Board permits a school district to provide access to communication facilities to the union selected for the discharge of the exclusive representative duties of representing the bargaining unit and its individual members without having to provide equal access to rival unions. Following the election, PEA and the School District negotiated a labor contract in which the School Board gave PEA "access to teachers' mailboxes in which to insert material" and the right to use the interschool mail delivery system to the extent that the School District incurred no extra expense by such use. The labor agreement noted that these access rights were being accorded to PEA "acting as the representative of the teachers" and went on to stipulate that these access rights shall not be granted to any other "school employee organization"—a term of art defined by Indiana law to mean "any organization which has school employees as members and one of whose primary purposes is representing school employees in dealing with their school employer." The PEA contract with these provisions was renewed in 1980 and is presently in force.

The exclusive-access policy applies only to use of the mailboxes and school mail system. PLEA is not prevented from using other school facilities to communicate with teachers. PLEA may post notices on school bulletin boards; may hold meetings on school property after school hours; and may, with approval of the building principals, make announcements on the public address system. Of course, PLEA also may communicate with teachers by word of mouth, telephone, or the United

States mail. Moreover, under Indiana law, the preferential access of the bargaining agent may continue only while its status as exclusive representative is insulated from challenge. * * * While a representation contest is in progress, unions must be afforded equal access to such communication facilities.

PLEA and two of its members filed this action under 42 U.S.C. § 1983 against PEA and individual members of the Perry Township School Board. Plaintiffs contended that PEA's preferential access to the internal mail system violates the First Amendment and the Equal Protection Clause of the Fourteenth Amendment. They sought injunctive and declaratory relief and damages. Upon cross-motions for summary judgment, the District Court entered judgment for the defendants. * * *

The Court of Appeals for the Seventh Circuit reversed. * * * The court held that once the School District "opens its internal mail system to PEA but denies it to PLEA, it violates both the Equal Protection Clause and the First Amendment." It acknowledged that PEA had "legal duties to the teachers that PLEA does not have" but reasoned that "[w]ithout an independent reason why equal access for other labor groups and individual teachers is undesirable, the special duties of the incumbent do not justify opening the system to the incumbent alone." * * *

* * *

The primary question presented is whether the First Amendment, applicable to the States by virtue of the Fourteenth Amendment, is violated when a union that has been elected by public school teachers as their exclusive bargaining representative is granted access to certain means of communication, while such access is denied to a rival union. There is no question that constitutional interests are implicated by denying PLEA use of the interschool mail system. "It can hardly be argued that either students or teachers shed their constitutional rights to freedom of speech or expression at the schoolhouse gate." *Tinker* v. *Des Moines School District* * * * The First Amendment's guarantee of free speech applies to teacher's mailboxes as surely as it does elsewhere within the school, *Tinker* v. *Des Moines School District, supra*, and on sidewalks outside * * * . But this is not to say that the First Amendment requires equivalent access to all parts of a school building in which some form of communicative activity occurs. "[N]owhere else [have we] suggested that students, teachers, or anyone else has an absolute constitutional right to use all parts of a school building or its immediate environs for . . . unlimited expressive purposes." * * * The existence of a right of access to public property and the standard by which limitations upon such a right must be evaluated differ depending on the character of the property at issue.

In places which by long tradition or by government fiat have been devoted to assembly and debate, the rights of the State to limit expressive activity are sharply circumscribed. At one end of the spectrum are streets and parks which "have immemorially been held in trust for the use of the public and, time out of mind, have been used for purposes of assembly, communicating thoughts between citizens, and discussing public questions." * * * In these quintessential public forums, the government may not prohibit all communicative activity. For the State to enforce a content-based exclusion it must show that its regulation is necessary to serve a compelling state interest and that it is narrowly drawn to achieve that end. * * * The State may also enforce regulations of the time, place, and manner of expression which are content-neutral, are narrowly tailored to serve a significant government interest, and leave open ample alternative channels of communication. * * *

A second category consists of public property which the State has opened for use by the public as a place for expressive activity. The Constitution forbids a State to enforce certain exclusions from a forum generally open to the public even if it was not required to create the forum in the first place. * * * Although a State is not required to indefinitely retain the open character of the facility, as long as it does so it is bound by the same standards as apply in a traditional public forum. Reasonable time, place, and manner regulations are permissible, and a content-based prohibition must be narrowly drawn to effectuate a compelling state interest. * * *

Public property which is not by tradition or designation a forum for public communication is governed by different standards. We have recognized that the "First Amendment does not guarantee access to property simply because it is owned or controlled by the government." * * * In addition to time, place, and manner regulations, the State may reserve the forum for its intended purposes, communicative or otherwise, as long as the regulation on speech is reasonable and not an effort to suppress expression merely because public officials oppose the speaker's view. * * * As we have stated on several occasions, "[t]he State, no less than a private owner of property, has power to preserve the property under its control for the use to which it is lawfully dedicated." * * *

The school mail facilities at issue here fall within this third category. The Court of Appeals recognized that Perry School District's interschool mail system is not a traditional public forum: "We do not hold that a school's internal mail system is a public forum in the sense that a school board may not close it to all but official business if it chooses." * * *

The internal mail system, at least by policy, is not held open to the general public. It is instead PLEA's position that the school mail facilities have become a "limited public forum" from which it may not be excluded because of the periodic use of the system by private non-school-connected groups, and PLEA's own unrestricted access to the system prior to PEA's certification as exclusive representative.

Neither of these arguments is persuasive. The use of the internal school mail by groups not affiliated with the schools is no doubt a relevant consideration. If by policy or by practice the Perry School District has opened its mail system for indiscriminate use by the general public, then PLEA could justifiably argue a public forum has been created. This, however, is not the case. As the case comes before us, there is no indication in the record that the school mailboxes and interschool delivery system are open for use by the general public. Permission to use the system to communicate with teachers must be secured from the individual building principal. There is no court finding or evidence in the record which demonstrates that this permission has been granted as a matter of course to all who seek to distribute material. We can only conclude that the schools do allow some outside organizations such as the YMCA, Cub Scouts, and other civic and church organizations to use the facilities. This type of selective access does not transform government property into a public forum. In *Greer* v. *Spock* * * * the fact that other civilian speakers and entertainers had sometimes been invited to appear at Fort Dix did not convert the military base into a public forum. And in *Lehman* v. *Shaker Heights,* * * * a plurality of the Court concluded that a city transit system's rental of space in its vehicles for commercial advertising did not require it to accept partisan political advertising.

Moreover, even if we assume that by granting access to the Cub Scouts, YMCA's, and parochial schools, the School District has created a "limited" public forum, the constitutional right of access would in any event extend only to other entities of similar character. While the school mail facilities thus might be a forum generally open for use by the Girl Scouts, the local boys' club, and other organizations that engage in activities of interest and educational relevance to students, they would not as a consequence be open to an organization such as PLEA, which is concerned with the terms and conditions of teacher employment.

* * *

We believe it is more accurate to characterize the access policy as based on the *status* of the respective unions rather than their views. Implicit in the concept of the nonpublic forum is the right to make distinctions in access on the basis of subject matter and speaker identity. These distinctions may be impermissible in a public forum but are inherent and inescapable in the process of limiting a nonpublic forum to activities compatible with the intended purpose of the property. The touchstone for evaluating these distinctions is whether they are reasonable in light of the purpose which the forum at issue serves.

* * *

We observe that providing exclusive access to recognized bargaining representatives is a permissible labor practice in the public sector. We have previously noted that the "designation of a union as exclusive representative carries with it great responsibilities. The tasks of negotiating and administering a collective-bargaining agreement and representing the interests of employees in settling disputes and processing grievances are continuing and difficult ones." * * * Moreover, exclusion of the rival union may reasonably be considered a means of insuring labor peace within the schools. The policy "serves to prevent the District's schools from becoming a battlefield for inter-union squabbles."

* * *

* * * The judgment of the Court of Appeals is

Reversed.

Notes

Prior to **Perry,** courts had allowed the granting of exclusive rights to use bulletin boards, school mailboxes, and meeting rooms to teacher organizations to which a majority of teachers belonged. See *Connecticut State Federation of Teachers* v. *Board of Education Members,* 538 F.2d 471 (2d Cir. 1976), and *Memphis American Federation of Teachers* v. *Board of Education of Memphis City Schools,* 534 F.2d 699 (6th Cir. 1976).

A controversy grew out of attempts by a teacher association to disseminate documents to teachers, to send speakers to school meetings, and to arrange meetings at the schools. A federal appellate court held the policy concerning literature distribution to be unconstitutional both facially and as applied; however, the policy regulating visitors on school campuses was held not to be facially unconstitutional. See *Hall* v. *Board of School Commissioners of Mobile County,* 681 F.2d 965 (5th Cir. 1982).

III. Academic Freedom

Academic freedom is difficult to conceptualize definitively, since its extent is influenced by such factors as grade level and the nature of certain courses. Litigation often occurs when a school system's views regarding academic freedom are not in congruence with a teacher's perception of autonomy in determining specific subject matter for a particular class, appropriate teaching methods, and the selection of appropriate materials. In this type of litigation, teachers generally allege that they have a constitutional right to present material to which students, parents, or school officials may object. Although courts have recognized that teachers have the right to academic freedom, as with other constitutional rights, it is not absolute and must be balanced against the competing interests of the larger society.

A. Appropriate Materials

Fowler v. Board of Education of Lincoln County

United States Court of Appeals, Sixth Circuit, 1987
819 F.2d 657
cert. denied, 484 U.S. 986 (1987)

MILBURN, Circuit Judge.

Defendants, The Board of Education of Lincoln County, Kentucky, individual board members, and the Superintendent of the Lincoln County Schools, appeal from the judgment of the district court awarding reinstatement and damages to plaintiff Jacqueline Fowler on the ground that her employment was terminated in violation of her First Amendment rights. Plaintiff cross-appeals on the ground that K.R.S. § 161.-790(1), which proscribes conduct unbecoming a teacher, is unconstitutionally vague as applied to her conduct. For the reasons that follow, we vacate the judgment of the district court and dismiss plaintiff's action.

Plaintiff Jacqueline Fowler was a tenured teacher employed by the Lincoln County, Kentucky, school system for fourteen years. She was discharged in July, 1984 for insubordination and conduct unbecoming a teacher. The basis for this action was that she had an "R" rated movie, *Pink Floyd—The Wall,* shown to her high school students on the last day of the 1983–84 school year. The students in Fowler's classes were in grades nine through eleven and were of the ages fourteen through seventeen.

The day on which the movie was shown, May 31, 1984, was a noninstructional day used by teachers for completing grade cards. A group of students requested that Fowler allow the movie to be shown while she was completing the grade cards. Fowler was unfamiliar with the movie and asked the students whether it was appropriate for viewing at school. Charles Bailey, age fifteen, who had seen the movie on prior occasions, indicated that the movie had "one bad place in it." * * *

* * *

When Fowler had the movie shown on the morning of May 31, 1984, she instructed Charles Bailey, the fifteen-year-old student who had seen the movie, to edit out any parts that were unsuitable for viewing at school. He did so by attempting to cover the 25″ screen with an 8½″ by 11″ letter-sized file folder.

There is conflicting testimony as to whether, or how much, nudity was seen by the students. At the administrative hearing, several students testified that they saw no nudity. One student testified that she saw "glimpses" of nudity, but "nothing really offending." * * * It is undisputed that the audio portion of the movie, which contained enough offensive language to mandate an automatic "R" rating under motion picture industry standards, was played through the entire movie.

There is also conflicting testimony regarding the amount of sexual innuendo existing in the "unedited" version of the film. Because some parts of the film are animated, they are susceptible to varying interpretations. One particularly controversial segment of scenes is animated in which flowers appear on the screen, are transformed into the shape of male and female sex organs and then engage in an act of intercourse. This segment of the film was shown in the morning session. Other segments involving a violent rape, nudity, a suggestion of oral sex, and a naked woman and naked man in bed engaging in foreplay and intercourse were also shown in the morning.

* * *

In addition to the sexual aspects of the movie, there is a great deal of violence. One scene involves a bloody battlefield. Another shows police brutality. Another shows the protagonist cutting his chest with a razor. Another scene shows children being fed into a giant sausage machine. * * *

* * *

On July 10, 1984, plaintiff Fowler appeared with counsel at the administrative hearing. She testified that, despite the fact that she had never seen the movie before having it shown to her students, and despite the fact that she was posting grades on report cards and left the room several times while the movie was being shown, she believed it had significant value. She believed the movie portrayed the dangers of alienation between people and of repressive educational systems. She testified that she would show an edited version of the movie again if given the opportunity to explain it. She stated that she did not at any time discuss the movie with her students because she did not have enough time.

The board viewed the movie once in its entirety and once as it had been edited in the classroom. The board then retired into executive session. Following this executive session, the board returned to open session and voted unanimously to terminate plaintiff's employment for insubordination and conduct unbecoming a teacher.

* * *

The district court concluded that Fowler's conduct was protected by the First Amendment, and that she was discharged for exercising her constitutionally protected rights. Consequently, it awarded her reinstatement, back pay with interest, reimbursement of funds necessary for her reinstatement with the Kentucky Teachers Retirement System, damages for emotional distress and damage to professional reputation, compensatory damages for costs incurred in seeking new employment, costs, and attorney's fees.

* * *

The Supreme Court has consistently recognized the importance of the exercise of First Amendment rights in the context of public schools.

> First Amendment rights, applied in light of the special characteristics of the school environment, are available to teachers and students. It can hardly be argued that either students or teachers shed their constitutional rights to freedom of speech or expression at the schoolhouse gate. This has been the unmistakable holding of this Court for almost 50 years. Tinker, * * *

* * *

* * * Many courts have recognized that a teacher's First Amendment rights encompass the notion of "academic freedom" to exercise professional judgment in selecting topics and materials for use in the course of the educational process. * * *

Among the "special circumstances" which must be considered in defining the *scope* of First Amendment protection inside the classroom is the "inculcat[ion of] fundamental values necessary to the maintenance of a democratic political system." * * *

> Indeed, the "fundamental values necessary to the maintenance of a democratic political system" disfavor the use of terms of debate highly offensive or highly threatening to others. Nothing in the Constitution prohibits the states from insisting that certain modes of expression are inappropriate and subject to sanctions. The inculcation of these values is truly the "work of the schools." *Fraser* * * *

The single most important element of this inculcative process is the teacher. *Consciously or otherwise, teachers . . . demonstrate the appropriate form of civil discourse and political expression by their conduct and deportment in and out of class. Inescapably, like parents, they are role models. Fraser* (emphasis supplied). * * *

The accommodation of these sometimes conflicting fundamental values has caused great tension, particularly when the conflict arises within the classroom. * * * In the final analysis,

> [t]he ultimate goal of school officials is to insure that the discipline necessary to the proper functioning of the school is maintained among both teachers and students. Any limitation on the exercise of constitutional rights can be justified only by a conclusion, based upon reasonable inferences flowing from concrete facts and not abstractions, that the interests of discipline or sound education are materially and substantially justified. . . . "The problem in any case is to arrive at a balance between the interests of the teacher, as a citizen, in commenting upon matters of public concern and the interest of the State, as an employer, in promoting the efficiency of the public services it performs through its employees." *James*, 461 F.2d at 571–72 (quoting *Pickering* v. *Board of Education*)

* * *

I conclude that Fowler's conduct in having the movie shown under the circumstances present here did not constitute expression protected by the First Amendment. It is undisputed that Fowler was discharged for the showing of the movie, *Pink Floyd—The Wall.* Such conduct, under the circumstances involved, clearly is not "speech" in the traditional sense of the expression of ideas through use of the spoken or written word.

* * *

In the present case, plaintiff Fowler had a fifteen-year-old student show a controversial, highly suggestive and somewhat sexually explicit movie to a group of high school students aged fourteen to seventeen. She did not preview the movie, despite the fact that she had been warned that portions were unsuitable for viewing in this context. She made no attempt at any time to explain the meaning of the movie or to use it as an educational tool. Rather, she had it shown for the purpose of keeping her students occupied during a noninstructional day while she was involved in posting grades on report cards. We conclude that the statute proscribing "conduct unbecoming a teacher" gave her adequate notice that such conduct would subject her to discipline. Accordingly, we conclude that the statute is not unconstitutionally vague as applied to Fowler's conduct.

* * *

We conclude that plaintiff's conduct, although not illegal, constituted serious misconduct. Moreover, there was a direct connection between this misconduct and Fowler's work as a teacher. She introduced a controversial and sexually explicit movie into a classroom of adolescents without preview, preparation or discussion. In the process, she abdicated her function as an educator. Her having the movie shown under the circumstances involved demonstrates a blatant lack of judgment. Having considered the entire record, including the viewing of the movie, which we describe as gross and bizarre and containing material completely unsuitable for viewing by a classroom of students aged fourteen to seventeen, we conclude that such conduct falls within the concept of conduct unbecoming a teacher under Kentucky law.

Accordingly, for the reasons stated, the judgment of the district court is *vacated*, and this cause is *dismissed*.

* * *

MERRITT, Circuit Judge, dissenting.

Federal judges and local school boards do not make good movie critics or good censors of movie content. What one judge sees as "gross and bizarre," another may find, * * * mild and not very "sexually suggestive."

The movie here seems to me to present a message similar to that expounded by Dr. Spock: abuse of sex and drugs as well as various forms of mental instability and anti-social conduct are associated with an overly authoritarian society. The message is that unloving, overly rigid and authoritarian parents, teachers, judges and officials create disturbed individuals and societies. This lack of love is the figurative "wall" shown in the movie.

* * *

* * * Mrs. Fowler was not discharged because she entertained her students: she was discharged because the school board did not like the content of the movie. Mrs. Fowler proved at trial * * * that she was discharged because the board members regarded the movie as "immoral, antieducation, antifamily, antijudiciary, and antipolice." There is no support for the proposition—nor does the school board argue—that a teacher's academic freedom or a student's right to hear may be abridged simply because a school board dislikes the content of the protected speech. Furthermore, since this was a "free day" for the students, no departure from a board-mandated curriculum occurred. It is obvious, therefore, that Mrs. Fowler's discharge was prompted by the content of the movie.

Assuming that the school board could have properly discharged Mrs. Fowler for poor judgment and lack of remorse in showing an "R-rated" movie which had short scenes depicting nudity and sexual foreplay, but not for the other reasons given, this case must be decided under the "mixed-motive" analysis of *Mt. Healthy City School Dist. Bd. of Educ.* v. *Doyle.* * * * Where a plaintiff can show that her constitutionally-protected conduct was a "substantial" or "motivating" factor in the discharge decision, the employer must prove "by a preponderance of the evidence that it would have reached the same decision as to . . . re-employment even in the absence of the protected conduct." *Mt. Healthy,* * * *

* * *

In *Cohen* v. *California* * * * the Supreme Court held constitutionally protected the act of wearing a jacket bearing the words "!?X! the Draft" into a courthouse corridor. Writing for the Court, Justice Harlan stated that "while the particular four-letter word being litigated here is perhaps more distasteful than most others of its genre, it is nevertheless often true that one man's vulgarity is another's lyric. Indeed, we think it is largely because governmental officials cannot make principled distinctions in this area that the Constitution leaves matters of taste and style so largely to the individual." * * *

Therefore, I disagree with the distinction between instruction and entertainment drawn by Judge Milburn and the conflation of vulgarity and anti-establishment ideas set forth by Judge Peck. As the District Court correctly found, the school board in this case had to negate the testimony of its own members that the determinative causative factor in Mrs. Fowler's discharge was her decision to allow "antieducation, antifamily, antijudiciary, and antipolice" views to be expressed in her classroom. The District Court held that the school board failed to carry this *Mt. Healthy* burden. I agree with both of these findings. Therefore, I would affirm the judgment of the District Court.

Notes and Questions

The majority held that Fowler's conduct was not expressive or communicative and therefore was not protected by the First Amendment. Additionally, they declared that the statute proscribing "conduct unbecoming a teacher" was not unconstitutionally vague. On the other hand, the district court judge and the dissenting court of appeals judge contended that the case should have been decided under the "mixed-motive" analysis of **Mt. Healthy City School District Board of Education v. Doyle.** What is the distinction between these differing legal viewpoints?

A badly divided Supreme Court, as evidenced by seven separate opinions, addressed the issue of a school board's authority to remove books from a school library. Although there was no majority opinion, the plurality opinion does offer some guidance. School authorities may not exercise their discretion in the removal of books for narrow partisan or political purposes or to deny students access to ideas with which school authorities disagree. Additionally, the justices suggested several constitutionally legitimate standards that could be applied in determining a book's candidacy for removal, such as the book's educational suitability. Specific suitability criteria could include relevance to the curriculum and appropriateness for an age level. A book considered obscene for minors, pervasively vulgar, or offensive in its language could also be legitimately excluded. See *Board of Education, Island Trees Union Free School District No. 26 v. Pico,* 457 U.S. 853 (1982).

B. Political Speakers

Wilson v. Chancellor

United States District Court, District of Oregon, 1976
418 F. Supp. 1358

BURNS, District Judge.

Plaintiffs Wilson and Logue seek declaratory and injunctive relief from a school board order banning "all political speakers" from Molalla Union High School (MHS). They contend that the order violates the First Amendment and the equal protection clause of the Fourteenth Amendment, and is unconstitutionally vague and overbroad. * * *

Wilson teaches the political science class at MHS in which Logue was a student. This dispute arose when Wilson invited a Communist, Anton Kchmareck, to speak to that class. Wilson already and without objection had presented a Democrat, a Republican, and a member of the John Birch Society. The Communist was to be the last of this quadrumvirate through which Wilson hoped to present, in the words of the adherent, each of four points of view.

Wilson followed customary procedure and reported this invitation to the principal. The principal approved. Defendant school board discussed the invitation at its November 1975 meeting and also approved. This procedure was neither unprecedented nor customary.

The board's approval inspired mixed reviews. Two severe critics called a community meeting on December 4 where they circulated a petition asking the board to reverse the decision; approximately 800 persons eventually signed it. Several townsfolk, in letters to the local newspaper, mentioned the possibility of voting down all school budgets and voting out the members of the board.

Faced with this petition and many outraged residents, the board on December 11 reversed its decision and issued orally an order banning "all political speakers" from the high school.

*   *   *

Miss Logue contends the order violates her First Amendment right to hear the speech of others.

The right to hear customarily is invoked by prisoners denied access to periodicals, * * * members of a potential audience for a speaker prohibited from speaking, * * * or persons asserting either the public's "right to know," * * * or the emerging right of privacy * * * .

Of these cases, only the potential audience cases are applicable here. * * * These cases and my recognition that the First Amendment exists to protect a broad range of interests persuade me that Logue suffered an infringement of her First Amendment rights. * * *

Few courts have considered whether and to what extent the First Amendment protects academic freedom. Honored in Germanic tradition and prominent in academic debates, the theory rarely surfaces in legal opinions. Moreover, even its most enthusiastic advocates usually distinguish between the freedom to be accorded university professors and that to be accorded elementary and secondary school teachers. It seems to be assumed that the former engage in the search for knowledge and therefore should have far greater freedom than the latter who merely disseminate knowledge.

The Supreme Court of the United States has discussed academic freedom in "eloquent and isolated statements." * * * Lower courts have spoken more frequently, but none has clearly defined the theory's legal contours. Nor will I. This case can be decided by using purely conventional freedom of expression analysis.

A teacher's teaching is expression to which the First Amendment applies. The right to freedom of expression is not absolute; it may be restricted, and restrictions on a teacher's expression should be judged in light of the "special characteristics of the school environment."

* * *

In imposing restrictions and making other decisions, school boards should be allowed great discretion. No court should intervene merely because a board's decision seems unwise. But if school boards, in exercising their discretion, act so as to interfere impermissibly with the constitutional rights of students or teachers, or both, courts must and will intervene if their jurisdiction is properly invoked.

These considerations in mind, I address two pivotal questions: First, is a teaching method or vehicle a form of expression protected by the First Amendment? Second, if so, is the restriction at issue here reasonable?

Three cases have treated teaching methods as protected forms of expression: *Keefe* v. *Geanakos*, 418 F.2d 359 (1st Cir. 1969), *Parducci* v. *Rutland*, 316 F. Supp. 352 (M.D. Ala. 1970), and *Sterzing* v. *Fort Bend Independent School District*, 376 F. Supp. 657 (S.D. Tex. 1972).

The teacher in *Keefe* assigned his class an *Atlantic Monthly* article containing a word which "admittedly highly offensive, is a vulgar term for an incestuous son."

A school committee summoned Keefe to defend his conduct. When he was asked to agree not to use the word again, he declined. He subsequently was suspended, and sought a temporary injunction against the committee's dismissal hearing.

The district court denied an interlocutory injunction pending a decision on the merits. The court of appeals reversed, holding that plaintiff had demonstrated he probably would succeed on his lack of notice and academic freedom claims.

In *Parducci*, the teacher assigned her eleventh grade English class a Kurt Vonnegut, Jr. short story, "Welcome to the Monkey House." Several parents complained. School officials admonished the teacher not to use the story in any of her classes, and threatened to dismiss her if she refused. The teacher resigned. In her suit for injunctive relief she contended that the school's action violated her First Amendment rights.

The court recognized such a right, but concluded that it must be balanced against competing societal interests, most prominently the "state's vital interest in protecting its young people from any form of extreme propagandism in the classroom." * * * The court also recognized that *Tinker* * * * requires the state to demonstrate that

"[T]he forbidden conduct would 'materially and substantially interfere with the requirements of appropriate discipline in the operation of the school.' "
* * *

The court then held that because the assignment was appropriate and presented no threat of disruption, the teacher's dismissal for assigning the short story violated her First Amendment rights.

In *Sterzing* a teacher disclosed to his civics class his lack of opposition to interracial marriage. After several parents complained, school officials urged Sterzing to confine his teaching to the assigned textbook. He ignored this request and several times departed from the text during the ensuing five months. Shortly after Sterzing administered an allegedly propagandistic test on race relations, the school board voted to discharge him for insubordination.

The district court ordered that Sterzing be reinstated. It held that a teacher has a substantive right to choose teaching methods which serve a demonstrated educational purpose. "A responsible teacher," wrote the court, "must have freedom to use the tools of his profession as he sees fit." * * *

* * *

These cases also recognize the validity of a popular maxim, "the medium is the message." The expresser's medium can affect the persuasiveness of his message, the duration of its influence, and the size and type of audience which it reaches. The act of teaching is a form of expression, and the methods used in teaching are media. Wilson's use of political speakers was his medium for teaching; similarly, the short story was Parducci's medium, the pamphlets were Sterzing's media, and the article containing the controversial words was Keefe's medium. The various school boards which restricted the media employed by Wilson here, and by Keefe, Parducci, and Sterzing in the cases cited, suppressed expression which the First Amendment protects.

But the school boards may restrict teachers' expression if the restrictions are reasonable in light of the special circumstances of the school environment. Thus, question two: was this order reasonable?

I conclude that the order was not reasonable and therefore violated the First Amendment.

The order barred political speakers absolutely, yet no disruptions had occurred in Wilson's classes, or at other school gatherings where political subjects were discussed. Further, none were expected in the future.

The defendants have not shown that outside speakers impair high school education. If they did, the board still would lack justification for banning only outside *political* speakers. Moreover, the evidence demonstrated that the use of outside speakers is widely recommended, widely practiced, and professionally accepted.

The boards cannot justify the ban by contending that political subjects are inappropriate in a high school curriculum. Political subjects frequently are discussed at Molalla High School and other schools throughout the country, as required by law. Nor does the board have a valid interest in suppressing, as it did, political expression occurring in the course of recognized extracurricular activities.

The board cannot contend it was acting within its discretionary power to exclude incompetent speakers. It acted under pressure from those who feared, rather than doubted, the speaker's competence by banning all speakers without regard to competence.

The board's only apparent reason for issuing the order which suppressed protected speech was to placate angry residents and taxpayers. The First Amendment forbids this; neither fear of voter reaction nor personal disagreement with views to be expressed justifies a suppression of free expression, at least in the absence of any reasonable fear of material and substantial interference with the educational process.

The order, by granting school officials discretion to bar political speakers before those persons speak, creates a system of prior restraint.

Prior restraints are not unconstitutional per se, but their invalidity is heavily presumed. * * * They are valid only if they include criteria to be followed by school authorities in determining whether to allow or forbid the expression and procedural safeguards in the form of an expeditious review procedure. * * *

The Molalla board order was completely bare; it failed to include either criteria by which to define "political speakers" or procedural safeguards in any form.

The order therefore constitutes an invalid prior restraint. Although our language contains many words and phrases which require no further definition, the phrase "political speakers" is not among them. * * *

* * *

Classifications which restrain conduct protected by the First Amendment are unconstitutional unless they suitably further an appropriate governmental interest. * * * Appropriate governmental interests include the desire to promote effective education by preventing material disruptions of classroom work, substantial disorders, or invasions of the rights of others, * * * or by averting a clear and present danger * * *.

Because I already have concluded that the order did not further any appropriate governmental interests, and therefore violated the First Amendment, I must also conclude that it violated the equal protection clause. The order exists to silence absolutely the expression of an unpopular political view, solely out of fear that some will listen. This the government, acting through the school board, cannot do.

The board discriminated in a third way. It allowed Wilson to invite a Republican, a Democrat, and a member of the John Birch Society to speak to his class, but it forbade him from inviting a Communist.

The effect was discriminatory. Persons with palatable views could speak; those with less readily digestible views could not.

An order prohibiting Wilson from inviting a Republican to class after a Democrat had spoken there clearly would be discriminatory. That Wilson invited a Communist rather than a champion of the current political orthodoxy has no constitutional significance.

* * *

I do not imply that members of a community now may sue to compel schools to open their doors to particular outside speakers. Such compulsion would restrict a teacher's freedom rather than protect it, contrary to the important policies that I have outlined.

Nor do I suggest that Federal courts stand ready to regulate the regimen and to control the curricula of our public schools. A teacher is not required to have outside speakers contribute to class. I hold only that this regulation, as it applied in this particular set of facts, does not withstand constitutional scrutiny.

And I do not malign the defendant board members. Their position is sensitive, at once both a challenge and an opportunity. They serve a community in which many persons equate Communism with violence, deception, and imperialism. Yet violence, deception, and imperialism have occurred under many flags and in the name of many creeds. School boards could eliminate much of the high schools' curricula by restricting them to theories, philosophies, and practices of resolutely pacifistic, honest, nonexpansionist societies.

It seems these same residents fear that young Molallans will become young Marxists and Maoists, virtually overnight. Because Oregon law * * * requires the schools to specially emphasize our form of government, respect for the flag, and obedience to our laws, this fear seems ill-founded. Moreover, today's high school students are surprisingly sophisticated, intelligent, and discerning. They are far from easy prey to even the most forcefully expressed, cogent, and persuasive words.

Finally, I am firmly convinced that a course designed to teach students that a free and democratic society is superior to those in which freedoms are sharply curtailed will fail entirely if it fails to teach one important lesson: that the power of the state is never so great that it can silence a man or woman simply because there are those who disagree. Perhaps that carries with it a second lesson: that those who enjoy the blessings of a free society must occasionally bear the burden of listening to others with whom they disagree, even to the point of outrage.

*   *   *

Notes and Questions

Who has the *ultimate* authority to decide what will or will not take place in a classroom? a teacher? building-level administrators? central office administrators? the local school board? state department of education? state legislature? the Department of Education? courts? What factors would influence your decision? Does grade level and/or nature of the subject matter being taught affect the decision?

Apparently, academic freedom may be bargained away. A teacher's association negotiated an agreement with a provision that the board shall have the right to "determine the processes, techniques, methods and means of teaching any and all subjects." Several English teachers challenged the school board's action in directing that certain books not be purchased or assigned. The court held for the school board but contended it would have held for the teachers if the negotiated agreement had not existed. See *Cary* v. *Board of Education of Adams-Arapahoe School District 28-J*, 598 F.2d 535 (10th Cir. 1979).

IV. Drug Testing

In reaction to the alleged prevalence of drugs in American society, some school systems have attempted to screen teachers for drug use. Based on a 1966 Supreme Court decision, however, courts construe mandatory urine sampling as a search and, thus, as subject to the Fourth Amendment's prohibition of unreasonable searches. In that decision, *Schmerber* v. *California*, 384 U.S. 757 (1966), the Court held that Fourth Amendment restrictions applied to a blood test of an intoxicated driver against his will.

In assessing the reasonableness of a contested search, courts weigh several factors: the intrusiveness of the search (urine sampling in this case), the necessity of conducting the search, and the degree of suspicion that triggered the search. The necessity of testing teachers has been found to be less compelling than the need to test other governmental employees, such as police officers and bus drivers, whose use of controlled substances would pose an imminent and grave danger to public safety. Accordingly, courts have rejected blanket testing programs for teachers, that is, programs in which there was no individualized suspicion that a specific employee was using drugs. Courts have contended that a "reasonable suspicion," not the higher standard of "probable cause," is necessary when teachers are requested to undergo urinalysis to determine use of controlled substances. See *Patchogue-Medford Congress of Teachers v. Board of Education of Patchogue-Medford Union Free School District*, 119 A.D.2d 35, 505 N.Y.S.2d 888 (1986) for an exposition of these issues.

V. Dress

Personal appearance of teachers in respect to dress and grooming has received considerable attention in the courts. School authorities generally contend that proper dress and grooming establish a professional image for teachers, promote good grooming among students, and aid in the maintenance of respect and decorum in the classroom. Teachers, on the other hand, generally allege that local regulations governing their personal appearance invade their rights of privacy and liberty. Issues raised in these conflicts include the wearing of "long" hair or sideburns for males, wearing of a beard, wearing of a tie and/or jacket for a male, and improper skirt length for a female.

East Hartford Education Association v. Board of Education of Town of East Hartford

United States Court of Appeals, Second Circuit, 1977
562 F.2d 838

* * *

Before KAUFMAN, Chief Judge, and SMITH, FEINBERG, MANSFIELD, MULLIGAN, OAKES, TIMBERS, GURFEIN, VAN GRAAFEILAND and MESKILL, Circuit Judges.
On petition for Rehearing En Banc
MESKILL, Circuit Judge:
Although this case may at first appear too trivial to command the attention of a busy court, it raises important issues concerning the proper scope of judicial oversight of local affairs. The appellant here, Richard

Brimley, is a public school teacher reprimanded for failing to wear a necktie while teaching his English class. Joined by the teachers union, he sued the East Hartford Board of Education, claiming that the reprimand for violating the dress code deprived him of his rights of free speech and privacy. Chief Judge Clarie granted summary judgment for the defendants. * * * A divided panel of this Court reversed and remanded for trial. 562 F.2d at 838-856 (1977). At the request of a member of the Court, a poll of the judges in regular active service was taken to determine if the case should be reheard *en banc.* A majority voted for rehearing. We now vacate the judgment of the panel majority and affirm the judgment of the district court.

The facts are not in dispute. In February, 1972, the East Hartford Board of Education adopted "Regulations for Teacher Dress." At that time, Mr. Brimley, a teacher of high school English and filmmaking, customarily wore a jacket and sport-shirt, without a tie. His failure to wear a tie constituted a violation of the regulation and he was reprimanded for his delict. Mr. Brimley appealed to the school principal and was told that he was to wear a tie while teaching English, but that his informal attire was proper during filmmaking classes. He then appealed to the superintendent and the board without success, after which he began formal arbitration proceedings, which ended in a decision that the dispute was not arbitrable. This lawsuit followed. Although Mr. Brimley initially complied with the code while pursuing his remedies, he has apparently returned to his former mode of dress. * * *

In the vast majority of communites, the control of public schools is vested in locally-elected bodies. This commitment to local political bodies requires significant public control over what is said and done in school. * * * It is not the federal courts, but local democratic processes, that are primarily responsible for the many routine decisions that are made in public school systems. Accordingly, it is settled that "[c]ourts do not and cannot intervene in the resolution of conflicts which arise in the daily operation of school systems and which do not directly and sharply implicate basic constitutional values." * * *

* * *

Because the appellant's clash with his employer has failed to "directly and sharply implicate basic constitutional values," we refuse to upset the policies established by the school board.

Mr. Brimley claims that by refusing to wear a necktie he makes a statement on current affairs which assists him in his teaching. In his brief, he argues that the following benefits flow from his tielessness:

(a) He wishes to present himself to his students as a person who is not tied to "establishment conformity."

(b) He wishes to symbolically indicate to his students his association with the ideas of the generation to which those students belong, including the rejection of many of the customs and values, and of the social outlook, of the older generation.

(c) He feels that dress of this type enables him to achieve closer rapport with his students, and thus enhances his ability to teach.

Appellant's claim, therefore, is that his refusal to wear a tie is "symbolic speech," and, as such, "is protected against governmental interference by the First Amendment."

We are required here to balance the alleged interest in free expression against the goals of the school board in requiring its teachers to dress somewhat more formally than they might like. * * * When this test is applied, the school board's position must prevail.

Obviously, a great range of conduct has the symbolic, "speech-like" aspect claimed by Mr. Brimley. To state that activity is "symbolic" is only the beginning, and not the end, of constitutional inquiry. * * * Even though intended as expression, symbolic speech remains conduct, subject to regulation by the state. * * *

As conduct becomes less and less like "pure speech" the showing of governmental interest required for its regulation is progressively lessened. * * * In those cases where governmental regulation of expressive conduct has been struck down, the communicative intent of the actor was clear and "closely akin to 'pure speech.'" * * * Thus, the First Amendment has been held to protect wearing a black armband to protest the Vietnam War, * * * burning an American Flag to highlight a speech denouncing the government's failure to protect a civil rights leader, * * * or quietly refusing to recite the Pledge of Allegiance. * * *

In contrast, the claims of symbolic speech made here are vague and unfocused. Through the simple refusal to wear a tie, Mr. Brimley claims that he communicates a comprehensive view of life and society. It may well be, in an age increasingly conscious of fashion, that a significant portion of the population seeks to make a statement of some kind through its clothes. * * * However, Mr. Brimley's message is sufficiently vague to place it close to the "conduct" end of the "speech-conduct" continuum described above. * * * While the regulation of the school board must still pass constitutional muster, the showing required to uphold it is significantly less than if Mr. Brimley had been punished, for example, for publicly speaking out on an issue concerning school administration. * * *

At the outset, Mr. Brimley had other, more effective means of communicating his social views to his students. He could, for example, simply have told them his views on contemporary America; if he had done this in a temperate way, without interfering with his teaching duties, we would be confronted with a very different First Amendment case. * * * The existence of alternative, effective means of communication, while not conclusive, is a factor to be considered in assessing the validity of a regulation of expressive conduct. * * *

Balanced against appellant's claim of free expression is the school board's interest in promoting respect for authority and traditional values, as well as discipline in the classroom, by requiring teachers to dress in a professional manner. A dress code is a rational means of promoting these goals. * * *

This balancing test is primarily a matter for the school board. Were we local officials, and not appellate judges, we might find Mr. Brimley's arguments persuasive. However, our role is not to choose the better educational policy. We may intervene in the decisions of school authorities only when it has been shown that they have strayed outside the area committed to their discretion. If Mr. Brimley's argument were to prevail, this policy would be completely eroded. Because teaching is by definition an expressive activity, virtually every decision made by school authorities would raise First Amendment issues calling for federal court intervention.

The very notion of public education implies substantial public control. Educational decisions must be made by someone; there is no reason to create a constitutional preference for the views of individual teachers over those of their employers. * * * [T]he First Amendment claim made here is so insubstantial as to border on the frivolous. We are unwilling to expand First Amendment protection to include a teacher's sartorial choice.

Mr. Brimley also claims that the "liberty" interest grounded in the due process clause of the Fourteenth Amendment protects his choice of attire. * * * This claim will not withstand analysis.

* * *

* * * If Mr. Brimley has any protected interest in his neckwear, it does not weigh very heavily on the constitutional scales. As with most legislative choices, the board's dress code is presumptively constitutional. It is justified by the same constitutional concerns for respect, discipline and traditional values described in our discussion of the First Amendment claim.

The rights of privacy and liberty in which appellant seeks refuge are important and evolving constitutional doctrines. To date, however, the Supreme Court has extended their protection only to the most basic personal decisions. * * * Nor has the Supreme Court been quick to expand these rights to new fields. * * * As with any other constitutional provision, we are not given a "roving commission" to right wrongs and impose our notions of sound policy upon society. There is substantial danger in expanding the reach of due process to cover cases such as this. By bringing trivial activities under the constitutional umbrella, we trivialize the constitutional provision itself. If we are to maintain the vitality of this new doctrine, we must be careful not to "cry wolf" at every minor restraint on a citizen's liberty. * * *

The two other Courts of Appeals which have considered this issue have reached similar conclusions. In *Miller* v. *School District,* 495 F.2d 658 (7th Cir. 1974), the Seventh Circuit upheld a grooming regulation for teachers. * * * The First Circuit reached the same result in *Tardif* v. *Quinn,* 545 F.2d 761 (1st Cir. 1976), where a school teacher was dismissed for wearing short skirts. * * *

Both *Miller* and *Tardif* are stronger cases for the plaintiff's position than the instant case. Both involved dismissals rather than, as here, a reprimand. Moreover, *Miller* involved a regulation of hair and beards, as well as dress. Thus, Miller was forced to appear as his employers wished both on and off the job. In contrast, Mr. Brimley can remove his tie as soon as the school day ends. If the plaintiffs in *Miller* and *Tardif* could not prevail, neither can Mr. Brimley.

Each claim of substantive liberty must be judged in the light of that case's special circumstances. In view of the uniquely influential role of the public school teacher in the classroom, the board is justified in imposing this regulation. As public servants in a special position of trust, teachers may properly be subjected to many restrictions in their professional lives which would be invalid if generally applied. * * * We join the sound views of the First and Seventh Circuits, and follow *Kelley* [425 U.S. 238 (1976), a challenge to a police department's hair grooming regulations], by holding that a school board may, if it wishes, impose reasonable regulations governing the appearance of the teachers it employs. There being no material factual issue to be decided, the grant of summary judgment is affirmed.

Notes and Questions

Other federal courts of appeals have held similarly to the **East Hartford** decision. Some observers find it incongruous that school authorities have more control over teachers' dress than they do over students' dress. How would you explain this seeming incongruity?

VI. Teacher as Exemplar

Not too many years ago a teacher's lifestyle was determined to a large extent by a school system's formal or informal, often rigid rules. An example is Rules of Conduct for Teachers, which was published by a local West Virginia Board of Education in 1915.

Rules of Conduct for Teachers

1. You will not marry during the term of your contract.
2. You are not to keep company with men.
3. You must be home between the hours of 8:00 P.M. and 6:00 A.M. unless attending a school function.
4. You may not loiter downtown in ice cream stores.
5. You may not travel beyond the city limits unless you have the permission of the chairman of the board.
6. You may not ride in a carriage or automobile with any man unless he is your father or brother.
7. You may not smoke cigarettes.
8. You may not dress in bright colors.
9. You may under no circumstances dye your hair.
10. You must wear at least two petticoats.
11. Your dresses must not be any shorter than two inches above the ankle.
12. To keep the schoolroom neat and clean, you must sweep the floor at least once daily; scrub the floor at least once a week with hot, soapy water; clean the blackboards at least once a day, and start the fire at 7:00 A.M. so the room will be warm by 8:00 A.M.

All school teachers did not work under such restrictive rules. However, a belief had developed over the years that teachers should act as examples to their charges and that they should be exemplars to their students in such areas as dress, grooming, the social amenities, and morals.

Although it may at times have been difficult for a teacher to uphold the community's view of exemplary conduct, this expectation was generally well known to the teacher. In those days a teacher knew that improper dress or grooming, being seen drunk in public, and, for females, divorce would result not only in school authorities' disapproval but possibly in dismissal. The same rules applied to extramarital affairs, "improper" or "immoral" conduct on the part of single teachers, and homosexuality.

Changing lifestyles and frequent lack of agreement regarding not necessarily exemplary but merely "proper" conduct may make it difficult for a teacher to know when a norm is transgressed or exceeds school authorities' or a community's zone of acceptance. This problem is further heightened by the fact that teacher conduct which may be tolerated in a metropolitan area may not be in a small town with a homogeneous population that considers itself conservative.

Since state statutes may cite "immorality" as a ground for teacher dismissal, courts have been called upon repeatedly to adjudicate issues dealing with controversial lifestyles. Some of these issues have included homosexuality, adultery, unmarried members of the opposite sex living together, unwed pregnant teachers, sex-change operations, and sexual advances by teachers toward students. Although court decisions have not been consistent, they have determined that in certain areas of personal conduct, teachers do not necessarily have to be exemplars. An overriding factor in most of the cases is whether or not a questionable lifestyle or persuasion hampers a teacher's effectiveness. Courts have demonstrated a reluctance to enforce or bar conduct solely on the basis of conformity, historical precedent, or "expert" opinion. Rather, they have required that there be a connection between the conduct in question and actual teaching performance.

To date courts have been inconsistent in their treatment of adulterous teachers or unmarried couples living together. However, they have generally not upheld dismissals of teachers for being unmarried and pregnant but have consistently upheld dismissals based on homosexuality or sexual advances toward students. In one instance, *In re Grossman*, 127 N.J. Super. 13, 316 A.2d 39 (1974), a court upheld the dismissal of a male tenured teacher who underwent sex-reassignment surgery to change his external anatomy to that of a female.

A. Homosexual Teacher

Gaylord v. Tacoma School District No. 10

Supreme Court of Washington, 1977
88 Wash. 2d 286, 559 P.2d 1340, *cert. denied*,
434 U.S. 879 (1977)

HOROWITZ, Associate Justice.

Plaintiff-appellant, James Gaylord, appeals a judgment of the trial court upholding Gaylord's discharge from employment as a high school teacher by defendant school district. * * *

* * *

We need consider only the assignments of error which raise two basic issues: (1) whether substantial evidence supports the trial court's conclusion plaintiff-appellant Gaylord was guilty of immorality; (2) whether substantial evidence supports the findings, that as a known homosexual,

Gaylord's fitness as a teacher was impaired to the injury of the Wilson High School, justifying his discharge by the defendant school district's board of directors. The relevant findings of the trial court may be summarized as follows.

Gaylord knew of his homosexuality for 20 years prior to his trial, actively sought homosexual company for the past several years, and participated in homosexual acts. He knew his status as a homosexual, if known, would jeopardize his employment, damage his reputation and hurt his parents.

Gaylord's school superior first became aware of his sexual status on October 24, 1972, when a former Wilson High student told the school's vice-principal he thought Gaylord was a homosexual. The vice-principal confronted Gaylord at his home that same day with a written copy of the student's statement. Gaylord admitted he was a homosexual and attempted unsuccessfully to have the vice-principal drop the matter.

On November 21, 1972, Gaylord was notified the board of directors of the Tacoma School Board had found probable cause for his discharge due to his status as a publicly known homosexual. This status was contrary to school district policy No. 4119(5), which provides for discharge of school employees for "immorality." After hearing, the defendant board of directors discharged Gaylord effective December 21, 1972.

The court found an admission of homosexuality connotes illegal as well as immoral acts, because "sexual gratification with a member of one's own sex is implicit in the term 'homosexual.' " These acts were proscribed by RCW 9.79.120 (lewdness) and RCW 9.79.100 (sodomy).

After Gaylord's homosexual status became publicly known, it would and did impair his teaching efficiency. A teacher's efficiency is determined by his relationship with his students, their parents, the school administration and fellow teachers. If Gaylord had not been discharged after he became known as a homosexual, the result would be fear, confusion, suspicion, parental concern and pressure on the administration by students, parents and other teachers.

The court concluded "appellant was properly discharged by respondent upon a charge of immorality upon his admission and disclosure that he was a homosexual" and that relief sought should be denied.

Was Gaylord guilty of immorality?

Our concern here is with the meaning of immorality in the sense intended by school board policy No. 4119(5). School boards have broad management powers. * * * Under RCW 28A.58.100(1) the school board may discharge teachers for "sufficient cause." Policy No. 4119(5) adopted by the school board and in effect during the term of Gaylord's teaching contract with defendant school district permits the Tacoma

School Board of Directors to treat "immorality" as sufficient cause for discharge.

"Immorality" as used in policy No. 4119(5) does not stand alone. RCW 28A.67.110 makes it the duty of all teachers to "endeavor to impress on the minds of their pupils the principles of morality, truth, justice, temperance, humanity, and patriotism . . . " RCW 28A.70.140 requires an applicant for a teacher's certificate be "a person of good moral character." RCW 28A.70.160 makes "immorality" a ground for revoking a teacher's certificate. Other grounds include the commission of "crimes against the laws of the state." The moral conduct of a teacher is relevant to a consideration of that person's fitness or ability to function adequately as a teacher of the students he is expected to teach—in this case high school students. * * *

"Immorality" as a ground of teacher discharge would be unconstitutionally vague if not coupled with resulting actual or prospective adverse performance as a teacher. * * * The basic statute permitting discharge for "sufficient cause" (RCW 38A.58.100(1)) has been construed to require the cause must adversely affect the teacher's performance before it can be invoked as a ground for discharge. * * *

* * *

When, as in the case here, the term "immorality" has not been defined in policy No. 4119(5), it would seem reasonable to give the term its ordinary, common, everyday meaning as we would when construing an undefined term in a statute. * * *

* * *

The medical and psychological and psychiatric literature on the subject of homosexuality distinguishes between the overt homosexual and the passive or latent homosexual. An overt homosexual has homosexual inclinations consciously experienced and expressed in actual homosexual behavior as opposed to latent. A latent homosexual is one who has "an erotic inclination toward members of the same sex, not consciously experienced or expressed in overt action; opposite of overt." * * *

* * *

In the instant case Gaylord "admitted his status as a homosexual" * * * [a]nd "from appellant's own testimony it is unquestioned that homosexual acts were participated in by him, although there was no evidence of any overt act having been committed." * * *

* * *

This rule of construction concerning his admission of homosexuality is supported by evidence that Gaylord was and had been a homosexual for 20 years. He also testified that in the 2-year period before his discharge, he actively sought out the company of other male homosexuals and participated actively as a member of the Dorian Society (a society of homosexuals). He responded to a blind advertisement in the society's paper for homosexual company. He concealed his homosexuality from his parents until compelled to reveal it by the present dispute.

If Gaylord meant something other than homosexual in the usual sense, he failed to explain what he meant by his admission of homosexuality or being a homosexual so as to avoid any adverse inference, although he had adequate opportunity at trial to do so. He clearly had a right to explain that he was not an overt homosexual and did not engage in the conduct the court ascribed to him which the court found immoral and illegal. Evidence that explains the admission or qualifies it is clearly admissible. * * * There was uncontroverted evidence plaintiff was a competent and intelligent teacher so the court could reasonably assume Gaylord knew what homosexuality could mean. It was not a word to be thoughtlessly or lightly used. Gaylord's precaution for 20 years to keep his status of being a homosexual secret from his parents is eloquent evidence of his knowledge of the serious consequences attendant upon an undefined admission of homosexuality.

He testified that in June 1970 he realized that if he was "ever going to have [homosexual] friends . . . that I needed, that I was going to have to make more efforts of my own to find these people because I wasn't going to stumble across them by accident as I expected." It was about that time he joined the Dorian Society. He testified he "felt very comfortable with the people there." Eventually he began to attend a good many of their functions. On one occasion a high school boy conferred with the plaintiff about homosexuality and learned that plaintiff was "deeply involved" for a period of a month with a person whose advertisement he had answered. It would have been a simple matter for Gaylord to have explained the physical side, if any, of his relationship but he did not do so.

Our next inquiry is whether homosexuality as commonly understood is considered immoral. Homosexuality is widely condemned as immoral and was so condemned as immoral during biblical times. * * *

A sociologist testified in the instant case: "A majority of people and adults in this country react negatively to homosexuality." A psychiatrist testified "I would say in our present culture and certainly, in the last few hundred years in Western Europe and in America this [homosexuality] has been a frightening idea . . ."

The court found "sexual gratification with a member of one's own sex is implicit in the term 'homosexual.'" * * * This finding would not necessarily apply to latent homosexuals, however, the court in effect found from the evidence and reasonable inferences therefrom, it applied to Gaylord. These acts—sodomy and lewdness—were crimes during the period of Gaylord's employment and at the time of his discharge. * * *

Volitional choice is an essential element of morality. One who has a disease, for example, cannot be held morally responsible for his condition. Homosexuality is not a disease, however. Gaylord's witness, a psychiatrist, testified on cross-examination that homosexuality except in a case of hormonal or congenital defect (not shown to be present here) is not inborn. Most homosexuals have a "psychological or acquired orientation." Only recently the Board of the American Psychiatric Association has stated: "homosexuality . . . by itself does not necessarily constitute a psychiatric disorder." * * *

Nevertheless it is a disorder for those who wish to change their homosexuality which is acquired after birth. In the instant case plaintiff desired no change and has sought no psychiatric help because he feels comfortable with his homosexuality. He has made a voluntary choice for which he must be held morally responsible. * * *

The remaining question on this point is whether the repeal of the sodomy statute (RCW 9.79.100), while this case was pending, deprives sodomy of its immoral character. In the first place the repeal did not go into effect until July 1, 1976, sometime after Gaylord's discharge. Sodomy between consenting adults is no longer a crime. * * * Generally the fact that sodomy is not a crime no more relieves the conduct of its immoral status than would consent to the crime of incest.

The next question is whether the plaintiff's performance as a teacher was sufficiently impaired by his known homosexuality to be the basis for discharge. The court found that Gaylord, prior to his discharge on December 21, 1972, had been a teacher at the Wilson High School in the Tacoma School District No. 10 for over 12 years, and had received favorable evaluations of his teaching throughout this time. * * *

First, he argues his homosexuality became known at the school only after the school made it known and that he should not be responsible therefore so as to justify his discharge as a homosexual. The difficulty with this argument is twofold. First, by seeking out homosexual company he took the risk his homosexuality would be discovered. It was he who granted an interview to the boy who talked to him about his homosexual problems. The boy had been referred to Gaylord for that purpose by the homosexual friend to whom Gaylord had responded favorably in answering his advertisement in the paper of the Dorian Society. As a result of that interview the boy came away with the impression plaintiff was a homosexual and later told the assistant high school principal about the matter. The latter in turn conferred with plaintiff for the purpose of verifying the charge that had been made. It was the vice-principal's duty to report the information to his superiors because it involved the performance capabilities of Gaylord. The school cannot be charged with making plaintiff's condition known so as to defeat the school board's duty to protect the school and the students against the impairment of the learning process in all aspects involved.

Second, there is evidence that at least one student expressly objected to Gaylord teaching at the high school because of his homosexuality. Three fellow teachers testified against Gaylord remaining on the teaching staff, testifying it was objectionable to them both as teachers and parents. The vice-principal and the principal, as well as the retired superintendent of instruction, testified his presence on the faculty would create problems. There is conflicting evidence on the issue of impairment but the court had the power to accept the testimony it did on which to base complained of findings. * * * The testimony of the school teachers and administrative personnel constituted substantial evidence sufficient to support the findings as to the impairment of the teacher's efficiency.

It is important to remember that Gaylord's homosexual conduct must be considered in the context of his position of teaching high school students. Such students could treat the retention of the high school teacher by the school board as indicating adult approval of his homosexuality. It would be unreasonable to assume as a matter of law a teacher's ability to perform as a teacher required to teach principles of morality * * * is not impaired and creates no danger of encouraging expression of approval and of imitation. Likewise to say that school directors must wait for prior specific overt expression of homosexual conduct before they act to prevent harm from one who chooses to remain "erotically attracted to a notable degree towards persons of his own sex and is psychologically, if not actually disposed to engage in sexual activity prompted by this attraction" is to ask the school directors to take an unacceptable risk in discharging their fiduciary responsibility of managing the affairs of the school district.

* * * It must be shown that "the conduct of the individual may reasonably be expected to interfere with the ability of the person's fitness in the job or against the ability to discharge its responsibility." * * * These principles are similar to those applicable here. The challenged findings and conclusions are supported by substantial evidence.

Affirmed.

DOLLIVER, Associate Justice (dissenting).

The appellant, Mr. Gaylord, had been a teacher at Wilson High School for over 12 years at the time of his discharge. In college, he had been an outstanding scholar: he graduated Phi Beta Kappa from the University of Washington and was selected "Outstanding Senior" in the political science department. He later received a masters degree in librarianship. As a teacher, the evaluations made of Mr. Gaylord were consistently favorable. The most recent evaluation of this teaching performance stated that "Mr. Gaylord continues his high standards and thorough teaching performance. He is both a teacher and student in his field."

Despite this outstanding record, the trial court found that Mr. Gaylord should be discharged for "immorality." To uphold this dismissal, we must find substantial evidence supporting the finding that Mr. Gaylord was discharged for "sufficient cause."

*   *   *

There is not a shred of evidence in the record that Mr. Gaylord participated in any of the acts stated above. While we have held in the past that "sufficient cause" requires certain *conduct* * * * , we are presented here with a record showing no illegal or immoral conduct; we have only an admission of a homosexual status and Gaylord's testimony that he sought male companionship. * * *

Undoubtedly there are individuals with a homosexual identity as there are individuals with a heterosexual identity, who are not sexually active. Mr. Gaylord, for all we know, may be one of these individuals. Certainly in this country we should be beyond drawing severe and far-reaching inferences from the admission of a status—a status which may be no more than a state of mind. Furthermore, there are homosexual activities involving a physical relationship which are not prohibited by statute. * * *

The trial court made a most puzzling finding that, "From appellant's own testimony it is unquestioned that homosexual acts were participated in by him, although there was no evidence of any overt acts having been committed." The trial court essentially found that, as an admitted homosexual, unless Mr. Gaylord denied doing a particular immoral or illegal act, he can be assumed to have done the act. The court has placed upon the appellant the burden to negate what it asserts are the implications that may be drawn from his testimony although he never was accused of participating in acts of sodomy or lewdness.

We must require here, as we have done in the past, proof of conduct to justify a dismissal. The only conceivable testimony on conduct was the comment of the student that Gaylord and another male were "deeply involved" for about a month. This hardly qualifies as testimony either as to "immorality," sodomy or lewdness. Finding no conduct, I am unwilling to take the leap in logic accepted by the majority that admission of a status or identity implies the commission of certain illegal or immoral acts.

* * *

Surely the majority has adopted a novel approach. Mr. Gaylord was never at any time accused of performing any "homosexual acts." Yet because of his declared status, he must assume the burden of proving he did not commit certain illegal or immoral acts which have at no time been referred to or mentioned, much less described, by the school board. Presumably under this reasoning, an unmarried male who declares himself to be heterosexual will be held to have engaged in "illegal or immoral acts." The opportunities for industrious school districts seem unlimited.

The majority goes to great lengths to differentiate between an overt and a latent homosexual. Authority is cited that overt homosexuality is "consciously experienced and expressed in actual homosexual behavior." Yet there is no evidence in the record of any actual behavior of acts, and the findings of the trial court specifically state "there was no evidence of any overt act having been committed." The real problem faced by the majority is that the term "homosexual" is not mentioned once in the Revised Code of Washington. There is no law in this state against being a homosexual. All that is banned (prior to July 1, 1976) are certain acts, none of which Mr. Gaylord was alleged to have committed and none of which can it be either assumed or inferred he committed simply because of his status as a homosexual.

The second glaring error in this proceeding is the respondent's failure to establish that Mr. Gaylord's performance as a teacher was impaired by his homosexuality. As pointed out by the trial court in its findings, the evidence is quite clear that, having been a homosexual for the entire time he taught at Wilson High School, the fact of Mr. Gaylord's homosexuality did not impair his performance as a teacher. In other words, homosexuality per se does not preclude competence. * * *

The evidence before the court is uncontroverted—Mr. Gaylord carefully kept his private life quite separate from the school. * * * He made no sexual advances toward his professional contemporaries or his students. There is absolutely no evidence that Mr. Gaylord failed in any way to perform the duties listed in RCW 28A.67.110. In over 12 years of teaching at the same school, his best friends on the teaching staff were unaware of his homosexuality until the time of his discharge. Gaylord did not use his classroom as a forum for discussing homosexuality. Given the discretion with which Gaylord conducted his private life, it appears that public knowledge of Gaylord's homosexuality occurred, as the trial court found, at the time of his dismissal. * * *

At the trial, a variety of witnesses speculated on the effect that Gaylord's homosexuality might have on his effectiveness in the classroom. The speculation varied considerably. Certainly there were witnesses who testified that Gaylord's effectiveness would be damaged. There were also those who testified to the contrary. As a result, the trial court found that "the continued employment of appellant after he became known as a homosexual would result, had he not been discharged, in confusion, suspicion, fear, expressed parental concern and pressure upon the administration." The question this court must ask is whether a finding of detrimental effect can be made on the basis of conjecture alone.

* * *

Historically, the private lives of teachers have been controlled by the school districts in many ways. There was a time when a teacher could be fired for a marriage, a divorce, or for the use of liquor or tobacco. * * * Although the practice of firing teachers for these reasons has ceased, there are undoubtedly those who could speculate that any of these practices would have a detrimental effect on a teacher's classroom efficiency as well as cause adverse community reaction. I find such speculation to be an unacceptable method for justifying the dismissal of a teacher who has a flawless record of excellence in his classroom performance. * * *

What if Mr. Gaylord's status was as a black, a Roman Catholic, or a young heterosexual single person, instead of a male homosexual? Would his dismissal be handled in such a manner? Mere speculation coupled with status alone is not enough. * * * In this finding, substitute the words "black" or "female" for "homosexual" and the defect of the majority approach is brought into sharp focus.

* * *

Notes and Questions

Tangential to the issue of dismissal of a homosexual teacher for unfitness or immorality is a freedom-of-expression issue; namely, may teachers express their sexual preferences or advocate homosexuality? Courts have addressed these issues in several decisions.

A nontenured vocational guidance counselor informed several colleagues that she was bisexual and had a female lover. In upholding her nonrenewal a federal appellate court held that her First Amendment rights had not been violated. In citing *Connick* v. *Meyers*, 461 U.S. 138 (1983), the court stated, "If a public employee's statement cannot be fairly characterized as constituting speech on a matter of public concern, it is unnecessary to scrutinize the reasons for the discharge." The court opined that the teacher was speaking in her personal interest and that there was no evidence of any public concern in the high school or community with the issue of bisexuality among school personnel. See *Rowland* v. *Mad River School District*, 730 F.2d 444 (6th Cir. 1984), *cert. denied*, 470 U.S. 1009 (1985). Justice Brennan, joined by Justice Marshall in a lengthy dissent, chastised the Court's majority for not accepting the case for review.

The Tenth Circuit Court of Appeals upheld a portion of an Oklahoma statute proscribing homosexual activity, but it declared unconstitutional the portion prohibiting the advocacy of such activity. Specifically, the court found fault with a section that barred "advocating, soliciting, imposing, encouraging or promoting public or private homosexual activity in a manner that creates a substantial risk that such conduct will come to the attention of school children or school employees . . ." The court stated that this provision purported to regulate "pure speech" and that the first amendment protects advocacy of legal as well as illegal conduct as long as such advocacy does not incite imminent lawlessness. See *National Gay Task Force* v. *Board of Education of Oklahoma City*, 729 F.2d 1270 (10th Cir. 1984), *aff'd. by an equally divided Court*, 470 U.S. 903 (1985).

A number of other decisions have addressed the issue of dismissing or revoking certificates of homosexual teachers. See *Ross* v. *Springfield School District No. 19*, 71 Or. App. 111, 691 P.2d 509 (1984), *Gish* v. *Board of Education of the Borough of Paramus*, 145 N.J. Super. 108, 366 A.2d 1337 (1977), *cert. denied*, 434 U.S. 879 (1977), *Board of Education of Long Beach Unified School District* v. *Jack M.*, 566 P.2d 602 (Cal. 1977), *Burton* v. *Cascade School District Union High School No. 5*, 512 F.2d 850 (9th Cir. 1975), *Acanfora* v. *Board of Education of Montgomery County*, 491 F.2d 498 (4th Cir. 1974), *McConnell* v. *Anderson*, 451 F.2d 193 (8th Cir. 1971), and *Morrison* v. *State Board of Education*, 1 Cal. 3d 214, 461 P.2d 375 (1969).

The United States Supreme Court, in a sharply disputed five-to-four decision, upheld a Georgia law proscribing sodomy. Under the statute consenting adults who engage in oral or anal sexual relations are guilty of a felony punishable by twenty years in prison. See *Bowers* v. *Hardwick*,

478 U.S. 186 (1986). Approximately two dozen states have laws under which substantial jail sentences may be imposed for sodomy.

Do school authorities have a duty to ferret out homosexual teachers? A reading of several decisions suggests that teaching effectiveness is impaired if homosexual teachers bring undue attention to themselves. Does this suggest that homosexuality among teachers is acceptable if it is not admitted or overt?

B. Adulterous Teacher

Erb v. Iowa State Board of Public Instruction

Supreme Court of Iowa, 1974
216 N.W.2d 339

McCORMICK, Justice.

In this appeal plaintiff Richard Arlan Erb challenges the revocation of his teaching certificate. The certificate was revoked by defendant Board of Educational Examiners after a hearing on July 16, 1971. Erb brought an action in certiorari alleging the board's action was illegal. After the trial the writ of certiorari was annulled. Erb appealed. We reverse.

* * *

Erb, a native Iowan, military veteran, and holder of a master's degree in fine arts, received his Iowa teaching certificate in 1963. Since then he has taught art in the Nishna Valley Community School which serves an area including the towns of Strahn, Emerson, Hastings, and Stanton. He resides in Emerson, is married and has two young sons. In addition to teaching he has coached wrestling, assisted with football, and acted as senior class sponsor.

The complaint against Erb was made by Robert M. Johnson, a farmer whose wife Margaret taught home economics in the Nishna Valley School. Johnson told the board his goal was removal of Erb from the school and not revocation of his teaching certificate. He read an extensive statement in which he detailed his observations relating to an adulterous liaison between Erb and Johnson's wife which began and ended in spring 1970.

Margaret planned to quit teaching and open a boutique in Red Oak. Her association with Erb began in early spring when he agreed to assist her with design of the store. They saw each other often. By May, Johnson became suspicious of Margaret's frequent late-night absences from home. He suspected Margaret and Erb were meeting secretly and engaging in illicit activity in the Johnson automobile. One night in May he hid in the trunk of the car. Margaret drove the car to school, worked there for some time, and later drove to a secluded area in the country where she met Erb. Margaret and Erb had sexual intercourse in the back seat of the car while Johnson remained hidden in the trunk. Johnson did not disclose his presence or his knowledge of the incident.

Instead he consulted a lawyer with a view toward divorcing Margaret. He told the board he was advised his interests in a divorce action would be better served if he had other witnesses to his wife's misconduct. After several days of fruitless effort to catch Margaret and Erb in a compromising situation, he and his "raiding party" eventually located them one night in June parked in a remote area. Johnson and the others surrounded the car and took photographs of Margaret and Erb who were partially disrobed in the back seat. Johnson told Margaret not to come home and that further communication would be through lawyers. He told Erb to disclose the affair to his wife.

Erb did so. He and Margaret terminated their affair. Erb offered to resign his teaching position, but the local school board unanimously decided not to accept his resignation. The board president testified Erb's teaching was highly rated by his principal and superintendent, he had been forgiven by his wife and the student body, and he had maintained the respect of the community. Erb was retained for the ensuing school year and continued to teach in the Nishna Valley school.

Witnesses before the board included Erb's past and present high school principals, his minister, a parent of children in the school, and a substitute teacher. All vouched for his character and fitness to teach. His superintendent gave essentially the same testimony in district court. The board refused to allow Erb's attorney to cross-examine Johnson or two witnesses in support of Erb's character and fitness to teach. Trial court ruled in its pretrial order that under the admitted record Erb's teacher-student relationship had not been impaired by his conduct.

The board voted five to four to revoke Erb's teaching certificate and, without making any findings of fact or conclusions of law, ordered it revoked. Revocation was stayed by trial court and then by this court pending outcome of the certiorari action and appeal. Trial court held Erb's admitted adulterous conduct was sufficient basis for revocation of his certificate and annulled the writ.

* * * In this appeal Erb contends the board acted illegally (1) in denying his right to cross-examine witnesses against him and limiting the number of his witnesses, (2) in failing to make findings, and (3) in revoking his teaching certificate without substantial evidence that he is not morally fit to teach.

Limitations at the hearing. Erb did not object before the board to the board's denial of his right of cross-examination and limitation on the number of his witnesses. These questions cannot be presented for the first time here. Erb was obliged to raise them before the board and the trial court. * * * Since he did not do so he failed to preserve error in these respects for review here.

Failure of the board to make findings. A different situation exists concerning the board's failure to make findings of fact. Erb's first opportunity to complain of the absence of board findings was in his certiorari action, and he did raise the issue there. We hold the board acted illegally in failing to make findings of fact.

Although Iowa does not have an administrative procedure act to guide administrative boards, we have held such boards are required, even without statutory mandate, to make findings of fact on issues presented in any adjudicatory proceeding. Such findings must be sufficiently certain to enable a reviewing court to ascertain with reasonable certainty the factual basis and legal principle upon which the administrative body acted. * * *

The board violated this precept in the present case. No findings were made. This would be sufficient basis to hold trial court should have sustained the writ of certiorari. However, reversing the case on that basis would return the case to the board which could make its findings on the present record and would not answer the remaining issue whether there is substantial evidence in the record which would permit the board to find Erb is not morally fit to teach. If that issue is resolved favorably to Erb, the case will be ended now in his favor rather than sent back to the board for findings.

Sufficiency of the evidence. Since the board made no findings there is no intelligible way to determine what interpretation the board gave to its statutory authorization to revoke the certificate of one not "morally fit to teach." But nothing prevents us from determining whether there is substantial evidence in the record which would have supported revocation if the proper standard had been applied. Erb contends there is not. We agree. We will first examine the standard and then the sufficiency of the evidence.

This court has not previously been called upon to decide what constitutes moral unfitness to teach. The legislature provided no definition in code chapter 260.

* * *

The board contends the fact Erb admitted adultery is sufficient in itself to establish his unfitness to teach. This assumes such conduct automatically and invariably makes a person unfit to teach. We are unwilling to make that assumption. It would vest the board with unfettered power to revoke the certificate of any teacher whose personal, private conduct incurred its disapproval regardless of its likely or actual effect upon his teaching. The legislature did not give the board that kind of power in Code § 260.23. The label applied to the teacher's conduct is only a lingual abstraction until given content by its likely or actual effect on his fitness to teach. *Morrison* v. *State Board of Education,* 1 Cal. 3d 214, 82 Cal. Rptr. 175, 194, 461 P.2d 375, 394 (1969); * * * 68 Am Jur. 2d Schools § 134 at 465 ("Where the courts have been presented with the question whether or not specific conduct of a teacher constitutes moral unfitness which would justify revocation, they have apparently required that the conduct must adversely affect the teacher-student relationship before revocation will be approved.").

As observed by the Morrison court, "Surely incidents of extramarital heterosexual conduct against a background of years of satisfactory teaching would not constitute 'immoral conduct' sufficient to justify revocation of a life diploma without any showing of an adverse effect on fitness to teach." * * *

We emphasize the board's power to revoke teaching certificates is neither punitive nor intended to permit exercise of personal moral judgment by members of the board. Punishment is left to the criminal law, and the personal moral views of board members cannot be relevant. A subjective standard is impermissible and contrary to obvious legislative intent. The sole purpose of the board's power under § 260.23 is to provide a means of protecting the school community from harm. Its exercise is unlawful to the extent it is exercised for any other purpose.

In Morrison the California court discussed factors relevant to application of the standard:

"In determining whether the teacher's conduct thus indicates unfitness to teach the board may consider such matters as the likelihood that the conduct may have adversely affected students or fellow teachers, the degree of such adversity anticipated, the proximity or remoteness in time of the conduct, the type of teaching certificate held by the party involved, the extenuating or aggravating circumstances, if any, surrounding the conduct, the praiseworthiness or blameworthiness of the motives resulting in the conduct, the likelihood of the recurrence of the questioned conduct, and the extent to which disciplinary action may inflict an adverse impact or chilling effect upon the constitutional rights of the teacher involved or other teachers."
* * *

These factors have relevance in deciding whether a teacher is morally fit to teach under Code § 260.2. Since the same standard is applicable in determining whether a certificate should be revoked under Code § 260.23, a certificate can be revoked only upon a showing before the board of a reasonable likelihood that the teacher's retention in the profession will adversely affect the school community.

There was no evidence of such adverse effect in the present case. No one even asserted such an effect. The complainant himself acknowledged his purpose was to remove Erb from the school rather than from teaching. The evidence showed Erb to be a teacher of exceptional merit. He is dedicated, hardworking and effective. There was no evidence to show his affair with Margaret Johnson had or is likely to have an adverse effect upon his relationship with the school administration, fellow teachers, the student body, or the community. Overwhelming and uncontroverted evidence of local regard and support for Erb is a remarkable testament to the ability of a community to understand, forgive and reconcile.

There was no evidence other than that Erb's misconduct was an isolated occurrence in an otherwise unblemished past and is not likely to recur. The conduct itself was not an open or public affront to community mores; it became public only because it was discovered with considerable effort and made public by others. * * * Erb made no effort to justify it; instead he sought to show he regretted it, it did not reflect his true character, and it would not be repeated.

* * * [W]e are persuaded the evidence adduced before the board would not support a finding that Erb is morally unfit to teach in Iowa.

The board acted illegally in revoking his certificate. Trial court erred in annulling the writ of certiorari.

Reversed.

Notes and Questions

Would a state supreme court have ruled the same way in the *Erb* case fifty years ago?

A school board's dismissal, in midterm, of a single female elementary school teacher who was openly living with a man was upheld. The court in *Sullivan* v. *Meade Independent School District No. 101*, 530 F.2d 799 (8th Cir. 1976), contended that

> . . . Ms. Sullivan's conduct violated local mores, that her students were aware of this, and that, because of the size of the town, this awareness would continue. . . . Ms. Sullivan was shown to have generated deep affection from her students, increasing the probability of emulation. . . .
> (P. 804)

* * *

. . . [however,] the parameters of the newly evolving constitutional right to privacy are not yet clear. While the right of a couple to live together without benefit of matrimony eventually may be held to fall within the penumbra of the constitutional right to privacy, it had not been so held at the time the Board dismissed the appellant. . . . (P. 806)

Would the dismissal by the school board of a male in similar circumstances have been upheld by this court?

See *Fisher* v. *Snyder,* 476 F.2d 375 (8th Cir. 1973), in which the court did not uphold the dismissal of a high school teacher accused of having men not related to her staying in her apartment. This court concluded that:

. . . while a school board may legitimately inquire into the character and integrity of its teachers, . . . it must be certain that it does not arbitrarily or capriciously dismiss a teacher based on unsupported conclusions drawn from such inquiries.

* * *

But here, there is no proof of improper conduct. The only whit of evidence offered as support for the board's conclusion that Mrs. Fisher was guilty of unbecoming conduct was the fact that she had overnight guests. But the presence of these guests in her home provides no inkling beyond subtle implication and innuendo which would impugn Mrs. Fisher's morality. Idle speculation certainly does not provide a basis in fact for the board's conclusory inference that "there was strong potential of sexual misconduct" and that, therefore Mrs. Fisher's activity was "social misbehavior that is not conducive to the maintenance of the integrity of the public school system." We agree with the district court that "At most, the evidence may be said to raise a question of Mrs. Fisher's good judgment in her personal affairs, when measured against an undefined standard which someone could suppose exists in a small town in Nebraska." (Pp. 377–78)

What appears to be the reason for the seemingly opposite holdings in *Sullivan* and *Fisher?*

C. Criminal Activities

Gillett v. Unified School District No. 276

Supreme Court of Kansas, 1980
605 P.2d 105

PRAGER, Justice:

This case involves a controversy between a school teacher and school board over the nonrenewal of her teaching contract. Unified school district No. 276 appeals from a judgment of the district court reversing the school board's decision not to renew the teacher's employment contract. The trial court ordered the teacher to be reinstated with back pay.

The facts in the case are not greatly in dispute and essentially are as follows: Unified school district No. 276 is located in Jewell County. Jessie Mae Gillett is a tenured teacher who had been continuously employed by the school district for a period of seven years. Her last term of employment covered the 1976–77 school year. On March 11, 1977, the school board delivered to Mrs. Gillett a notice of nonrenewal of her teaching contract for the following year pursuant to K.S.A. 1977 Supp. 72–5437. The notice, which was contained in a letter from the president and clerk of the school board, was in the form required by statute. The reason given for nonrenewal was the existence of criminal charges of shoplifting pending against Mrs. Gillett in Hastings, Nebraska. Mrs. Gillett promptly filed a request for a due process hearing on the matter. On May 5, 1977, the board served on the teacher a notice which contained a supplemental list of reasons for nonrenewal including the following:

1. Inability to properly handle school funds;
2. Excessive absences from teaching school duties for allegedly being ill;
3. Improper use of sick leave;
4. Physical and mental instability; and
5. Loss of community, student, and school board respect for this teacher.

Mrs. Gillett, through her counsel, objected to the consideration of the supplemental reasons contending they were not timely served. The hearing committee overruled the objection, stating that it would consider the supplementary reasons.

* * *

The recommendation of the hearing committee was delivered to the school board, which considered all of the evidence presented in the case together with arguments and briefs of counsel. The board unanimously decided to follow its previous decision of nonrenewal of Mrs. Gillett's contract. The board made no findings of fact and gave no specific reason in writing for rejecting the committee's recommendation. Mrs. Gillett then appealed the school board's decision to the district court, using K.S.A. 60–2101(d) as required by K.S.A. 1977 Supp. 72–5443. The district court reviewed the transcript of the evidence presented at the due process hearing and heard arguments of counsel. The district court entered judgment in favor of Mrs. Gillett, ordering her reinstated with back pay. * * *

* * *

The primary issue raised on this appeal is whether the district court erred in holding that the school board had failed to present substantial evidence to support its reason for nonrenewal. From the evidentiary record in the case, we have concluded that there was substantial competent evidence showing good cause which justified the school board in its decision not to renew the teaching contract of Mrs. Gillett. In the original notice of nonrenewal served on the teacher on March 11, 1977, the reason given for nonrenewal was the criminal charges pending against Mrs. Gillett in Hastings, Nebraska. The evidence of the pendency of these two criminal cases was undisputed. Although Mrs. Gillett did not take the stand herself, the evidence presented on her behalf showed without question that she had taken articles at two stores in Hastings, Nebraska, on October 16, and November 17, 1976. The teacher did not deny that she took the articles of property. Her defense to the accusation was that, because of her mental condition at the time, she was not criminally responsible for her actions. Dr. Dale W. Peters, a practicing psychiatrist, testified that he was a consultant to the Sunflower Guidance Center in Concordia. Mrs. Gillett was referred to that center for psychiatric evaluation in March of 1977. Dr. Peters examined her to determine her mental capacity and state of health, primarily for determining her mental state in relationship to the shoplifting incidents in Hastings, Nebraska. From these examinations, he concluded that, although she was not mentally ill, she was subject to altered states of consciousness resulting from sensitive reactions to a wide variety of foods. Various tests showed her sensitive to numerous foods which at times interfered with the functioning of her brain cells. During these attacks, she would become mentally disturbed and her judgment adversely affected.

At the time of her arrests in Hastings, Nebraska, it appeared that Mrs. Gillett was acting strangely and out of touch with reality. The thrust of Dr. Peters testimony was that, at the time of the shoplifting incidents in Hastings, Nebraska, Mrs. Gillett, being in an altered state of consciousness, was not responsibile for her actions. The evidence showed that she had been involved in another shoplifting incident in 1973. Apparently on a number of occasions, she had become confused and lost while driving her motor vehicle. Each of these situations involved an altered state of consciousness which came on gradually. Dr. Peters testified that acute episodes can be dramatic. Such episodes could last up to one hour and could occur at any time, including during classroom hours. Dr. Peters conceded that Mrs. Gillett could again be involved in shoplifting incidents in the future and that she was still under treatment at the time of the hearing. Although Dr. Peters was of the opinion that there was no danger to the students in the classroom, he indicated an attack during class could be disruptive. Similar attacks could occur either from the consumption of certain foods or from a withdrawal from such foods. At the time of the hearing Mrs. Gillett was in the course of an elimination diet which, hopefully, might eliminate her problem. If it did not work, then additional testing and treatment would be required. Dr. Peters mentioned over 80 foods which could cause Mrs. Gillett to go into an altered state of consciousness. He further stated that this list was inconclusive and that there might be other foods which could affect her in the same way.

A teacher testified that at one time she had observed Mrs. Gillett in an altered state of consciousness while seated in her automobile. After the arrests at Hastings, she heard a student discussing the fact that Mrs. Gillett had been arrested. Another teacher testified that she had also heard students mention the fact that Mrs. Gillett had been arrested. This was the first time the teacher had known about it. There was no evidence presented at the hearing as to the ultimate outcome of the criminal actions. There was testimony tending to show that Mrs. Gillett had been careless in keeping candy sale proceeds in her desk drawer and in failing to make daily deposits at the bank as directed by the school superintendent. However, there was no proof of any misappropriation or loss of any money as the result of Mrs. Gillett's handling of the school funds. In regard to excessive absences from teaching duties for allegedly being ill, the record is devoid of any misconduct on the part of the teacher in this regard. In regard to loss of community, student, and school respect for the teacher, the president of the school board testified that in his opinion the school board had community support in the nonrenewal of Mrs. Gillett's contract. A substitute teacher testified about a classroom incident where students were caught copying. When she told them copying wasn't allowed, the students responded: "The teacher can get away with it."

Mr. Ralph Hooten, who was president of the school board at the time the letter of nonrenewal was delivered to Mrs. Gillett, testified that the school board had unanimously decided that Mrs. Gillett's teaching contract should not be renewed because of the criminal charges of shoplifting pending in Nebraska. This conclusion was reached only after substantial discussion by the board over a period of hours. The board had concluded that these shoplifting charges reduced her efficiency as a teacher. It appeared to him that, with the charges pending, the learning atmosphere would be improved if her contract was not renewed. Mr. Hooten stated that the board was aware of a similar charge of shoplifting in the year 1973 which was subsequently dismissed. At the time the board decided not to pursue the matter further. When the charges came up again in 1976, the board felt that they could not ignore those charges, having knowledge of the prior incident in 1973. It is fair to conclude, from

Mr. Hooten's testimony, that the school board was very much concerned about the criminal charges against Mrs. Gillett, that the board spent hours discussing the situation, and that they decided to nonrenew her contract rather than to terminate her in midyear.

The issue to be determined here is whether there is substantial evidence in the record sufficient to establish good cause, justifying the school board's decision of nonrenewal of the teaching contract. The district court found that there was not. We have concluded there was. The problem presented in this case was obviously one of great difficulty for the school board. The trial court specifically found that the school board had not arbitrarily and fraudulently refused to accept the findings of the hearing committee. The district court was correct in that finding. It is difficult to reconcile that finding with the additional finding that there was no substantial evidence to support the board's reason for nonrenewal. Here the evidence was undisputed that, for a period of at least three years, the teacher had been subject to altered states of consciousness, during which she did not know what she was doing and her judgment and her conduct were adversely affected. At the time of the hearing, a testing and treatment program for Mrs. Gillett had been undertaken but not completed. She was attempting to get to the cause of her problem and was taking appropriate action to do something about it. However, we do not believe that, at that time, the school board acted unreasonably in concluding that it would be for the best interests of the school system to nonrenew Mrs. Gillett's teaching contract for the following school year.

We think it significant that in this case the teacher did not personally take the witness stand to give her own explanation as to her physical and mental condition or to deny that she, knowingly with larcenous intent, took property from the stores in Hastings, Nebraska. She did not testify that the treatment then being administered was effective or was beginning to solve her problem. She did not testify as to her relationship with the students, or with other teachers, or with the school administrators. Not a single witness testified as to any contributions she was making to the educational program of the school district.

We cannot in good conscience find from the evidence that the board's action was not taken in good faith, or that it was arbitrary, irrational, unreasonable, or irrelevant to the school board's objective of maintaining an efficient school system for the students in the school district. It follows that the judgment of the district court must be reversed and the case remanded to the district court with directions to enter judgment in favor of the school board.

It is so ordered.

Note

In a similar case a permanent teacher's indefinite contract was terminated because of three instances of alleged immoral conduct: stealing a teapot that was a prop in a school play, twenty dollars from a basketball game's receipts, and a set of the school's books. See *Kimble* v. *Worth County R-III Board of Education*, 669 S.W.2d 949 (Mo. App. 1984).

D. Impropriety with Students

Barcheski v. Board of Education of Grand Rapids Public Schools

Court of Appeals of Michigan, 1987
162 Mich. App. 388, 412 N.W.2d 296

PER CURIAM.

* * *

On October 18, 1976, the Board of Education of the Grand Rapids Public Schools voted to proceed on three charges brought against petitioner. * * * Those charges were as follows:

"1. That on or about August 10, 1976, Mr. Barcheski invited two female members of his driver education class to a party to be held on Friday night, August 13, 1976, the night before the raft race.
"2. The two female students attended the party and drank beer and smoked pot during the evening in the presence of Mr. Barcheski.
"3. Mr. Barcheski took one of the female students, Mary . . . , home in his automobile after leaving the party. Mary . . . was 15 years of age at the time in question. On the way to the residence of Mary . . . , Mr. Barcheski parked his automobile and had sexual intercourse with [her] in his automobile.

* * *

Our review of the record discloses that the tenure commission's findings are supported by substantial, material and competent evidence, and we therefore affirm.

Regarding the first finding, i.e., that petitioner invited two female members of his driver's education class to a party, Commissioner Gibson's majority opinion relied heavily on the credibility of one of petitioner's students, "Mary." Mary admitted to the board of education that she had originally misled board investigators in her account of the party and petitioner's invitation, but stated that shortly thereafter she told them the truth. Mary testified before the board of education that on about August 10, 1976, she discussed an upcoming raft race with petitioner and that petitioner told her that he was going to a party on Friday, August 13, 1976, the night before the raft race. She stated that petitioner invited her and Wendy to attend the party and that the three of them talked about the party "every day" that week. At the tenure commission hearing, Mary's testimony concerning petitioner's alleged invitation was substantially the same as that offered before the board of education.

* * *

Petitioner testified before the board of education that he had never invited the two students to the party. He said that when they asked him one day at the driving range whether he was going to attend the upcoming raft race he told them "no," but explained to them that he went to an annual pre-raft-race party at the Michigan Wheel Test Basin. When they asked where Michigan Wheel was located, he simply gave them directions. Moreover, although he did not specifically remember having written down a telephone number on Wendy's book, he said he often provided his number to students in case they needed a ride home from driver's training classes. Petitioner conceded that, out of fear, he had originally lied to board of education investigators about the girls' presence at the party.

In the tenure commission's decision, Commissioner Gibson gave little weight to the testimony of Wendy and petitioner, finding that the former's midstream change in story which had apparently been precipitated by prior meetings with petitioner and the latter's attempts to persuade Wendy to falsify her testimony seriously jeopardized the credibility of these witnesses. On the other hand, Commissioner Gibson saw no reason not to credit Mary's testimony, even though Mary herself had experienced many personal problems, such as drug and alcohol use and unwed motherhood.

* * *

We believe that the tenure commission majority's finding that petitioner invited at least one female student to the party was supported by competent, material and substantial evidence on the record when viewed as a whole.

* * *

The tenure commission's second finding, i.e., that the two female students drank beer and smoked marijuana in petitioner's presence at the party, is also supported by competent, material and substantial evidence.

Petitioner stated that he arrived at the party at about 7:30 p.m. with two male friends and that about one-half hour later the students arrived. Two friends of petitioner who were at the party said petitioner looked surprised to see the students. There was conflicting testimony as to what occurred when the two students first came in contact with petitioner at the party. Petitioner testified that the students said they were "out partying" and that they looked somewhat "loose," like they had been drinking. Petitioner said that he introduced the students to his friends and chatted with them for about ten minutes, after which they disappeared. Petitioner said he never told the students to leave because he thought they had left on their own. He acknowledged that fifteen minutes after he initially saw the two students he saw Wendy standing down near the cement foundation of a metal derrick constructed on the riverbank, but that thereafter he saw neither of the students until preparing to leave the party several hours later. He testified that he spent most of the party in an out-of-the-way spot behind a wrecker parked next to the Michigan Wheel building, some seventy feet from the derrick where the students allegedly spent most of their evening. It was undisputed that many of those attending the party were drinking alcoholic beverages and smoking marijuana.

Mary admitted to the board of education that she and Wendy had smoked two "bowls" (two pipes full) of marijuana and had drunk several beers before having arrived at the party. She also testified that when they arrived, petitioner gave them some beer and that, during the course of the evening, they smoked marijuana in petitioner's presence. Before the tenure commission, Mary altered her testimony somewhat and testified that petitioner had not handed them their first beer but had, instead, directed them to a refrigerator where they could get their own. Petitioner and several of his friends denied that petitioner had ever given the students beer at the party.

* * *

Both before the board of education and the tenure commission Mary testified that she had smoked marijuana and had drunk beer in petitioner's presence at the party. At the board of education hearing, Wendy also affirmed that Mary had smoked marijuana and had drunk beer in front of petitioner. She noted, however, that she intentionally hid her own marijuana smoking from petitioner out of embarrassment.

Before the tenure commission, Wendy recanted part of her board of education testimony. She testified that neither she nor Mary smoked marijuana or drank beer in petitioner's presence during the party. Six of petitioner's friends testified that although each had seen the students smoke marijuana and drink beer at the party, this had never taken place in petitioner's presence.

Some of Wendy's unrecanted testimony weakened petitioner's blanket denial that he had lost sight of the two students through most of the middle portion of the party. Wendy testified before the tenure commission that during the party petitioner and Wendy would sometimes see each other and acknowledge each other's presence with a smile. Wendy also reluctantly testified before the tenure commission that she had seen a blonde-haired woman next to petitioner and later at the party, or at some later time, had asked petitioner if the woman was his wife. Petitioner's wife testified before the board of education that she arrived at the party at about 8:30 p.m. and that she and her husband spent most of their time in the cement area down by the river, an area very near the derrick where the two students spent most of their evening.

Wendy also gave unrecanted testimony before the board of education that just before leaving the party, Mary was sitting in a police car with her arm around petitioner and at one point reached over and kissed him. Wendy said that both she and Mary drank beer during this time by the police car. Petitioner conceded before the tenure commission that just as he was leaving the party he saw the two students standing next to a police car drinking beer. Observing that the students were intoxicated, petitioner convinced a friend to drive the students home. Petitioner, two of his male friends, Mary and Wendy then left the party together in a car.

Thus, besides the direct testimony of Mary, who flatly asserted that she had smoked marijuana and had drunk beer in petitioner's presence at the party, there was also testimony suggesting that petitioner maintained some visual contact with the students during the party and had spent at least some of his time near where the students were smoking and drinking. Under these circumstances, we cannot conclude that the tenure commission's finding that the students drank beer and smoked marijuana in petitioner's presence is not supported by substantial evidence.

* * *

Next, petitioner argues that the tenure commission improperly made its third finding regarding petitioner's having driven Mary home alone after the party because he was never put on notice that taking the student home by itself constituted a basis for a charge of wrongful conduct.

*   *   *

Based on petitioner's own testimony, however, we believe that petitioner was, or should have been, well aware that taking Mary, a young, intoxicated female student home alone in his car constituted, by itself, grounds for discipline. Petitioner stated that the students appeared intoxicated when they arrived at the party and were in even worse shape when he found them several hours later as he was leaving the party. Moreover, petitioner testified that on previous occasions, he had asked another driver's training instructor to give Mary a ride home because he thought she had a "crush" on him. Petitioner also explained that on one occasion Mary had placed her head on his shoulder while his class was watching a movie. As noted previously, Wendy testified that at the end of the party Mary put her arm around petitioner and kissed him. Wendy gave unrecanted testimony that when petitioner's friend, Michael Maxim, gave the two students and petitioner a ride to the social hall where petitioner had left his car, Mary kept her hand near the zipper of petitioner's pants and that petitioner made no effort to remove it. Mary herself said that she and petitioner kissed passionately while riding in the back seat of Maxim's car.

Given this factual scenario and the earlier findings of the board of education on this issue, petitioner was adequately put on notice that driving Mary home alone constituted by itself conduct supporting a charge of improper or wrongful conduct which could properly be considered in deciding whether a penalty would be appropriate.

*   *   *

For the foregoing reasons, the circuit court's affirmance of the tenure commission's ruling that petitioner's discharge was based on reasonable and just cause is affirmed.

Affirmed.

Note

A teacher's dismissal, which was based on a grand jury's indictment for sexual misconduct with teenage pupils, was upheld. Although the teacher was not provided a hearing before the school board to refute the allegations of misconduct, the court ruled that the dismissal did not violate his right of due process. In the event that the school board brought the charges, the court held, the teacher would have been entitled to a hearing before the board. The court stated:

After the grand jury had acted, the issue for the board was not whether Moore had committed the acts charged by the girls or whether he was guilty or innocent under the indictments but whether the existence and pendency of the indictments justified his suspension and the refusal to act upon the matter of his contract renewal. (P. 1073)

See *Moore* v. *Knowles,* 482 F.2d 1069 (5th Cir. 1973).

VII. Employment Discrimination

Certain personnel practices that have an impact on racial minorities, women, pregnant women, religious groups, older persons, and the handicapped have been challenged as being discriminatory. Although it has been argued that some of these practices may have reflected custom and did not have an overt discriminatory intent when instituted, those directly affected by them have alleged that they were in fact discriminatory.

In addition to constitutional protections under the Fourteenth Amendment's Equal Protection and Due Process Clauses, several federal statutes protect public school personnel against employment discrimination. These statutes include: Sections 1981 through 1983 of Title 42, United States Code; Title IX of the Education Amendments of 1972; Section 504 of the Rehabilitation Act of 1973; the Pregnancy Discrimination Act of 1978; the Age Discrimination in Employment Act of 1967 and its amendments; and Title VII of the Civil Rights Act of 1964.* The Civil Rights Act of 1964 was the seminal legislative enactment of the movement to eradicate discrimination in the United States. Title VII, the section dealing with discrimination in the workplace, provides in part:

SECTION 703
(a) It shall be an unlawful employment practice for an employer
   (1) to . . . discriminate against any individual with respect to his compensation, terms, conditions, or privileges of employment, because of such individual's race, color, religion, sex, or national origin; or
   (2) to limit, segregate, or classify his employees or applicants for employment in any way which would deprive or tend to deprive any individual of employment opportunities or otherwise adversely affect his status as an employee, because of such individual's race, color, religion, sex, or national origin.
(e) (1) it shall not be an unlawful employment practice . . . to hire and employ employees . . . on the basis of . . . religion, sex, or national origin in those certain instances where religion, sex, or national

---

* See Appendix D for these statutes.

origin is a bona fide occupational qualification reasonably necessary to the normal operation of that particular business or enterprise.

(h) It shall not be an unlawful employment practice . . . to [use] a bona fide seniority or merit system . . . provided that such differences are not the result of an intention to discriminate. . . . Nor shall it be an unlawful employment practice . . . to give and to act upon the results of any professionally developed ability test, provided that such test, its administration, or action upon the results is not designed, intended, or used to discriminate.

(j) Nothing contained in this Title shall be interpreted to require any employer . . . to grant preferential treatment to an individual or to any group because of the race, color, religion, sex, or national origin of such individual or group on account of an imbalance which may exist [between] the percentage employed by any employer [and] the percentage . . . in any community, State, section, or other area.

SECTION 706

(g) If the court finds that the [employer] has intentionally engaged in . . . an unlawful employment practice . . . the court . . . may order such affirmative action as may be appropriate.

A. Racial Discrimination

Racial discrimination against teachers has been a much litigated issue since the Supreme Court's decision in **Brown v. Board of Education of Topeka,** 347 U.S. 483 (1954), in which de jure segregation was declared to be a violation of the Equal Protection Clause of the Fourteenth Amendment. Court-ordered desegregation plans subsequent to **Brown** often contain provisions effectively regulating the hiring, promotion, and dismissal of minority school personnel. Courts also may impose affirmative action plans on school districts that have violated Title VII.

Involuntary termination of black teachers in school systems that have been under court order to desegregate has resulted in severe action against offending school systems. Court action in such cases has included awarding monetary damages, back pay, and attorneys' fees to minority plaintiffs; assessing court costs against defendant school districts; reinstating personnel; freezing the hiring of white teachers; and requiring districts to report all personnel actions to the court for a specified time. Such severe judicial enforcement of desegregation remedies, coupled with the vigorous application of Title VII, has been effective in reducing discriminatory employment practices against black teachers. Desegregation issues are examined in additional detail in Chapter 5.

Several Supreme Court decisions have addressed the limits of affirmative action plans. Although not a decision dealing with educators, a six-to-three Supreme Court decision upheld the "last-hired—first-fired" principle as applied to Memphis firefighters. The Court asserted that seniority systems, as long as they are unbiased, may not be disrupted to save the jobs of newly hired minority workers. The decision states: "It is inappropriate to deny an innocent employee the benefits of his seniority in order to provide a remedy in a pattern or practice suit such as this." *Firefighters Local Union No. 1784* v. *Stotts,* 467 U.S. 561 (1984).

Additionally, the Supreme Court did not uphold a layoff plan that was part of a school district's collective bargaining agreement. Although the plan called for retaining teachers by seniority, it also stipulated that minorities were not to be dismissed in proportions greater than their representation in the district. When, in accordance with the racially sensitive stipulation, white teachers were terminated instead of less-senior black teachers, the displaced white teachers claimed reverse discrimination. In its five-to-four decision, the Court agreed, holding that the policy was a violation of the non-minority teachers' constitutional equal protection. Racial classifications such as that imposed by the policy were justified only when narrowly tailored to accomplish a compelling state purpose. However, the Court found that other, less intrusive, means were available to the district to accomplish its purpose—for example, the adoption of hiring goals. Although the policy would have been allowable to remedy past de jure discrimination, no such finding had been made in court. See *Wygant* v. *Jackson Board of Education,* 476 U.S. 267 (1986).

Title VII was employed by a black assistant principal who had been denied the position of director of vocational education in favor of a white applicant. In upholding the white's selection, a court recognized that superior qualifications were a valid, nondiscriminatory reason. See *Clark* v. *Huntsville City Board of Education,* 717 F.2d 525 (11th Cir. 1983).

A high school band teacher who failed to have his contract renewed claimed that his discharge was racially discriminatory. Reasons for the nonrenewal included: parental concern over disorder and inconsistency in the band program; failure to care for the band's equipment and facilities; the program's being loosely structured; failure to provide leadership or to command respect; and deficiency of organizational skills. The federal appellate court held that "the reasons asserted by the school district may have been based partly on subjective considerations, but they were premised on objective factual observations that clearly constitute legitimate reasons for not renewing the plaintiff's contract." See *Tyler* v. *Hot Springs School District No. 6,* 827 F.2d 1227 (8th Cir. 1987).

Concern over excellence in the public schools has brought increased attention to the quality of teachers and to the adequacy of teacher-training programs. One result of this concern has been the increased use of competency testing of both prospective and practicing teachers, prior to their certification, hiring, promotion, or retention. Such tests have raised racial discrimination issues since these tests have often had a disproportionate impact on racial minorities. It should be noted that Title VII specifically condones professionally developed employment tests where such tests are not used to discriminate.

To date, teacher competency tests have been challenged, primarily in southern states, on a variety of constitutional and statutory grounds, including alleged racially biased content and alleged failure sufficiently to validate the tests' job relatedness. Courts have found that such testing fulfills a legitimate state function, and they have upheld tests and cutoff scores that objective validation has shown to be indicative of actual job qualifications. The decision in *United States* v. *South Carolina*, 445 F. Supp. 1094 (S.C. 1977), upheld the use of the National Teacher Examination as a requirement for state certification, despite the fact that its use disproportionately disqualified blacks. And in *United States* v. *LULAC*, 793 F.2d 636 (5th Cir. 1986), the Texas Pre-Professional Skills Test, which college students were required to pass before scheduling more than six hours of professional education courses at any state college or university, was upheld. The testing of veteran teachers was upheld in *Texas* v. *Project Principle*, 724 S.W.2d 387 (Tex. 1987).

B. Sex Discrimination

Although not challenged on the basis of Title VII, **Marshall v. Kirkland** addresses the issue of sex-based discrimination in not hiring females for administrative and specialty positions.

Marshall v. Kirkland

United States Court of Appeals, Eighth Circuit, 1979
602 F.2d 1282

HANSON, Senior District Judge.

* * *

Appellants' complaint . . . alleges gender-based discrimination. Women have predominated as teachers in Barton-Lexa School District by a ratio of between three and four to one. Evidence was presented to the district court which indicated that the assignment to "specialty" positions (a position with extra duties for which an increment in compensation was provided), and promotion to one of the three administrative positions in the district (principal of the elementary school, principal of the high school, and superintendent of the district) was influenced by the sex of the employee and statistically favored males with a concomitant differential in pay as between men and women.

The district court concluded:

the plaintiffs have failed in their burden of presenting any testimony to the effect that discrimination due to sex existed within a period of 3 years from the commencement of this litigation.

* * * Plaintiffs appeal from this determination that they failed to prove a prima facie case of sex discrimination.

* * *

* * * The district court held that a prima facie case of unconstitutional sex discrimination had not been made and that no rebuttable presumption arose. We conclude that the district court's finding in this regard is clearly erroneous and contrary to recently articulated constitutional principles with respect to the assignment of specialty personnel and promotion of teachers to administrative positions.

Appellants do not distinguish the elements involved in a constitutional as opposed to a Title VII statutory claim of sex discrimination. The two actions are different, however, as the Supreme Court has recently made clear. The evidence raises the question of whether defendants violated the right of female teachers, administrators, and applicants to equal protection of the law, a claim cognizable under 42 U.S.C. § 1983. Title VII is not involved.

As a general proposition, the equal protection clause of the Fourteenth Amendment, substantively inherent in the Fifth Amendment, grants to public employees "a federal constitutional right to be free from gender discrimination" unless a gender classification serves important governmental objectives and is substantially related to the achievement of those objectives. * * *

In *Feeney* the Supreme Court elaborated on what constitutes "discriminatory purpose": "It implies that the decisionmaker . . . selected or reaffirmed a particular course of action at least in part 'because of,' not merely 'in spite of,' its adverse effects upon an identifiable group."— U.S. at—, 99 S. Ct. at 2296. If employment decisions or policies in the public employment area are made in part "because it would accomplish the collateral goal of keeping women in a stereotypic and predefined place," the Constitution is violated. * * *

* * *

The record indicates that during the relevant years there were ten or eleven administrative and specialty positions. As noted, the administrative positions were the superintendent and the elementary and high school principals. The seven or eight specialty positions, which carried an increment in pay because of extra duties involved, consisted of various jobs—coaching, physical education, counselor, agriculture and home economics teachers. The practice of the school district was that the three administrators usually came from the ranks of teachers, and the specialists were of course teachers compensated for extra duties.

With regard to the specialty positions, the home economics and girls' physical education teacher positions were occupied by women during the relevant years, while the other specialty positions were filled by men. Women teachers outnumbered men by a ratio of three or four to one with the net result that all or nearly all male teachers in the district had specialty positions while the great majority of women did not. With regard to pay, the women specialty teachers received less than the males, though this evidence was poorly developed. School board president W. F. Burney testified that "[i]t has . . . been the policy of the school to hire men" for coaching positions, * * * and he agreed "that the men always get specialty jobs and the women almost never get specialty jobs." * * * School superintendent Kirkland, prior to 1973 the principal at the high school and like Burney, a decisionmaker, agreed that the football, basketball, and track coaches had traditionally been men and that, with the exception of the girls' basketball coach (a special pay job established relatively recently), should continue to be men. * * * Kirkland candidly testified:

> [T]here is no evidence, to indicate that only men could perform those jobs, but again, this is something that has been traditionally done in this Country and I concur with it.

* * * He also testified that men had previously taught girls' physical education and that men would be capable of coaching girls' basketball. In contrast, women were not qualified to coach male athletic teams because "I just feel that a man could do [a] better job of handling a group of young men like that, than a woman." * * *

With respect to administrators, the evidence suggests that at the time of trial women were virtually disqualified from holding the position of high school principal and, as a consequence, superintendent. Mrs. Todd, the elementary principal during the relevant years, was the lowest paid of the three administrators. In 1973 David Bagley, a high school teacher, was promoted to high school principal to replace Mr. Kirkland who assumed the duties of superintendent. Mrs. Todd was concededly better qualified than Bagley, * * * but was not considered for the job. Mrs. Todd testified and did not indicate any interest in the high school principal or superintendent positions. However, Superintendent Kirkland did not indicate in his testimony that Todd's lack of interest was a factor in failing to consider her for the position. Instead, he testified that Todd was not considered "[b]ecause with the situation we had, and the students we had, I felt that we needed a man for the job." * * * Thereupon occurred the following colloquy between appellants' counsel and Mr. Kirkland:

> Q Now, fully explain that please. The situation you had and the students you had . . .
> A Because with high school students I feel that men are stronger disciplinarians than women are, and this particular instance I felt we needed a man in this position because part of the job was to be at athletic events, this sort of thing . . . to see that things . . . everything goes off as it should and I felt that a man could do a better job than a woman.
> Q Well, what is the objective evidence that you have for arriving at the conclusion that a woman can't do those things?
> A I don't have any, Mr. Walker.
> Q Is that just a natural bias?
> A I suppose it is. * * *

Coupled with objective evidence showing a clear pattern of disproportionate gender representation in administrative and specialty positions, the testimony of school board president Burney and former principal and superintendent Kirkland strongly indicates that the sex of a teacher was an important part of assignment and promotion decisions in this area of the school district's employment. At the very least, appellants made a prima facie showing that decisionmakers in the school district sought to maintain women teachers in a "stereotypic and predefined place" in the school district and the district court clearly erred in finding otherwise. * * * Indeed, the testimony of Burney and Kirkland would support a factual finding that the school district had a discernible policy or practice of hiring only men (or women) for certain specific administrative or specialty jobs. Such a finding would raise the question of whether the non-neutral gender classification could be justified as bearing a close and substantial relationship to important governmental objectives. * * *

* * *

The district court observed that the school district "presented substantial testimony that no sex discrimination existed in the operation of the school system," but the court did not elaborate in view of its finding on the prima facie issue. Accordingly, on remand the district court should, on the basis of the present record, determine (1) by appropriate order whether the named plaintiffs may sue as representative parties on behalf of the class of all female teachers and applicants; (2) if the cause may be maintained as a class action, whether the evidence of no sex discrimination referred to by the district court rebuts the presumption in favor of class-wide equitable relief * * * ; and (3) whether the presumption in favor of individual relief has been rebutted with respect to those women who testified. Judgment may then be entered on the district court's supplemental findings and conclusions.

* * *

* * * We reverse the district court's dismissal of the class and individual claims for relief predicated on alleged unconstitutional sex discrimination to the extent it relates to the assignment of female teachers to specialty positions and promotion to administrative positions. We remand the cause to the district court for further proceedings consistent with this opinion.

Though the results here are mixed, because on this appeal appellants' counsel has successfully established a prima facie case of sex discrimination, we award costs on appeal to appellants including $500 in attorney fees. 42 U.S.C. § 1988.

* * *

Notes

See *Jepsen* v. *Florida Board of Regents*, 610 F.2d 1379 (5th Cir. 1980) for an action brought under Title VII.

Title IX regulations were vague on the question of whether the amendment covered employment practices of schools and colleges. A six-to-three decision by the United States Supreme Court reasoned that Congress had intended Title IX to cover employment. See *North Haven Board of Education* v. *Bell*, 456 U.S. 512 (1982).

In *Grove City College* v. *Bell*, 465 U.S. 555 (1984), the Supreme Court, referring to private institutions, declared that Title IX did not apply to schools and colleges as a whole but only to those parts of an institution that received federal aid directly. However, provisions of the Civil Rights Restoration Act of 1988 were designed to overturn the *Grove City College* decision. The act made it clear that if one part of an entity receives federal funds, then the entire entity is covered.

Title VII prohibits unequal treatment with respect to "conditions of employment." Courts have construed "conditions" to include insulting and degrading treatment; therefore, Title VII applies to sexual harassment on the job.

A Supreme Court decision provides impetus for affirmative action. In a six-to-three ruling the Court upheld the concept that employers, both private and public, voluntarily can adopt hiring and promotion goals to benefit women, even at the expense of more-qualified men. By permitting self-imposed affirmative action plans when women are under-represented, the decision sends a strong signal to men who are inclined to sue for reverse discrimination. See *Johnson* v. *Transportation Agency, Santa Clara,* 480 U.S. 616 (1987).

C. Pregnancy

A challenge to local school board policies that provided for mandatory leave at a particular time in a pregnancy and rules pertaining to reemployment after delivery has been heard by the United States Supreme Court. In its decision in *Cleveland Board of Education* v. *La Fleur,* 414 U.S. 632 (1974), the Court held that mandatory maternity termination provisions stating the number of months before anticipated childbirth violated the Due Process Clause of the Fourteenth Amendment. The court reasoned that arbitrary cutoff dates have no valid relationship to the state's interest in preserving continuity of instruction, as long as the teacher is required to give substantial advance notice that she is pregnant. And the Court stated that the challenged provisions created a conclusive presumption that every teacher is physically incapable of continuing her duties at a specified time in her pregnancy. Additionally, the Court struck down the provision that a mother could not return to work until the next regular semester after her child was three months old.

Shortly after this decision many court challenges were brought against policies pertaining to disability benefits, sick leave, and health insurance involving pregnancy. The issue was addressed by the United States Supreme Court in a non-educator-related case, *General Electric Company* v. *Gilbert,* 429 U.S. 125 (1976). Largely as a result of the *Gilbert* decision, which upheld the exclusion of pregnancy-related disabilities from General Electric's comprehensive disability plan, Congress passed the Pregnancy Discrimination Act, which went into effect in 1979.

This act is an amendment to Title VII. The Pregnancy Discrimination Act stipulates that employment discrimination "because of sex" or "on the basis of sex," as prohibited by Title VII, includes discrimination "because of or on the basis of pregnancy, childbirth or related medical conditions." Women so situated must be treated as other applicants or employees are: on the basis of their ability to work. Women may not be fired, be denied promotions, or be refused employment as a consequence of their being pregnant or having an abortion. They may not be forced to take leave while they still can work. They may not be required to exhaust their vacation benefits prior to receiving sick leave or disability benefits, unless the same policy applies to other disabled employees. If other employees are entitled to resume their jobs after disability leave, so too are women who have been absent because of pregnancy. Usually, however, they have no guarantee of returning to their former positions or schools.

In the area of fringe benefits, such as disability benefits, sick leave, and health insurance, the same principle applies. A woman unable to work for pregnancy-related reasons is entitled to disability benefits or sick leave on the same basis as employees unable to work for other temporary medical reasons. Also, any health insurance provided must cover expenses for pregnancy-related conditions on the same basis as coverage given for other medical conditions. However, health insurance for expenses resulting from abortion is not required, except where the life of the mother would be endangered if the fetus were carried to term or where medical complications have arisen from such an abortion.

Ponton v. Newport News School Board

United States District Court, Eastern District of Virginia, 1986
632 F. Supp. 1056

MERHIGE, District Judge.

Plaintiff, Pamela Brown Ponton, a teacher in the Newport News Public School System, has filed this action against the Newport News School Board and various employees of the Newport News Public School System. Plaintiff alleges that the defendants violated her rights by forcing her to take a leave of absence from her teaching position because she was single and pregnant. Plaintiff contends that this coerced leave constituted a violation of her constitutional rights to equal protection, privacy and due process and her statutory rights under 42 U.S.C. §§ 1981 and 1983, 20 U.S.C. § 1681 (Title IX of the Education Amendments of 1972) and 42 U.S.C. § 2000e et seq. (Title VII of the Civil Rights Act of 1964).

* * *

The first issue that must be decided is whether plaintiff was in fact forced to take the leave of absence, for if she took the leave voluntarily, plaintiff would have no claim against the defendants. The defendants contend that plaintiff agreed that she should not be teaching while she was single and pregnant and that she voluntarily took the leave of absence.

* * *

First, although plaintiff did not file a grievance with the school system, she did file a complaint with the EEOC a few weeks after the commencement of her leave, charging the Newport News School District with sex discrimination. Such action would seem to have been reasonable, for an appeal through the school system's grievance procedure would have been futile if, as plaintiff believed, the discrimination against single, pregnant teachers was the product of a School Board policy.

Second, plaintiff was told by Crawford Smith that the Personnel Department dealt with single, pregnant women by presenting them with three options: (1) resign, (2) get married, or (3) take a leave of absence. Smith told plaintiff that a previous unwed, pregnant teacher had been dealt with in this manner.

* * *

It therefore must be determined whether this involuntary leave constituted a violation of any of plaintiff's rights. The Court finds that the coerced leave did in fact violate at least two of plaintiff's rights; her constitutional right of privacy and her statutory right under Title VII against discrimination on the basis of sex. * * *

* * *

It is clear that the right to bear a child out of wedlock is protected by the Constitution. The Supreme Court has repeatedly noted that the right to privacy encompasses decisions regarding whether to have a child. See, *e.g., Roe* v. *Wade,* 410 U.S. 113 (1973) * * *; *Eisenstadt* v. *Baird,* 405 U.S. 438 (1972) * * *; *Griswold* v. *Connecticut,* 381 U.S. 479 (1965) * * *. This right to bear children extends to both single and married persons for, as the Supreme Court stated in *Eisenstadt* v. *Baird,* "[i]f the right of privacy means anything, it is the right of the individual, *married or single,* to be free from unwarranted governmental intrusion into matters so fundamentally affecting a person as the decision whether to bear or beget a child." * * * (emphasis added).

Plaintiff therefore had a constitutional right to bear a child while unmarried. It is undisputed that plaintiff's exercise of this right was the reason she was forced to take a leave of absence, for if she had been either married and pregnant or single and non-pregnant she would not have been forced to take the leave. It must therefore be determined whether plaintiff's interest in exercising her right to become pregnant out of wedlock was outweighed by the School District's asserted interest in excluding plaintiff from the classroom.

It is now well established that public employment is not a privilege that can be made subject to unreasonable conditions. *See, e.g., Connick* v. *Meyers; Pickering* v. *Board of Education.* * * * Accordingly, public employees may not be compelled to forfeit all of their constitutional rights when they accept such employment. There are limits, however, to the extent to which public employees may exercise their constitutional rights when such excercise conflicts with their performance of their duties as employees. The Supreme Court has developed a balancing test for determining when the state may legitimately discharge a public employee for the exercise of her constitutional rights. Under this test, the teacher's interest in exercising her rights is balanced against the state's interest in promoting the efficiency of the public services it performs through its employees. *See, e.g., Connick* v. *Meyers,* * * * *Pickering* v. *Board of Education.*

* * *

In this case, the particular state interest which has been alleged is that of protecting schoolchildren from exposure to a single, pregnant teacher. The Court has serious doubt as to whether this is in fact a legitimate interest. Even assuming that the asserted state interest is a valid one, however, the Court finds that it does not outweigh plaintiff's interest in exercising her constitutional right to bear a child out of wedlock.

It has not been alleged that the fact that plaintiff became pregnant out of wedlock indicated some moral defect in plaintiff which made her unfit to teach. Nor has it been alleged that plaintiff intended to openly advocate the virtues of pregnancy out of wedlock. Indeed, the evidence establishes that plaintiff was both desirous and anxious to marry her child's father. Rather, the sole allegation is that the mere sight of an unmarried, pregnant teacher would have a sufficiently undesirable influence on schoolchildren to justify excluding the teacher from the classroom. The Court finds this allegation to be meritless, for the effect on students of the mere sight of a single, pregnant teacher would be negligible, at best. To begin with, it is unclear whether plaintiff's students would have even been aware that plaintiff was unmarried. Moreover, even if plaintiff's students would have known that she was single, the mere knowledge that their teacher had gotten pregnant out of wedlock would seem to have a fairly minimal impact on them. There was no evidence that plaintiff intended to proselytize her students regarding the issue of unwed pregnancy. Plaintiff's pregnancy would not have affected the School Board's authority to prescribe the curriculum for plaintiff's students, nor would it have affected plaintiff's ability to implement this curriculum in her classes. Finally, there was no danger that plaintiff's single, pregnant status could in any way be perceived as representing a School Board-sponsored statement regarding the desirability of pregnancy out of wedlock; rather, such status could only be viewed as representing a personal decision made by plaintiff in her private capacity.

* * *

In 1978, Congress amended Title VII of the Civil Rights Act of 1964 by adding the Pregnancy Discrimination Act, 42 U.S.C. § 2000e(k). This amendment provides that "[t]he terms 'because of sex' or 'on the basis of sex' include, but are not limited to, because of or on the basis of pregnancy, childbirth, or related medical conditions; and women affected by pregnancy, childbirth, or related medical conditions shall be treated the same for all employment-related purposes . . . as other persons not so affected but similar in their ability or inability to work." The Supreme Court, in considering the implications of this amendment, stated that, "[t]he Pregnancy Discrimination Act has now made clear that, for all Title VII purposes, discrimination based on a woman's pregnancy is, on its face, discrimination because of her sex."

* * *

It seems clear that, in this case, plaintiff was discriminated against on the basis of her pregnancy, for plaintiff would not have been forced to take the leave of absence if she had not become pregnant. A policy such as that invoked by the Personnel Department could apply only to pregnant teachers.

Since plaintiff has established a prima facie case of sex discrimination, the burden shifts to the defendants to articulate a legitimate, nondiscriminatory reason for the manner in which plaintiff was treated. Indeed, the defendants do not advance any reason for the plaintiff's having taken leave as she did, other than that was her wish. The Court reiterates its rejection of this position. It is beyond question, in the Court's view, that the *true* reason was her pregnancy and unmarried status coupled with the expressed view that her teaching under those conditions would have been a bad moral example for her students. The Court has already discussed why such a concern is not a legitimate one.

* * *

* * * The discrimination in the instant case was based on both an immutable sex characteristic—pregnancy—and a constitutionally protected activity—the right to bear a child out of wedlock. Accordingly, such discrimination must be considered a violation of Title VII.

* * *

Notes and Questions

Several other courts have ruled similarly to **Ponton.** See *Avery* v. *Homewood City Board of Education,* 674 F.2d 337 (5th Cir. 1982); *Cochran* v. *Chidester School District,* 456 F. Supp. 390 (Ark. 1978); *Brown* v. *Bathke,* 566 F.2d 588 (8th Cir. 1977); *New Mexico State Board of Education* v. *Stoudt,* 571 P.2d 1186 (N.M. 1977); *Andrews* v. *Drew Municipal Separate School District,* 507 F.2d 611 (5th Cir. 1975); and *Drake* v. *Covington County Board of Education,* 371 F. Supp. 974 (Ala. 1974).

In a seven-to-two decision the Court established that an insurance plan violated the 1964 Civil Rights Act and the Pregnancy Discrimination Act because it offered full hospitalization benefits to husbands of female workers but excluded pregnancy from the full coverage offered to the wives of male workers. The decision stated that under the plan "husbands of female employees receive a specified level of hospitalization coverage for all conditions; the wives of male employees receive such coverage except for pregnancy-related conditions. . . . The 1978 act makes clear that it is discriminatory to treat pregnancy-related conditions less favorably than other medical conditions." Therefore, the plan "unlawfully gives married male employees a benefit package for their dependents that is less inclusive than the dependency coverage provided to married female employees." See *Newport News Shipbuilding and Dry Dock Company* v. *Equal Employment Opportunity Commission,* 462 U.S. 669 (1983).

A sectarian private school did not renew a pregnant teacher's contract because the school's tenet included "the importance of the mother in the home during the early years of child growth." When the teacher's lawyer threatened the school with court action, the school terminated her in accordance with her contractual agreement to acquiesce to the decisions of the school's board of directors in the "Biblical chain of command." Citing its freedom of religion, the board sought a federal court injunction against the intervention of the Ohio Civil Rights Commission. The Supreme Court, however, ruled that the federal courts must abstain from entering pending state administrative proceedings except to prevent great and immediate irreparable injury. See *Ohio Civil Rights Commission* v. *Dayton Christian Schools*, 477 U.S. 619 (1986).

A Fifth Circuit Court of Appeals recognized that a teacher's decision to breastfeed her baby had some constitutional dimensions. In its decision the court contended that the teacher's right to breastfeed her baby could be limited if this practice interfered with important educational interests that were furthered by the rules that prohibited teachers from bringing their children to work with them for any reason. See *Dike* v. *School Board of Orange County*, 650 F.2d 783 (5th Cir. 1981).

Two other Court decisions addressed issues related to pregnancy. In *California Federal Savings and Loan Association* v. *Guerra*, 479 U.S. 272 (1987), a six-to-three decision, the Court upheld a California law granting four months of unpaid maternity leave to pregnant workers and guaranteeing that they could return to their former jobs. However, a unanimous Supreme Court decision upheld a Missouri law that did not provide either reinstatement or unemployment benefits to a woman who left her job because of pregnancy. Under the law, benefits were available only to those who left work for job-related reasons. Layoffs or illnesses caused by a job were considered job-related; pregnancy was not. See *Wimberly* v. *Labor and Industrial Relations Commission of Missouri*, 479 U.S. 511 (1987).

What would be the status of a single female teacher who had been artificially inseminated or who became a surrogate mother?

D. Religious Discrimination

Title VII of the Civil Rights Act of 1964 provides in part that an employer must "reasonably accommodate to an employee's . . . religious observances or practice without undue hardship on the conduct of the employer's business." In *Ansonia Board of Education* v. *Philbrook*, 479 U.S. 60 (1986), the Court considered a teacher's request to use, for religious purposes, his allotment of "necessary personal business" leave. The teacher's collective-bargaining agreement allowed three days of paid religious leave and three days of paid personal business leave; religious observances were not included among the enumerated reasons for taking a leave of absence for personal business. The school board required the teacher to take unpaid leave for all religious observances exceeding three days. Upholding the board, the Court declared the policy to be a "reasonable accommodation" under Title VII.

Most states have laws that, like Title VII, require employers to accommodate employees' religious practices. However, a point exists at which such accommodation may violate the Establishment Clause of the

United States Constitution's First Amendment. The Supreme Court struck down a Connecticut statute that allowed employees to absent themselves from work on any day that they claimed as their Sabbath. The Court found that the statute imposed on employers the absolute duty to conform their business practices to the religious practices of their employees. The statute allowed no exceptions, for example, in the event of a teacher's claiming a Friday Sabbath. The Court concluded that the law's primary effect was the advancement of a particular religious practice. See *Estate of Thornton* v. *Caldor, Inc.,* 472 U.S. 703 (1985).

Oregon laws that disallowed the wearing of religious dress while teaching and that provided for suspension and teaching certificate revocation were upheld. In this instance the teacher wore the white clothes and turban of a Sikh Hindu. See *Cooper* v. *Eugene School District No. 4J,* 301 Or. 358, 723 P.2d 298 (1986).

Teachers' use of school facilities for religious meetings has also come under judicial review. An Indiana school-district policy that banned religious meetings of teachers on school property, before the teachers were to report for duty, was upheld. See *May* v. *Evansville-Vanderburgh School Corporation,* 787 F.2d 1105 (7th Cir. 1986).

E. Age Discrimination

Under the Age Discrimination in Employment Act of 1967 it is unlawful for an employer to discriminate against any employee or potential employee on the basis of age except "where age is a bona fide occupational qualification reasonably necessary to the normal operation of the particular business, or where the differentiation is based on reasonable factors other than age." As originally passed in 1967, the act did not apply to the federal government, to the states and their political subdivisions, or to private employers with fewer than twenty-five employees. In 1974, however, Congress extended the act's substantive prohibitions to employers having at least twenty workers and to the federal and state governments and, thus, to public school employees.

Coverage of the act is limited to employees within a specified range of ages. An important effect of the range's upper limit is to define the minimum age for mandatory retirement. Coverage in 1967 was limited to workers between the ages of forty and sixty-five. Amendments of 1978 raised the upper limit to age seventy and removed the cap entirely for federal workers. Amendments of 1986 will, after 1994, remove the cap for tenured faculty in higher education.*

* See Appendix D for material pertaining to this legislation.

Whether or not a school board's policy favoring the hiring of less experienced teachers violated the Age Discrimination in Employment Act was addressed in *Geller v. Markham.*

Geller v. Markham

United States Court of Appeals, Second Circuit, 1980
635 F.2d 1027, *cert. denied,* 451 U.S. 945 (1981)

MANSFIELD, Circuit Judge:

Miriam Geller, a 55-year-old teacher, brought a class action in the District Court for the District of Connecticut under the Age Discrimination in Employment Act of 1967 (ADEA), * * * claiming that defendants-appellants violated her rights by denying her employment as a teacher because of her age. She sought damages, equitable relief (including reinstatement, pension rights, benefits and seniority) and attorney's fees. A jury trial before Judge M. Joseph Blumenfeld resulted in an award of $15,190 damages. Following the trial, Judge Blumenfeld denied her application for equitable relief but awarded attorney's fees. From this denial she appeals. * * *

We affirm the finding of defendants' liability, since the record reveals that defendants subjected Ms. Geller to a hiring practice with both discriminatory impact, * * * and illegally disparate treatment, * * * the principles of which may be applied in ADEA cases. * * * We also affirm the district court's refusal to award reinstatement, but reverse its decision not to award pension benefits.

Ms. Geller applied for a position as a teacher at Bugbee School in West Hartford in late August, 1976. She was then 55 years old. She had gained considerable experience as a tenured teacher in New Jersey, where she had lived until shortly before applying for the Bugbee job, and she had done some work as a substitute teacher in the Connecticut schools. She was interviewed for a permanent position to fill a "sudden opening" in the Bugbee School on September 3, 1976, and was told to be ready to begin teaching art on September 7. Meanwhile, school officials continued to interview other candidates for the job.

Ms. Geller prepared the art room over Labor Day weekend, and taught school until September 17, when she was replaced by a 25-year-old woman who had not applied for the job until September 10. Shortly thereafter, Ms. Geller brought the present suit, alleging violations of ADEA, and pointing in particular to the "Sixth Step Policy" adopted by the West Hartford Board of Education ("Board"). This cost-cutting policy, which was derived from a statement included by the previous Bugbee School Superintendent in his budget report to the Board, read:

"Except in special situations and to the extent possible, teachers needed in West Hartford next year will be recruited at levels below the sixth step of the salary schedule."

The sixth step is the salary grade reached by teachers with more than five years' experience.

At trial plaintiff introduced expert statistical testimony establishing that 92.6% of Connecticut teachers between 40 and 65 years old (the protected age group under ADEA) have more than 5 years experience, while only 62% of teachers under 40 have taught more than five years. She also presented considerable evidence in the form of witnesses' testimony that individual defendants had discussed the "sixth step" policy with her, and had taken the policy into account when deciding to replace her. Defendants countered that the ratio of hirees over 40 years of age to under-40 hirees had not changed substantially since the announcement of the "sixth step" policy. From these latter statistics, which were offered not by an expert statistician but by Mr. Hedrick, a named defendant, defendants argued that the "sixth step" policy had never been applied to discriminate on the basis of age. They claimed that Ms. Geller had been replaced by a younger woman because hiring officials considered the younger woman more qualified, not because the school board was unwilling to pay a woman with her experience. Defendants also argue that even if the "sixth step" was applied, they were justified in applying it because an "experience-cost criterion" for hiring was necessary in view of declining enrollments and rising school costs.

Largely on the strength of plaintiff's expert statistical evidence, Judge Blumenfeld found that defendants' "sixth step" policy was discriminatory as a matter of law. * * * He declined to accept defendants' contention that proof of a violation of ADEA required establishment of discriminatory motive. With respect to plaintiff's claim of disparate treatment, * * * however, he took the view that to sustain this claim plaintiff must ultimately prove a discriminatory motive on the defendants' part and that proof that they discharged her because of the application of the "sixth step" policy was insufficient * * * .

After instructing the jury that the "sixth step" policy was discriminatory on the basis of age as a matter of law, Judge Blumenfeld submitted to it the question of whether this policy had been applied to Ms. Geller. First, in his oral instructions to the jury, he asked it to determine "if the decision about Mrs. Geller was made in whole or in part, because she was above the fifth step," and if the "sixth step" policy "made a difference" in the decision to replace her with the younger woman, stating:

There could have been more than one reason for defendants' decision about [Mrs. Geller's] employment but she is nevertheless entitled to recover if one factor was her [age] and if it made a difference in determining whether she would be employed. If it did not make any difference, if it was not a reason that entered into the decision, then of course she has not proved her case. But if it did, then she has.

"If defendants' decision about Mrs. Geller was made in whole or in part because she was above the fifth step on the salary scale, . . . Mrs. Geller is entitled to recover. . . ."

*   *   *

As the Supreme Court pointed out, * * * discriminatory or disparate treatment in violation of Title VII occurs where "[t]he employer simply treats some people less favorably than others because of their race, color, religion, sex or national origin. Proof of discriminatory motive is critical, although it can in some situations be inferred from the mere fact of differences in treatment." "Disparate impact," on the other hand, results from the use of "employment practices that are facially neutral in their treatment of different groups but that in fact fall more harshly on one group than another and cannot be justified by business necessity." * * * Proof of motive is not required to sustain a claim of disparate impact.

*   *   *

A prima facie case of discriminatory impact may be established by showing that an employer's facially neutral practice has a disparate impact upon members of plaintiff's class, in this case teachers over 40 years of age. * * * Such a discriminatory impact is frequently evidenced by statistics from which it may be inferred that an employer's selection methods or employment criteria result in employment of a larger share of one group (here, teachers under 40 years of age) than of another (teachers over 40). * * * The employer may defend by showing that the employment practice is justified by business necessity or need and is related to successful performance of the job for which the practice is used. * * * In that event the plaintiff must be given an opportunity to show that other selection methods having less discriminatory effects would serve the employer's legitimate interest in competent performance of the job. * * *

A prima facie case of discriminatory treatment may be made out by the plaintiff's showing:

"(i) that he belongs to a racial minority; (ii) that he applied and was qualified for a job for which the employer was seeking applicants; (iii) that, despite his qualifications, he was rejected; and (iv) that, after his rejection, the position remained open and the employer continued to seek applicants from persons of complainant's qualifications." * * * The burden then shifts to the employer to go forward with evidence of "some legitimate, nondiscriminatory reason for the employee's rejection," * * * in which event the plaintiff, who has the ultimate burden, must be afforded the opportunity to demonstrate by competent evidence that the employer's presumptively valid reasons are a cover-up or pretext. * * * If the plaintiff succeeds in this showing the employer's articulated reason will not stand. * * *

Turning to the present case, the plaintiff showed through an accredited expert (Dr. Alan Hunt), based on his statistical analysis of the relationship between age and years of experience for teachers in Connecticut, that 92.6% of all teachers over 40 years of age have five or more years of teaching experience, which he characterized as "very significant" statistically or about "600 times the level generally required for statistical significance." Although the significance of the 92.6% figure is somewhat weakened by evidence that over 60% of teachers under 40 also have had more than five years' experience, we agree with Judge Blumenfeld's finding that the high correlation between experience and membership in the protected age group (40 to 65 years of age) would render application of the "sixth step" policy discriminatory as a matter of law, * * * since, absent countervailing statistics, the likelihood of a person over 40 being selected under the policy would be substantially less than that of a person under 40. The purpose of the "sixth step" policy was to economize by employing less experienced teachers, which would inevitably open more teaching opportunities to younger less experienced applicants than to the older, who were more experienced.

Defendants have offered two lines of defense, both of which are unpersuasive. First they contend that, although the "sixth step" policy appears to be correlated strongly to membership in the group over 40, the policy did not in fact result in discrimination against this group since the percentage of over-40 teachers hired to fill job openings before and after the application of the policy was about the same. The uncorroborated statistics offered in support of this contention, however, were so defective as to justify the district court's refusal to give them any weight. They were prepared by a named defendant in the case, a former Personnel Director for the West Hartford schools who had no expertise as a statistician and had a direct interest in the outcome of the case. He not only failed to produce any competent evidence of the applicant pool for the periods, which is essential to a statistical determination of hiring patterns, but he employed such dubious analytical techniques as obtaining an overall percentage figure by averaging annual percentages for several different years, thus contravening the basic, well-recognized principle that such averaging by percentages produces meaningless and often misleading results. Moreover it appears that there were dramatic changes in the size of the applicant pool and in the number of teachers hired in the West Hartford School District during the mid-1970's, which cast serious doubt upon the statistical significance of the defendants' evidence of allegedly unchanging hiring patterns. In 1968 and 1969, according to defendants' own figures, West Hartford hired 129 and 136 teachers, of whom 28 and 33, respectively, were above the fifth step, and 17 (13%) and 15 (8%), respectively, were over 40. In 1975 and 1976, by contrast, the District hired only 35 and 53 teachers, a substantially smaller group, of whom 7 and 10 were above the fifth step and 2 (6%) and 4 (8%), respectively, were over 40.

* * *

Here Judge Blumenfeld rightly found that the "sixth step" policy was discriminatory on its face. From there, he apparently declined to rely on statistics either to establish as a matter of law plaintiff's position that the policy was applied or to support defendants' position that it was not applied. Absent statistics regarding any changes in the applicant pool for teaching jobs as over-all hiring decreased, comparative evidence of overall hiring percentages carries little weight, since these percentages may have remained constant despite an increase or fall-off in over-40 applicants. In the face of these deficiencies in the statistical proof and the existence of testimony that the "sixth step" policy was applied in Ms. Geller's individual case, which was disputed, Judge Blumenfeld properly submitted the issue of whether it was applied to the jury, which resolved the question in her favor by finding that the "sixth step" policy was one reason for the hiring of a younger replacement.

Defendants' second line of defense, somewhat inconsistent with their contention that the "sixth step" policy was never followed, is that the policy, if applied, was supportable as a necessary cost-cutting gesture in the face of tight budgetary constraints. This cost justification must fail, however, because of the clear rule that

"a general assertion that the average cost of employing older workers as a group is higher than the average cost of employing younger workers as a group will not be recognized as a differentiation under the terms and provisions of the Act, unless one of the other statutory exceptions applies. To classify or group employees solely on the basis of age for the purpose of comparing costs, or for any other purpose, necessarily rests on the assumption that the age factor alone may be used to justify a differentiation—an assumption plainly contrary to the terms of the Act and the purpose of Congress in enacting it. Differentials so based would serve only to perpetuate and promote the very discrimination at which the Act is directed." * * *

* * *

The record also reveals that, in addition to making out a case of disparate impact, Ms. Geller established a prima facie case of discriminatory treatment * * * satisfying the oft-repeated four conditions prescribed by the Court. * * * At age 55 she was clearly within the protected group under ADEA. She applied for the teaching job, was concededly qualified for it, and was even hired temporarily to perform it. She was then released, and saw a younger person placed in the job for which she was concededly qualified. These undisputed facts are sufficient to place upon the defendants the burden of rebutting her prima facie case. For reasons already stated, the defenses that the "sixth step" policy was not applied to Ms. Geller and that, if applied, it was cost-justified, must be rejected. The only other defense, that the discharge of Ms. Geller in favor of a younger teacher, was not motivated by the policy but by the superior competence of the latter candidate, was rejected by the jury's findings.

This leads us to defendants' final contention, that the court erred in instructing the jury as to the part age must play in determining whether they violated ADEA in discharging Ms. Geller. In order to make out a case under ADEA, Ms. Geller was not required to show that age discrimination was the *sole* cause of her discharge. Where an employer acts out of mixed motives in discharging or refusing to hire an employee, the plaintiff must show that age was a causative or determinative factor, one that made a difference in deciding whether the plaintiff should be employed. * * *

* * *

We next turn to Ms. Geller's contention that the district court erred in denying her equitable relief beyond the damages awarded by the jury. * * *

* * *

Judge Blumenfeld viewed reinstatement as inappropriate because he interpreted the jury's decision granting damages equal to one year's salary at Bugbee School as a factual conclusion that Ms. Geller was deprived of only one year's employment by the defendants' discriminatory action. We agree with this conclusion. Ms. Geller had never formally been hired as a permanent teacher during the time she was working but had merely been told to get started. Permanent reinstatement therefore is unwarranted.

On the other hand, we disagree with the trial judge's refusal to consider Ms. Geller's request for lost pension benefits on the ground that "[d]amages for lost pension benefits are one component of the overall damages suffered by a plaintiff, which a jury may assess in ADEA actions."

* * *

The judgment appealed from by the defendants is affirmed. The district court's order denying equitable relief to the plaintiff is affirmed except as to the denial of pension benefits which is reversed to the extent indicated.

Notes and Question

Although *Geller* deals with age discrimination, it has implications for other types of discrimination litigation. The significance of the discriminatory impact of system practices, the necessity for legally sound school-system policy, and the importance of adequate and appropriate statistics are demonstrated in this decision.

Courts have generally held that those teaching beyond a specified retirement age do so on a year-to-year basis. In addressing this issue, the South Dakota Supreme Court in *Monnier* v. *Todd County Independent School District*, 245 N.W.2d 503 (S.D. 1976) has contended that

> after a school district has adopted a mandatory retirement policy, teachers within that district who attain the age of retirement specified in the policy are no longer entitled to the benefits of the continuing contract law. By its very terms the concept of mandatory retirement is inconsistent with the concept of continuing contract rights. . . . (P. 505)

Periodic changes in the federal age discrimination acts tend to include more workers and to increase the minimum age for mandatory retirement. Is it likely that teachers over the age of seventy will contest present law?

F. Discrimination against the Handicapped

Section 504 of the Vocational Rehabilitation Act of 1973 prohibits discrimination against handicapped persons. It states in part:

> No otherwise qualified handicapped individual in the United States shall, solely by reason of his handicap, be excluded from participation in, be

denied the benefits of, or be subjected to discrimination under any program or activity receiving Federal financial assistance. . . .

Covered employers must make "reasonable accommodation" to the limitations of handicapped employees who are otherwise qualified to do the job. Reasonable accommodation may mean restructuring physical access in work areas, redistributing tasks among jobs such that handicapped employees can function in their positions, and eliminating unnecessary job qualifications. It does not mean that employers must tolerate substandard job performance or must hire persons whose employment would threaten the safety of others.

A visually handicapped and hearing-impaired teacher's discharge was upheld by the Washington Supreme Court after substantial evidence showed that the handicap affected his performance. The teacher experienced problems with student discipline, exhibited deficient professional preparation, failed to establish appropriate educational objectives, and generally, jeopardized the welfare and safety of the students in his charge. See *Clark* v. *Shoreline School District No. 412,* 720 P.2d 793 (Wash. 1986). Also see *Upshur* v. *Love,* 474 F. Supp. 332 (Cal. 1979), which discusses a handicapped teacher's being denied an administrative position.

The Supreme Court addressed the issue of whether having a contagious disease, tuberculosis in this instance, is a handicapping condition under Section 504. In its decision in *School Board of Nassau County* v. *Arline,* 480 U.S. 273 (1987), the Court stated:

> Allowing discrimination based on the contagious effects of a physical impairment would be inconsistent with the basic purpose of § 504, which is to ensure that handicapped individuals are not denied jobs or other benefits because of the prejudiced attitudes or the ignorance of others. By amending the definition of "handicapped individual" to include not only those who are actually physically impaired, but also those who are regarded as impaired and who, as a result, are substantially limited in a major life activity, Congress acknowledged that society's accumulated myths and fears about disability and disease are as handicapping as are the physical limitations that flow from actual impairment. Few aspects of a handicap give rise to the same level of public fear and misapprehension as contagiousness. Even those who suffer or have recovered from such noninfectious diseases as epilepsy or cancer have faced discrimination based on the irrational fear that they might be contagious. The Act is carefully structured to replace such reflexive reactions to actual or perceived handicaps with actions based on reasoned and medically sound judgments: the definition of "handicapped individual" is broad, but only those individuals who are both handicapped and otherwise qualified are eligible for relief. The fact that some persons who have contagious diseases may pose a serious health threat to others under certain circumstances does not justify excluding from the coverage of the Act all persons with actual or perceived contagious diseases. Such exclusion would mean that those accused of being contagious would never

have the opportunity to have their condition evaluated in light of medical evidence and a determination made as to whether they were "otherwise qualified." Rather, they would be vulnerable to discrimination on the basis of mythology—precisely the type of injury Congress sought to prevent. (Pp. 284–85)

The Court cited several "well established" criteria to be used to determine whether a handicapped person is an "otherwise qualified" employee: whether, given "reasonable accommodation," the person can meet all of a program's requirements or can perform "the essential functions" of the job. Accommodation is not reasonable if it imposes "undue financial and administrative burdens" on the employer or requires a fundamental alteration in the "nature of the program."

A teacher diagnosed as having AIDS (Acquired Immune Deficiency Syndrome) alleged that his reassignment to an administrative position violated Section 504. In a decision filled with references to *Arline,* a federal court of appeals upheld the teacher's motion for a preliminary injunction reinstating him to classroom duties. The court noted the overwhelming consensus of medical testimony, which revealed that the teacher posed no significant risk of spreading the disease. Additionally, the court found that the reassignment to an administrative position, although involving no monetary deprivation, failed to utilize the teacher's skills and, thus, injured him emotionally and psychologically. See *Chalk v. United States District Court,* 840 F.2d 701 (9th Cir. 1988).

VIII. Teacher Bargaining

A wide range of practices exists among the fifty states pertaining to school employee-employer relations. These practices vary from states that either have no statutory provisions or prohibit collective bargaining to those that mandate bargaining and allow teachers to strike. Although the majority of states have statutory provisions addressing issues surrounding school employee-employer relations, several states rely on the authority of case law, and a handful of states rely on attorney general opinions.

The statutes of the approximately 60 percent of states having provisions pertaining to school employee-employer relations vary considerably. Some, for instance, leave teacher negotiation or bargaining rights to the discretion of local school boards while others provide bargaining rights that compare favorably with those held by employees in the private sector. The range of issues addressed in the various statutes include whether or not there are exclusive bargaining rights for one teacher group, who may be included in the bargaining unit, dues check-off, the establishment of agency shops, "service fees," the scope of bargaining, impasse procedures, and strike provisions.

Approximately half of the states have statutes providing for good-faith bargaining between local school boards and bargaining groups. A handful of states have statutes requiring that a school board "meet and confer" with representatives of educator organizations or authorize local boards to deal with educator organizations' representatives.

Some state statutes either exclude supervisory personnel from collective bargaining or require them to be in a unit separate from teachers. Yet other states allow supervisory personnel to be included in the teacher bargaining unit, although those statutes often allow principals and other supervisory personnel to form separate bargaining units if they so desire. The vast majority of states with collective-bargaining provisions allow for exclusive bargaining rights for those groups having such rights.

The right of public school teachers to strike is a highly controversial subject. Not all school employee-employer statutory provisions address the issue of strikes. However, in several states (Hawaii, Illinois, Montana, Ohio, Oregon, Pennsylvania, and Wisconsin) statutory provisions allow teachers to strike under certain conditions. Statutes in approximately half of the states specifically prohibit strikes by teachers, and in some instances penalties for striking are specified.

A. Dismissal of Striking Teachers

Hortonville Joint School District No. 1 v. Hortonville Education Association

Supreme Court of the United States, 1976
426 U.S. 482

MR. CHIEF JUSTICE BURGER delivered the opinion of the Court.

We granted certiorari in this case to determine whether School Board members vested by state law with the power to employ and dismiss teachers could, consistent with the Due Process Clause of the Fourteenth Amendment, dismiss teachers engaged in a strike prohibited by state law.

The petitioners are a Wisconsin school district, the seven members of its School Board, and three administrative employees of the district. Respondents are teachers suing on behalf of all teachers in the district and the Hortonville Education Association (HEA), the collective-bargaining agent for the district's teachers.

During the 1972–1973 school year Hortonville teachers worked under a master collective-bargaining agreement; negotiations were conducted for renewal of the contract, but no agreement was reached for the 1973–1974 school year. The teachers continued to work while negotiations proceeded during the year without reaching agreement. On March 18, 1974, the members of the teachers' union went on strike, in direct violation of Wisconsin law. On March 20, the district superintendent sent all teachers a letter inviting them to return to work; a few did so. On March 23, he sent another letter, asking the 86 teachers still on strike to return, and reminding them that strikes by public employees were illegal; none of these teachers returned to work. After conducting classes with substitute teachers on March 26 and 27, the Board decided to conduct disciplinary hearings for each of the teachers on strike. Individual notices were sent to each teacher setting hearings for April 1, 2, and 3.

On April 1, most of the striking teachers appeared before the Board with counsel. Their attorney indicated that the teachers did not want individual hearings, but preferred to be treated as a group. Although counsel agreed that the teachers were on strike, he raised several procedural objections to the hearings. He also argued that the Board was not sufficiently impartial to exercise discipline over the striking teachers and that the Due Process Clause of the Fourteenth Amendment required an independent, unbiased decisionmaker. An offer of proof was tendered to demonstrate that the strike had been provoked by the Board's failure to meet teachers' demands, and respondents' counsel asked to cross-examine Board members individually. The Board rejected the request, but permitted counsel to make the offer of proof, aimed at showing that the Board's contract offers were unsatisfactory, that the Board used coercive and illegal bargaining tactics, and that teachers in the district had been locked out by the Board.

* * *

The sole issue in this case is whether the Due Process Clause of the Fourteenth Amendment prohibits this School Board from making the decision to dismiss teachers admittedly engaged in a strike and persistently refusing to return to their duties. The Wisconsin Supreme Court held that state law prohibited the strike and that termination of the striking teachers' employment was within the Board's statutory authority. * * * We are, of course, bound to accept the interpretation of Wisconsin law by the highest court of the State. * * * The only decision remaining for the Board therefore involved the exercise of its discretion as to what should be done to carry out the duties the law placed on the Board.

Respondents argue, and the Wisconsin Supreme Court held, that the choice presented for the Board's decision is analogous to that involved in revocation of parole in *Morrissey* v. *Brewer,* * * * that the decision could be made only by an impartial decisionmaker, and that the Board was not impartial. In *Morrissey* the Court considered a challenge to state procedures employed in revoking the parole of state prisoners. There we noted that the parole revocation decision involved two steps: first, an inquiry whether the parolee had in fact violated the conditions of his parole; second, determining whether the violations found were serious enough to justify revocation of parole and the consequent deprivation of the parolee's conditional liberty. * * * Nothing in this case is analogous to the first step in *Morrissey,* since the teachers admitted to being on strike. But respondents argue that the School Board's decision in this case is, for constitutional purposes, the same as the second aspect of the decision to revoke parole. The Board cannot make a "reasonable" decision on this issue, the Wisconsin Supreme Court held and respondents argue, because its members are biased in some fashion that the due process guarantees of the Fourteenth Amendment prohibit.

* * * A school board is not to be equated with the parole officer as an arresting officer; the school board is more like the parole board, for it has ultimate plenary authority to make its decisions derived from the state legislature. General language about due process in a holding concerning revocation of parole is not a reliable basis for dealing with the School Board's power as an employer to dismiss teachers for cause. We must focus more clearly on, first, the nature of the bias respondents attribute to the Board, and, second, the nature of the interests at stake in this case.

Respondents' argument rests in part on doctrines that have no application to this case. They seem to argue that the Board members had some personal or official stake in the decision whether the teachers should be dismissed, * * * and that the Board has manifested some personal bitterness toward the teachers, aroused by teacher criticism of the Board during the strike. * * * Even assuming that those cases state the governing standards when the decisionmaker is a public employer dealing with employees, the teachers did not show, and the Wisconsin courts did not find, that the Board members had the kind of personal or financial stake in the decision that might create a conflict of interest, and there is nothing in the record to support charges of personal animosity. The Wisconsin Supreme Court was careful "not to suggest . . . that the board members were anything but dedicated public servants, trying to provide the district with quality education . . . within its limited budget." * * * That court's analysis would seem to be confirmed by the Board's repeated invitations for striking teachers to return to work, the final invitation being contained in the letter that notified them of their discharge.

The only other factor suggested to support the claim of bias is that the School Board was involved in the negotiations that preceded and precipitated the striking teachers' discharge. Participation in those negotiations was a statutory duty of the Board. The Wisconsin Supreme Court held that this involvement, without more, disqualified the Board from deciding whether the teachers should be dismissed. * * * Mere familiarity with the facts of a case gained by an agency in the performance of its statutory role does not, however, disqualify a decisionmaker. * * * Nor is a decisionmaker disqualified simply because he has taken a position, even in public, on a policy issue related to the dispute, in the absence of a showing that he is not "capable of judging a particular controversy fairly on the basis of its own circumstances." * * *

Respondents' claim and the Wisconsin Supreme Court's holding reduce to the argument that the Board was biased because it negotiated with the teachers on behalf of the school district without reaching agreement and learned about the reasons for the strike in the course of negotiating. From those premises the Wisconsin court concluded that the Board lost its statutory power to determine that the strike and persistent refusal to terminate it amounted to conduct serious enough to warrant discharge of the strikers. Wisconsin statutes vest in the Board the power to discharge its employees, a power of every employer, whether it has negotiated with the employees before discharge or not. The Fourteenth Amendment permits a court to strip the Board of the otherwise remarkable power the Wisconsin Legislature has given it only if the Board's prior involvement in negotiating with the teachers means that it cannot act consistently with due process.

Due process, as this Court has repeatedly held, is a term that "negates any concept of inflexible procedures universally applicable to every imaginable situation." * * * Determining what process is due in a given setting requires the Court to take into account the individual's stake in the decision at issue as well as the State's interest in a particular procedure for making it. * * * Our assessment of the interests of the parties in this case leads to the conclusion that * * * the Board's prior role as negotiator does not disqualify it to decide that the public interest in maintaining uninterrupted classroom work required that teachers striking in violation of state law be discharged.

The teachers' interest in these proceedings is, of course, self-evident. They wished to avoid termination of their employment, obviously an important interest, but one that must be examined in light of several factors. Since the teachers admitted that they were engaged in a work stoppage, there was no possibility of an erroneous factual determination on this critical threshold issue. Moreover, what the teachers claim as a property right was the expectation that the jobs they had left to go and remain on strike in violation of law would remain open to them. The Wisconsin court accepted at least the essence of that claim in defining the property right under state law, and we do not quarrel with its conclusion. * * *

* * * The Board's decision whether to dismiss striking teachers involves broad considerations, and does not in the main turn on the Board's view of the "seriousness" of the teachers' conduct or the factors they urge mitigated their violation of state law. It was not an adjudicative decision, for the Board had an obligation to make a decision based on its own answer to an important question of policy: What choice among the alternative responses to the teachers' strike will best serve the interests of the school system, the interests of the parents and children who depend on the system, and the interests of the citizens whose taxes support it? The Board's decision was only incidentally a disciplinary decision; it had significant governmental and public policy dimensions as well. * * *

State law vests the governmental, or policymaking function exclusively in the School Board and the State has two interests in keeping it there. First, the Board is the body with overall responsibility for the governance of the school district; it must cope with the myriad day-to-day problems of a modern public school system including the severe consequences of a teachers' strike; by virtue of electing them the constituents have declared the Board members qualified to deal with these problems, and they are accountable to the voters for the manner in which they perform. Second, the state legislature has given to the Board the power to employ and dismiss teachers, as a part of the balance it has struck in the area of municipal labor relations; altering those statutory powers as a matter of federal due process clearly changes that balance. Permitting the Board to make the decision at issue here preserves its control over school district affairs, leaves the balance of power in labor relations where the state legislature struck it, and assures that the decision whether to dismiss the teachers will be made by the body responsible for that decision under state law.

Respondents have failed to demonstrate that the decision to terminate their employment was infected by the sort of bias that we have held to disqualify other decisionmakers as a matter of federal due process. A showing that the Board was "involved" in the events preceding this decision, in light of the important interest in leaving with the Board the power given by the state legislature, is not enough to overcome the presumption of honesty and integrity in policymakers with decision-making power. * * * Accordingly, we hold that the Due Process Clause of the Fourteenth Amendment did not guarantee respondents that the decision to terminate their employment would be made or reviewed by a body other than the School Board.

The judgment of the Wisconsin Supreme Court is reversed, and the case is remanded for further proceedings not inconsistent with this opinion.

Reversed and remanded.

B. Compulsory Union Dues

Abood v. Detroit Board of Education

Supreme Court of the United States, 1977
431 U.S. 209

MR. JUSTICE STEWART delivered the opinion of the Court.

The State of Michigan has enacted legislation authorizing a system for union representation of local governmental employees. A union and a local government employer are specifically permitted to agree to an "agency shop" arrangement, whereby every employee represented by a union—even though not a union member—must pay to the union, as a condition of employment, a service fee equal in amount to union dues. The issue before us is whether this arrangement violates the constitutional rights of government employees who object to public-sector unions as such or to various union activities financed by the compulsory service fees.

After a secret ballot election, the Detroit Federation of Teachers (Union) was certified in 1967 pursuant to Michigan law as the exclusive representative of teachers employed by the Detroit Board of Education (Board). The Union and the Board thereafter concluded a collective-bargaining agreement effective from July 1, 1969, to July 1, 1971. Among the agreement's provisions was an "agency shop" clause, requiring every teacher who had not become a Union member within 60 days of hire (or within 60 days of January 26, 1970, the effective date of the clause) to pay the Union a service charge equal to the regular dues required of Union members. A teacher who failed to meet this obligation was subject to discharge. Nothing in the agreement, however, required any teacher to join the Union, espouse the cause of unionism, or participate in any other way in Union affairs.

* * *

The designation of a union as exclusive representative carries with it great responsibilities. The tasks of negotiating and administering a collective-bargaining agreement and representing the interests of employees in settling disputes and processing grievances are continuing and difficult ones. They often entail expenditure of much time and money. * * * The services of lawyers, expert negotiators, economists, and a research staff, as well as general administrative personnel, may be required. Moreover, in carrying out these duties, the union is obliged "fairly and equitably to represent all employees . . . , union and nonunion," within the relevant unit. * * * A union-shop arrangement has been thought to distribute fairly the cost of these activities among those who benefit, and it counteracts the incentive that employees might otherwise have to become "free riders"—to refuse to contribute to the union while obtaining benefits of union representation that necessarily accrue to all employees. * * *

To compel employees financially to support their collective-bargaining representative has an impact upon their First Amendment interests. Any employee may very well have ideological objections to a wide variety of activities undertaken by the union in its role as exclusive representative. His moral or religious views about the desirability of abortion may not square with the union's policy in negotiating a medical benefits plan. One individual might disagree with a union policy of negotiating limits on the right to strike, believing that to be the road to serfdom for the working class, while another might have economic or political objections to unionism itself. An employee might object to the union's wage policy because it violates guidelines designed to limit inflation, or might object to the union's seeking a clause in the collective-bargaining agreement proscribing racial discrimination. The examples could be multiplied. To be required to help finance the union as a collective bargaining agent might well be thought, therefore, to interfere in some way with an employee's freedom to associate for the advancement of ideas, or to refrain from doing so, as he sees fit. * * *

* * *

Finally, decisionmaking by a public employer is above all a political process. The officials who represent the public employer are ultimately responsible to the electorate, which for this purpose can be viewed as comprising three overlapping classes of voters—taxpayers, users of particular government services, and government employees. Through exercise of their political influence as part of the electorate, the employees have the opportunity to affect the decisions of government representatives who sit on the other side of the bargaining table. Whether these representatives accede to a union's demands will depend upon a blend of political ingredients, including community sentiment about unionism generally and the involved union in particular, the degree of taxpayer resistance, and the views of voters as to the importance of the service involved and the relation between the demands and the quality of service. It is surely arguable, however, that permitting public employees to unionize and a union to bargain as their exclusive representative gives the employees more influence in the decisionmaking process than is possessed by employees similarly organized in the private sector.

* * *

Public employees are not basically different from private employees; on the whole, they have the same sort of skills, the same needs, and seek the same advantages. "The uniqueness of public employment is *not in the employees* nor in the work performed; the uniqueness is in the special character of the employer." * * * The very real differences between exclusive-agent collective bargaining in the public and private sectors are not such as to work any greater infringement upon the First Amendment interests of public employees. A public employee who believes that a union representing him is urging a course that is unwise as a matter of public policy is not barred from expressing his viewpoint. Besides voting in accordance with his convictions, every public employee is largely free to express his views, in public or private, orally or in writing. With some exceptions not pertinent here, public employees are free to participate in the full range of political activities open to other citizens. * * *

There can be no quarrel with the truism that because public employee unions attempt to influence governmental policymaking, their activities—and the views of members who disagree with them—may be properly termed political. But that characterization does not raise the ideas and beliefs of public employees onto a higher plane than the ideas and beliefs of private employees. It is no doubt true that a central purpose of the First Amendment " 'was to protect the free discussion of governmental affairs.' " * * * But our cases have never suggested that expression about philosophical, social, artistic, economic, literary, or ethical matters—to take a nonexhaustive list of labels—is not entitled to full First Amendment protection. Union members in both the public and private sectors may find that a variety of union activities conflict with their beliefs. * * * Nothing in the First Amendment or our cases discussing its meaning makes the question whether the adjective "political" can properly be attached to those beliefs the critical constitutional inquiry.

The differences between public- and private-sector collective bargaining simply does not translate into differences in First Amendment rights.

Even those commentators most acutely aware of the distinctive nature of public-sector bargaining and most seriously concerned with its policy implications agree that "[t]he union security issue in the public sector . . . is fundamentally the same issue . . . as in the private sector . . . No special dimension results from the fact that a union represents public rather than private employees." * * *

* * *

Our decisions establish with unmistakable clarity that the freedom of an individual to associate for the purpose of advancing beliefs and ideas is protected by the First and Fourteenth Amendments. * * * Equally clear is the proposition that a government may not require an individual to relinquish rights guaranteed him by the First Amendment as a condition of public employment. * * * The appellants argue that they fall within the protection of these cases because they have been prohibited, not from actively associating, but rather from refusing to associate. They specifically argue that they may constitutionally prevent the Union's spending a part of their required service fees to contribute to political candidates and to express political views unrelated to its duties as exclusive bargaining representative. We have concluded that this argument is a meritorious one.

* * *

The fact that the appellants are compelled to make, rather than prohibited from making, contributions for political purposes works no less an infringement of their constitutional rights. For at the heart of the First Amendment is the notion that an individual should be free to believe as he will, and that in a free society one's beliefs should be shaped by his mind and his conscience rather than coerced by the State. * * *
These principles prohibit a State from compelling any individual to affirm his belief in God * * * or to associate with a political party * * * as a condition of retaining public employment. They are no less applicable to the case at bar, and they thus prohibit the appellees from requiring any of the appellants to contribute to the support of an ideological cause he may oppose as a condition of holding a job as a public school teacher.
We do not hold that a union cannot constitutionally spend funds for the expression of political views, on behalf of political candidates, or toward the advancement of other ideological causes not germane to its duties as collective-bargaining representative. Rather, the Constitution requires only that such expenditures be financed from charges, dues or

assessments paid by employees who do not object to advancing those ideas and who are not coerced into doing so against their will by the threat of loss of governmental employment.

There will, of course, be difficult problems in drawing lines between collective-bargaining activities, for which contributions may be compelled, and ideological activities unrelated to collective bargaining, for which such compulsion is prohibited. * * * The process of establishing a written collective-bargaining agreement prescribing the terms and conditions of public employment may require not merely concord at the bargaining table, but subsequent approval by other public authorities; related budgetary and appropriations decisions might be seen as an integral part of the bargaining process. We have no occasion in this case, however, to try to define such a dividing line. * * *

* * *

The judgment is vacated, and the case is remanded for further proceedings not inconsistent with this opinion.

It is so ordered.

Note

A subsequent Court decision, *Chicago Teachers Union Local No. 1* v. *Hudson,* 475 U.S. 292 (1986), addressed fair procedures governing a union's collection of agency fees from nonmembers. The Court held that the Constitution requires (1) an adequate explanation of the basis for the fee; (2) a reasonably prompt opportunity to challenge, before an impartial decision maker, the amount of the fee; and (3) an escrow for the amounts reasonably in dispute while such a challenge is pending.

IX. Political Activities

Not many states have addressed the issue of whether restrictions should be placed on the political activities of public school teachers. Although several states have statutes covering the political candidacy of public school employees, most of the statutory provisions are far from comprehensive.

Four significant legal issues are involved when a public school employee becomes a candidate for public office or campaigns for other political candidates and issues. These issues are (1) the school employee's First

Amendment rights of freedom of expression and association, (2) incompatibility of office provisions, (3) conflict-of-interest provisions, and (4) nepotism provisions.

Although a public school employee has the First Amendment right to run for public office, a distinction must be made between the employee's right to run for public office and the right to continue school employment while holding a public office. Well-settled case law has established that a public school employee may not simultaneously hold a public office and his or her school employment if this is against (1) incompatibility-of-office provisions, (2) conflict-of-interest provisions, or (3) provisions providing for the tripartite separation of the divisions of government. Courts have consistently held that these provisions represent a compelling state need that justifies infringements upon the school employee's political rights.

Under state incompatibility-of-office and conflict-of-interest provisions, courts have established that public school employees may not maintain their employment while holding office on (1) their employing board of education or (2) any governmental body, or while holding an office that has supervisory powers over their employing school district. However, in the absence of statutory prohibitions, public school employees may serve on a board of education that is not their employing board.

Whether public school employees may maintain their employment and serve in the state legislature depends on the conflict-of-interest statute covering the state's legislators. In those states that prohibit legislators from having a direct or indirect interest in any contract dependent upon funds appropriated while they serve in the legislature, school employees may not be able to continue school employment. However, in states that do not have this type of statutory provisions, courts have held that the school employee may serve in the legislature but that it is reasonable for the board of education to require the employee to take an unpaid leave of absence while so serving. Under incompatibility-of-office provisions, courts have held that there is no incompatibility between local school employment and serving in the state legislature. However, some courts have held that it is incompatible for employees of the state university system to serve simultaneously in the legislature and hold their university jobs.

Under state nepotism provisions, a school employee's continued employment may be in jeopardy when a relative is elected to his or her employing board of education. Or the board member's continuation in office may be in jeopardy if he or she has relatives who are employed by the school board. Some state courts, under general nepotism statutes, do not strictly apply nepotism provisions to certificated school personnel. These courts have applied the rationale that state certification requirements and teacher tenure acts prevent nepotism practices in the hiring of school employees. On the other hand, where an education statute addresses nepotism issues on the part of members of a board of education, the courts strictly apply the language of such a statute.

Public school employees have the First Amendment right to campaign for other political candidates and issues; however, this right is not absolute. Courts have held that these types of activities (1) may not take place during working hours, (2) may not take place in the classroom, (3) may not interfere with the school employee's job performance, and (4) are not permissible if the employee uses his or her position of employment to influence the outcome of a political election. Further, courts have held that these activities can be restricted if they result in material disruption of the normal administrative operations of the school system.

school desegregation

Introduction

A Supreme Court decision in 1896 established the "separate but equal" doctrine regarding public facilities and services used by blacks. This decision, *Plessy* v. *Ferguson,* established a legal basis for segregated public facilities and services, including public education. Where there were no state statutory and/or constitutional provisions pertaining to segregation, **Plessy** enabled custom to be affirmed by also providing a legal basis for dual school systems in which black and white students were segregated. Although generally associated with the southern states, dual school systems were operated in several nonsouthern states. Under the dual school system, black students in a community attended all-black schools, which were staffed by blacks, and white students attended schools exclusively for whites. Little or no intercourse took place between the schools serving blacks and those attended by whites. Such de jure segregation, which had its most rigid codification and practice in the southern public schools, had the force of the law behind it since it was mandated by state constitutional and/or statutory provisions and official local school policies.

A 1954 United States Supreme Court decision, **Brown v. Board of Education,** reversed the *Plessy* doctrine as it pertained to public schools by declaring that in the field of education the doctrine of "separate but equal" had no place. This landmark reversal by the Supreme Court held de jure public school segregation to be unconstitutional. Since this decision, courts have had a veritable stream of cases brought before them in which they have had to determine whether alleged segregative policies in southern schools, nonsouthern schools, and private schools were unconstitutional.

I. Historical Perspective

A. Separate but Equal Doctrine

Plessy v. Ferguson

Supreme Court of the United States, 1896
163 U.S. 537

MR. JUSTICE BROWN, after stating the case, delivered the opinion of the court.

This case turns upon the constitutionality of an act of the General Assembly of the State of Louisiana, passed in 1890, providing for separate railway carriages for the white and colored races. * * *

The first section of the statute enacts "that all railway companies carrying passengers in their coaches in this State, shall provide equal but separate accommodations for the white, and colored races, by providing two or more passenger coaches for each passenger train, or by dividing the passenger coaches by a partition so as to secure separate accommodations: *Provided,* That this section shall not be construed to apply to street railroads. No person or persons, shall be admitted to occupy seats in coaches, other than, the ones, assigned, to them on account of the race they belong to."

By the second section it was enacted "that the officers of such passenger trains shall have the power and are hereby required to assign each passenger to the coach or compartment used for the race to which such passenger belongs; any passenger insisting on going into a coach or compartment to which by race he does not belong, shall be liable to a fine of twenty-five dollars, or in lieu thereof to imprisonment for a period of not more than twenty days in the parish prison, and any officer of any railroad insisting on assigning a passenger to a coach or compartment other than the one set aside for the race to which said passenger belongs, shall be liable to a fine of twenty-five dollars, or in lieu thereof to imprisonment for a period of not more than twenty days in the parish prison; and should any passenger refuse to occupy the coach or compartment to which he or she is assigned by the officer of such railway, said officer shall have power to refuse to carry such passenger on his train, and for such refusal neither he nor the railway company which he represents shall be liable for damages in any of the courts of this State."

The third section provides penalties for the refusal or neglect of the officers, directors, conductors and employes of railway companies to comply with the act, with a proviso that "nothing in this act shall be construed as applying to nurses attending children of the other race." The fourth section is immaterial.

The information filed in the criminal District Court charged in substance that Plessy, being a passenger between two stations within the State of Louisiana, was assigned by officers of the company to the coach used for the race to which he belonged, but he insisted upon going into a coach used by the race to which he did not belong. Neither in the information nor the plea was his particular race or color averred.

The petition for the writ of prohibition averred that petitioner was seven eighths Caucasian and one eighth African blood; that the mixture of colored blood was not discernible in him, and that he was entitled to every right, privilege and immunity secured to citizens of the United States of the white race; and that, upon such theory, he took possession of a vacant seat in a coach where passengers of the white race were accommodated, and was ordered by the conductor to vacate said coach and take a seat in another assigned to persons of the colored race, and having refused to comply with such demand he was forcibly ejected with the aid of a police officer, and imprisoned in the parish jail to answer a charge of having violated the above act.

The constitutionality of this act is attacked upon the ground that it conflicts both with the Thirteenth Amendment of the Constitution, abolishing slavery, and the Fourteenth Amendment, which prohibits certain restrictive legislation on the part of the States.

1. That it does not conflict with the Thirteenth Amendment, which abolished slavery and involuntary servitude, except as a punishment for crime, is too clear for argument. Slavery implies involuntary servitude— a state of bondage; the ownership of mankind as a chattel, or at least the control of the labor and services of one man for the benefit of another, and the absence of a legal right to the disposal of his own person, property and services. * * *

* * *

A statute which implies merely a legal distinction between white and colored races—a distinction which is founded in the color of the two races, and which must always exist so long as white men are distinguished from the other race by color—has no tendency to destroy the legal quality of the two races, or reestablish a state of involuntary servitude. Indeed, we do not understand that the Thirteenth Amendment is strenuously relied upon by the plaintiff in error in this connection.

2. By the Fourteenth Amendment, all persons born or naturalized in the United States, and subject to the jurisdiction thereof, are made citizens of the United States and of the State wherein they reside; and the States are forbidden from making or enforcing any law which shall abridge the privileges or immunities of citizens of the United States, or shall deprive any person or life, liberty or property without due process of law, or deny to any person within their jurisdiction the equal protection of the laws.

The proper construction of this amendment was first called to the attention of this court in the *Slaughter-house cases*, 16 Wall. 36, which involved, however, not a question of race, but one of exclusive privileges. The case did not call for any expression of opinion as to the exact rights it was intended to secure to the colored race, but it was said generally that its main purpose was to establish the citizenship of the negro; to give definitions of citizenship of the United States and of the States, and to protect from the hostile legislation of the States the privileges and immunities of citizens of the United States, as distinguished from those of citizens of the States.

The object of the amendment was undoubtedly to enforce the absolute equality of the two races before the law, but in the nature of things it could not have been intended to abolish distinctions based upon color, or to enforce social, as distinguished from political equality, or a commingling of the two races upon terms unsatisfactory to either. Laws permitting, and even requiring, their separation in places where they are liable to be brought into contact do not necessarily imply the inferiority of either race to the other, and have been generally, if not universally, recognized as within the competency of the state legislatures in the exercise of their police power. The most common instance of this is connected with the establishment of separate schools for white and colored children, which has been held to be a valid exercise of the legislative power even by courts of States where the political rights of the colored race have been longest and most earnestly enforced.

One of the earliest of these cases is that of *Roberts* v. *City of Boston*, 5 Cush. 198, in which the Supreme Judicial Court of Massachusetts held that the general school committee of Boston had power to make provision for the instruction of colored children in separate schools established exclusively for them, and to prohibit their attendance upon the other schools. * * * It was held that the powers of the committee extended to the establishment of separate schools for children of different ages, sexes and colors, and that they might also establish special schools for poor and neglected children, who have become too old to attend the primary school, and yet have not acquired the rudiments of learning, to enable them to enter the ordinary schools. Similar laws have been enacted by Congress under its general power of legislation over the District of Columbia, * * * as well as by the legislatures of many of the States, and have been generally, if not uniformly, sustained by the courts. * * *

Laws forbidding the intermarriage of the two races may be said in a technical sense to interfere with the freedom of contract, and yet have been universally recognized as within the police power of the State. * * *

The distinction between laws interfering with the political equality of the negro and those requiring the separation of the two races in schools, theatres and railway carriages has been frequently drawn by this court. Thus in *Strauder* v. *West Virginia*, 100 U.S. 303, it was held that a law of West Virginia limiting white male persons, 21 years of age and citizens of the State, the right to sit upon juries, was a discrimination which implied a legal inferiority in civil society, which lessened the security of the right of the colored race, and was a step toward reducing them to a condition of servility. Indeed, the right of the colored man that, in the selection of jurors to pass upon his life, liberty and property, there shall be no exclusion of his race, and no discrimination against them because of color, has been asserted in a number of cases. * * *

*   *   *

So far, then, as a conflict with the Fourteenth Amendment is concerned, the case reduces itself to the question of whether the statute of Louisiana is a reasonable regulation, and with respect to this there must necessarily be a large discretion on the part of the legislature. In determining the question of reasonableness it is at liberty to act with reference to the established usages, customs and traditions of the people, and with a view to the promotion of their comfort, and the preservation of the public peace and good order. Gauged by this standard, we cannot say that a law which authorized or even requires the separation of the two races in public conveyances is unreasonable, or more obnoxious to the Fourteenth Amendment than the acts of Congress requiring separate schools for colored children in the District of Columbia, the constitutionality of which does not seem to have been questioned, or the corresponding acts of state legislatures.

We consider the underlying fallacy of the plaintiff's argument to consist in the assumption that the enforced separation of the two races stamps the colored race with a badge of inferiority. If this be so, it is not by reason of anything found in the act, but solely because the colored race chooses to put that construction upon it. The argument necessarily assumes that if, as had been more than once the case, and is not unlikely to be so again, the colored race should become the dominant power in the state legislature, and should enact a law in precisely similar terms, it would thereby relegate the white race to an inferior position. We imagine that the white race, at least, would not acquiesce in this assumption. The argument also assumes that social prejudices may be overcome by legislation, and that equal rights cannot be secured to the negro except by an enforced commingling of the two races. We cannot accept this proposition. If the two races are to meet upon terms of social equity, it must be the result of natural affinities, a mutual appreciation of each other's merits and a voluntary consent of individuals. * * * Legislation is powerless to eradicate racial instincts or to abolish distinctions based upon physical differences, and the attempt to do so can only result in accentuating the difficulties of the present situation. If the civil and political rights of both races be equal one cannot be inferior to the other civilly or politically. If one race be inferior to the other socially, the Constitution of the United States cannot put them upon the same plane.

It is true that the question of the proportion of colored blood necessary to constitute a colored person, as distinguished from a white person, is one upon which there is a difference of opinion in the different States, some holding that any visible admixture of black blood stamps the person as belonging to the colored race, * * * others that it depends upon the preponderance of blood, * * * and still others that the predominance of white blood must only be in the proportion of three fourths. * * * But these are questions to be determined under the laws of each State and are not properly put in issue in this case. Under the allegations of his petition it may undoubtedly become a question of importance whether, under the laws of Louisiana, the petitioner belongs to the white or colored race.

The judgment of the court below is, therefore,

Affirmed.

MR. JUSTICE HARLAN dissenting.

* * *

* * * [W]e have before us a state enactment that compels, under penalties, the separation of the two races in railroad passenger coaches, and makes it a crime for a citizen of either race to enter a coach that has been assigned to citizens of the other race.

* * *

However apparent the injustice of such legislation may be, we have only to consider whether it is consistent with the Constitution of the United States.

* * *

In respect of civil rights, common to all citizens, the Constitution of the United States does not, I think, permit any public authority to know the race of those entitled to be protected in the enjoyment of such rights. Every true man has pride of race, and under appropriate circumstances when the rights of others, his equals before the law, are not to be affected, it is his privilege to express such pride and to take such action based upon it as to him seems proper. But I deny that any legislative body or judicial tribunal may have regard to the race of citizens when the civil rights of those citizens are involved. Indeed, such legislation, as that here in question, is inconsistent not only with that equality of rights which pertains to citizenship, National and State, but with the personal liberty enjoyed by every one within the United States.

The Thirteenth Amendment does not permit the withholding or the deprivation of any right necessarily inhering in freedom. It not only struck down the institution of slavery as previously existing in the United States, but it prevents the imposition of any burdens or disabilities that constitute badges of slavery or servitude. It decreed universal civil freedom in this country. This court has so adjudged. But that amendment having been found inadequate to the protection of the rights of those who had been in slavery, it was followed by the Fourteenth Amendment, which added greatly to the dignity and glory of American citizenship, and to the security of personal liberty, by declaring that "all persons born or naturalized in the United States, and subject to the jurisdiction thereof, are citizens of the United States and of the State wherein they reside," and that "no State shall make or enforce any law which shall abridge the privileges or immunities of citizens of the United States; nor shall any State deprive any person of life, liberty or property without due process of law, nor deny to any person within its jurisdiction the equal protection of the laws." These two amendments, if enforced according to their true intent and meaning, will protect all the civil rights that pertain to freedom and citizenship. Finally, and to the end that no citizen should be denied, on account of his race, the privilege of participating in the political control of his country, it was declared by the Fifteenth Amendment that "the right of the citizens of the United States to vote shall not be denied or abridged by the United States or by any State on account of race, color or previous condition of servitude."

These notable additions to the fundamental law were welcomed by the friends of liberty throughout the world. They removed the race line from our governmental systems. They had, as this court has said, a common purpose, namely, to secure "to a race recently emancipated, a race that through many generations have been held in slavery, all the civil rights that the superior race enjoy." They declared, in legal effect, this court has further said, "that the law in the States shall be the same for the black as for the white; that all persons, whether colored or white, shall stand equal before the laws of the States, and, in regard to the colored race, for whose protection the amendment was primarily designed, that no discrimination shall be made against them by law because of their color." We also said: "The words of the amendment, it is true, are prohibitory, but they contain a necessary implication of a positive immunity, or right, most valuable to the colored race—the right to exemption from unfriendly legislation against them distinctively as colored—exemption from legal discriminations, implying inferiority in civil society, lessening the security of their enjoyment of the rights which others enjoy, and discriminations which are steps towards reducing them to the condition of a subject race." It was, consequently, adjudged that a state law that excluded citizens of the colored race from juries, because of their race and however well qualified in other respects to discharge the duties of jurymen, was repugnant to the Fourteenth Amendment. * * *

* * *

It was said in argument that the statute of Louisiana does not discriminate against either race, but prescribes a rule applicable alike to white and colored citizens. But this argument does not meet the difficulty. Every one knows that the statute in question had its origins in the purpose, not so much to exclude white persons from railroad cars occupied by blacks, as to exclude colored people from coaches occupied by or assigned to white persons. Railroad corporations of Louisiana did not make discrimination among whites in the matter of accommodation for travellers. The thing to accomplish was, under the guise of giving equal accommodation for whites and blacks, to compel the latter to keep to themselves while travelling in railroad passenger coaches. No one would be so wanting in candor as to assert the contrary. The fundamental objection, therefore, to the statute is that it interferes with the personal freedom of citizens. * * * If a white man and a black man choose to occupy the same public conveyance on a public highway, it is their right to do so, and no government proceeding alone on grounds of race can prevent it without infringing the personal liberty of each.

* * *

The white race deems itself to be the dominant race in this country. And so it is, in prestige, in achievements, in education, in wealth and power. So, I doubt not, it will continue to be for all time, if it remains true to its great heritage and holds fast to the principles of constitutional liberty. But in view of the Constitution, in the eye of the law, there is in this country no superior, dominant, ruling class of citizens. There is no caste here. Our Constitution is color-blind, and neither knows nor tolerates classes among citizens. In respect of civil rights, all citizens are equal before the law. The humblest is the peer of the most powerful. The law regards man as man, and takes no account of his surroundings or of his color when his civil rights as guaranteed by the supreme law of the land are involved. It is, therefore, to be regretted that this high tribunal, the final expositor of the fundamental law of the land, has reached the conclusion that it is competent for a State to regulate the enjoyment by citizens of their civil rights solely upon the basis of race.

In my opinion, the judgment this day rendered will, in time, prove to be quite as pernicious as the decision made by this tribunal in the *Dred Scott case.* It was adjudged in that case that the descendants of Africans who were imported into this country and sold as slaves were not included nor intended to be included under the word "citizens" in the Constitution, and could not claim any of the rights and privileges which that instrument provided for and ensured to citizens of the United States; that at the time of the adoption of the Constitution they were "considered as a subordinate and inferior class of beings, who had been subjugated by the dominant race, and, whether emancipated or not, yet remained subject to their authority, and had no rights or privileges but such as those who held the power and the government might choose to grant them." * * * The recent amendments of the Constitution, it was supposed, had eradicated these principles from our institutions. But it seems that we have yet, in some of the States, a dominant race— a superior class of citizens, which assumes to regulate the enjoyment of civil rights, common to all citizens, upon the basis of race. The present decision, it may well be apprehended, will not only stimulate aggressions, more or less brutal and irritating, upon the admitted rights of colored citizens, but will encourage the belief that it is possible, by means of state enactments, to defeat the beneficent purposes which the people of the United States had in view when they adopted the recent amendments of the Constitution, by one of which the blacks of this country were made citizens of the United States and of the States in which they respectively reside, and whose privileges and immunities, as citizens, the States are forbidden to abridge. Sixty millions of whites are in no danger from the presence here of eight millions of blacks. The destinies of the two races, in this country, are indissolubly linked together, and the interests of both require that the common government of all shall not permit the seeds of race hate to be planted under the sanction of law. What can more certainly arouse race hate, what more certainly create and perpetuate a feeling of distrust between these races, than state enactments, which, in fact, proceed on the ground that colored citizens are so inferior and degraded that they cannot be allowed to sit in public coaches occupied by white citizens? That, as all will admit, is the real meaning of such legislation as was enacted in Louisiana.

* * *

There is a race so different from our own that we do not permit those belonging to it to become citizens of the United States. Persons belonging to it are, with few exceptions, absolutely excluded from our country. I allude to the Chinese race. But by the statute in question, a Chinaman can ride in the same passenger coach with white citizens of the United States, while citizens of the black race in Louisiana, many of whom, perhaps, risked their lives for the preservation of the Union, who are entitled, by law, to participate in the political control of the State and nation, who are not excluded, by law or by reason of their race, from public stations of any kind, and who have all the legal rights that belong to white citizens, are yet declared to be criminals, liable to imprisonment, if they ride in a public coach occupied by citizens of the white race. * * *

* * *

I do not deem it necessary to review the decisions of state courts to which reference was made in argument. Some, and the most important, of them are wholly inapplicable, because rendered prior to the adoption of the last amendment of the Constitution, when colored people had very few rights which the dominant race felt obliged to respect. Others were made at a time when public opinion, in many localities, was dominated by the institution of slavery; when it would not have been safe to do justice to the black man; and when, so far as the rights of blacks were concerned, race prejudice was, practically, the supreme law of the land. Those decisions cannot be guides in the era introduced by the recent amendments of the supreme law, which established universal civil freedom, gave citizenship to all born or naturalized in the United States and residing here, obliterated the race line from our systems of governments, National and State, and placed our free institutions upon the broad and sure foundation of the equality of all men before the law.

* * *

For the reasons stated, I am constrained to withhold my assent from the opinion and judgment of the majority.

Notes and Questions

Justice Harlan's dissenting opinion has proven to be prophetic. As we shall see, it is an example of how a dissent's rationale, in time, may be adopted as a majority view.

What did the "equal" in "separate but equal" mean? Did it mean that black facilities and services would be equal to those provided whites, or did it mean services and facilities afforded blacks should be equal? Could "equal" have had any other meaning than the latter one, since at the time of the decision whites dominated political, economic, and social life?

Given the racial attitudes of that day, some argue that a contrary decision in *Plessy* would have been widely flouted, thereby weakening the status of the Court as an institution. Do you think it possible that the Court would take such factors into consideration in rendering a decision?

The Court drew a distinction between "social" and "political" equality. Is the key to this distinction the involvement of state action? Do you agree that the Constitution should protect only "political" equality?

It was not until 1927 that the Court specifically extended the *Plessy* doctrine to public education. See *Gong Lum* v. *Rice*, 275 U.S. 78 (1927).

B. De Jure Public School Segregation Unconstitutional *(Brown I)*

Several United States Supreme Court decisions dealing with higher education segregative practices successfully eroded the *Plessy* doctrine before it received a mortal blow from *Brown* v. *Board of Education.* In one of these cases a black law-school applicant challenged a policy under which he had to attend an out-of-state law school because his home state did not have a "separate" law school for blacks. The Court held that such an arrangement did not meet the "separate but equal" doctrine. See *Missouri ex rel. Gaines* v. *Canada*, 305 U.S. 337 (1938). In another decision, *Sweatt* v. *Painter*, 339 U.S. 629 (1950), the Court contended that "separate" law schools in Texas were not "equal" to those attended by whites. In its decision the Court not only compared tangible factors between the black and white law schools, but also such intangible factors as prestige, faculty reputation, and experience of the administration.

Decisions such as *Gaines, Sweatt,* and others set the stage for a challenge to the de jure segregative practices in the primary and secondary public schools. This challenge was presented in **Brown,** and the Court declared that segregation in public education was a denial of the Fourteenth Amendment's guarantee of the equal protection of the laws.

Brown v. Board of Education of Topeka

Supreme Court of the United States, 1954
347 U.S. 483

MR. CHIEF JUSTICE WARREN delivered the opinion of the Court.

These cases come to us from the States of Kansas, South Carolina, Virginia, and Delaware. They are premised on different facts and different local conditions, but a common legal question justifies their consideration together in this consolidated opinion.

In each of the cases, minors of the Negro race, through their legal representatives, seek the aid of the courts in obtaining admission to the public schools of their community on a nonsegregated basis. In each instance, they had been denied admission to schools attended by white children under laws requiring or permitting segregation according to race. This segregation was alleged to deprive the plaintiffs of the equal protection of the laws under the Fourteenth Amendment. In each of the cases other than the Delaware case, a three-judge federal district court denied relief to the plaintiffs on the so-called "separate but equal" doctrine announced by this Court in *Plessy* v. *Ferguson*, 163 U.S. 537. Under that doctrine, equality of treatment is accorded when the races are provided substantially equal facilities, even though these facilities be separate. In the Delaware case, the Supreme Court of Delaware adhered to that doctrine, but ordered that the plaintiffs be admitted to the white schools because of their superiority to the Negro schools.

The plaintiffs contend that segregated public schools are not "equal" and cannot be made "equal," and that hence they are deprived of the equal protection of the laws. Because of the obvious importance of the question presented, the Court took jurisdiction. Argument was heard in the 1952 Term, and reargument was heard this Term on certain questions propounded by the Court.

Reargument was largely devoted to the circumstances surrounding the adoption of the Fourteenth Amendment in 1868. It covered exhaustively consideration of the Amendment in Congress, ratification by the states, then existing practices in racial segregation, and the views of proponents and opponents of the Amendment. This discussion and our own investigation convince us that, although the sources cast some light, it is not enough to resolve the problem with which we are faced. At best, they are inconclusive. The most avid proponents of the post-War Amendments undoubtedly intended them to remove all legal distinctions among "all persons born or naturalized in the United States." Their opponents, just as certainly, were antagonistic to both the letter and the spirit of the Amendments and wished them to have the most limited effect. What others in Congress and the state legislatures had in mind cannot be determined with any degree of certainty.

An additional reason for the inconclusive nature of the Amendment's history, with respect to segregated schools, is the status of public education at that time. In the South, the movement toward free common schools, supported by general taxation, had not yet taken hold. Education of white children was largely in the hands of private groups. Education of Negroes was almost nonexistent, and practically all of the race were illiterate. In fact, any education of Negroes was forbidden by law in some states. Today, in contrast, many Negroes have achieved outstanding success in the arts and sciences as well as in the business and professional world. It is true that public school education at the time of the Amendment had advanced further in the North, but the effect of the Amendment on Northern States was generally ignored in the congressional debates. Even in the North, the conditions of public education did not approximate those existing today. The curriculum was usually rudimentary; ungraded schools were common in rural areas; the school term was but three months a year in many states; and compulsory school attendance was virtually unknown. As a consequence, it is not surprising that there should be so little in the history of the Fourteenth Amendment relating to its intended effect on public education.

In the first cases in this Court construing the Fourteenth Amendment, decided shortly after its adoption, the Court interpreted it as proscribing all state-imposed discriminations against the Negro race. The doctrine of "separate but equal" did not make its appearance in this Court until 1896 in the case of *Plessy* v. *Ferguson, supra,* involving not education but transportation. American courts have since labored with the doctrine for over half a century. In this Court, there have been six cases involving the "separate but equal" doctrine in the field of public education. In *Cumming* v. *County Board of Education,* 175 U.S. 528, and *Gong Lum* v. *Rice,* 275 U.S. 78, the validity of the doctrine itself was not challenged. In more recent cases, all on the graduate school level, inequality was found in that specific benefits enjoyed by white students were denied to Negro students of the same educational qualifications. *Missouri ex rel. Gaines* v. *Canada,* 305 U.S. 337; *Sipuel* v. *Oklahoma,* 332 U.S. 631; *Sweatt* v. *Painter,* 339 U.S. 629; *McLaurin* v. *Oklahoma State Regents,* 339 U.S. 637. In none of these cases was it necessary to re-examine the doctrine to grant relief to the Negro plaintiff. And in *Sweatt* v. *Painter, supra,* the Court expressly reserved decision on the question whether *Plessy* v. *Ferguson* should be held inapplicable to public education.

In the instant cases, that question is directly presented. Here, unlike *Sweatt* v. *Painter,* there are findings below that the Negro and white schools involved have been equalized, or are being equalized, with respect to buildings, curricula, qualifications and salaries of teachers, and other "tangible" factors. Our decision, therefore, cannot turn on merely a comparison of these tangible factors in the Negro and white schools involved in each of the cases. We must look instead to the effect of segregation itself on public education.

In approaching this problem, we cannot turn the clock back to 1868 when the Amendment was adopted, or even to 1896 when *Plessy* v. *Ferguson* was written. We must consider public education in the light of its full development and its present place in American life throughout the Nation. Only in this way can it be determined if segregation in public schools deprives these plaintiffs of the equal protection of the laws.

Today, education is perhaps the most important function of state and local governments. Compulsory school attendance laws and the great expenditures for education both demonstrate our recognition of the importance of education to our democratic society. It is required in the performance of our most basic public responsibilities, even service in the armed forces. It is the very foundation of good citizenship. Today it is a principal instrument in awakening the child to cultural values, in preparing him for later professional training, and in helping him to adjust normally to his environment. In these days, it is doubtful that any child may reasonably be expected to succeed in life if he is denied the opportunity of an education. Such an opportunity, where the state has undertaken to provide it, is a right which must be made available to all on equal terms.

We come then to the question presented: Does segregation of children in public schools solely on the basis of race, even though the physical facilities and other "tangible" factors may be equal, deprive the children of the minority group of equal educational opportunities? We believe that it does.

In *Sweatt* v. *Painter, supra,* in finding that a segregated law school for Negroes could not provide them equal educational opportunities, this Court relied in large part on "those qualities which are incapable of objective measurement but which make for greatness in a law school." In *McLaurin* v. *Oklahoma State Regents, supra,* the Court, in requiring that a Negro admitted to a white graduate school be treated like all other students, again resorted to intangible considerations: ". . . his ability to study, to engage in discussions and exchange views with other students, and, in general, to learn his profession." Such considerations apply with added force to children in grade school and high schools. To separate them from others of similar age qualifications solely because of their race generates a feeling of inferiority as to their status in the community that may affect their hearts and minds in a way unlikely ever to be undone. The effect of this separation on their educational opportunities was well stated by a finding in the Kansas case by a court which nevertheless felt compelled to rule against the Negro plaintiffs:

"Segregation of white and colored children in public schools has a detrimental effect upon the colored children. The impact is greater when it has the sanction of the law; for the policy of separating the races is usually interpreted as denoting the inferiority of the negro group. A sense of inferiority affects the motivation of a child to learn. Segregation with the sanction of law, therefore, has a tendency to [retard] the educational and mental development of negro children and to deprive them of some of the benefits they would receive in a racial[ly] integrated school system."

Whatever may have been the extent of psychological knowledge at the time of *Plessy* v. *Ferguson,* this finding is amply supported by modern authority. Any language in *Plessy* v. *Ferguson* contrary to this finding is rejected.

We conclude that in the field of public education the doctrine of "separate but equal" has no place. Separate educational facilities are inherently unequal. Therefore, we hold that the plaintiffs and others similarly situated for whom the actions have been brought are, by reason of the segregation complained of, deprived of the equal protection of the laws guaranteed by the Fourteenth Amendment. This disposition makes unnecessary any discussion whether such segregation also violates the Due Process Clause of the Fourteenth Amendment.

Because these are class actions, because of the wide applicability of this decision, and because of the great variety of local conditions, the formulation of decrees in these cases presents problems of considerable complexity. On reargument, the consideration of appropriate relief was necessarily subordinated to the primary question—the constitutionality of segregation in public education. We have now announced that such segregation is a denial of the equal protection of the laws. * * *

Notes and Questions

Brown may be one of the most significant decisions rendered by the United States Supreme Court. By declaring de jure segregation in the schools unconstitutional, the decision had reverberations far beyond the public schools. It was a catalyst that forced Americans to examine many forms of government-condoned separation of the races.

It should be emphasized that the consolidated opinion in *Brown* addressed de jure segregation in the public schools. Constitutional and statutory provisions in South Carolina, Virginia, and Delaware and statutory provisions in Kansas required the segregation of black and white students. Consequently, *Brown* applied only to those states having government-imposed segregation at the time of the decision. It did not have applicability to de facto segregated public schools outside the South.

The decision was widely criticized by those opposed to desegregation and applauded by those who were for it. Criticism on legalistic grounds focused on the fact that the Court relied on sociological evidence to establish the negative effect of segregation on black students rather than relying on precedent. This raises the question of what factors the Court should take into consideration when attempting to determine whether or not a person has received "equal protection of the laws" guaranteed by the Fourteenth Amendment to the Constitution.

Proponents of "judicial activism" argued that since the executive and legislative branches were apparently unwilling to address this issue, it was the duty of the judiciary to ensure that all persons, in this instance blacks, receive their constitutional rights. Opponents of the decision contended that nine appointed judges, as opposed to elected officials, should not have the power to institute such fundamental social change. Which view do you hold?

C. Implementation *(Brown II)*

Brown discussed the broad issue of public school segregation and declared de jure segregation to be unconstitutional. However, the decision did not provide a remedy for those whom it affected. As the Court stated:

> Because these are class actions, because of the wide applicability of this decision, and because of the great variety of local conditions, the formulation

of decrees in these cases presents problems of considerable complexity. (P. 495)

Therefore, the Court addressed this question in a separate opinion in *Brown II.*

Brown v. Board of Education of Topeka

Supreme Court of the United States, 1955
349 U.S. 294

MR. CHIEF JUSTICE WARREN delivered the opinion of the Court.

These cases were decided on May 17, 1954. The opinions of that date, declaring the fundamental principle that racial discrimination in public education is unconstitutional, are incorporated herein by reference. All provisions of federal, state, or local law requiring or permitting such discrimination must yield to this principle. There remains for consideration the manner in which relief is to be accorded.

Because these cases arose under different local conditions and their disposition will involve a variety of local problems, we requested further argument on the question of relief. * * *

These presentations were informative and helpful to the Court in its consideration of the complexities arising from the transition to a system of public education freed of racial discrimination. The presentations also demonstrated that substantial steps to eliminate racial discrimination in public schools have already been taken, not only in some of the communities in which these cases arose, but in some of the states appearing as *amici curiae,* and in other states as well. Substantial progress has been made in the District of Columbia and in the communities in Kansas and Delaware involved in this litigation. The defendants in the cases coming to us from South Carolina and Virginia are awaiting the decision of this Court concerning relief.

Full implementation of these constitutional principles may require solution of varied local school problems. School authorities have the primary responsibility for elucidating, assessing, and solving these problems; courts will have to consider whether the action of school authorities constitutes good faith implementation of the governing constitutional principles. Because of their proximity to local conditions and the possible need for further hearings, the courts which originally heard these cases can best perform this judicial appraisal. Accordingly, we believe it appropriate to remand the cases to those courts.

In fashioning and effectuating the decrees, the courts will be guided by equitable principles. Traditionally, equity has been characterized by a practical flexibility in shaping its remedies and by a facility for adjusting and reconciling public and private needs. These cases call for the exercise of these traditional attributes of equity power. At stake is the personal interest of the plaintiffs in admission to public schools as soon as practicable on a nondiscriminatory basis. To effectuate this interest may call for elimination of a variety of obstacles in making the transition to school systems operated in accordance with the constitutional principles set forth in our May 17, 1954, decision. Courts of equity may properly take into account the public interest in the elimination of such obstacles in a systematic and effective manner. But it should go without saying that the vitality of these constitutional principles cannot be allowed to yield simply because of disagreement with them.

While giving weight to these public and private considerations, the courts will require that the defendants make a prompt and reasonable start toward full compliance with our May 17, 1954, ruling. Once such a start has been made, the courts may find that additional time is necessary to carry out the ruling in an effective manner. The burden rests upon the defendants to establish that such time is necessary in the public interest and is consistent with good faith compliance at the earliest practicable date. To that end, the courts may consider problems related to administration, arising from the physical condition of the school plant, the school transportation system, personnel, revision of school districts and attendance areas into compact units to achieve a system of determining admission to the public schools on a nonracial basis, and revision of local laws and regulations which may be necessary in solving the foregoing problems. They will also consider the adequacy of any plans the defendants may propose to meet these problems and to effectuate a transition to a racially nondiscriminatory school system. During this period of transition, the courts will retain jurisdiction of these cases.

The judgments below, except that in the Delaware case, are accordingly reversed and the cases are remanded to the District Courts to take such proceedings and enter such orders and decrees consistent with this opinion as are necessary and proper to admit to public schools on a racially nondiscriminatory basis with all deliberate speed the parties to these cases. The judgment in the Delaware case—ordering the immediate admission of plaintiffs to schools previously attended only by white children—is affirmed on the basis of the principles stated in our May 17, 1954, opinion, but the case is remanded to the Supreme Court of Delaware for such further proceedings as that Court may deem necessary in light of this opinion.

It is so ordered.

Notes and Questions

Did *Brown II* temper the original decision by employing such an imprecise standard as "all deliberate speed"? In this regard Justice Frankfurter suggested: "Nothing could be worse from my point of view than for this court to make an abstract declaration that segregation is bad and then to have it evaded by tricks." Would the establishment of a specific time frame, for instance, have been enforceable?

In addition to not setting a time frame, why do you believe the Court did not offer specific desegregation guidelines to the lower courts that were effecting desegregation? Do *Brown I* and *Brown II* provide sufficient instructions and guidance from the Supreme Court to the lower federal courts for the latter to have effected desegregation adequately? Since the Court did not provide a test for compliance with the desegregation ruling, what criteria would one use to determine if a school system was in compliance with *Brown I?*

II. Desegregation in the South

Under the *Brown II* formula local school authorities were given the primary responsibility for fashioning desegregation plans. Lower-level federal courts were to determine whether such plans constituted good faith implementation of the principles enunciated in *Brown I*. However, the Court's abstract doctrine, lack of clear guidance, and imprecise time frame, especially in those areas of the South where there was considerable animosity to the decision, all contributed to attempts at delay if not outright noncompliance with *Brown I.*

Consequently, lower federal courts in the South were inundated with school desegregation cases. Some of these cases represented resistance in complying with *Brown I* on the part of local school systems, yet in other instances local authorities were thwarted in their attempt to desegregate by state-level action. An example of this latter problem, which gained nationwide notoriety at the time, is the events in Little Rock, Arkansas. Here the local school system had made good-faith efforts to desegregate; however, the governor ordered the national guard to prevent black students from entering the school to which they had been assigned. Under the circumstances, the local authorities sought a postponement of the desegregation plan by citing preservation of the public peace. In addressing this issue, the Supreme Court, in *Cooper* v. *Aaron*, 358 U.S. 1 (1958), declared that while the Court was sympathetic to the authorities' good-faith efforts that had been hindered by state action, desegregation of the schools could not be postponed.

In Virginia that state's compulsory-education laws were repealed, and school attendance was made a matter of local option. Prince Edward County closed its schools, and private schools for whites only were operated in their place with state and county assistance. The Supreme Court rejected such a course in *Griffin* v. *County School Board of Prince Edward County*, 377 U.S. 218 (1964), by instructing the local district court to require the authorities to levy taxes, thereby raising funds to reopen and operate a nondiscriminatory public school system such as those in other Virginia counties.

A so-called freedom-of-choice plan was another method school systems employed to comply with the necessity to desegregate. Under such a plan parents had the choice of determining which school their children would attend, with the result that there was often little or no actual desegregation within a school system.

A. Freedom of Choice

Green v. County School Board of New Kent County

Supreme Court of the United States, 1968
391 U.S. 430

MR. JUSTICE BRENNAN delivered the opinion of the Court.

The question for decision is whether, under all the circumstances here, respondent School Board's adoption of a "freedom-of-choice" plan which allows a pupil to choose his own public school constitutes adequate compliance with the Board's responsibility "to achieve a system of determining admission to the public schools on a non-racial basis. . . ." *Brown* v. *Board of Education*, 349 U.S. 294, 300–301 *(Brown II)*.

Petitioners brought this action in March 1965 seeking injunctive relief against respondent's continued maintenance of an alleged racially segregated school system. New Kent County is a rural county in Eastern Virginia. About one-half of its population of some 4,500 are Negroes. There is no residential segregation in the county; persons of both races reside throughout. The school system has only two schools, the New Kent school on the east side of the county and the George W. Watkins school on the west side. In a memorandum filed May 17, 1966, the District Court found that the "school system serves approximately 1,300 pupils, of which 740 are Negro and 550 are White. The School Board operates one white combined elementary and high school [New Kent], and one Negro combined elementary and high school [George W. Watkins]. There are no attendance zones. Each school serves the entire county." The record indicates that 21 school buses—11 serving the Watkins school and 10 serving the New Kent school—travel overlapping routes throughout the county to transport pupils to and from the two schools.

The segregated system was initially established and maintained under the compulsion of Virginia constitutional and statutory provisions mandating racial segregation in public education. * * * These provisions were held to violate the Federal Constitution in *Davis* v. *County School Board of Education of Prince Edward County,* decided with *Brown* v. *Board of Education,* 347 U.S. 483, 487 *(Brown I).* The respondent School Board continued the segregated operation of the system after the *Brown* decisions, presumably on the authority of several statutes enacted by Virginia in resistance to those decisions. Some of these statutes were held to be unconstitutional on their face or as applied. One statute, the Pupil Placement Act, Va. Code § 22–232.1 *et seq.* (1964), not repealed until 1966, divested local boards of authority to assign children to particular schools and placed that authority in a State Pupil Placement Board. Under that Act children were each year automatically reassigned to the school previously attended unless upon their application the State Board assigned them to another school; students seeking enrollment for the first time were also assigned at the discretion of the State Board. To September 1964, no Negro pupil had applied for admission to the New Kent school under this statute and no white pupil had applied for admission to the Watkins school.

The School Board initially sought dismissal of this suit on the ground that petitioners had failed to apply to the State Board for assignment to New Kent school. However on August 2, 1965, five months after the suit was brought, respondent School Board, in order to remain eligible for federal financial aid, adopted a "freedom-of-choice" plan for desegregating the schools. Under that plan, each pupil, except for those entering the first and eighth grades, may annually choose between the New Kent and Watkins schools and pupils not making a choice are assigned to the school previously attended; first and eighth grade pupils must affirmatively choose a school. * * *

The pattern of separate "white" and "Negro" schools in the New Kent County school system established under compulsion of state laws is precisely the pattern of segregation to which *Brown I* and *Brown II* were particularly addressed, and which *Brown I* declared unconstitutionally denied Negro school children equal protection of the laws. Racial identification of the system's schools was complete, extending not just to the composition of student bodies at the two schools but to every facet of school operations—faculty, staff, transportation, extracurricular activities and facilities. In short, the State, acting through the local school board and school officials, organized and operated a dual system, part "white" and part "Negro."

It was such dual systems that 14 years ago *Brown I* held unconstitutional and a year later *Brown II* held must be abolished; school boards operating such school systems were *required* by *Brown II* "to effectuate a transition to a racially nondiscriminatory school system." 349 U.S., at 301. It is of course true that for the time immediately after *Brown II* the concern was with making an initial break in a long-established pattern of excluding Negro children from schools attended by white children. The principal focus was on obtaining for those Negro children courageous enough to break with tradition a place in the "white" schools. See, *e.g., Cooper* v. *Aaron,* 358 U.S. 1. Under *Brown II* that immediate goal was only the first step, however. The transition to a unitary, nonracial system of public education was and is the ultimate end to be brought about; it was because of the "complexities arising from the transition to a system of public education freed of racial discrimination" that we provided for "all deliberate speed" in the implementation of the principles of *Brown I.* * * * Thus we recognized the task would necessarily involve solution of "varied local school problems." * * * In referring to the "personal interest of the plaintiffs in admission to public schools as soon as practicable on a nondiscriminatory basis," we also noted that "[t]o effectuate this interest may call for elimination of a variety of obstacles in making the transition. . . ." * * * Yet we emphasized that the constitutional rights of Negro children required school officials to bear the burden of establishing that additional time to carry out the ruling in an effective manner "is necessary in the public interest and is consistent with good faith compliance at the earliest practicable date." * * * We charged the district court in their review of particular situations to

> "consider problems related to administration, arising from the physical condition of the school plant, the school transportation system, personnel, revision of school districts and attendance areas into compact units to achieve a system of determining admission to the public schools on a nonracial basis, and revision of local laws and regulations which may be necessary in solving the foregoing problems. They will also consider the adequacy of any plans the defendants may propose to meet these problems and to effectuate a transition to a racially nondiscriminatory school system." * * *

It is against this background that 13 years after *Brown II* commanded the abolition of dual systems we must measure the effectiveness of respondent School Board's "freedom-of-choice" plan to achieve that end. The School Board contends that it has fully discharged its obligation by adopting a plan by which every student, regardless of race, may "freely" choose the school he will attend. The Board attempts to cast the issue in its broadest form by arguing that its "freedom-of-choice" plan may be faulted only by reading the Fourteenth Amendment as universally requiring "compulsory integration," a reading it insists the wording of the Amendment will not support. But that argument ignores the thrust of *Brown II*. In the light of the command of that case, what is involved here is the question whether the Board has achieved the "racially nondiscriminatory school system" *Brown II* held must be effectuated in order to remedy the established unconstitutional deficiencies of its segregated system. In the context of the state-imposed segregated pattern of long standing, the fact that in 1965 the Board opened the doors of the former "white" school to Negro children and of the "Negro" school to white children merely begins, not ends, our inquiry whether the Board has taken steps adequate to abolish its dual, segregated system. *Brown II* was a call for the dismantling of well-entrenched dual systems tempered by an awareness that complex and multifaceted problems would arise which would require time and flexibility for a successful resolution. School boards such as the respondent then operating state-compelled dual systems were nevertheless clearly charged with the affirmative duty to take whatever steps might be necessary to convert to a unitary system in which racial discrimination would be eliminated root and branch. * * * The constitutional rights of Negro school children articulated in *Brown I* permit no less than this; and it was to this end that *Brown II* commanded school boards to bend their efforts.

In determining whether respondent School Board met that command by adopting its "freedom-of-choice" plan, it is relevant that this first step did not come until some 11 years after *Brown I* was decided and 10 years after *Brown II* directed the making of a "prompt and reasonable start." This deliberate perpetuation of the unconstitutional dual system can only have compounded the harm of such a system. Such delays are no longer tolerable, for "the governing constitutional principles no longer bear the imprint of newly enunciated doctrine." * * * Moreover, a plan that at this late date fails to provide meaningful assurance of prompt and effective disestablishment of a dual system is also intolerable. "The time for mere 'deliberate speed' has run out," *Griffin* v. *County School Board,* 377 U.S. 218, 234; "the context in which we must interpret and apply this language [of *Brown II*] to plans for desegregation has been significantly altered." * * * The burden on a school board today is to come forward with a plan that promises realistically to work, and promises realistically to work *now*.

The obligation of the district courts, as it always has been, is to assess the effectiveness of a proposed plan in achieving desegregation. There is no universal answer to complex problems of desegregation; there is obviously no one plan that will do the job in every case. The matter must be assessed in light of the circumstances present and the options available in each instance. It is incumbent upon the school board to establish that its proposed plan promises meaningful and immediate progress toward disestablishing state-imposed segregation. It is incumbent upon the district court to weigh that claim in light of the facts at hand and in light of any alternatives which may be shown as feasible and more promising in their effectiveness. Where the court finds the board to be acting in good faith and the proposed plan to have real prospects for dismantling the state-imposed dual system "at the earliest practicable date," then the plan may be said to provide effective relief. Of course, the availability to the board of other more promising courses of action may indicate a lack of good faith; and at the least it places a heavy burden upon the board to explain its preference for an apparently less effective method. Moreover, whatever plan is adopted will require evaluation in practice, and the court should retain jurisdiction until it is clear that state-imposed segregation has been completely removed. * * *

We do not hold that "freedom of choice" can have no place in such a plan. We do not hold that a "freedom-of-choice" plan might of itself be unconstitutional, although that argument has been urged upon us. Rather all we decide today is that in desegregating a dual system a plan utilizing "freedom of choice" is not an end in itself. * * * Although the general experience under "freedom of choice" to date has been such as to indicate its ineffectiveness as a tool of desegregation, there may well be instances in which it can serve as an effective device. Where it offers real promise of aiding a desegregation program to effectuate conversion of a state-imposed dual system to a unitary, nonracial system there might be no objection to allowing such a device to prove itself in operation. On the other hand, if there are reasonably available other ways, such for illustration as zoning, promising speedier and more effective conversion to a unitary, nonracial school system, "freedom of choice" must be held unacceptable.

The New Kent School Board's "freedom-of-choice" plan cannot be accepted as a sufficient step to "effectuate a transition" to a unitary system. In three years of operation not a single white child has chosen to attend Watkins school and although 115 Negro children enrolled in New Kent school in 1967 (up from 35 in 1965 and 111 in 1966) 85% of the Negro children in the system still attend the all-Negro Watkins school. In other words, the school system remains a dual system. Rather than further the dismantling of the dual system, the plan has operated simply to burden children and their parents with a responsibility which *Brown II* placed squarely on the School Board. The Board must be required to formulate a new plan and, in light of other courses which appear open to the Board, such as zoning, fashion steps which promise realistically to convert promptly to a system without a "white" school and a "Negro" school, but just schools.

It is so ordered.

Notes and Questions

Does the opinion in **Green** suggest that in the future a school system must engage in affirmative action in order to desegregate schools? Do you think the school board's failure to take any steps to eliminate segregation for eleven years after **Brown I** influenced the Court's decision?

In a per curiam opinion one year after **Green,** the Court declared that with respect to continued operation of racially segregated schools, the standard of "all deliberate speed" was no longer constitutionally permissible and that school districts must immediately terminate dual school systems based on race or color. See *Alexander* v. *Holmes County Board of Education,* 396 U.S. 19 (1969).

B. Defining the Scope of the Duty to Eliminate the Dual School System

Swann v. Charlotte-Mecklenburg Board of Education

Supreme Court of the United States, 1971
402 U.S. 1

MR. CHIEF JUSTICE BURGER delivered the opinion of the Court.

* * *

This case and those argued with it arose in States having a long history of maintaining two sets of schools in a single school system deliberately operated to carry out a governmental policy to separate pupils in schools solely on the basis of race. That was what *Brown* v. *Board of Education* was all about. These cases present us with the problem of defining in more precise terms than heretofore the scope of the duty of school authorities and district courts in implementing *Brown I* and the mandate to eliminate dual systems and establish unitary systems at once. Meanwhile district courts and courts of appeals have struggled in hundreds of cases with a multitude and variety of problems under this Court's general directive. Understandably, in an area of evolving remedies, those courts had to improvise and experiment without detailed or specific guidelines. This Court, in *Brown I,* appropriately dealt with the large constitutional principles; other federal courts had to grapple with the flinty, intractable realities of day-to-day implementation of those constitutional commands. Their efforts, of necessity, embraced a process of "trial and error," and our effort to formulate guidelines must take into account their experience.

The Charlotte-Mecklenburg school system, the 43d largest in the Nation, encompasses the city of Charlotte and surrounding Mecklenburg County, North Carolina. The area is large—550 square miles—spanning roughly 22 miles east-west and 36 miles north-south. During the 1968–1969 school year the system served more than 84,000 pupils in 107 schools. Approximately 71% of the pupils were found to be white and 29% Negro. As of June 1969 there were approximately 24,000 Negro students in the system, of whom 21,000 attended schools within the city of Charlotte. Two-thirds of those 21,000—approximately 14,000 Negro students—attended 21 schools which were either totally Negro or more than 99% Negro.

* * *

In April 1969 the District Court ordered the school board to come forward with a plan for both faculty and student desegregation. Proposed plans were accepted by the court in June and August 1969 on an interim basis only, and the board was ordered to file a third plan by November 1969. In November the board moved for an extension of time until February 1970, but when that was denied the board submitted a partially completed plan. In December 1969 the District Court held that the Board's submission was unacceptable and appointed an expert in education administration, Dr. John Finger, to prepare a desegregation plan. Thereafter in February 1970, the District Court was presented with two alternative pupil assignment plans—the finalized "board plan" and the "Finger plan."

The Board Plan. As finally submitted, the school board plan closed seven schools and reassigned their pupils. It restructured school attendance zones to achieve greater racial balance but maintained existing grade structures and rejected techniques such as pairing and clustering as part of a desegregation effort. The plan created a single athletic league, eliminated the previously racial basis of the school bus system, provided racially mixed faculties and administrative staffs, and modified its free-transfer plan into an optional majority-to-minority transfer system.

The board plan proposed substantial assignment of Negroes to nine of the system's 10 high schools, producing 17% to 36% Negro population in each. The projected Negro attendance at the 10th school, Independence, was 2%. The proposed attendance zones for the high schools were typically shaped like wedges of a pie, extending outward from the center of the city to the suburban and rural areas of the county in order to afford residents of the center city area access to outlying schools.

As for junior high schools, the board rezoned the 21 school areas so that in 20 the Negro attendance would range from 0% to 38%. The other school, located in the heart of the Negro residential area, was left with an enrollment of 90% Negro.

The board plan with respect to elementary schools relied entirely upon gerry-mandering of geographic zones. More than half of the Negro elementary pupils were left in nine schools that were 86% to 100% Negro; approximately half of the white elementary pupils were assigned to schools 86% to 100% white.

The Finger Plan. The plan submitted by the court-appointed expert, Dr. Finger, adopted the school board zoning plan for senior high schools with one modification: it required that an additional 300 Negro students be transported from the Negro residential area of the city to the nearly all-white Independence High School.

The Finger plan for the junior high schools employed much of the rezoning plan of the board, combined with the creation of nine "satellite" zones. Under the satellite plan, inner-city Negro students were assigned by attendance zones to nine outlying predominantly white junior high schools, thereby substantially desegregating every junior high school in the system.

The Finger plan departed from the board plan chiefly in its handling of the system's 76 elementary schools. Rather than relying solely upon geographic zoning, Dr. Finger proposed use of zoning, pairing, and grouping techniques, with the result that student bodies throughout the system would range from 9% to 38% Negro.

* * * Under the Finger plan, nine inner-city Negro schools were grouped in this manner with 24 suburban white schools.

On February 5, 1970, the District Court adopted the board plan, as modified by Dr. Finger, for the junior and senior high schools. The court rejected the board elementary school plan and adopted the Finger plan as presented. * * *

On appeal the Court of Appeals affirmed the District Court's order as to faculty desegregation and the secondary school plans, but vacated the order respecting elementary schools. * * *

* * *

Nearly 17 years ago this Court held, in explicit terms, that state-imposed segregation by race in public schools denies equal protection of the laws. At no time has the Court deviated in the slightest degree from that holding or its constitutional underpinnings. * * *

* * *

Over the 16 years since *Brown II,* many difficulties were encountered in implementation of the basic constitutional requirement that the State not discriminate between public school children on the basis of their race. Nothing in our national experience prior to 1955 prepared anyone for dealing with changes and adjustments of the magnitude and complexity encountered since then. Deliberate resistance of some to the Court's mandates has impeded the good-faith efforts of others to bring school systems into compliance. The detail and nature of these dilatory tactics have been noted frequently by this Court and other courts.

* * *

The problems encountered by the district courts and courts of appeals make plain that we should now try to amplify guidelines, however incomplete and imperfect, for the assistance of school authorities and courts. The failure of local authorities to meet their constitutional obligations aggravated the massive problem of converting from the state-enforced discrimination of racially separate school systems. This process has been rendered more difficult by changes since 1954 in the structure and patterns of communities, the growth of student population, movement of families, and other changes, some of which had marked impact on school planning, sometimes neutralizing or negating remedial action before it was fully implemented. Rural areas accustomed for half a century to the consolidated school systems implemented by bus transportation could make adjustments more readily than metropolitan areas with dense and shifting population, numerous schools, congested and complex traffic patterns.

* * *

This allocation of responsibility once made, the Court attempted from time to time to provide some guidelines for the exercise of the district judge's discretion and for the reviewing function of the courts of appeals. However, a school desegregation case does not differ fundamentally from other cases involving the framing of equitable remedies to repair the denial of a constitutional right. The task is to correct, by a balancing of the individual and collective interests, the condition that offends the Constitution.

In seeking to define even in broad and general terms how far this remedial power extends it is important to remember that judicial powers may be exercised only on the basis of a constitutional violation. Remedial judicial authority does not put judges automatically in the shoes of school authorities whose powers are plenary. Judicial authority enters only when local authority defaults.

* * *

We turn now to the problem of defining with more particularity the responsibilities of school authorities in desegregating a state-enforced dual school system in light of the Equal Protection Clause. Although the several related cases before us are primarily concerned with problems of student assignment, it may be helpful to begin with a brief discussion of other aspects of the process.

In *Green*, we pointed out that existing policy and practice with regard to faculty, staff, transportation, extracurricular activities, and facilities were among the most important indicia of a segregated system. 391 U.S., at 435. Independent of student assignment, where it is possible to identify a "white school" or a "Negro school" simply by reference to the racial composition of teachers and staff, the quality of school buildings and equipment, or the organization of sports activities, a *prima facie* case of violation of substantive constitutional rights under the Equal Protection Clause is shown.

When a system has been dual in these respects, the first remedial responsibility of school authorities is to eliminate invidious racial distinctions. With respect to such matters as transportation, supporting personnel, and extracurricular activities, no more than this may be necessary. Similar corrective action must be taken with regard to the maintenance of buildings and the distribution of equipment. In these areas, normal administrative practice should produce schools of like quality, facilities, and staffs. Something more must be said, however, as to faculty assignment and new school construction.

* * *

In *United States* v. *Montgomery County Board of Education*, 395 U.S. 225 (1969), the District Court set as a goal a plan of faculty assignment in each school with a ratio of white to Negro faculty members substantially the same throughout the system. * * *

The District Court in *Montgomery* then proceeded to set an initial ratio for the whole system of at least two Negro teachers out of each 12 in any given school. The Court of Appeals modified the order by eliminating what it regarded as "fixed mathematical" ratios of faculty and substituted an initial requirement of *"substantially or approximately"* a five-to-one ratio. With respect to the future, the Court of Appeals held that the numerical ratio should be eliminated and that compliance should not be tested solely by the achievement of specified proportions. * * *

We reversed the Court of Appeals and restored the District Court's order in its entirety. * * * The principles of *Montgomery* have been properly followed by the District Court and the Court of Appeals in this case.

The construction of new schools and the closing of old ones are two of the most important functions of local school authorities and also two of the most complex. They must decide questions of location and capacity in light of population growth, finances, land values, site availability, through an almost endless list of factors to be considered. The result of this will be a decision which, when combined with one technique or another of student assignment, will determine the racial composition of the student body in each school in the system. Over the long run, the consequences of the choices will be far reaching. People gravitate toward school facilities, just as schools are located in response to the needs of people. The location of schools may thus influence the patterns of residential development of a metropolitan area and have important impact on composition of inner-city neighborhoods.

In the past, choices in this respect have been used as a potent weapon for creating or maintaining a state-segregated school system. In addition to the classic pattern of building schools specifically intended for Negro or white students, school authorities have sometimes, since *Brown,* closed schools which appeared likely to become racially mixed through changes in neighborhood residential patterns. This was sometimes accompanied by building new schools in the areas of white suburban expansion farthest from Negro population centers in order to maintain the separation of the races with a minimum departure from the formal principles of "neighborhood zoning." Such a policy does more than simply influence the short-run composition of the student body of a new school. It may well promote segregated residential patterns which, when combined with "neighborhood zoning," further lock the school system into the mold of separation of the races. Upon a proper showing a district court may consider this in fashioning a remedy.

In ascertaining the existence of legally imposed school segregation, the existence of a pattern of school construction and abandonment is thus a factor of great weight. In devising remedies where legally imposed segregation has been established, it is the responsibility of local authorities and district courts to see to it that future school construction and abandonment are not used and do not serve to perpetuate or reestablish the dual system. * * *

The central issue in this case is that of student assignment, and there are essentially four problem areas:

court orders in this and the companion *Davis* case now provide such an option.

[3] Remedial Altering of Attendance Zones

The maps submitted in these cases graphically demonstrate that one of the principal tools employed by school planners and by courts to break up the dual school system has been a frank—and sometimes drastic—gerrymandering of school districts and attendance zones. An additional step was pairing, "clustering," or "grouping" of schools with attendance assignments made deliberately to accomplish the transfer of Negro students out of formerly segregated Negro schools and transfer of white students to formerly all-Negro schools. More often than not, these zones are neither compact nor contiguous; indeed, they may be on opposite ends of the city. As an interim corrective measure, this cannot be said to be beyond the broad remedial powers of a court.

Absent a constitutional violation there would be no basis for judicially ordering assignment of students on a racial basis. All things being equal, with no history of discrimination, it might well be desirable to assign pupils to schools nearest their homes. But all things are not equal in a system that has been deliberately constructed and maintained to enforce racial segregation. The remedy for such segregation may be administratively awkward, inconvenient, and even bizarre in some situations and may impose burdens on some; but all awkwardness and inconvenience cannot be avoided in the interim period when remedial adjustments are being made to eliminate the dual school systems.

No fixed or even substantially fixed guidelines can be established as to how far a court can go, but it must be recognized that there are limits. The objective is to dismantle the dual school system. "Racially neutral" assignment plans proposed by school authorities to a district court may be inadequate; such plans may fail to counteract the continuing effects of past school segregation resulting from discriminatory location of school sites or distortion of school size in order to achieve or maintain an artificial racial separation. When school authorities present a district court with a "loaded game board," affirmative action in the form of remedial altering of attendance zones is proper to achieve truly non-discriminatory assignments. In short, an assignment plan is not acceptable simply because it appears to be neutral.

* * *

We hold that the pairing and grouping of noncontiguous school zones is a permissible tool and such action is to be considered in light of the objectives sought. * * * Maps do not tell the whole story since non-contiguous school zones may be more accessible to each other in terms of critical travel time, because of traffic patterns and good highways, than schools geographically closer together. Conditions in different localities will vary so widely that no rigid rules can be laid down to govern all situations.

[4] Transportation of Students

The scope of permissible transportation of students as an implement of a remedial decree has never been defined by this Court and by the very nature of the problem it cannot be defined with precision. No rigid guidelines as to student transportation can be given for application to the infinite variety of problems presented in thousands of situations. Bus transportation has been an integral part of the public education system for years, and was perhaps the single most important factor in the transition from the one-room schoolhouse to the consolidated school. Eighteen million of the Nation's public school children, approximately 39%, were transported to their schools by bus in 1969–1970 in all parts of the country.

The importance of bus transportation as a normal and accepted tool of educational policy is readily discernible in this and the companion case, *Davis, supra*. The Charlotte school authorities did not purport to assign students on the basis of geographically drawn zones until 1965 and then they allowed almost unlimited transfer privileges. The District Court's conclusion that assignment of children to the school nearest their home serving their grade would not produce an effective dismantling of the dual system is supported by the record.

Thus the remedial techniques used in the District Court's order were within that court's power to provide equitable relief; implementation of the decree is well within the capacity of the school authority.

The decree provided that buses used to implement the plan would operate on direct routes. Students would be picked up at schools near their homes and transported to the schools they were to attend. The trips for elementary school pupils average about seven miles and the District Court found that they would take "not over 35 minutes at the most." This system compares favorably with the transportation plan previously operated in Charlotte under which each day 23,600 students on all grade levels were transported an average of 15 miles one way for an average trip requiring over an hour. In these circumstances, we find no basis for holding that the local school authorities may not be required to employ bus transportation as one tool of school desegregation. Desegregation plans cannot be limited to the walk-in school.

An objection to transportation of students may have validity when the time or distance of travel is so great as to either risk the health of the children or significantly impinge on the educational process. * * * It hardly needs stating that the limits on time of travel will vary with many factors, but probably with none more than the age of the students. The reconciliation of competing values in a desegregation case is, of course, a difficult task with many sensitive facets but fundamentally no more so than remedial measures courts of equity have traditionally employed.

The Court of Appeals, searching for a term to define the equitable remedial power of the district courts, used the term "reasonableness." In *Green, supra*, this Court used the term "feasible" and by implication, "workable," "effective," and "realistic" in the mandate to develop "a plan that promises realistically to work, and . . . to work *now*." On the facts of this case, we are unable to conclude that the order of the District Court is not reasonable, feasible or workable. However, in seeking to define the scope of remedial power or the limits on remedial power of courts in an area as sensitive as we deal with here, words are poor instruments to convey the sense of basic fairness inherent in equity. Substance, not semantics, must govern, and we have sought to suggest the nature of limitations without frustrating the appropriate scope of equity.

At some point, these school authorities and others like them should have achieved full compliance with this Court's decision in *Brown I*. The systems would then be "unitary" in the sense required by our decisions in *Green* and *Alexander*.

It does not follow that the communities served by such systems will remain demographically stable, for in a growing, mobile society, few will do so. Neither school authorities nor district courts are constitutionally required to make year-by-year adjustments of the racial composition of student bodies once the affirmative duty to desegregate has been accomplished and racial discrimination through official action is eliminated from the system. This does not mean that federal courts are without power to deal with future problems; but in the absence of a showing that either the school authorities or some other agency of the State has deliberately attempted to fix or alter demographic patterns to affect the racial composition of the schools, further intervention by a district court should not be necessary.

* * *

Notes and Questions

Swann represented another example of the Supreme Court's continued effort to render decisions that unequivocally reflected its desire to eliminate the dual school system. The unanimous decision contended that the dismantling of the dual school system could be accomplished by assigning teachers so as to achieve a particular degree of faculty desegregation; ensuring that future school construction and abandonment would not perpetuate or reestablish a dual system; scrutinizing one-race schools to ensure that the racial composition did not result from present or past discriminatory action; altering attendance zones and employing pairing and grouping of noncontiguous zones to counteract past segregation; and although not requiring it, employing bus transportation as a constitutionally permissible method of dismantling the dual system. Would the path to eliminating de jure segregation have been smoother if *Brown II* had contained such guidelines?

III. Desegregation in Nonsouthern States

Continued and successful desegregation efforts in the southern states clearly revealed the lack of similar efforts in many nonsouthern states where public school racial segregation existed. The legitimate question was often raised of why one section of the country was required to desegregate its schools while obviously segregated school systems continued to operate in the northern and western portions of the United States. From a legal standpoint a partial answer to this question lies in the Supreme Court's reliance on the distinction between de jure and de facto segregation.

As we have noted, the presence of constitutional and/or statutory provisions and local policies mandating segregated schools in the southern states made it possible to address this form of state-sanctioned de jure segregation. Segregated school systems existed outside the South, and although such segregation was not always based on officially stated state or local policy, in some areas it had been. Several nonsouthern states had statutes authorizing separate but equal public schools, and although eventually repealed, such statutes remained on the books in New York until 1938, in Wyoming until 1954, and in Indiana until 1959. The presence of such statutes established persistent patterns of segregated schools that were not always easily changed.

Segregation outside the South existed for other reasons. In some instances long-standing "customs" were present at the local level, which also contributed to racial attitudes and resultant segregated schools.

Perhaps the most significant force, however, contributing to segregated schools outside the South resulted from housing patterns, which in some areas found blacks living in all-black neighborhoods and black students attending all-black neighborhood schools. Such de facto segregation was often based on housing patterns that allegedly were not the result of direct state action. Since the Supreme Court had not considered de facto segregation violative of the *Brown I* edict, nonsouthern public schools that were segregated on that basis were not immediately challenged in the courts. However, in time, segregative practices of nonsouthern school systems were examined by the judiciary. One of the contentions made against segregated nonsouthern school systems was that they had engaged in a form of de jure segregation, perhaps not as blatant as in the South but nevertheless resulting in impermissible racial discrimination.

A. Nonsouthern Segregation

Keyes v. School District No. 1

Supreme Court of the United States, 1973
413 U.S. 189

MR. JUSTICE BRENNAN delivered the opinion of the Court.

This school desegregation case concerns the Denver, Colorado, school system. That system has never been operated under a constitutional or statutory provision that mandated or permitted racial segregation in public education. Rather, the gravamen of this action, brought in June 1969 in the District Court for the District of Colorado by parents of Denver schoolchildren, is that respondent School Board alone, by use of various techniques such as the manipulation of student attendance zones, schoolsite selection and a neighborhood school policy, created or maintained racially or ethnically (or both racially and ethnically) segregated schools throughout the school district, entitling petitioners to a decree directing desegregation of the entire school district.

The boundaries of the school district are coterminous with the boundaries of the city and county of Denver. There were in 1969, 119 schools with 96,580 pupils in the school system. * * * The District Court found that by the construction of a new, relatively small elementary school, Barrett, in the middle of the Negro community west of Park Hill, by the gerrymandering of student attendance zones, by the use of so-called "optional zones," and by the excessive use of mobile classroom units, among other things, the respondent School Board had engaged over almost a decade after 1960 in an unconstitutional policy of deliberate racial segregation with respect to the Park Hill schools. The court therefore ordered the Board to desegregate those schools through the implementation of the three rescinded resolutions. * * *

Segregation in Denver schools is not limited, however, to the schools in the Park Hill area, and not satisfied with their success in obtaining relief for Park Hill, petitioners pressed their prayer that the District Court order desegregation of all segregated schools in the city of Denver, particularly the heavily segregated schools in the core city area. But that court concluded that its finding of a purposeful and systematic program of racial segregation affecting thousands of students in the Park Hill area did not, in itself, impose on the School Board the affirmative duty to eliminate segregation throughout the school district. Instead, the court fractionated the district and held that the petitioners had to make a fresh showing of *de jure* segregation in each area of the city for which they sought relief. Moreover, the District Court held that its finding of intentional segregation in Park Hill was not in any sense material to the question of segregative intent in other areas of the city. * * *

* * *

Before turning to the primary question we decide today, a word must be said about the District Court's method of defining a "segregated" school. Denver is a tri-ethnic, as distinguished from a bi-racial, community. The overall racial and ethnic composition of the Denver public schools is 66% Anglo, 14% Negro, and 20% Hispano. * * * What is or is not a segregated school will necessarily depend on the facts of each particular case. In addition to the racial and ethnic composition of a school's student body, other factors, such as the racial and ethnic composition of faculty and staff and the community and administration attitudes toward the school, must be taken into consideration. The District Court has recognized these specific factors as elements of the definition of a "segregated" school, * * * and we may therefore infer that the court will consider them again on remand.

We conclude, however, that the District Court erred in separating Negroes and Hispanos for purposes of defining a "segregated" school. We have held that Hispanos constitute an identifiable class for purposes of the Fourteenth Amendment. * * * Indeed, the District Court recognized this in classifying predominantly Hispano schools as "segregated" schools in their own right. But there is also much evidence that in the Southwest Hispanos and Negroes have a great many things in common. The United States Commission on Civil Rights has recently published two Reports on Hispano education in the Southwest. Focusing on students in the States of Arizona, California, Colorado, New Mexico, and Texas, the Commission concluded that Hispanos suffer from the same educational inequities as Negroes and American Indians. In fact, the District Court itself recognized that "[o]ne of the things which the Hispano has in common with the Negro is economic and cultural deprivation and discrimination." * * *

In our view, the only other question that requires our decision at this time is * * * whether the District Court and the Court of Appeals applied an incorrect legal standard in addressing petitioners' contention that respondent School Board engaged in an unconstitutional policy of deliberate segregation in the core city schools. Our conclusion is that those courts did not apply the correct standard in addressing that contention.

Petitioners apparently concede for the purpose of this case that in the case of a school system like Denver's, where no statutory dual system has ever existed, plaintiffs must prove not only that segregated schooling exists but also that it was brought about or maintained by intentional state action. Petitioners proved that for almost a decade after 1960 respondent School Board had engaged in an unconstitutional policy of deliberate racial segregation in the Park Hill schools. Indeed, the District Court found that "[b]etween 1960 and 1969 the Board's policies with respect to these northeast Denver schools show an undeviating purpose to isolate Negro students" in segregated schools "while preserving the Anglo character of [other] schools." * * * This finding did not relate to any unsubstantial or trivial fragment of the school system. On the contrary, respondent School Board was found guilty of following a deliberate segregation policy at schools attended, in 1969, by 37.69% of Denver's total Negro school population, including one-fourth of the Negro elementary pupils, over two-thirds of the Negro junior high pupils, and over two-fifths of the Negro high school pupils. In addition, there was uncontroverted evidence that teachers and staff had for years been assigned on the basis of a minority teacher to a minority school throughout the school system. Respondent argues, however, that a finding of state-imposed segregation as to a substantial portion of the school system can be viewed in isolation from the rest of the district, and that even if state-imposed segregation does exist in a substantial part of the Denver school system, it does not follow that the District Court could predicate on that fact a finding that the entire school system is a dual system. We do not agree. We have never suggested that plaintiffs in school desegregation cases must bear the burden of proving the element of *de jure* segregation as to each and every school or each and every student within the school system. Rather, we have held that where plaintiffs prove that a current condition of segregated schooling exists within a school district where a dual system was compelled or authorized by statute at the time of our decision in *Brown* v. *Board of Education*, 347 U.S. 483 (1954) *(Brown I)*, the State automatically assumes an affirmative duty "to effectuate a transition to a racially nondiscriminatory school system," *Brown* v. *Board of Education*, 349 U.S. 294, 301 (1955) *(Brown II)*, see also *Green* v. *County School Board*, 391 U.S. 430, 437–438 (1968), that is, to eliminate from the public schools within their school system "all vestiges of state-imposed segregation." *Swann* v. *Charlotte-Mecklenburg Board of Education*, 402 U.S. 1, 15 (1971).

This is not a case, however, where a statutory dual system has ever existed. Nevertheless, where plaintiffs prove that the school authorities have carried out a systematic program of segregation affecting a substantial portion of the students, schools, teachers, and facilities within the school system, it is only common sense to conclude that there exists a predicate for a finding of the existence of a dual school system. Several considerations support this conclusion. First, it is obvious that a practice of concentrating Negroes in certain schools by structuring attendance zones or designating "feeder" schools on the basis of race has the reciprocal effect of keeping other nearby schools predominantly white. Similarly, the practice of building a school—such as the Barrett Elementary School in this case—to a certain size and in a certain location, "with conscious knowledge that it would be a segregated school" * * * has a substantial reciprocal effect on the racial composition of other nearby schools. So also, the use of mobile classrooms, the drafting of student transfer policies, the transportation of students, and the assignment of faculty and staff, on racially identifiable bases, have the clear effect of earmarking schools according to their racial composition, and this, in turn, together with the elements of student assignment and school construction, may have a profound reciprocal effect on the racial composition of residential neighborhoods within a metropolitan area, thereby causing further racial concentration within the schools. * * *

In short, common sense dictates the conclusion that racially inspired school board actions have an impact beyond the particular schools that are the subjects of those actions. This is not to say, of course, that there can never be a case in which the geographical structure of, or the natural boundaries within, a school district may have the effect of dividing the district into separate, identifiable and unrelated units. Such a determination is essentially a question of fact to be resolved by the trial court in the first instance, but such cases must be rare. In the absence of such a determination, proof of state-imposed segregation in a substantial portion of the district will suffice to support a finding by the trial court of the existence of a dual system. Of course, where that finding is made, as in cases involving statutory dual systems, the school authorities have an affirmative duty "to effectuate a transition to a racially nondiscriminatory school system." *Brown II, supra,* at 301.

* * *

On the question of segregative intent, petitioners presented evidence tending to show that the Board, through its actions over a period of years, intentionally created and maintained the segregated character of the core city schools. Respondents countered this evidence by arguing that the segregation in these schools is the result of a racially neutral "neighborhood school policy" and that the acts of which petitioners complain are explicable within the bounds of that policy. Accepting the School Board's explanation, the District Court and the Court of Appeals agreed that a finding of *de jure* segregation as to the core city schools was not permissible since petitioners had failed to prove "(1) a racially discriminatory purpose and (2) a causal relationship between the acts complained of and the racial imbalance admittedly existing in those schools." * * * This assessment of petitioners' proof was clearly incorrect.

Although petitioners had already proved the existence of intentional school segregation in the Park Hill schools, this crucial finding was totally ignored when attention turned to the core city schools. Plainly, a finding of intentional segregation as to a portion of a school system is not devoid of probative value in assessing the school authorities' intent with respect to other parts of the same school system. On the contrary, where, as here, the case involves one school board, a finding of intentional segregation on its part in one portion of a school system is highly relevant to the issue of the board's intent with respect to other segregated schools in the system. This is merely an application of the well-settled evidentiary principle that "the prior doing of other similar acts, whether clearly a part of a scheme or not, is useful as reducing the possibility that the act in question was done with innocent intent." * * *

Applying these principles in the special context of school desegregation cases, we hold that a finding of intentionally segregative school board actions in a meaningful portion of a school system, as in this case, creates a presumption that other segregated schooling within the system is not adventitious. It establishes, in other words, a prima facie case of unlawful segregative design on the part of school authorities, and shifts to those authorities the burden of proving that other segregated schools within the system are not also the result of intentionally segregative actions. This is true even if it is determined that different areas of the school district should be viewed independently of each other because, even in that situation, there is high probability that where school authorities have effectuated an intentionally segregative policy in a meaningful portion of the school system, similar impermissible considerations have motivated their actions in other areas of the system. We emphasize that the differentiating factor between *de jure* segregation and so-called *de facto* segregation to which we referred in *Swann* is *purpose* or *intent* to segregate. Where school authorities have been found to have practiced purposeful segregation in part of a school system, they may be expected to oppose system-wide desegregation, as did the respondents in this case, on the ground that their purposefully segregative actions were isolated and individual events, thus leaving plaintiffs with the burden of proving otherwise. But at that point where an intentionally segregative policy is practiced in a meaningful segment of a school system, as in this case, the school authorities cannot be heard to argue that plaintiffs have proved only "isolated and individual" unlawfully segregative actions. In that circumstance, it is both fair and reasonable to require that the school authorities bear the burden of showing that their actions as to other segregated schools within the system were not also motivated by segregative intent.

* * *

In discharging that burden, it is not enough, of course, that the school authorities rely upon some allegedly logical, racially neutral explanation for their actions. Their burden is to adduce proof sufficient to support a finding that segregative intent was not among the factors that motivated their actions. The courts below attributed much significance to the fact that many of the Board's actions in the core city area antedated our decision in *Brown.* We reject any suggestion that remoteness in time has any relevance to the issue of intent. If the actions of school authorities were to any degree motivated by segregative intent and the segregation resulting from those actions continues to exist, the fact of remoteness in time certianly does not make those actions any less "intentional."

* * *

The respondent School Board invoked at trial its "neighborhood school policy" as explaining racial and ethnic concentrations within the core city schools, arguing that since the core city area population had long been Negro and Hispano, the concentrations were necessarily the result of residential patterns and not of purposefully segregative policies. We have no occasion to consider in this case whether a "neighborhood school policy" of itself will justify racial or ethnic concentrations in the absence of a finding that school authorities have committed acts constituting *de jure* segregation. It is enough that we hold that the mere assertion of such a policy is not dispositive where, as in this case, the school authorities have been found to have practiced *de jure* segregation in a meaningful portion of the school system by techniques that indicate that the "neighborhood school" concept has not been maintained free of manipulation. * * *

* * *

The judgment of the Court of Appeals is modified to vacate instead of reverse the parts of the Final Decree that concern the core city schools, and the case is remanded to the District Court for further proceedings consistent with this opinion.

It is so ordered.

MR. JUSTICE DOUGLAS.

While I join the opinion of the Court, I agree with my Brother Powell that there is, for the purposes of the Equal Protection Clause of the Fourteenth Amendment as applied to the school cases, no difference between *de facto* and *de jure* segregation. The school board is a state agency and the lines that it draws, the locations it selects for school sites, the allocation it makes of students, the budgets it prepares are state action for Fourteenth Amendment purposes.

* * *

I think it is time to state that there is no constitutional difference between *de jure* and *de facto* segregation, for each is the product of state actions or policies. If a "neighborhood" or "geographical" unit has been created along racial lines by reason of the play of restrictive covenants that restrict certain areas to "the elite," leaving the "undesirables" to move elsewhere, there is state action in the constitutional sense because the force of law is placed behind those convenants.

There is state action in the constitutional sense when public funds are dispersed by urban development agencies to build racial ghettoes.

Where the school district is racially mixed and the races are segregated in separate schools, where black teachers are assigned almost exclusively to black schools, where the school board closed existing schools located in fringe areas and built new schools in black areas and in distant white areas, where the school board continued the "neighborhood" school policy at the elementary level, these actions constitute state action. They are of a kind quite distinct from the classical *de jure* type of school segregation. Yet calling them *de facto* is a misnomer, as they are only more subtle types of state action that create or maintain a wholly or partially segregated school system. * * *

When a State forces, aids, or abets, or helps creat a racial "neighborhood," it is a travesty of justice to treat that neighborhood as sacrosanct in the sense that its creation is free from the taint of state action.

* * *

MR. JUSTICE POWELL concurring in part and dissenting in part.

I concur in the remand of this case for further proceedings in the District Court, but on grounds that differ from those relied upon by the Court.

This is the first school desegregation case to reach the Court which involves a major city outside the South. It comes from Denver, Colorado, a city and a State which have not operated public schools under constitutional or statutory provisions which mandated or permitted racial segregation. Nor has it been argued that any other legislative actions (such as zoning and housing laws) contributed to the segregation which is at issue. The Court has inquired only to what extent the Denver public school authorities may have contributed to the school segregation which is acknowledged to exist in Denver.

* * *

The situation in Denver is generally comparable to that in other large cities across the country in which there is a substantial minority population and where desegregation has not been ordered by the federal courts. There is segregation in the schools of many of these cities fully as pervasive as that in southern cities prior to the desegregation decrees of the past decade and a half. The focus of the school desegregation problem has now shifted from the South to the country as a whole. Unwilling and footdragging as the process was in most places, substantial progress toward achieving integration has been made in Southern States. No comparable progress has been made in many nonsouthern cities with large minority populations primarily because of the *de facto/de jure* distinction nurtured by the courts and accepted complacently by many of the same voices which denounced the evils of segregated schools in the South. But if our national concern is for those who attend such schools, rather than for perpetuating a legalism rooted in history rather than present reality, we must recognize that the evil of operating separate schools is no less in Denver than in Atlanta.

In my view we should abandon a distinction which long since has outlived its time, and formulate constitutional principles of national rather than merely regional application. When *Brown* v. *Board of Education*, 347 U.S. 483 (1954) *(Brown I)*, was decided, the distinction between *de jure* and *de facto* segregation was consistent with the limited constitutional rationale of that case. The situation confronting the Court, largely confined to the Southern States, was officially imposed racial segregation in the schools extending back for many years and usually embodied in constitutional and statutory provisions.

The great contribution of *Brown I* was its holding in unmistakable terms that the Fourteenth Amendment forbids state-compelled or state-authorized segregation of public schools. 347 U.S., at 488, 493–495. Although some of the language was more expansive, the holding in *Brown I* was essentially negative: It was impermissible under the Constitution for the States, or their instrumentalities, to force children to attend segregated schools. The forbidden action was *de jure*, and the opinion in *Brown I* was construed—for some years and by many courts—as requiring only state neutrality, allowing "freedom of choice" as to schools to be attended so long as the State itself assured that the choice was genuinely free of official restraint.

But the doctrine of *Brown I*, as amplified by *Brown II*, * * * did not retain its original meaning. In a series of decisions extending from 1954 to 1971 the concept of state neutrality was transformed into the present constitutional doctrine requiring affirmative state action to desegregate school systems. The keystone case was *Green* v. *County School Board* * * * where school boards were declared to have "the affirmative duty to take whatever steps might be necessary to convert to a unitary system in which racial discrimination would be eliminated root and branch." * * * The Court properly identified the freedom-of-choice program there as a subterfuge, and the language in *Green* imposing an affirmative duty to convert to a unitary system was appropriate on the facts before the Court. There was, however, reason to question to what extent this duty would apply in the vastly different factual setting of a large city with extensive areas of residential segregation, presenting problems and calling for solutions quite different from those in the rural setting of New Kent County, Virginia.

But the doubt as to whether the affirmative-duty concept would flower into a new constitutional principle of general application was laid to rest by *Swann* v. *Charlotte-Mecklenburg Board of Education*, * * * in which the duty articulated in *Green* was applied to the urban school system of metropolitan Charlotte, North Carolina. * * *

* * *

Whereas *Brown I* rightly decreed the elimination of state-imposed segregation in that particular section of the country where it did exist, *Swann* imposed obligations on southern school districts to eliminate conditions which are not regionally unique but are similar both in origin and effect to conditions in the rest of the country. As the remedial obligations of *Swann* extend far beyond the elimination of the outgrowths of the state-imposed segregation outlawed in *Brown*, the rationale of *Swann* points inevitably toward a uniform, constitutional approach to our national problem of school segregation.

The Court's decision today, while adhering to the *de jure/de facto* distinction, will require the application of the *Green/Swann* doctrine of "affirmative duty" to the Denver School Board despite the absence of any history of state-mandated school segregation. The only evidence of a constitutional violation was found in various decisions of the School Board. I concur in the Court's position that the public school authorities are the responsible agency of the State, and that if the affirmative-duty doctrine is sound constitutional law for Charlotte, it is equally so for Denver. I would not, however, perpetuate the *de jure/de facto* distinction nor would I leave to petitioners the initial tortuous effort of identifying "segregation acts" and deducing "segregative intent." I would hold, quite simply, that where segregated public schools exist within a school district to a substantial degree, there is a prima facie case that the duly constituted public authorities (I will usually refer to them collectively as the "school board") are sufficiently responsible to warrant imposing upon them a nationally applicable burden to demonstrate they nevertheless are operating a genuinely integrated school system.

* * *

* * * In *Brown II*, the Court identified the "fundamental principle" enunciated in *Brown I* as being the unconstitutionality of "racial discrimination in public education" * * * and spoke of "the personal interest of the plaintiffs in admission to public schools as soon as practicable on a nondiscriminatory basis." * * * Although this and similar language is ambiguous as to the specific constitutional right, it means— as a minimum—that one has the right not to be compelled by state action to attend a segregated school system. In the evolutionary process since 1954, decisions of this Court have added a significant gloss to this original right. Although nowhere expressly articulated in these terms, I would now define it as the right, derived from the Equal Protection Clause, to expect that once the State has assumed responsibility for education, local school boards will operate *integrated school systems* within their respective districts. This means that school authorities, consistent with the generally accepted educational goal of attaining quality education for all pupils, must make and implement their customary decisions with a view toward enhancing integrated school opportunities.

The term "integrated school system" presupposes, of course, a total absence of any laws, regulations, or policies supportive of the type of "legalized" segregation condemned in *Brown*. A system would be integrated in accord with constitutional standards if the responsible authorities had taken appropriate steps to (i) integrate faculties and administration; (ii) scrupulously assure equality of facilities, instruction, and curriculum opportunities throughout the district; (iii) utilize their authority to draw attendance zones to promote integration; and (iv) locate new schools, close old ones, and determine the size and grade categories with this same objective in mind. Where school authorities decide to undertake the transportation of students, this also must be with integrative opportunities in mind.

The foregoing prescription is not intended to be either definitive or all-inclusive, but rather an indication of the contour characteristics of an *integrated school system* in which all citizens and pupils may justifiably be confident that racial discrimination is neither practiced nor tolerated. An integrated school system does not mean—and indeed could not mean in view of the residential patterns of most of our major metropolitan areas—that *every school* must in fact be an integrated unit. A school which happens to be all or predominantly white or all or predominantly black is not a "segregated" school in an unconstitutional sense if the system itself is a genuinely integrated one.

Having school boards operate an integrated school system provides the best assurance of meeting the constitutional requirement that racial discrimination, subtle or otherwise, will find no place in the decisions of public school officials. Courts judging past school board actions with a view to their *general integrative effect* will be best able to assure an absence of such discrimination while avoiding the murky, subjective judgments inherent in the Court's search for "segregative intent." Any test resting on so nebulous and elusive an element as a school board's segregative "intent" provides inadequate assurance that minority children will not be short-changed in the decisions of those entrusted with the nondiscriminatory operation of our public schools.

Public schools are creatures of the State, and whether the segregation is state-created or state-assisted or merely state-perpetuated should be irrelevant to constitutional principle. The school board exercises pervasive and continuing responsibility over the long-range planning as well as the daily operations of the public school system. It sets policies on attendance zones, faculty employment and assignments, school construction, closings and consolidations, and myriad other matters. School board decisions obviously are not the sole cause of segregated school conditions. But if, after such detailed and complete public supervision, substantial school segregation still persists, the presumption is strong that the school board, by its acts or omission, is in some part responsible. Where state action and supervision are so pervasive and where, after years of such action, segregated schools continue to exist within the district to a substantial degree, this Court is justified in finding a prima facie case of a constitutional violation. The burden then must fall on the school board to demonstrate it is operating an "integrated school system."

It makes little sense to find prima facie violations and the consequent affirmative duty to desegregate solely in those States with state-imposed segregation at the time of the *Brown* decision. The history of state-imposed segregation is more widespread in our country than the *de jure/de facto* distinction has traditionally cared to recognize. * * *

* * *

The Court today does move for the first time toward breaking down past sectional disparities, but it clings tenuously to its distinction. It searches for *de jure* action in what the Denver School Board has done or failed to do, and even here the Court does not rely upon the results or effects of the Board's conduct but feels compelled to find segregative intent. * * *

* * *

The issue in these cases will not be whether segregated education exists. This will be conceded in most of them.* * *

* * *

MR. JUSTICE REHNQUIST, dissenting.

* * *

Underlying the Court's entire opinion is its apparent thesis that a district judge is at least permitted to find that if a single attendance zone between two individual schools in the large metropolitan district is found by him to have been "gerrymandered," the school district is guilty of operating a "dual" school system, and is apparently a candidate for what is in practice a federal receivership. * * *

* * *

The drastic extension of *Brown* which *Green* represented was barely, if at all, explicated in the latter opinion. To require that a genuinely "dual" system be disestablished, in the sense that the assignment of a child to a particular school is not made to depend on his race, is one thing. To require that school boards affirmatively undertake to achieve racial mixing in schools where such mixing is not achieved in sufficient degree by neutrally drawn boundary lines is quite obviously something else.

The Court's own language in *Green* makes it unmistakably clear that this significant extension of *Brown's* prohibition against discrimination, and the conversion of that prohibition into an affirmative duty to integrate, was made in the context of a school system which had for a number of years rigidly excluded Negroes from attending the same schools as were attended by whites. Whatever may be the soundness of that decision in the context of a genuinely "dual" system, where segregation of the races had once been mandated by law, I can see no constitutional justification for it in a situation such as that which the record shows to have obtained in Denver.

* * *

The Court has taken a long leap in this area of constitutional law in equating the district-wide consequences of gerrymandering individual attendance zones in a district where separation of the races was never required by law with statutes or ordinances in other jurisdictions which did so require. It then adds to this potpourri a confusing enunciation of evidentiary rules in order to make it more likely that the trial court will on remand reach the result which the Court apparently wants it to reach. Since I believe neither of these steps is justified by prior decisions of this Court, I dissent.

Notes and Questions

Although admonished by Justices Powell and Douglas to abandon the distinction between de jure and de facto segregation in its decisions, the Court relied on the distinction in its decision in **Keyes.** Does **Keyes** represent a broadening of the concept of de jure segregation?

Subsequent Court decisions reveal a continued reliance on the de jure/de facto distinction. In decisions involving Columbus and Dayton, Ohio, the Court upheld lower court-ordered desegregation measures on the basis that both school systems had operated racially segregated dual school systems at the time of **Brown I.** The majority of the Court maintained that since the schools were intentionally segregated in 1954, the boards of education had an "affirmative duty" not to engage in actions that would impede the desegregation process. In these cases, the Court declared that the respective boards of education took actions which assured the continuance of racial separation in the schools. See *Columbus Board of Education* v. *Penick*, 443 U.S. 449 (1979), a seven-to-two decision, and *Dayton Board of Education* v. *Brinkman*, 443 U.S. 526 (1979), a five-to-four decision. Do these decisions suggest a further broadening of the concept of de jure segregation?

Although commentators disagree on the significance of Supreme Court denials of certiorari, examination of two such denials reveals the Court's continuing strong stance on effecting desegregation. In *Tasby* v. *Estes*, 572 F.2d 1010 (5th Cir. 1978), *cert. denied*, 444 U.S. 437 (1980), the Court refused to review the Fifth Circuit's overturning of a district court order substituting certain educational remedies and neighborhood schools in Dallas for systemwide busing based on black-white student population ratios. Additionally the appellate court required mandatory pupil reassignment unless "the natural boundaries and traffic considerations preclude either the pairing and clustering of schools or the use of transportation to eliminate the large number of one race schools still existing." In *Kelley* v. *Metropolitan County Board of Education of Nashville and Davidson County*, 687 F.2d 814 (6th Cir. 1982), *cert. denied*, 459 U.S. 1183 (1983), the Court denied certiorari to the Sixth Circuit's decision that the Nashville School Board had a continuing obligation to ensure that modifications in desegregation remedies reflected current black-white student population ratios.

B. Interdistrict Integration

Milliken v. Bradley

Supreme Court of the United States, 1974
418 U.S. 717

MR. CHIEF JUSTICE BURGER delivered the opinion of the Court.

We granted certiorari in these consolidated cases to determine whether a federal court may impose a multidistrict, areawide remedy to a single-district *de jure* segregation problem absent any finding that the other included school districts have failed to operate unitary school systems within their districts, absent any claim or finding that the boundary lines of any affected school district were established with the purpose of fostering racial segregation in public schools, absent any finding that the included districts committed acts which effected segregation within the other districts, and absent a meaningful opportunity for the included neighboring school districts to present evidence or be heard on the propriety of a multidistrict remedy or on the question of constitutional violations by those neighboring districts.

* * *

The District Court found that the Detroit Board of Education created and maintained optional attendance zones within Detroit neighborhoods undergoing racial transition and between high school attendance areas of opposite predominant racial compositions. These zones, the court found, had the "natural, probable, foreseeable and actual effect" of allowing white pupils to escape identifiably Negro schools. Similarly, the District Court found that Detroit school attendance zones had been drawn along north-south boundary lines despite the Detroit Board's awareness that drawing boundary lines in an east-west direction would result in significantly greater desegregation. Again, the District Court concluded, the natural and actual effect of these acts was the creation and perpetuation of school segregation within Detroit.

The District Court found that in the operation of its school transportation program, which was designed to relieve overcrowding, the Detroit Board had admittedly bused Negro Detroit pupils to predominantly Negro schools which were beyond or away from closer white schools with available space. * * *

With respect to the Detroit Board of Education's practices in school construction, the District Court found that Detroit school construction generally tended to have a segregative effect with the great majority of schools being built in either overwhelmingly all-Negro or all-white neighborhoods so that the new schools opened as predominantly one-race schools. Thus, of the 14 schools opened for use in 1970–1971, 11 opened over 90% Negro and one opened less than 10% Negro.

The District Court also found that the State of Michigan had committed several constitutional violations with respect to the exercise of its general responsibility for, and supervision of, public education. The State, for example, was found to have failed, until the 1971 Session of Michigan Legislature, to provide authorization or funds for the transportation of pupils within Detroit regardless of their poverty or distance from the school to which they were assigned; during this same period the State provided many neighboring, mostly white, suburban districts the full range of state-supported transportation.

The District Court found that the State, through Act 48 acted to "impede, delay and minimize racial integration in Detroit schools." The first sentence of § 12 of Act 48 was designed to delay the April 7, 1970, desegregation plan originally adopted by the Detroit Board. The remainder of § 12 sought to prescribe for each school in the eight districts criteria of "free choice" and "neighborhood schools," which, the District Court found, "had as their purpose and effect the maintenance of segregation." * * *

The District Court also held that the acts of the Detroit Board of Education, as a subordinate entity of the State, were attributable to the

State of Michigan, thus creating a vicarious liability on the part of the State. Under Michigan law, Mich. Comp. Laws § 388.851 (1970), for example, school building construction plans had to be approved by the State Board of Education, and, prior to 1962, the State Board had specific statutory authority to supervise schoolsite selection. The proofs concerning the effect of Detroit's school construction program were, therefore, found to be largely applicable to show state responsibility for the segregative results.

Turning to the question of an appropriate remedy for these several constitutional violations, the District Court deferred a pending motion by intervening parent defendants to join as additional parties defendant the 85 outlying school districts in the three-county Detroit metropolitan area on the ground that effective relief could not be achieved without their presence. The District Court concluded that this motion to join was "premature," since it "has to do with relief" and no reasonably specific desegregation plan was before the court. * * * Accordingly, the District Court proceeded to order the Detroit Board of Education to submit desegregation plans limited to the segregation problems found to be existing within the city of Detroit. At the same time, however, the state defendants were directed to submit desegregation plans encompassing the three-county metropolitan area despite the fact that the 85 outlying school districts of these three counties were not parties to the action and despite the fact that there had been no claim that these outlying districts had committed constitutional violations. * * *

* * *

On June 12, 1973, a divided Court of Appeals, sitting en banc, affirmed in part, vacated in part, and remanded for further proceedings. * * * The Court of Appeals held, first, that the record supported the District Court's findings and conclusions on the constitutional violations committed by the Detroit Board * * * and by the state defendants * * *. It stated that the acts of racial discrimination shown in the record are "causally related to the substantial amount of segregation found in the Detroit school system," * * * and that "the District Court was therefore authorized and required to take effective measures to desegregate the Detroit Public School System." * * *

The Court of Appeals also agreed with the District Court that "any less comprehensive a solution than a metropolitan area plan would result in an all black school system immediately surrounded by practically all white suburban school systems, with an overwhelmingly white majority population in the total metropolitan area." * * * The court went on to state that it could "not see how such segregation can be any less harmful to the minority students than if the same result were accomplished within one school district." * * *

Accordingly, the Court of Appeals concluded that "the only feasible desegregation plan involves the crossing of the boundary lines between the Detroit School District and adjacent or nearby school districts for the limited purpose of providing an effective desegregation plan." * * * It reasoned that such a plan would be appropriate because of the State's violations, and could be implemented because of the State's authority to control local school districts. * * * An interdistrict remedy was thus held to be "within the equity powers of the District Court." * * *

* * *

Viewing the record as a whole, it seems clear that the District Court and the Court of Appeals shifted the primary focus from a Detroit remedy to the metropolitan area only because of their conclusion that total desegregation of Detroit would not produce the racial balance which they perceived as desirable. Both courts proceeded on an assumption that the Detroit schools could not be fully desegregated—in their view of what constituted desegregation—unless the racial composition of the student body of each school substantially reflected the racial composition of the population of the metropolitan area as a whole. The metropolitan area was then defined as Detroit plus 53 of the outlying school districts.* * *

Here the District Court's approach to what constituted "actual desegregation" raised the fundamental question, not presented in *Swann*, as to the circumstances in which a federal court may order desegregation relief that embraces more than a single school district. The court's analytical starting point was its conclusion that school district lines are no more than arbitrary lines on a map drawn "for political convenience." Boundary lines may be bridged where there has been a constitutional violation calling for interdistrict relief, but the notion that school district lines may be casually ignored or treated as a mere administrative convenience is contrary to the history of public education in our country. No single tradition in public education is more deeply rooted than local control over the operation of schools; local autonomy has long been thought essential both to the maintenance of community concern and support for public schools and to quality of the educational process. * * * [L]ocal control over the educational process affords citizens an opportunity to participate in decisionmaking, permits the structuring of school programs to fit local needs, and encourages "experimentation, innovation, and a healthy competition for educational excellence."

The Michigan educational structure involved in this case, in common with most States, provides for a large measure of local control, and a review of the scope and character of these local powers indicates the extent to which the interdistrict remedy approved by the two courts could disrupt and alter the structure of public education in Michigan. The metropolitan remedy would require, in effect, consolidation of 54 independent school districts historically administered as separate units into a vast new super school district. * * * Entirely apart from the logistical and other serious problems attending large-scale transportation of students, the consolidation would give rise to an array of other problems in financing and operating this new school system. Some of the more obvious questions would be: What would be the status and authority of the present popularly elected school boards? Would the children of Detroit be within the jurisdiction and operating control of a school board elected by the parents and residents of other districts? What board or boards would levy taxes for school operations in these 54 districts constituting the consolidated metropolitan area? What provisions could be made for assuring substantial equality in tax levies among the 54 districts, if this were deemed requisite? What provisions would be made for financing? Would the validity of long-term bonds be jeopardized unless approved by all of the component districts as well as the State? What body would determine that portion of the curricula now left to the discretion of local school boards? Who would establish attendance zones, purchase school equipment, locate and construct new schools, and indeed attend to all the myriad day-to-day decisions that are necessary to school operations affecting potentially more than three-quarters of a million pupils? * * *

It may be suggested that all of these vital operational problems are yet to be resolved by the District Court, and that this is the purpose of the Court of Appeals' proposed remand. But it is obvious from the scope of the interdistrict remedy itself that absent a complete restructuring of the laws of Michigan relating to school districts the District Court will become first, a *de facto* "legislative authority" to resolve these complex questions, and then the "school superintendent" for the entire area. This is a task which few, if any, judges are qualified to perform and one which would deprive the people of control of schools through their elected representatives.

Of course, no state law is above the Constitution. School district lines and the present laws with respect to local control, are not sacrosanct and if they conflict with the Fourteenth Amendment federal courts have a duty to prescribe appropriate remedies. * * * But our prior holdings have been confined to violations and remedies within a single school district. We therefore turn to address, for the first time, the validity of a remedy mandating cross-district or inter-district consolidation to remedy a condition of segregation found to exist in only one district.

The controlling principle consistently expounded in our holdings is that the scope of the remedy is determined by the nature and extent of the constitutional violation. *Swann*, 402 U.S., at 16. Before the boundaries of separate and autonomous school districts may be set aside by consolidating the separate units for remedial purposes or by imposing a cross-district remedy, it must first be shown that there has been a constitutional violation within one district that produces a significant segregative effect in another district. Specifically, it must be shown that racially discriminatory acts of the state or local school districts, or of a single school district have been a substantial cause of interdistrict segregation. Thus an interdistrict remedy might be in order where the racially discriminatory acts of one or more school districts caused racial segregation in an adjacent district, or where district lines have been deliberately drawn on the basis of race. In such circumstances an interdistrict remedy would be appropriate to eliminate the interdistrict segregation directly caused by the constitutional violation. Conversely, without an interdistrict violation and interdistrict effect, there is no constitutional wrong calling for an interdistrict remedy.

The record before us, voluminous as it is, contains evidence of *de jure* segregated conditions only in the Detroit schools; indeed, that was the theory on which the litigation was initially based and on which the District Court took evidence. * * * With no showing of significant violation by the 53 outlying school districts and no evidence of any interdistrict violation or effect, the court went beyond the original theory of the case as framed by the pleading and mandated a metropolitan area remedy. To approve the remedy ordered by the court would impose on the outlying districts, not shown to have committed any constitutional violation, a wholly impermissible remedy based on a standard not hinted at in *Brown I* and *II* or any holding of this Court.

In dissent, MR. JUSTICE WHITE and MR. JUSTICE MARSHALL undertake to demonstrate that agencies having statewide authority participated in maintaining the dual school system found to exist in Detroit. They are apparently of the view that once such participation is shown, the District Court should have a relatively free hand to reconstruct school districts outside of Detroit in fashioning relief. Our assumption, *arguendo*, * * * that state agencies did participate in the maintenance of the Detroit system, should make it clear that it is not on this point that we part company. The difference between us arises instead from established doctrine laid down by our cases. *Brown, supra; Green, supra; Swann, supra; Scotland Neck, supra;* and *Emporia, supra*, each addressed the issue of constitutional wrong in terms of an established geographic and administrative school system populated by both Negro and white children. In such a context, terms such as "unitary" and "dual" systems, and "racially identifiable schools," have meaning, and the necessary federal authority to remedy the constitutional wrong is firmly established. But the remedy is necessarily designed, as all remedies are, to restore the victims of discriminatory conduct to the position they would have occupied in the absence of such conduct. Disparate treatment of white and Negro students occurred within the Detroit school system, and not elsewhere, and on this record the remedy must be limited to that system. * * *

The constitutional right of the Negro respondents residing in Detroit is to attend a unitary school system in that district. Unless petitioners drew the district lines in a discriminatory fashion, or arranged for white students residing in the Detroit District to attend schools in Oakland and Macomb Counties, they were under no constitutional duty to make provisions for Negro students to do so. The view of the dissenters, that the existence of a dual system in *Detroit* can be made the basis for a decree requiring cross-district transportation of pupils, cannot be supported on the grounds that it represents merely the devising of a suitably flexible remedy for the violation of rights already established by our prior decisions. It can be supported only by drastic expansion of the constitutional right itself, an expansion without any support in either constitutional principle or precedent.

* * *

We conclude that the relief ordered by the District Court and affirmed by the Court of Appeals was based upon an erroneous standard and was unsupported by record evidence that acts of the outlying districts effected the discrimination found to exist in the schools of Detroit. Accordingly, the judgment of the Court of Appeals is reversed and the case is remanded for further proceedings consistent with this opinion leading to prompt formulation of a decree directed to eliminating the segregation found to exist in Detroit city schools, a remedy which has been delayed since 1970.

Reversed and remanded.

* * *

MR. JUSTICE DOUGLAS; dissenting.

The Court of Appeals has acted responsibly in these cases and we should affirm its judgment * * *.

We have before us today no plan for integration. The only orders entered so far are interlocutory. No new principles of law are presented here. Metropolitan treatment of metropolitan problems is commonplace.

If this were a sewage problem or a water problem, or an energy problem, there can be no doubt that Michigan would stay well within federal constitutional bounds if she sought a metropolitan remedy. * * * The State controls the boundaries of school districts. The state supervised school site selection. The construction was done through municipal bonds approved by several state agencies. Education in Michigan is a state project with very little completely local control. * * *

* * *

As I indicated in *Keyes* * * * there is so far as the school cases go no constitutional difference between *de facto* and *de jure* segregation. Each school board performs state action for Fourteenth Amendment purposes when it draws the lines that confine it to a given area, when it builds schools at particular sites, or when it allocates students. The creation of the school districts in Metropolitan Detroit either maintained existing segregation or caused additional segregation. Restrictive covenants maintained by state action or inaction build black ghettos. It is state action when public funds are dispensed by housing agencies to build racial ghettos. Where a community is racially mixed and school authorities segregate schools, or assign black teachers to black schools or close schools in fringe areas and build new schools in black areas and in more distant white areas, the State creates and nurtures a segregated school system, just as surely as did those States involved in *Brown* v. *Board of Education,* * * * when they maintained dual school systems.

* * * The issue is not whether there should be racial balance but whether the State's use of various devices that end up with black schools and white schools brought the Equal Protection Clause into effect. Given the State's control over the educational system in Michigan, the fact that the black schools are in one district and the white schools are in another is not controlling—either constitutionally or equitably. No specific plan has yet been adopted. We are still at an interlocutory state of a long drawn-out judicial effort at school desegregation. It is conceivable that ghettos develop on their own without any hint of state action. But since Michigan by one device or another has over the years created black school districts and white school districts, the task of equity is to provide a unitary system for the affected area where, as here, the State washes its hands of its own creations.

MR. JUSTICE WHITE, with whom MR. JUSTICE DOUGLAS, MR. JUSTICE BRENNAN, and MR. JUSTICE MARSHALL join, dissenting.

* * *

Regretfully, and for several reasons, I can join neither the Court's judgment nor its opinion. The core of my disagreement is that deliberate acts of segregation and their consequences will go unremedied, not because a remedy would be infeasible or unreasonable in terms of the usual criteria governing school desegregation cases, but because an effective remedy would cause what the Court considers to be undue administrative inconvenience to the State. The result is that the State of Michigan, the entity at which the Fourteenth Amendment is directed, has successfully insulated itself from its duty to provide effective desegregation remedies by vesting sufficient power over its public schools in its local school districts. If this is the case in Michigan, it will be the case in most States.

There are undoubted practical as well as legal limits to the remedial powers of federal courts in school desegregation cases. The Court has made it clear that the achievement of any particular degree of racial balance in the school system is not required by the Constitution; nor may it be the primary focus of a court in devising an acceptable remedy for *de jure* segregation. A variety of procedures and techniques are available to a district court engrossed in fashioning remedies in a case such as this; but the courts must keep in mind that they are dealing with the process of *educating* the young, including the very young. The task is not to devise a system of pains and penalties to punish constitutional violations brought to light. Rather, it is to desegregate an *educational* system in which the races have been kept apart, without, at the same time, losing sight of the central *educational* function of the schools.

Viewed in this light, remedies calling for school zoning, pairing, and pupil assignments, become more and more suspect as they require that school children spend more and more time in buses going to and from school and that more and more educational dollars be diverted to transportation systems. Manifestly, these considerations are of immediate and urgent concern when the issue is the desegregation of a city school system where residential patterns are predominantly segregated and the respective areas occupied by blacks and whites are heavily populated and geographically extensive. Thus, if one postulates a metropolitan school system covering a sufficiently large area, with the population evenly divided between whites and Negroes and with the races occupying identifiable residential areas, there will be very real practical limits on the extent to which racially identifiable schools can be eliminated within the school district. It is also apparent that the larger the proportion of Negroes in the area, the more difficult it would be to avoid having a substantial number of all-black or nearly all-black schools.

The Detroit school district is both large and heavily populated. * * * If "racial balance" were achieved in every school in the district, each school would be approximately 64% Negro. A remedy confined to the district could achieve no more desegregation.* * *

* * *

I am * * * mystified how the Court can ignore the legal reality that the constitutional violations, even if occurring locally, were committed by governmental entities for which the State is responsible and that it is the State that must respond to the command of the Fourteenth Amendment. An interdistrict remedy for the infringements that occurred in this case is well within the confines and powers of the State, which is the governmental entity ultimately responsible for desegregating its schools. * * *

* * *

The Court draws the remedial line at the Detroit School District boundary, even though the Fourteenth Amendment is addressed to the State and even though the *State* denies equal protection of the laws when its public agencies, acting in its behalf, invidiously discriminate. * * * I cannot understand, nor does the majority satisfactorily explain, why a federal court may not order an appropriate interdistrict remedy, if this is necessary or more effective to accomplish this constitutionally mandated task. * * *

* * *

MR. JUSTICE MARSHALL, with whom MR. JUSTICE DOUGLAS, MR. JUSTICE BRENNAN, and MR. JUSTICE WHITE join, dissenting.

* * *

The great irony of the Court's opinion and, in my view, its most serious analytical flaw may be gleaned from its concluding sentence, in which the Court remands for "prompt formulation of a decree directed to eliminating the segregation found to exist in Detroit city schools, a remedy which has been delayed since 1970." * * * The majority, however, seems to have forgotten the district Court's explicit finding that a Detroit only decree, the only remedy permitted under today's decision, "would not accomplish desegregation."

Nowhere in the Court's opinion does the majority confront, let alone respond to, the District Court's conclusion that a remedy limited to the city of Detroit would not effectively desegregate the Detroit city schools. * * *

* * *

Desegregation is not and was never expected to be an easy task. Racial attitudes ingrained in our Nation's childhood and adolescence are not quickly thrown aside in its middle years. But just as the inconvenience of some cannot be allowed to stand in the way of the rights of others, so public opposition, no matter how strident, cannot be permitted to divert this Court from the enforcement of the constitutional principles at issue in this case. Today's holding, I fear, is more a reflection of a perceived public mood that we have gone far enough in enforcing the Constitution's guarantee of equal justice than it is the product of neutral principles of law. In the short run, it may seem to be the easier course to allow our great metropolitan areas to be divided up each into two cities—one white, the other black—but it is a course, I predict, our people will ultimately regret. I dissent.

Notes and Questions

Milliken was a five-to-four decision. Would suburbanite parents have complied with the Metropolitan Plan if the Court had upheld it? Would black parents have allowed their children to be bussed to the suburbs?

Is the following an accurate description of the attitude of many white suburbanites living adjacent to cities having a large minority concentration? Their preference for suburban life stemmed from the perception that an absence of congestion, lack of crime, and "good" schools all contributed to the "good life." A move to an often "lily-white" suburb was considered to be a partial fulfillment of the American dream, whereby a person may improve his or her lot by sheer hard work and dedication. Central to this fulfillment was the sending of children to "good" neighborhood schools, which in many instances attempted to emulate the better private schools. Would persons having such attitudes allow their children to be bussed, often long distances, into predominantly black inner-city schools? If not, could a court-mandated metropolitan plan have been enforced?

Is there an assumption that black parents agree with plans whereby their children would be bussed into the suburbs for schooling? Does evidence exist that sustains such an assumption? One noted black educator and chairman of the Atlanta Board of Education for many years, Dr. Benjamin Mays, for instance, agreed with the Supreme Court's affirmation of a lower-court decision not to order a metropolitan solution for Atlanta. See *Armour* v. *Nix*, 446 U.S. 930 (1980).

On remand, the district court approved a desegregation plan that included educational components in the areas of reading, inservice teacher training, testing, and counseling. Costs were to be borne by both the Detroit School Board and the state. The Supreme Court upheld the lower court's action, and stated that such a remedy was reasonable in the light of past acts of de jure segregation. See *Milliken* v. *Bradley,* 433 U.S. 267 (1977) *(Milliken II).*

IV. Litigation after *Milliken*

Many observers consider *Milliken I* as marking an end to the Supreme Court's unwavering support of desegregation efforts. Subsequent to this decision the Court has been viewed decreasingly as a friendly and receptive forum for achieving school desegregation.

As we have seen, desegregation litigation in the two decades after *Brown I* was focused primarily on dismantling dual school systems in the rural South. Since the mid-1970s school desegregation is said to have entered its "second generation," and the locus of school desegregation efforts has shifted to outside the South and to the nation's large urban centers. Proving de jure segregation in such cases has grown increasingly complex, as courts often are asked to consider the effects of exogenous factors such as public housing policies. School districts that have labored under court desegregation orders have petitioned for release from such orders. In those cases, courts have had to determine what criteria evince school districts' achievement of "unitary status" and whether the attainment of that status releases districts from their remedial orders.

A. Release from Court Order

Several federal courts of appeals have litigated whether or not school districts should remain under court order once they have achieved unitary status or have made significant progress in eradicating the vestiges of de jure segregation. These decisions, however, have not been uniform among the federal circuits. Courts have had to deal with difficult issues in these cases, and their decisions reveal their varying interpretations of the district court's role.

In the long-standing Boston school desegregation litigation, the First Circuit Court of Appeals held that the district court should relinquish its supervision of the student assignment portion of the school district's desegregation plan, despite the fact that the system was not completely unitary. Although the court found the schools to be unitary in the area of student assignments, racial imbalance in faculty hiring continued to exist. The court declared that hiring and recruitment efforts should continue until 25 percent of Boston's public school teachers were black. See *Morgan* v. *Nucci,* 831 F.2d 313 (1st Cir. 1987).

Decisions in the Fourth and Fifth Circuits, dealing with Norfolk, Virginia, and Austin, Texas, clearly proclaim that in these jurisdictions the district court's role ends once the goal of a unitary school system is achieved. One of the courts observed that the idea that a school district can be declared unitary and yet continue to be answerable to the federal courts "is at war with itself." Thus, school districts found to be unitary are restored to a status equal to other districts; they may adopt racially neutral policies and alter former desegregation plans as long as their motivation is not to discriminate. See *Riddick* v. *School Board of City of Norfolk*, 784 F.2d 521 (4th Cir. 1986), *cert. denied*, 479 U.S. 938 (1986), and *United States* v. *Overton*, 834 F.2d 1171 (5th Cir. 1987).

A contrary view was adopted by the Tenth Circuit Court of Appeals in *Dowell* v. *Board of Education of the Oklahoma City Public Schools*, 795 F.2d 1516 (10th Cir. 1986), *cert. denied*, 479 U.S. 938 (1986). This court observed:

> While there are sound reasons for courts to seek the earliest opportunity to return control of school district affairs to the local body elected for that purpose, those reasons do not require abandonment of the inherent equitable power of any court to enforce orders which it has never vacated. The court's authority is not diminished once the original case has been closed because the viability of a permanent injunction does not depend upon this ministerial procedure. * * * Therefore, termination of active supervision of a case does not prevent the court from enforcing its orders. If such were the case, it would give more credence to the ministerial function of "closing" a case and less credence to the prospective operation of a mandatory injunction. (P. 1521)

Another decision emanating from the Tenth Circuit—*Brown* v. *Board of Education of Topeka*, __F.2d __(10th Cir. 1989) (Brown III), a progeny of the landmark school desegregation case—overturned a lower court by pronouncing the Topeka schools not to be a racially unitary system. The court held that since implementing its desegregation plan in the 1950s the school district had exercised a form of benign neglect by insufficiently attending to further desegregation efforts.

A more flexible approach appears to have been taken by the Eleventh Circuit Court of Appeals in *United States* v. *Board of Education of Jackson County*, 794 F.2d 1541 (11th Cir. 1986), which observed:

> That school districts have become unitary, however, does not inevitably require the courts to vacate the orders upon which the parties had relied in reaching that state. Our cases do not require the premature termination of those long-term orders that are part of a remedy "tailored to cure" a particular constitutional wrong. In some situations, such orders make possible the long term commitment needed to start the desegregation process. (P. 1543)

Taken by itself, this statement apparently allows district courts either to vacate or not to vacate desegregation orders under which schools have achieved unitary status. However, given the particular facts of this case, the implications of this decision remain uncertain.

B. Effect of Public Housing

Segregated conditions in the schools often are associated with segregated neighborhoods, which in turn, may stem from deliberate discrimination by public-housing and other governmental officials. Courts have been reluctant to hold school districts accountable for such practices except when school district complicity has been proved. In *Bell* v. *Board of Education, Akron Schools,* 683 F.2d 963 (6th Cir. 1982), the court held that a school board innocent of segregative intent is not liable for the discriminatory housing practices of other agencies. Schools, the court insisted, should not be held responsible for the actions of courts, churches, the Congress, or other institutions. It cited Justice Powell's statement in *Austin Independent School District* v. *United States,* 429 U.S. 990 (1976), in which he maintained:

> The principal cause of racial and ethnic imbalance in urban public schools across the country—North and South—is the imbalance in residential patterns. Such residential patterns are typically beyond the control of school authorities. For example, discrimination in housing—whether public or private—cannot be attributed to school authorities. Economic pressures and voluntary preferences are the primary determinants of residential patterns. (P. 994)

Also see *Jenkins* v. *State of Missouri,* 807 F.2d 657 (8th Cir. 1986), *cert. denied,* 484 U.S. 816 (1987), in which the same issue was raised.

A federal appellate court held that various actions and inactions of the Yonkers, New York, Board of Education reinforced the city's intentional discrimination in public housing, and thus, constituted de jure segregation. The court stated, however, that a school district with no prior history of de jure segregation is not required to abandon its neighborhood school policy merely because its adherence to the policy perpetuates segregated schools. Other action was taken against the Yonkers city council for refusing to approve a public housing desegregation plan. A fine was levied against the city that was $100 on the first day and that doubled daily thereafter. Additionally, each council member voting against the plan was fined $500 per day and threatened with jail. See *United States* v. *Yonkers Board of Education,* 837 F.2d 1181 (2d Cir. 1987), *cert. denied,* 486 U.S. __(1988). After much political posturing, local authorities complied with the court order to approve the public housing desegregation plan.

VI

school finance reform

Introduction

Court decisions involving racial segregation in the public schools over the last several decades revealed that the judiciary would deal with issues that other branches of government were unwilling to be concerned with or were reluctant to recognize. Consequently, many persons who perceived that they were being denied rights owing to governmental action or inaction increasingly employed the courts in an attempt to redress alleged grievances. One such group of persons brought the issue of equality of educational opportunity before the courts. Their contention was that many state methods of financing public education were unconstitutional because they violated the Equal Protection Clause for certain classes of people.

Reliance on local revenue to support a large portion of the total public school budget, it was alleged, was unfair because of the disparity in taxable wealth among local school systems.* Since the property tax is the most commonly used local school tax, many school finance experts have defined school system wealth as the ratio of taxable property divided by the number of students. Consequently, a "wealthy" school system would achieve such status by having much valuable taxable property, such as factories, utilities, or natural resources, and few children to educate. Conversely, a "poor" school system would have little valuable property and many children to educate. A school system composed largely of trailer parks, where each trailer contained several school-age children, would be an example of a poor system. School-district wealth is based on property wealth and not on income wealth; consequently, there may or may not be a relationship in poor or wealthy school systems with the income wealth of its inhabitants.

Those who contend that a state's method of financing the public schools is unfair often argue that wealthy school systems can raise large amounts of money with lower tax rates than can poor systems. Allowing this situation under a state-authorized method of financing public education, it is alleged, is unfair to both taxpayers and the recipients of school services in poor systems. For example, assume that the wealthiest school system in a state has a taxable assessed valuation per student (usually expressed on the basis of average daily attendance or membership) of $400,000 and the poorest school system has a taxable assessed valuation per student of $25,000. A levy of one mill (one-tenth of one percent, also expressed as a tax rate of $1 per $1,000 of property value) would raise $400 per student in the wealthiest system and only $25 per student in the poorest school system. Since education is a responsibility of the state, school finance reformers allege that a state's allowing a school-financing system in which such disparities operate in favor of wealthy school systems denies equality of educational opportunity to those students in poorer school systems.

Widely diverse school finance issues have been raised since the earliest court cases. These issues include the effects of municipal overburden, the higher costs of urban education, the greater concentrations of disadvantaged children in urban schools, and the necessity in some states to raise local funds by referenda. However, the issue that has received the greatest court attention addressed the alleged inequality of educational opportunity resulting from statewide school finance systems that

---

* Nationally, through 1987, local revenue made up approximately 44 percent of the total revenue for elementary and secondary schools, while state revenue made up approximately 50 percent and federal revenue 6 percent. Across the country local support for public elementary and secondary education ranged from a high of approximately 90 percent to a low of approximately 10 percent. Hawaii is the only state having no official local support for education.

make educational funding a function of district property wealth. Court attention to this issue will be the subject of the remainder of this chapter.

I. Early Decisions

In one of the earliest decisions, *McInnis v. Shapiro*, 293 F. Supp. 327 (Ill. 1968), *aff'd sub nom. McInnis v. Ogilvie*, 394 U.S. 322 (1969), the Illinois method of financing public education was described by plaintiffs as being particularly inequitable, since it permitted wide variations in expenditures per student and did not apportion funds according to the educational needs of students. In rejecting this contention, the court declared that the controversy was essentially nonjusticiable because of a lack of judicially manageable standards. The court contended that equal expenditures per student were inappropriate as a standard and that courts were ill-equipped to devise an equitable financing plan for the public schools. A virtually indistinguishable case, *Burruss v. Wilkerson*, 310 F. Supp. 572 (Va. 1969), *aff'd mem.*, 397 U.S. 44 (1970), essentially reached the same conclusion as *McInnis*.

Questions raised in these early cases revealed the lack of empirical data necessary to have a clear and accurate understanding of the effects of a state's finance system. Additionally, these cases revealed other methodological shortcomings, such as the lack of consensus over the goals of schooling and especially what constituted a "basic" education, an absence of meaningful cost-effectiveness analysis, a clear definition of educational need, and the inexactitude of measurement technology. Courts, it soon became evident, had great difficulty in dealing with broad generalizations or abstractions concerning education, requiring, instead, quantifiable evidence.

II. Fiscal Neutrality

Lack of success in *McInnis* and *Burruss* did not dissuade others interested in school finance reform from continuing a legal assault on interdistrict resource inequality. A California case, *Serrano v. Priest*, 5 Cal. 3d 584, 487 P.2d 1241 (1971) (*Serrano I*), provided the court with a judicially manageable standard, which had been missing in *McInnis* and *Burruss*. In this case the plaintiffs attempted to demonstrate that the California method of financing public education allowed substantial disparities among the various school districts in the amount of revenue available for education, thereby denying students equal protection of the laws under both the United States and California constitutions.

Furthermore, plaintiffs alleged that under this system parents were required to pay taxes at a higher rate than taxpayers in many other districts in order to provide the same or lesser educational opportunities for their children. In its decision, the California Supreme Court established that education was a constitutionally protected fundamental interest and that "wealth" was a "suspect classification." When a fundamental interest or suspect classification is involved, the court contended, the state must establish not only that it has a compelling interest that justifies the law, but that the distinctions drawn by the law are necessary to further its purpose. Employing this line of reasoning places the so-called burden of proof on the state. Perhaps most important in this decision was the standard established by the court to determine whether or not a school finance plan was constitutional. Under this standard, which the court called fiscal neutrality, the quality of a child's education could not be based on the wealth of the child's local school district but rather had to be based on the wealth of the state as a whole. This provided the court with a judicially manageable standard, in contrast to the "needs" standard in *McInnis*, since the court merely had to reject the present financing plan as unconstitutional, thereby placing the burden of adopting a constitutionally acceptable finance plan with the state.*

III. *Rodriguez*

Suits were filed in both state and federal courts in over three dozen states after the California *Serrano I* decision. In many of these suits plaintiffs were successful in their request that the court endorse the fiscal neutrality standard adopted in *Serrano I* to remedy wealth disparity. One of these cases, **San Antonio Independent School District v. Rodriguez,** provided the United States Supreme Court with an opportunity to address this issue.

San Antonio Independent School District v. Rodriguez
Supreme Court of the United States, 1973
411 U.S. 1

MR. JUSTICE POWELL delivered the opinion of the Court.
This suit attacking the Texas system of financing public education was initiated by Mexican-American parents whose children attend the

---

* A subsequent decision by the California Supreme Court in *Serrano II*, 18 Cal. 3d 728, 135 Cal. Rptr. 345 (1976), *cert. denied*, 432 U.S. 907 (1977), again affirmed the trial court's finding that the California school finance system was unconstitutional under the equal protection provision of the state constitution. *Serrano III*, 226 Cal. Rptr. 584 (1986) held that there had been full compliance with the original *Serrano* mandate to improve equity.

elementary and secondary schools in the Edgewood Independent School District, an urban school district in San Antonio, Texas. They brought a class action on behalf of schoolchildren throughout the State who are members of minority groups or who are poor and reside in school districts having a low property tax base. * * * The complaint was filed in the summer of 1968 and a three-judge court was impaneled in January 1969. In December 1971 the panel rendered its judgment in a *per curiam* opinion holding the Texas school finance system unconstitutional under the Equal Protection Clause of the Fourteenth Amendment. The State appealed, and we noted probable jurisdiction to consider the far-reaching constitutional questions presented. * * * For the reasons stated in this opinion, we reverse the decision of the District Court.

The first Texas State Constitution, promulgated upon Texas' entry into the Union in 1845, provided for the establishment of a system of free schools. Early in its history, Texas adopted a dual approach to the financing of its schools, relying on mutual participation by the local school districts and the State. * * *

Until recent times, Texas was a predominantly rural State and its population and property wealth were spread relatively evenly across the State. Sizable differences in the value of assessable property between local school districts became increasingly evident as the State became more industrialized and as rural-to-urban population shifts became more pronounced. The location of commercial and industrial property began to play a significant role in determining the amount of tax resources available to each school district. These growing disparities in population and taxable property between districts were responsible in part for increasingly notable differences in levels of local expenditure for education.

* * *

Recognizing the need for increased state funding to help offset disparities in local spending and to meet Texas' changing educational requirements, the state legislature in the late 1940's undertook a thorough evaluation of public education with an eye toward major reform. * * * [It established] the Texas Minimum Foundation School Program. Today, this Program accounts for approximately half of the total educational expenditures in Texas.

The Program calls for state and local contributions to a fund earmarked specifically for teacher salaries, operating expenses, and transportation costs. The State, supplying funds from its general revenues, finances approximately 80% of the Program, and the school districts are responsible—as a unit—for providing the remaining 20%. The districts' share, known as the Local Fund Assignment, is apportioned among the school districts under a formula designed to reflect each district's relative taxpaying ability. * * *

* * *

The school district in which appellees reside, the Edgewood Independent School District, has been compared throughout this litigation with the Alamo Heights Independent School District. This comparison between the least and most affluent districts in the San Antonio area serves to illustrate the manner in which the dual system of finance operates and to indicate the extent to which substantial disparities exist despite the State's impressive progress in recent years. Edgewood is one of seven public school districts in the metropolitan area. Approximately 22,000 students are enrolled in its 25 elementary and secondary schools. The district is situated in the core-city sector of San Antonio in a residential neighborhood that has little commercial or industrial property. The residents are predominantly of Mexican-American descent: approximately 90% of the student population is Mexican-American and over 6% is Negro. The average assessed property value per pupil is $5,960—the lowest in the metropolitan area—and the median family income ($4,686) is also the lowest. At an equalized tax rate of $1.05 per $100 of assessed property—the highest in the metropolitan area— the district contributed $26 to the education of each child for the 1967–1968 school year above its Local Fund Assignment for the Minimum Foundation Program. The Foundation Program contributed $222 per pupil for a state-local total of $248. Federal funds added another $108 for a total of $356 per pupil.

Alamo Heights is the most affluent school district in San Antonio. Its six schools, housing approximately 5,000 students, are situated in a residential community quite unlike the Edgewood District. The school population is predominantly "Anglo," having only 18% Mexican-Americans and less than 1% Negroes. The assessed property value per pupil exceeds $49,000, and the median family income is $8,001. In 1967–1968 the local tax rate of $.85 per $100 of valuation yielded $333 per pupil over and above its contribution to the Foundation Program. Coupled with the $225 provided from that Program, the district was able to supply $558 per student. Supplemented by a $36 per-pupil grant from federal sources, Alamo Heights spent $594 per pupil.

Although the 1967–1968 school year figures provide the only complete statistical breakdown for each category of aid, more recent partial statistics indicate that the previously noted trend of increasing state aid has been significant. For the 1970–1971 school year, the Foundation School Program allotment of Edgewood was $356 per pupil. * * * Alamo Heights enjoyed a similar increase under the Foundation Program, netting $491 per pupil in 1970–1971. These recent figures also reveal the extent to which these two districts' allotments were funded from their own required contributions to the Local Fund Assignment. Alamo Heights, because of its relative wealth, was required to contribute out of its local property tax collections approximately $100 per pupil, or about 20% of its Foundation grant. Edgewood, on the other hand, paid only $8.46 per pupil, which is about 2.4% of its grant. It appears then that, at least as to these two districts, the Local Fund Assignment does reflect a rough approximation of the relative taxpaying potential of each.

Despite these recent increases, substantial interdistrict disparities in school expenditures found by the District Court to prevail in San Antonio and in varying degrees throughout the State still exist. And it was these disparities, largely attributable to differences in the amounts of money collected through local property taxation, that led the District Court to conclude that Texas' dual system of public school financing violated the Equal Protection Clause. * * *

* * *

* * * We must decide, first, whether the Texas system of financing public education operates to the disadvantage of some suspect class or impinges upon a fundamental right explicitly or implicitly protected by the Constitution, thereby requiring strict judicial scrutiny. If so, the judgment of the District Court should be affirmed. If not, the Texas scheme must still be examined to determine whether it rationally furthers some legitimate, articulated state purpose and therefore does not constitute an invidious discrimination in violation of the Equal Protection Clause of the Fourteenth Amendment.

* * *

The wealth discrimination discovered by the District Court in this case, and by several other courts that have recently struck down school-financing laws in other states, is quite unlike any of the forms of wealth discrimination heretofore reviewed by this Court. * * *

The case comes to us with no definitive description of the classifying facts or delineation of the disfavored class. Examination of the District Court's opinion and of appellees' complaint, briefs, and contentions at oral arguments suggests, however, at least three ways in which the discrimination claimed here might be described. The Texas system of school financing might be regarded as discriminating (1) against "poor" persons whose incomes fall below some identifiable level of poverty or who might be characterized as functionally "indigent," or (2) against those who are relatively poorer than others, or (3) against all those who, irrespective of their personal incomes, happen to reside in relatively poorer school districts. Our task must be to ascertain whether, in fact, the Texas system has been shown to discriminate on any of these possible bases and, if so, whether the resulting classification may be regarded as suspect.

The precedents of this Court provide the proper starting point. The individuals, or groups of individuals, who constituted the class discriminated against in our prior cases shared two distinguishing characteristics: because of their impecunity they were completely unable to pay for some desired benefit, and as a consequence, they sustained an absolute deprivation of a meaningful opportunity to enjoy that benefit. * * *

* * *

Only appellees' first possible basis for describing the class disadvantaged by the Texas school-financing system—discrimination against a class of definably "poor" persons—might arguably meet the criteria established in these prior cases. Even a cursory examination, however, demonstrates that neither of the two distinguishing characteristics of wealth classifications can be found here. First, in support of their charge that the system discriminates against the "poor," appellees have made no effort to demonstrate that it operates to the peculiar disadvantage of any class fairly definable as indigent, or as composed of persons whose incomes are beneath any designated poverty level. Indeed, there is reason to believe that the poorest families are not necessarily clustered in the poorest property districts. A recent and exhaustive study of school districts in Connecticut concluded that "[i]t is clearly incorrect . . . to contend that the 'poor' live in 'poor' districts. . . . Thus, the major factual assumption of *Serrano*—that the educational financing system discriminates against the "poor"—is simply false in Connecticut." Defining "poor" families as those below the Bureau of the Census "poverty level," the Connecticut study found, not surprisingly, that the poor were clustered around commercial and industrial areas—those same areas that provide the most attractive sources of property tax income for school districts. Whether a similar pattern would be discovered in Texas is not known, but there is no basis on the record in this case for assuming that the poorest people—defined by reference to any level of absolute impecunity—are concentrated in the poorest districts.

Second, neither appellees nor the District Court addressed the fact that, unlike each of the foregoing cases, lack of personal resources had not occasioned an absolute deprivation of the desired benefit. The argument here is not that the children in districts having relatively low assessable property values are receiving no public education; rather, it is that they are receiving a poorer quality education than that available to children in districts having more assessable wealth. Apart from the unsettled and disputed question whether the quality of education may be determined by the amount of money expended for it, a sufficient answer to appellees' argument is that, at least where wealth is involved, the Equal Protection Clause does not require absolute equality or precisely equal advantages. * * *

For these two reasons—the absence of any evidence that the financing system discriminates against any definable category of "poor" people or that it results in the absolute deprivation of education—the disadvantaged class is not susceptible of identification in traditional terms.

As suggested above, appellees and the District Court may have embraced a second or third approach, the second of which might be characterized as a theory of relative comparative discrimination based on family income. Appellees sought to prove that a direct correlation exists between the wealth of families within each district and the expenditures therein for education. That is, along a continuum, the poorer the family the lower the dollar amount of education received by the family's children.

* * *

This brings us, then, to the third way in which the classification scheme might be defined—*district* wealth discrimination. Since the only correlation indicated by the evidence is between district property wealth and expenditures, it may be argued that discrimination might be found without regard to the individual income characteristics of district residents. * * *

However described, it is clear that appellees' suit asks this Court to extend its most exacting scrutiny to review a system that allegedly discriminates against a large, diverse, and amorphous class, unified only by the common factor of residence in its districts that happen to have less taxable wealth than other districts. The system of alleged discrimination and the class it defines have none of the traditional indicia of suspectness: the class is not saddled with such disabilities, or subjected to such a history of purposeful unequal treatment, or relegated to such a position of political powerlessness as to command extraordinary protection from the majoritarian political process.

We thus conclude that the Texas system does not operate to the peculiar disadvantage of any suspect class. But in recognition of the fact that this Court has never heretofore held that wealth discrimination alone provides an adequate basis for invoking strict scrutiny, appellees have not relied solely on this contention. They also assert that the State's system impermissibly interferes with the exercise of a "fundamental" right and that accordingly the prior decisions of this Court require the application of the strict standard of judicial review. * * * It is this question—whether education is a fundamental right, in the sense that it is among the rights and liberties protected by the Constitution— which has so consumed the attention of courts and commentators in recent years.

* * *

Nothing this Court holds today in any way detracts from our historic dedication to public education. We are in complete agreement with the conclusion of the three-judge panel below that "the grave significance of education both to the individual and to our society" cannot be doubted. But the importance of a service performed by the State does not determine whether it must be regarded as fundamental for purposes of examination under the Equal Protection Clause. * * *

* * *

* * * It is not the province of this Court to create substantive constitutional rights in the name of guaranteeing equal protection of the laws. Thus, the key to discovering whether education is "fundamental" is not to be found in comparisons of the relative societal significance of education as opposed to subsistence or housing. Nor is it to be found by weighing whether education is as important as the right to travel. Rather, the answer lies in assessing whether there is a right to education explicitly or implicitly guaranteed by the Constitution. * * *

Education, of course, is not among the rights afforded explicit protection under our Federal Constitution. Nor do we find any basis for saying it is implicitly so protected. As we have said, the undisputed importance of education will not alone cause this Court to depart from the usual standard for reviewing a State's social and economic legislation. It is appellees' contention, however, that education is distinguishable from other services and benefits provided by the State because it bears a peculiarly close relationship to other rights and liberties accorded protection under the Constitution. Specifically, they insist that education is itself a fundamental personal right because it is essential to the effective exercise of First Amendment freedoms and to intelligent utilization of the right to vote. In asserting a nexus between speech and education, appellees urge that the right to speak is meaningless unless the speaker is capable of articulating his thoughts intelligently and persuasively. The "marketplace of ideas" is an empty forum for those lacking basic communicative tools. Likewise, they argue that the corollary right to receive information becomes little more than a hollow privilege when the recipient has not been taught to read, assimilate, and utilize available knowledge.

*   *   *

Even if it were conceded that some identifiable quantum of education is a constitutionally protected prerequisite to the meaningful exercise of either right, we have no indication that the present levels of educational expenditures in Texas provides an education that falls short. Whatever merit appellees' argument might have if a State's financing system occasioned an absolute denial of educational opportunities to any of its children, that argument provides no basis for finding an interference with fundamental rights where only relative differences in spending levels are involved and where—as is true in the present case—no charge fairly could be made that the system fails to provide each child with an opportunity to acquire the basic minimal skills necessary for the enjoyment of the rights of speech and of full participation in the political process.

Furthermore, the logical limitations on appellees' nexus theory are difficult to perceive. How, for instance, is education to be distinguished from the significant personal interests in the basics of decent food and shelter? Empirical examination might well buttress an assumption that the ill-fed, ill-clothed, and ill-housed are among the most ineffective participants in the political process, and that they derive the least enjoyment from the benefits of the First Amendment. *   *   *

*   *   *

Thus, we stand on familiar ground when we continue to acknowledge that the Justices of this Court lack both the expertise and the familiarity with local problems so necessary to the making of wise decisions with respect to the raising and disposition of public revenues. Yet, we are urged to direct the States either to alter drastically the present system or to throw out the property tax altogether in favor of some other form of taxation. No scheme of taxation, whether the tax is imposed on property, income, or purchases of goods and services, has yet been devised which is free of all discriminatory impact. In such a complex arena in which no perfect alternatives exist, the Court does well not to impose too rigorous a standard of scrutiny lest all local fiscal schemes become subjects of criticism under the Equal Protection Clause.

In addition to matters of fiscal policy, this case also involves the most persistent and difficult questions of educational policy, another area in which this Court's lack of specialized knowledge and experience counsels against premature interference with the informed judgments made at the state and local levels. Education, perhaps even more than welfare assistance, presents a myriad of "intractable economic, social, and even philosophical problems." * * * The very complexity of the problems of financing and managing a statewide public school system suggests that "there will be more than one constitutionally permissible method of solving them," and that, within the limits of rationality, "the legislature's efforts to tackle the problems" should be entitled to respect. * * * On even the most basic questions in this area the scholars and educational experts are divided. Indeed, one of the major sources of controversy concerns the extent to which there is a demonstrable correlation between educational expenditures and the quality of education— an assumed correlation underlying virtually every legal conclusion drawn by the District Court in this case. Related to the questioned relationship between cost and quality is the equally unsettled controversy as to the proper goals of a system of public education. And the question regarding the most effective relationship between state boards of education and local school boards, in terms of their respective responsibilities and degrees of control, is now undergoing searching re-examination. The ultimate wisdom as to these and related problems of education is not likely to be divined for all time even by the scholars who now so earnestly debate the issues. In such circumstances, the judiciary is well advised to refrain from imposing on the States inflexible constitutional restraints that could circumscribe or handicap the continued research and experimentation so vital to finding even partial solutions to educational problems and to keeping abreast of ever-changing conditions.

* * *

The foregoing considerations buttress our conclusion that Texas' system of public school finance is an inappropriate candidate for strict judicial scrutiny. * * *

* * *

Appellees further urge that the Texas system is unconstitutionally arbitrary because it allows the availability of local taxable resources to turn on "happenstance." They see no justification for a system that allows, as they contend, the quality of education to fluctuate on the basis of the fortuitous positioning of the boundary lines of political subdivisions and the location of valuable commercial and industrial property. But any scheme of local taxation—indeed the very existence of identifiable local governmental units—requires the establishment of jurisdictional boundaries that are inevitably arbitrary. It is equally inevitable that some localities are going to be blessed with more taxable assets than others. Nor is local wealth a static quantity. Changes in the level of taxable wealth within any district may result from any number of events, some of which local residents can and do influence. For instance, commercial and industrial enterprises may be encouraged to locate within a district by various actions—public and private.

Moreover, if local taxation for local expenditures were an unconstitutional method of providing for education then it might be an equally impermissible means of providing for other necessary services customarily financed largely from local property taxes, including local police and fire protection, public health and hospitals, and public utility facilities of various kinds. We perceive no justification for such a severe denigration of local property taxation and control as would follow from appellees' contentions. It has simply never been within the constitutional prerogative of this Court to nullify statewide measures for financing public services merely because the burdens or benefits thereof fall unevenly depending upon the relative wealth of the political subdivisions in which citizens live.

* * * One also must remember that the system here challenged is not peculiar to Texas or to any other State. In its essential characteristics, the Texas plan for financing public education reflects what many educators for a half century have thought was an enlightened approach to a problem for which there is no perfect solution. We are unwilling to assume for ourselves a level of wisdom superior to that of legislators, scholars, and educational authorities in 50 States, especially where the alternatives proposed are only recently conceived and nowhere yet tested. * * *

* * *

* * * The consideration and initiation of fundamental reforms with respect to state taxation and education are matters reserved for the legislative processes of the various States, and we do no violence to the values of federalism and separation of powers by staying our hand. We hardly need add that this Court's action today is not to be viewed as placing its judicial imprimatur on the status quo. The need is apparent for reform in tax systems which may well have relied too long and too heavily on the local property tax. And certainly innovative thinking as to public education, its methods, and its funding is necessary to assure both a higher level of quality and greater uniformity of opportunity. These matters merit the continued attention of the scholars who already have contributed much by their challenges. But the ultimate solutions must come from the lawmakers and from the democratic pressures of those who elect them.

Reversed.

MR. JUSTICE STEWART, concurring.

The method of financing public schools in Texas, as in almost every other State, has resulted in a system of public education that can fairly be described as chaotic and unjust. It does not follow, however, and I cannot find, that this system violates the Constitution of the United States. I join the opinion and judgment of the Court because I am convinced that any other course would mark an extraordinary departure from principled adjudication under the Equal Protection Clause of the Fourteenth Amendment. * * *

* * *

MR. JUSTICE WHITE, with whom MR. JUSTICE DOUGLAS and MR. JUSTICE BRENNAN join, dissenting.

* * *

I cannot disagree with the proposition that local control and local decisionmaking play an important part in our democratic system of government. * * * Much may be left to local option, and this case would be quite different if it were true that the Texas system, while insuring minimum educational expenditures in every district through state funding, extended a meaningful option to all local districts to increase their per-pupil expenditures and so to improve their children's education to the extent that increased funding would achieve that goal. The system would then arguably provide a rational and sensible method of achieving the stated aim of preserving an area for local initiative and decision.

The difficulty with the Texas system, however, is that it provides a meaningful option to Alamo Heights and like school districts but almost none to Edgewood and those other districts with a low per-pupil real estate tax base. In these latter districts, no matter how desirous parents are of supporting their schools with greater revenues, it is impossible to do so through the use of the real estate property tax. In these districts, the Texas system utterly fails to extend a realistic choice to parents because the property tax, which is the only revenue-raising mechanism extended to school districts, is practically and legally unavailable. * * *

* * *

* * * If the State aims at maximizing local initiative and local choice, by permitting school districts to resort to the real property tax if they choose to do so, it utterly fails in achieving its purpose in districts with property tax bases so low that there is little if any opportunity for interested parents, rich or poor, to augment school district revenues. Requiring the State to establish only that unequal treatment is in furtherance of a permissible goal, without also requiring the State to show that the means chosen to effectuate that goal are rationally related to its achievement, makes equal protection analysis no more than an empty gesture. In my view, the parents and children in Edgewood, and in like districts, suffer from an invidious discrimination violative of the Equal Protection Clause.

This does not, of course, mean that local control may not be a legitimate goal of a school-financing system. Nor does it mean that the State must guarantee each district an equal per-pupil revenue from the state school-financing system. Nor does it mean, as the majority appears to believe, that, by affirming the decision below, this Court would be "imposing on the States inflexible constitutional restraints that could circumscribe or handicap the continued research and experimentation so vital to finding even partial solutions to educational problems and to keeping abreast of ever-changing conditions." On the contrary, it would merely mean that the State must fashion a financing scheme which provides a rational basis for the maximization of local control, if local control is to remain a goal of the system, and not a scheme with "different treatment be[ing] accorded to persons placed by a statute into different classes on the basis of criteria wholly unrelated to the objective of that statute." * * *

* * *

MR. JUSTICE MARSHALL, with whom MR. JUSTICE DOUGLAS concurs, dissenting.

The Court today decides, in effect, that a State may constitutionally vary the quality of education which it offers its children in accordance with the amount of taxable wealth located in the school districts within which they reside. The majority's decision represents an abrupt departure from the mainstream of recent state and federal court decisions concerning the unconstitutionality of state educational financing schemes dependent upon taxable local wealth. More unfortunately, though, the majority's holding can only be seen as a retreat from our historic commitment to equality of educational opportunity and as unsupportable acquiescence in a system which deprives children in their earliest years of the chance to reach their full potential as citizens. The Court does this despite the absence of any substantial justification for a scheme which arbitrarily channels educational resources in accordance with the fortuity of the amount of taxable wealth within each district.

In my judgment, the right of every American to an equal start in life, so far as the provision of a state service as important as education is concerned, is far too vital to permit state discrimination on grounds as tenuous as those presented by this record. Nor can I accept the notion that it is sufficient to remit these appellees to the vagaries of the political process which, contrary to the majority's suggestion, has proved singularly unsuited to the task of providing a remedy for this discrimination. I, for one, am unsatisfied with the hope of an ultimate "political" solution sometime in the indefinite future while, in the meantime, countless children unjustifiably receive inferior educations that "may affect their hearts and minds in a way unlikely ever to be undone."

*   *   *

The Court acknowledges that "substantial interdistrict disparities in school expenditures" exist in Texas, *   *   * and that these disparities are "largely attributable to differences in the amounts of money collected through local property taxation." *   *   * But instead of closely examining the seriousness of these disparities and the invidiousness of the Texas financing scheme, the Court undertakes an elaborate exploration of the efforts Texas has purportedly made to close the gaps between its districts in terms of level district wealth and resulting educational funding. Yet, however praiseworthy Texas' equalizing efforts, the issue in this case is not whether Texas is doing its best to ameliorate the worst features of a discriminatory scheme but, rather, whether the scheme itself is in fact unconstitutionally discriminatory in the face of the Fourteenth Amendment's guarantee of equal protection of the laws. When the Texas financing scheme is taken as a whole, I do not think it can be doubted that it produces a discriminatory impact on substantial numbers of the school-age children in the State of Texas.

*   *   *

*   *   * I must once more voice my disagreement with the Court's rigidified approach to equal protection analysis. *   *   * The Court seeks to establish today that equal protection cases fall into one of two neat categories which dictate the appropriate standard of review—strict scrutiny or mere rationality. But this Court's decisions in the field of equal protection defy such easy categorization. A principled reading of what this Court has done reveals that it has applied a spectrum of standards in reviewing discrimination allegedly violative of the Equal Protection Clause. This spectrum clearly comprehends variations in the degree of care with which the Court will scrutinize particular classifications, depending, I believe, on the constitutional and societal importance of the interest adversely affected and the recognized invidiousness of the basis upon which the particular classification is drawn. * * *

I therefore cannot accept the majority's labored efforts to demonstrate that fundamental interests which call for strict scrutiny of the challenged classification, encompass only established rights which we are somehow bound to recognize from the text of the Constitution itself. To be sure, some interests which the Court has deemed to be fundamental for purposes of equal protection analysis are themselves constitutionally protected rights. * * *

I would like to know where the Constitution guarantees the right to procreate, *Skinner* v. *Oklahoma*, 316 U.S. 535, 541 (1942), or the right to vote in state elections, *e.g.*, *Reynolds* v. *Sims*, 377 U.S. 533 (1964), or the right to an appeal from a criminal conviction, *e.g.*, *Griffin* v. *Illinois*, 351 U.S. 12 (1956). These are instances in which, due to the importance of the interests at stake, the Court has displayed a strong concern with the existence of discriminatory state treatment. But the Court has never said or indicated that these are interests which independently enjoy full-blown constitutional protection.

* * *

The study introduced in the District Court showed a direct inverse relationship between equalized taxable district property wealth and district tax effort with the result that the property-poor districts making the highest tax effort obtained the lowest per-pupil yield. * * * Since the funds received through the Minimum Foundation School Program are to be used only for minimum professional salaries, transportation costs, and operating expenses, it is not hard to see the lack of local choice—with respect to higher teacher salaries to attract more and better teachers, physical facilities, library books, and facilities, special courses, or participation in special state and federal matching funds programs—under which a property-poor district such as Edgewood is forced to labor. In fact, because of the difference in taxable local property wealth, Edgewood would have to tax itself almost nine times as heavily to obtain the same yield as Alamo Heights. At present, then, local control is a myth for many of the local school districts in Texas. As one district court has observed, "rather than reposing in each school district the economic power to fix its own level of per-pupil expenditure, the State has so arranged the structure as to guarantee that some districts will spend low (with high taxes) while others will spend high (with low taxes)." * * *

* * *

In conclusion, it is essential to recognize that an end to the wide variations in taxable district property wealth inherent in the Texas financing scheme would entail none of the untoward consequences suggested by the Court or by the appellants.

First, affirmance of the District Court's decisions would hardly sound the death knell for local control of education. It would mean neither centralized decisionmaking nor federal court intervention in the operation of public schools. Clearly, this suit has nothing to do with local decisionmaking with respect to educational policy or even educational spending. It involves only a narrow aspect of local control—namely, local control over the raising of educational funds. In fact, in striking down interdistrict disparities in taxable local wealth, the District Court took the course which is most likely to make true local control over educational decisionmaking a reality for *all* Texas school districts.

Nor does the District Court's decision even necessarily eliminate local control of educational funding. The District Court struck down nothing more than the continued interdistrict wealth discrimination inherent in the present property tax. Both centralized and decentralized plans for educational funding not involving such interdistrict discrimination have been put forward. The choice among these or other alternatives would remain with the State, not with the federal courts. * * *

* * *

The Court seeks solace for its action today in the possibility of legislative reform. The Court's suggestions of legislative redress and experimentation will doubtless be of great comfort to the schoolchildren of Texas' disadvantaged districts, but considering the vested interests of wealthy school districts in the preservation of the status quo, they are worth little more. The possibility of legislative action is, in all events, no answer to this Court's duty under the Constitution to eliminate unjustified state discrimination. In this case we have been presented with an instance of such discrimination, in a particularly invidious form, against an individual interest of large constitutional and practical importance. To support the demonstrated discrimination in the provision of educational opportunity the State has offered a justification which, on analysis, takes on at best an ephemeral character. Thus, I believe that the wide disparities in taxable district property wealth inherent in the local property tax element of the Texas financing scheme render that scheme violative of the Equal Protection Clause.

* * *

Notes and Questions

Rodriguez was a five-to-four decision. Joining Justice Powell in the majority opinion were Chief Justice Burger and Justices Stewart, Blackmun, and Rehnquist. In addition to upholding the constitutionality of the Texas method of financing public schools, the Court held that education was not a fundamental interest requiring strict scrutiny under the Equal Protection Clause. The Court also concluded that school finance reform should flow from state legislative processes.

Some observers have contended that, if the Court had mandated equality of educational opportunity for public school students, floodgates would have opened resulting in judicial attacks on statewide inequality in other government services, such as police and fire protection, recreational facilities, and health care. Do you agree with this contention? Does the fact that most state constitutions contain language committing the state to a responsibility for providing education negate this contention?

Despite the *Rodriguez* outcome, plaintiffs in Louisiana attempted to distinguish between practices in Louisiana and Texas in a suit alleging that the Equal Protection Clause of the Fourteenth Amendment was violated by the Louisiana school finance system. Nevertheless, a federal district court found the issues indistinguishable from *Rodriguez* and dismissed the case. See *Scarnato* v. *Parker,* 415 F. Supp. 272 (La. 1976), *aff'd,* 430 U.S. 960 (1977).

IV. Post-*Rodriguez* Litigation

Proponents of the school-finance-reform movement viewed the *Rodriguez* decision as essentially eliminating the federal courts as a viable battleground. Consequently, their attention turned to the state courts. In addition to relying on state equal protection grounds, litigation was brought under state constitutional provisions requiring public education to be "uniform," "adequate," or "thorough and efficient." The result has been much judicial activity among the states. However, largely because of the differences among states in the constitutional language or the specific statutory provisions that were challenged, state court holdings have not been uniform.

To date, supreme courts of ten states (Arizona, Colorado, Georgia, Idaho, Maryland, Michigan, Oklahoma, New York, Ohio, and Oregon) have concluded that state methods of financing public education are not constitutionally deficient. A federal appellate court in 1987 upheld the Louisiana finance plan. Additionally, lower courts in Pennsylvania (1987) and Wisconsin (1986) upheld challenged finance schemes. Many of these decisions espoused the legal rationale enunciated by the Supreme Court in *Rodriguez*. They agreed that education was unquestionably high on the list of priorities of governmental concern and responsibility; however, this did not automatically entitle public education to a classification as a fundamental right which would trigger a higher standard of judicial review for purposes of equal protection analysis. Public education in these cases was viewed as merely another public service battling for scarce resources in the political arena. The proper arena, these courts contended, was the legislature and not the courtroom. Additionally, decisions upholding existing state finance plans strongly favored the preservation of local control of education. Courts, in most instances, agreed that significant disparity in local wealth and expenditures existed and that reform was needed. However, it was emphasized that reform should be instituted by the legislative branch.*

To varying degrees, court decisions upholding school finance systems involved suits that were based on allegations of unconstitutional wealth and per-pupil expenditure disparities. Cases in Arizona, Idaho, and Oregon were filed soon after *Serrano I* and, although they were ultimately unsuccessful, plaintiffs closely patterned their arguments on the ones used in the California case.

Novel issues were addressed in several states. In New York State, New York City intervened on behalf of plaintiffs and added a "municipal overburden" issue to the case. "Municipal overburden" refers to the contention that city school systems have higher service costs than non-municipal districts, and intervenors alleged that this overburden represented a disequalizing force.

Several new issues were raised in Ohio. These included (1) the contention that voter control over tax levies should not have been permissible in a state that required a thorough and efficient educational program and (2) the argument that property-poor school districts tended to be income poor in that state and, therefore, constituted a more clearly identifiable suspect classification. Ohio plaintiffs also claimed that fiscal

---

* See listing of cases on pages 377–80.

capacity should not be represented solely by property value per student. In Maryland plaintiffs also attempted to base their case, in part, on a correlation between income and property wealth. Additionally, they sought to convince the court that a constitutional requirement of a "thorough and efficient" education should be construed as disallowing wide expenditure variations, even those resulting from factors other than local wealth disparity.

Decisions by the highest courts in eight states (Arkansas, California, Connecticut, Kentucky, New Jersey, Washington, West Virginia, and Wyoming) have held that statutes governing state and local financing of public education were unconstitutional. Although no decision rejected all features of a state's school finance legislation, each of these states was ordered to restructure the basic formula for the distribution of state funds or for the receipt of local revenues for education in order to eliminate or reduce local wealth disparity as a factor influencing expenditure variation among school districts.

Several legal rationales are woven through the decisions invalidating school finance schemes. Courts often held that either district wealth or per-pupil expenditure disparities, or both, were unconstitutional based either on equal protection grounds or on the wording pertaining to education in their state constitutions. Although these courts usually imposed "strict scrutiny" for equal protection analysis, they commonly declared that contested schemes failed to satisfy even the less stringent "rational basis" standard. In assessing the local control issue, these decisions usually reasoned that finance schemes, rather than preserving local control, thwarted it by requiring poor school systems merely to administer state-financed educational programs. However, the most pervasive theme threading through these decisions was the courts' recognition of the irrationality of the contested finance schemes.

Litigation continues in some of these states, generally as a consequence of dissatisfaction on the part of original plaintiffs or new parties with the quantity or quality of reforms enacted by legislatures in response to court orders. To date, no court has retreated from its initial requirement that inequities be corrected. Standards for alleviating disparities, after being promulgated by courts, have not been relaxed in subsequent orders. However, second- and third-generation decisions have in some instances declined to expand the scope or impact of earlier rulings, especially if new claims were brought by plaintiffs.

The legal controversy surrounding school finance wealth and per-pupil expenditure disparity continues unabated since the *Rodriguez* decision. This is clearly revealed by decisions at the state-supreme-court level in Oklahoma (1987), at the federal-appellate level in a case involving

Louisiana (1987), and at the lower-court levels in Texas (1987), Montana (1988), and Pennsylvania (1987).

Horton v. Meskill

Supreme Court of Connecticut, 1985
195 Conn. 24, 486 A.2d 1099

PETERS, Chief Justice.

These appeals are a sequel to *Horton v. Meskill,* 172 Conn. 615, 648–49, 376 A.2d 359 (1977) *(Horton I),* in which this court held unconstitutional the then existing statutory financing system for free public elementary and secondary school education in this state. Noting the difficulties of formulating appropriate orders of relief, we agreed in *Horton I* with the trial court's decision to retain jurisdiction while the General Assembly was afforded an opportunity to take responsive legislative action. * * * The legislature in 1979 enacted, and in subsequent years amended, a plan intended to achieve equity in educational financing. * * * The present litigation is a challenge by the original plaintiffs in *Horton I* and certain intervenors to the constitutionality of the new plan, both as originally enacted and as subsequently amended. The principal issue is whether this plan now provides the substantially equal educational opportunity for all Connecticut public school children that the Connecticut constitution requires. The trial court, *Spada, J.,* after extensive hearings, rendered judgments holding the plan constitutional in design but unconstitutional in part. * * *

The trial court examined in detail the provisions of the educational equity plan that the General Assembly enacted in 1979. * * * That plan has two principal components: (1) the guaranteed tax base grant formula (GTB) and (2) the minimum expenditure requirement (MER). The GTB formula is a plan of state grants designed to provide towns with a state-guaranteed tax base for the financing of public school education. It is designed to distribute equitably state aid to towns that establish their eligibility through the MER, a formula that sets the minimum acceptable level of per pupil town expenditures. The 1979 act did not commit any of the participants to immediate full implementation. Both state funding and local MER payments were to be phased-in over a five year period. In addition, property-poor towns were protected by a temporary "alternate" MER, which gave them access to GTB grants on the basis of their historical record of educational financing. Finally, all towns were guaranteed minimum-aid grants of $250 per pupil. The court concluded that this basic plan for financing of public school education provided a constitutionally appropriate mechanism to reduce state-wide disparity in educational resources. The court also found constitutional the state programs for equitable disbursement of categorical grants for transportation, special education and school construction.

The court nonetheless concluded that the salutary effect of these constitutional programs is being undermined by post-1979 destabilizing legislative action which has repeatedly postponed full implementation of the GTB program. The court thus declared unconstitutional: (1) the statute providing for continued minimum aid grants of $250 per pupil, regardless of town need; * * * (2) the statute requiring use of three year old data in the calculation of the guaranteed tax base; * * * (3) the statute postponing full funding of the guaranteed tax base to a seventh year; * * * and (4) the statute permitting towns to measure their minimum expenditure requirement (MER) by an alternate standard short of full funding. * * * In a further effort to achieve educational equity, the court concluded that the existing optional curriculum for secondary school students was unconstitutional; In each instance in which the court found the existing statutes to be constitutionally flawed, it ordered those of the defendants who had implementing responsibility to take designated appropriate action. * * *

* * *

* * * We noted in *Horton I* that "[t]he wealth discrimination found among school districts differs materially from the usual equal protection case where a fairly defined indigent class suffers discrimination to its peculiar disadvantage. The discrimination is relative rather than absolute." * * * We therefore defined the state's constitutional obligation as a duty to allocate governmental support to education so that state funds, instead of equally benefiting all the towns by way of a flat grant, would offset the demonstrated significant disparities in the financial ability of local communities to finance local education through the local property tax. * * * We held that the state was required to assure to all students in Connecticut's free public elementary and secondary schools "a substantially equal educational opportunity." * * * the sui generis nature of litigation involving school financing legislation militates against formalistic reliance on the usual standards of the law of equal protection, in particular against the requirement that the state must demonstrate a compelling state interest. * * *

* * *

We conclude that * * * educational financing legislation must be strictly scrutinized using a three-step process. First, the plaintiffs must make a prima facie showing that disparities in educational expenditures are more than de minimis in that the disparities continue to jeopardize the plaintiffs' fundamental right to education. If they make that showing, the burden then shifts to the state to justify these disparities as incident to the advancement of a legitimate state policy. If the state's justification is acceptable, the state must further demonstrate that the continuing disparities are nevertheless not so great as to be unconstitutional. In other words, to satisfy the mandate of *Horton I*, a school financing plan must, as a whole, further the policy of providing significant equalizing state support to local education. * * * However, no such plan will be constitutional if the remaining level of disparity continues "to emasculate the goal of substantial equality."

* * *

It is conceded by all parties that the evidence before the trial court demonstrates continued significant disparities in the funds that local communities spend on basic public education. The plaintiffs' evidence therefore suffices to shift to the state the burden of justification for the statute.

We next consider whether the state has met this burden. The trial court reasoned that the legislation enacted in 1979 was a constitutionally acceptable response to the problem of disparate local educational expenditures. The court determined that, if adequately funded, the GTB program would provide sufficient overall expenditures for public school education, that its five-year phase-in assured an efficient use of educational resources, and that its design would provide equity in the distribution of educational funds and a proper balance between state and local contributions thereto. In addition, the court found that the program retained a salutary role for local choice by guaranteeing minimum funds without imposing a ceiling on what a town might elect to spend for public education. Finally the court noted that a number of factors beyond direct state control had tended, in the recent past, to increase rather than diminish discrepancies in educational spending. The trial court identified several such factors: public school enrollment has decreased more rapidly in the wealthier than in the poorer towns; property values have increased more rapidly in the wealthier than in the poorer towns; and recent high rates of inflation have eroded the benefits of the GTB grants to the poorer towns. In light of all of these circumstances, Public Acts 1979, No. 79–128 was a reasonable response to the policy dictates of *Horton I*.

In assessing the adequacy of the challenged state legislation under the third step of the test, we can rely on the trial court's finding that the effect of the legislation was to narrow significantly disparities in the ability of local communities to finance local education and to increase significantly the state's share of overall educational costs for public schools. It was therefore reasonable for the trial court to conclude that the remaining disparities did not undermine the basic policy of equalizing state support for education.

* * *

We also agree with the conclusion of the trial court that the state plan for the distribution of categorical grants is constitutional. The court found that the categorical grant programs had not been shown to impinge upon the fundamental right to a substantially equal education.

* * *

The court's principal determinations of unconstitutionality relate to educational financing statutes enacted subsequent to the 1979 establishment of the GTB program which the court concluded had impermissibly undermined the capacity of that program to diminish continued disparities in educational expenditures. The court pointed to a variety of statutory enactments that served to perpetuate undesirable disparities. State funding has been phased in at a lower level and a slower rate than originally contemplated, so that for 1984–1985, funding has been provided at a 95 percent rather than a 100 percent level, and full funding postponed to a seventh year. Towns have been permitted to delay in moving to full MER contributions. The legislature has also amended the program to substitute three year old data for two year old data in the calculation of the relevant grants. The court determined that, although access to educational opportunities had been improved by the additional state and local educational funds generated by the GTB program, the post-1979 amendments resulted in continued financial disparities which, in the absence of a compelling state interest, unconstitutionally interfered with the plaintiffs' fundamental constitutional rights.

Relying on statistical evidence of continued significant disparities in local educational expenditures, the court declared that the gap between the educational resources of the property-rich towns and the property-poor towns must be narrowed by elimination of: (1) minimum aid grants, * * * (2) deferral of full GTB financing, * * * (3) alternate MER requirements, * * * and (4) three year old data in the calculation of GTB grants. * * * Accordingly, the court ordered, by way of remedy, that various designated governmental officials disburse or collect funds in order to implement the court's conclusions of unconstitutionality.

We agree with the trial court that the plaintiffs established a factual foundation for the court's conclusion that continued disparities in educational financing required strict scrutiny of the state statutes that have an impact on educational equity. We disagree, however, with the substantive standard by which the trial court tested the validity of the statutes and with the procedural failure of the trial court to afford all the interested parties an opportunity to be heard on the remedial implications of the court's decisions on unconstitutionality.

* * *

* * * As we have already indicated in this opinion, we believe that the proper test requires the state to prove that the amendments reasonably advanced a rational state policy and that they did not result in an unconstitutionally large disparity. For this reason, we must remand this case, as to the amendments only, for further proceedings in the trial court in accordance with the substantive standard which we have now articulated.

It is also clear that the trial court's judgment is procedurally flawed. Just as our decision in *Horton I* set the substantive parameters for assessment of the constitutionality of the present plan for state financing of public secondary school education, so our decision in *Horton v. Meskill*, 187 Conn. 187, 445 A.2d 579 (1982) *(Horton II)* set the procedural stage. There we discussed the role of the various municipalities who have an obvious interest in the outcome of this litigation. We noted first that "the rights at stake are the *students'* constitutional rights to equal protection and free public education. . . . The state's duty to provide education is owed to the students, not the municipalities." We referred also to our established case law that generally forbids municipalities, because they are creations of the state, from challenging the constitutionality of the state's laws. * * *

* * * Remand is therefore required to determine whether the challenged statutes are unconstitutional and to frame whatever orders for equitable relief may be appropriate.

There is error on the appeals; the judgments of the trial court are set aside and the cases are remanded for further proceedings in accordance with this opinion; there is no error on the cross appeals.

* * *

Notes and Questions

Horton demonstrates that relief regarding wealth disparity may be obtained in a state court although there was an opposite ruling in a similar situation by the United States Supreme Court in *Rodriguez*. This decision reveals that a state supreme court may grant greater protections to its citizenry under a state equal protection constitutional provision than is available under the federal Fourteenth Amendment provision. It also discloses that a state supreme court may establish education as a "fundamental" right. As we have seen, such a determination places the burden of proof on the defendant.

Does the **Horton** court provide a satisfactory test to determine what type of state finance plan would be an acceptable "constitutional system for financing public schools"?

Listing of Cases

Arizona

Shofstall v. *Hollins,* 110 Ariz. 88, 515 P.2d 590 (1973).

Arkansas

Dupree v. *Alma School District No. 30,* 279 Ark. 340, 651 S.W.2d 90 (1983).

California

Serrano v. *Priest,* 5 Cal. 3d 584, 487 P.2d 1241 (1971) *(Serrano I);* 18 Cal. 3d 728, 557 P.2d 929, 135 Cal. Rptr. 345 (1976), *cert. denied,* 432 U.S. 907 (1977) *(Serrano II);* 226 Cal. Rptr. 584 (1986) *(Serrano III).*

Colorado

Lujan v. *Colorado State Board of Education,* 649 P.2d 1005 (Colo. 1982).

Connecticut

Horton v. *Meskill,* 172 Conn. 615, 376 A.2d 359 (1977) *(Horton I);* 187 Conn. 187, 445 A.2d 579 (1982) *(Horton II);* 195 Conn. 24, 486 A.2d 1099 (1985) *(Horton III).*

Florida

School Board of Palm Beach County v. *State Board of Education of Florida,* No. 82–1435 (Leon County Cir. Ct. Nov. 30, 1982). (Suit dismissed in which equalizing factor in school finance formula was challenged by property-wealthy districts.)

Christensen v. *Graham,* No. 86–1390 (Leon County Cir. Ct., partial summary judgment rendered May 12, 1988), *appeal argued,* No. 88–69 (1st Dist. Ct. App. 1988).

Georgia

McDaniel v. *Thomas,* 248 Ga. 632, 285 S.E.2d 156 (1981).

Idaho

Thomas v. *Engelking,* 96 Idaho 793, 537 P.2d 635 (1975).

Illinois

McInnis v. *Shapiro*, 293 F. Supp. 327 (1968), *aff'd sub nom. McInnis* v. *Ogilvie*, 394 U.S. 322 (1969).

Blase v. *Illinois*, 55 Ill. 2d 94, 302 N.E.2d 46 (1973).

Kansas

Knowles v. *Kansas*, No. 77 CV 251 (Shawnee County Dist. Ct. 1981). (Suit dismissed in which equalizing factor in school finance formula was challenged by property-wealthy districts.)

Kentucky

Rose v. *Council for Better Education*, __Ky., __(1989).

Louisiana

Scarnato v. *Parker*, 415 F. Supp. 272 (1976), *aff'd*, 430 U.S. 961 (1977).

Livingston School Board v. *Louisiana State Board of Education*, 830 F.2d 563 (5th Cir. 1987), *cert. denied*, 487 U.S. __(1988).

Maine

Boothbay v. *Longley*, No. KEN-77-36 (Sup. Jud. Ct., dismissed without prejudice Feb. 9, 1978).

Maryland

Hornbeck v. *Somerset County Board of Education*, 295 Md. 597, 458 A.2d 758 (1983).

Massachusetts

Webby v. *Dukakis*, No. 78-179 Civil (Sup. Jud. Ct., statement of agreed facts filed July 10, 1985).

Michigan

Milliken v. *Green*, 389 Mich. 1, 203 N.W.2d 457 (1972) *(Governor I); vacated*, 390 Mich. 389, 212 N.W.2d 711 (1973) *(Governor II)*.

East Jackson Public Schools v. *Michigan*, 133 Mich. App. 132, 348 N.W.2d 303 (1984).

Minnesota

Van Dusartz v. *Hatfield*, 334 F. Supp. 870 (1971).

Montana

State ex rel. Woodahl v. *Straub*, 164 Mont. 141, 520 P.2d 776 (1974).

Helena Elementary School District No. 1 v. *Montana*, No. 85-370 (Lewis and Clark County Dist. Ct. Jan. 13, 1988).

New Hampshire

Jesseman v. *New Hampshire*, No. 82-E-038 (Merrimack County Super. Ct., plaintiffs' motion for voluntary nonsuit granted Sept. 4, 1985).

New Jersey

Robinson v. *Cahill*, 62 N.J. 473, 303 A.2d 273 (1973) *(Robinson I);* 63 N.J. 196, 306 A.2d 65 (1973), *cert. denied sub nom. Dickey* v. *Robinson*, 414 U.S. 976 (1973) *(Robinson II);* 67 N.J. 35, 335 A.2d 6 (1975) *(mem.)*, 67 N.J. 333, 339

A.2d 193 (1975) *(Robinson III);* 69 N.J. 133, 351 A.2d 713 (1975) *(Robinson IV);* 69 N.J. 449, 355 A.2d 129 (1976) *(Robinson V).*

Abbot v. *Burke,* 100 N.J. 269, 495 A.2d 376 (1985), *administrative law opinion rendered,* EDU 5581-85 (Aug. 24, 1988), Slip opinion decided by the Commissioner of Education (Feb. 22, 1989).

New York

Board of Education, Levittown Union Free School District v. *Nyquist,* 94 Misc. 2d 466, 408 N.Y.S.2d 606 (1978), *aff'd,* 83 A.D.2d 217, 443 N.Y.S.2d 843 (1981), *rev'd,* 57 N.Y.2d 27, 439 N.E.2d 359, 453 N.Y.S.2d 643 (1982), *appeal dismissed,* 459 U.S. 1139 (1983).

Ohio

Board of Education of City School District of Cincinnati v. *Walter,* 58 Ohio St. 2d 368, 390 N.E.2d 813 (1979), *cert. denied,* 444 U.S. 1015 (1980).

Oklahoma

Fair School Finance Council of Oklahoma v. *Oklahoma,* 746 P.2d 1135 (Okla. 1987).

Oregon

Olsen v. *Oregon,* 276 Or. 9, 554 P.2d 139 (1976).

Pennsylvania

Danson v. *Casey,* 484 Pa. 415, 399 A.2d 360 (1979).

Bensalem School District v. *Pennsylvania,* 105 Pa. Commw. 388, 524 A.2d 1027 (1987).

South Dakota

Oster v. *Kneip,* No. 77-555 (Hughes County Cir. Ct., filed 1977).

Texas

San Antonio Independent School District v. *Rodriguez,* 411 U.S. 1 (1973), *rev'g,* 337 F. Supp. 280 (1971).

Edgewood Independent School District v. *Kirby,* No. 362516 (Travis County Dist. Ct. June 1, 1987).

Virginia

Burruss v. *Wilkerson,* 310 F. Supp. 572 (1969), *aff'd,* 397 U.S. 44 (1970).

Washington

Northshore School District No. 417 v. *Kinnear,* 84 Wash. 2d 685, 530 P.2d 178 (1974).

Seattle School District No. 1 of King County v. *Washington,* 90 Wash. 2d 476, 585 P.2d 71 (1978).

West Virginia

Pauley v. *Kelly*, 162 W. Va. 672, 255 S.E.2d 859 (1979).

Pauley v. *Bailey*, 324 S.E.2d 128 (W. Va. 1984).

Wisconsin

Buse v. *Smith*, 74 Wis. 2d 550, 247 N.W.2d 141 (1976).

Kukor v. *Grover*, No. 79 CV 5252 (Dane County Cir. Ct. June 21, 1986), *cert. granted*, No. 86–1544 (Wis., oral arguments heard Mar. 29, 1988).

Wyoming

Washakie County School District No. 1 v. *Herschler*, 606 P.2d 310 (1980), *reh'g denied*, 606 P.2d 340 (1980), *cert. denied sub nom. Hot Springs County School District No. 1* v. *Washakie County School District No. 1*, 449 U.S. 824 (1980).

educator
and
school district
liability

Introduction

Educators are often concerned about the extent, if any, of their liability for damages as a result of their official action or inaction. The many types of concerns educators have in this area include possible liability on the part of the school district, individual board members, administrative personnel, and teachers for the injury or death of a child at school or while under school supervision; liability, if any, of a teacher or administrator for injuring a child while administering corporal punishment; school district, administrator, or teacher liability, if any, for depriving someone of his or her constitutional rights; and liability for malpractice.

The area of law that addresses these concerns is known as tort law. A tort is a civil wrong where one suffers loss as a result of the improper conduct of another. This branch of law is concerned with the compensation of losses suffered by an individual owing to an intentional or negligent act. Some torts may also be criminal, and if so, the person or persons charged may be prosecuted and punished by the state. Tort law is a specialized branch of law which laymen often perceive as being exceedingly complicated. Generalizing about tort law is difficult, if not bordering on the impossible, due to individual states' applicable case law and constitutional and statutory provisions. Consequently, the purpose of this chapter is to provide educators with a brief discussion of broad principles and major issues of general concern.

I. School District Immunity

A. Liability under State Law

In approximately half of the states school districts have governmental or sovereign immunity from liability for torts committed by the school district, school board members, or employees. Governmental immunity is grounded in the theory that the state and its agencies are sovereign and cannot be sued without consent. Such a view has its basis in the historic notion that "the king can do no wrong." Additionally, the doctrine seeks to protect the limited resources of government agencies. School districts in particular often have limited funds for other than educational purposes and frequently, therefore, are unable to pay high judgments rendered against them. Employment of the defense of sovereign immunity indicates that unless state courts or the legislature have modified or abrogated the doctrine, school districts cannot be sued for tort actions in a court of law. Many legal scholars, however, have been critical of the doctrine of sovereign immunity since it often leaves an injured party without any means to be compensated for losses. Consequently, governmental immunity has been substantially abrogated or modified in approximately thirty states, resulting in considerable variation regarding liability in those states.

Application of the doctrine of immunity differs from state to state: in most states where sovereign immunity has been preserved statutory law has been modified to allow limited liability, particularly for school-bus accidents. Although the majority of these states allow school districts to purchase liability insurance without waiving their immunity, some states have asserted that the purchase of insurance will constitute a waiver of immunity within the limits of insurance protection.

Individual liability also varies among the states. Generally, school board members or other officials may be held personally liable for the improper performance of so-called ministerial duties; they may not be liable, however, for the performance of discretionary responsibilities. Ministerial functions are defined as those having to do with the execution of policy as opposed to the formulation of policy represented by discretionary actions. If a school official is required to decide or act without established or readily ascertainable standards for guidance, that act is a discretionary function. Protection of discretionary activity follows from a desire to encourage governmental decision making; ministerial decisions, involving a lesser degree of discretion and judgment, require less protection or immunity. In school-related decisions courts have recognized a vital public interest in securing the free and independent judgment of school officials.

Historically, the immunity of school districts did not protect individual school employees from liability in tort. Many states, however, have reconsidered this notion, arguing that the individual school employees are least able to defend themselves in court. In Georgia, for instance, immunity has been extended to school principals and to classroom teachers. See *Hennessy* v. *Webb*, 245 Ga. 329, 264 S.E.2d 878 (1980), and *Truelove* v. *Wilson*, 159 Ga. App. 906, 285 S.E.2d 556 (1981).

B. Liability under Federal Law

A section of the Civil Rights Act of 1871 provides for liability if a "person" operating under the color of the state violates another person's civil rights. Specifically, the law states:

> Every person who, under color of any statute, ordinance, regulation, custom, or usage, of any State or Territory or the District of Columbia, subjects, or causes to be subjected, any citizen of the United States or other person within the jurisdiction thereof to the deprivation of any rights, privileges, or immunities secured by the Constitution and laws, shall be liable to the party injured in an action at law, suit in equity, or other proper proceeding for redress . . . 42 U.S.C. § 1983.

Although this law had not received much judicial attention for nearly a hundred years, several recent Supreme Court decisions have addressed school district and school officials' liability and the extent, if any, of damages under it. *Wood* **v.** *Strickland* addresses the issue of school board member immunity from liability under § 1983, while *Carey* **v.** *Piphus* clarifies the elements and prerequisites for recovery of damages under this act.

Wood v. Strickland

Supreme Court of the United States, 1975
420 U.S. 308

MR. JUSTICE WHITE delivered the opinion of the Court.

Respondents Peggy Strickland and Virginia Crain brought this lawsuit against petitioners, who were members of the school board at the time in question, two school administrators, and the Special School District of Mena, Ark., purporting to assert a cause of action under 42 U.S.C. § 1983, and claiming that their federal constitutional rights to due process were infringed under color of state law by their expulsion from the Mena Public High School on the grounds of their violation of a school regulation prohibiting the use or possession of intoxicating beverages at school or school activities. The complaint as amended prayed for compensatory and punitive damages against all petitioners, injunctive relief allowing respondents to resume attendance, preventing petitioners from imposing any sanctions as a result of the expulsion, and restraining enforcement of the challenged regulation, declaratory relief as to the constitutional invalidity of the regulation, and expunction of any record of their expulsion. * * *

The violation of the school regulation prohibiting the use or possession of intoxicating beverages at school or school activities with which respondents were charged concerned their "spiking" of the punch served at a meeting of an extra-curricular school organization attended by parents and students. At the time in question, respondents were 16 years old and were in the 10th grade. The relevant facts begin with their discovery that the punch had not been prepared for the meeting as previously planned. The girls then agreed to "spike" it. Since the county in which the school is located is "dry," respondents and a third girl drove across the state border into Oklahoma and purchased two 12-ounce bottles of "Right Time," a malt liquor. They then bought six 10-ounce bottles of a soft drink, and after having mixed the contents of the eight bottles in an empty milk carton, returned to school. Prior to the meeting, the girls experienced second thoughts about the wisdom of their prank, but by then they were caught up in the force of events and the intervention of other girls prevented them from disposing of the illicit punch. The punch was served at the meeting, without apparent effect.

Ten days later, the teacher in charge of the extracurricular group and meeting, Mrs. Curtis Powell, having heard something about the "spiking," questioned the girls about it. Although first denying any knowledge, the girls admitted their involvement after the teacher said that she would handle the punishment herself. The next day, however, she told the girls that the incident was becoming increasingly the subject of talk in the school and that the principal, P. T. Waller, would probably hear about it. She told them that her job was in jeopardy but that she would not force them to admit to Waller what they had done. If they did not go to him then, however, she would not be able to help them if the incident became "distorted." The three girls then went to Waller and admitted their role in the affair. He suspended them from school for a maximum two-week period, subject to the decision of the school board. Waller also told them that the board would meet that night, that the girls could tell their parents about the meeting, but that the parents should not contact any members of the board.

Neither the girls nor their parents attended the school board meeting that night. Both Mrs. Powell and Waller, after making their reports concerning the incident, recommended leniency. At this point, a telephone call was received by S. L. Inlow, then the superintendent of schools, from Mrs. Powell's husband, also a teacher at the high school, who reported that he had heard that the third girl involved had been in a fight that evening at a basketball game. Inlow informed the meeting of the news, although he did not mention the name of the girl involved. Mrs. Powell and Waller then withdrew their recommendations of leniency, and the board voted to expel the girls from school for the remainder of the semester, a period of approximately three months.

The board subsequently agreed to hold another meeting on the matter, and one was held approximately two weeks after the first meeting. The girls, their parents, and their counsel attended this session. The board began with a reading of a written statement of facts as it had found them. The girls admitted mixing the malt liquor into the punch with the intent of "spiking" it, but asked the board to forgo its rule punishing such violations by such substantial suspensions. Neither Mrs. Powell nor Waller was present at this meeting. The board voted not to change its policy and, as before, to expel the girls for the remainder of the semester.

* * *

Petitioners as members of the school board assert here, as they did below, an absolute immunity from liability under § 1983 and at the very least seek to reinstate the judgment of the District Court. If they are correct and the District Court's dismissal should be sustained, we need go no further in this case. Moreover, the immunity question involves the construction of a federal statute, and our practice is to deal with possibly dispositive statutory issues before reaching questions turning on the construction of the Constitution. * * * We essentially sustain the position of the Court of Appeals with respect to the immunity issue.

The nature of the immunity from awards of damages under § 1983 available to school administrators and school board members is not a question which the lower federal courts have answered with a single voice. There is general agreement on the existence of a "good faith" immunity, but the courts have either emphasized different factors as elements of good faith or have not given specific content to the good-faith standard.

* * *

Common-law tradition, recognized in our prior decisions, and strong public-policy reasons also lead to a construction of § 1983 extending a qualified good-faith immunity to school board members from liability for damages under that section. Although there have been different emphases and formulations of the common-law immunity of public school officials in cases of student expulsion or suspension, state courts have generally recognized that such officers should be protected from tort liability under state law for all good-faith, nonmalicious action taken to fulfill their official duties.

* * *

Liability for damages for every action which is found subsequently to have been violative of a student's constitutional rights and to have caused compensable injury would unfairly impose upon the school decisionmaker the burden of mistakes made in good faith in the course of exercising his discretion within the scope of his official duties. School board members, among other duties, must judge whether there have been violations of school regulations and, if so, the appropriate sanctions for the violations. Denying any measure of immunity in these circumstances "would contribute not to principled and fearless decisionmaking but to intimidation." * * * The imposition of monetary costs for mistakes which were not unreasonable in the light of all the circumstances would undoubtedly deter even the most conscientious school decisionmaker from exercising his judgment independently, forcefully, and in a manner best serving the long-term interest of the school and the students. The most capable candidates for school board positions might be deterred from seeking office if heavy burdens upon their private resources from monetary liability were a likely prospect during their tenure.

These considerations have undoubtedly played a prime role in the development by state courts of a qualified immunity protecting school officials from liability for damages in lawsuits claiming improper suspensions or expulsions. But at the same time, the judgment implicit in this common-law development is that absolute immunity would not be justified since it would not sufficiently increase the ability of school officials to exercise their discretion in a forthright manner to warrant the absence of a remedy for students subjected to intentional or otherwise inexcusable deprivations.

* * *

The disagreement between the Court of Appeals and the District Court over the immunity standard in this case has been put in terms of an "objective" versus a "subjective" test of good faith. As we see it, the appropriate standard necessarily contains elements of both. The official himself must be acting sincerely and with a belief that he is doing right, but an act violating a student's constitutional rights can be no more justified by ignorance or disregard of settled, indisputable law on the part of one entrusted with supervision of students' daily lives than by the presence of actual malice. To be entitled to a special exemption from the categorical remedial language of § 1983 in a case in which his action violated a student's constitutional rights, a school board member, who has voluntarily undertaken the task of supervising the operation of the school and the activities of the students, must be held to a standard of conduct based not only on permissible intentions, but also on knowledge of the basic, unquestioned constitutional rights of his charges. Such a standard imposes neither an unfair burden upon a person assuming a responsible public office requiring a high degree of intelligence and judgment for the proper fulfillment of its duties, nor an unwarranted burden in light of the value which civil rights have in our legal system. Any lesser standard would deny much of the promise of § 1983. Therefore, in the specific context of school discipline, we hold that a school board member is not immune from liability for damages under § 1983 if he knew or reasonably should have known that the action he took within his sphere of official responsibility would violate the constitutional rights of the student affected, or if he took the action with the malicious intention to cause a deprivation of constitutional rights or other injury to the student. * * * A compensatory award will be appropriate only if the school board member has acted with such an impermissible motivation or with such disregard of the student's clearly established constitutional rights that his action cannot reasonably be characterized as being in good faith.

*   *   *

Given the fact that there *was* evidence supporting the charge against respondents, the contrary judgment of the Court of Appeals is improvident. It is not the role of the federal courts to set aside decisions of school administrators which the court may view as lacking a basis in wisdom or compassion. Public high school students do have substantive and procedural rights while at school. * * * But § 1983 does not extend the right to relitigate in federal court evidentiary questions arising in school disciplinary proceedings or the proper construction of school regulations. The system of public education that has evolved in this Nation relies necessarily upon the discretion and judgment of school administrators and school board members, and § 1983 was not intended to be a vehicle for federal-court corrections of errors in the exercise of that discretion which do not rise to the level of violations of specific constitutional guarantees. * * *

* * *

The judgment of the Court of Appeals is vacated and the case remanded for further proceedings consistent with this opinion.

So ordered.

MR. JUSTICE POWELL, with whom THE CHIEF JUSTICE, MR. JUSTICE BLACKMUN, and MR. JUSTICE REHNQUIST join, concurring in part and dissenting in part.

I join in Parts I, III, and IV of the Court's opinion, and agree that the judgment of the Court of Appeals should be vacated and the case remanded. I dissent from Part II which appears to impose a higher standard of care upon public school officials, sued under § 1983, than that heretofore required of any other official.

* * * It would impose personal liability on a school official who acted sincerely and in the utmost good faith, but who was found—after the fact—to have acted in "ignorance . . . of settled, indisputable law." * * * Or, as the Court also puts it, the school official must be held to a standard of conduct based not only on good faith "but also on knowledge of the basic, unquestioned constitutional rights of his charges." * * * Moreover, ignorance of the law is explicitly equated with "actual malice." * * * This harsh standard, requiring knowledge of what is characterized as "settled, indisputable law," leaves little substance to the doctrine of qualified immunity. The Court's decision appears to rest on an unwarranted assumption as to what lay school officials know or can know about the law and constitutional rights. These officials will now act at the peril of some judge or jury subsequently finding that a good-faith belief as to the applicable law was mistaken and hence actionable.

The Court states the standard of required knowledge in two cryptic phrases: "settled, indisputable law" and "unquestioned constitutional rights." Presumably these are intended to mean the same thing, although the meaning of neither phrase is likely to be self-evident to constitutional law scholars—much less the average school board member. One need only look to the decisions of this Court—to our reversals, our recognition of evolving concepts, and our five-to-four splits—to recognize the hazard of even informed prophecy as to what are "unquestioned constitutional rights." * * *

* * *

There are some 20,000 school boards, each with five or more members, and thousands of school superintendents and school principals. Most of the school board members are popularly elected, drawn from the citizenry at large, and possess no unique competency in divining the law. Few cities and counties provide any compensation for service on school boards, and often it is difficult to persuade qualified persons to assume the burdens of this important function in our society. Moreover, even if counsel's advice constitutes a defense, it may safely be assumed that few school boards and school officials have ready access to counsel or indeed have deemed it necessary to consult counsel on the countless decisions that necessarily must be made in the operation of our public schools.

In view of today's decision significantly enhancing the possibility of personal liability, one must wonder whether qualified persons will continue in the desired numbers to volunteer for service in public education.

Notes and Questions

Although **Wood** specifically addresses school board member liability, the decision has implications for other school employees. Would the reasoning of the Court also apply to such school officials as superintendents and building-level administrators?

The majority opinion in **Wood** declared that ignorance of constitutional law pertaining to school discipline is no excuse. Do you agree, as the dissenters suggest, that the **Wood** standard is a "harsh" one that will place a board member's actions "at the peril of some judge or jury subsequently finding that a good-faith belief as to the applicable law was mistaken . . ."?

Subsequent Supreme Court decisions not dealing specifically with education issues have continued to address the issue of governmental immunity under § 1983. *Monell* v. *Department of Social Services of City of New York*, 436 U.S. 658 (1978), ruled that school districts are considered "persons" subject to suit under § 1983. Additionally, the Court held that

a local government may not be sued under § 1983 for an injury inflicted solely by its employees or agents. Instead, it is when execution of a government's policy or custom, whether made by its lawmakers or by those whose edicts or acts may fairly be said to represent official policy, inflicts the injury that the government as an entity is responsible under § 1983. . . . . (P. 694)

Monell reversed an earlier Court decision, *Monroe* v. *Pape,* 365 U.S. 167 (1961), which had held governmental bodies absolutely immune from liability under § 1983. Another decision, *Owen* v. *City of Independence,* 445 U.S. 622 (1980), which addressed the discharge of a police chief, held that

> there is no tradition of immunity for municipal corporations, and neither history nor policy support a construction of § 1983 that would justify the qualified immunity. . . . [T]he municipality may not assert the good faith of its officers or agents as a defense to liability under § 1983. (P. 638)

In *Harlow* v. *Fitzgerald,* 457 U.S. 800 (1982), the Court expanded government officials' immunity by abolishing the so-called subjective test. Under the Court's ruling an official who violates a right which was not "clearly established" at the time of the official's act will be immune from civil damages, even if the official acted with malice or with the knowledge that the official might be violating the law.

Potential areas of liability were expanded by the Court when it ruled that violations of federal statutory law as well as violations of constitutional provisions could be addressed under § 1983. See *Maine* v. *Thiboutot,* 448 U.S. 1 (1980). Additionally, the Court has ruled that state administrative remedies do not have to be exhausted before § 1983 claims are addressed in federal courts. See *Patsy* v. *Board of Regents of Florida,* 457 U.S. 496 (1982).

Carey v. Piphus

Supreme Court of the United States, 1978
435 U.S. 247

MR. JUSTICE POWELL delivered the opinion of the Court.

In this case, brought under 42 U.S.C. § 1983, we consider the elements and prerequisites for recovery of damages by students who were suspended from public elementary and secondary schools without procedural due process. The Court of Appeals for the Seventh Circuit held that the students are entitled to recover substantial nonpunitive damages even if their suspensions were justified, and even if they do not prove that any other actual injury was caused by the denial of procedural due process. We disagree, and hold that in the absence of proof of actual injury, the students are entitled to recover only nominal damages.

Respondent Jarius Piphus was a freshman at Chicago Vocational High School during the 1973–74 school year. On January 23, 1974, during school hours, the school principal saw Piphus and another student standing outdoors on school property passing back and forth what the principal described as an irregularly shaped cigarette. The principal approached the students unnoticed and smelled what he believed was the strong odor of burning marihuana. He also saw Piphus try to pass a packet of cigarette papers to the other student. When the students became aware of the principal's presence, they threw the cigarette into a nearby hedge.

The principal took the students to the school's disciplinary office and directed the assistant principal to impose the "usual" 20-day suspension for violation of the school rule against the use of drugs. The students protested that they had not been smoking marihuana, but to no avail. Piphus was allowed to remain at school, although not in class, for the remainder of the school day while the assistant principal tried, without success, to reach his mother.

A suspension notice was sent to Piphus' mother, and a few days later two meetings were arranged among Piphus, his mother, his sister, school officials, and representatives from a legal aid clinic. The purpose of the meetings was not to determine whether Piphus had been smoking marihuana, but rather to explain the reasons for the suspension. Following an unfruitful exchange of views, Piphus and his mother, as guardian *ad litem*, filed suit against petitioners in Federal District Court under 42 U.S.C. § 1983 * * * , charging that Piphus had been suspended without due process of law in violation of the Fourteenth Amendment. The complaint sought declaratory and injunctive relief, together with actual and punitive damages in the amount of $3,000. Piphus was readmitted to school under a temporary restraining order after eight days of his suspension.

Respondent Silas Brisco was in the sixth grade at Clara Barton Elementary School in Chicago during the 1973–74 school year. On September 11, 1973, Brisco came to school wearing one small earring. The previous school year the school principal had issued a rule against the wearing of earrings by male students because he believed that this practice denoted membership in certain street gangs and increased the likelihood that gang members would terrorize other students. Brisco was reminded of this rule, but he refused to remove the earring asserting that it was a symbol of black pride, not of gang membership.

The assistant principal talked to Brisco's mother, advising her that her son would be suspended for 20 days if he did not remove the earring. Brisco's mother supported her son's position, and a 20-day suspension was imposed. Brisco and his mother, as guardian *ad litem*, filed suit in Federal District Court under 42 U.S.C. § 1983 * * * , charging that Brisco had been suspended without due process of law in violation of the Fourteenth Amendment. The complaint sought declaratory and injunctive relief, together with actual and punitive damages in the amount of $5,000. Brisco was readmitted to school during the pendency of proceedings for a preliminary injunction after 17 days of his suspension.

* * *

Title 42 U.S.C. § 1983, Rev. Stat. § 1979, derived from § 1 of the Civil Rights Act of 1871, 17 Stat. 13, provides:

"Every person who, under color of any statute, ordinance, regulation, custom, or usage, of any State or Territory, subjects, or causes to be subjected, any citizen of the United States or other person within the jurisdiction thereof to the deprivation of any rights, privileges, or immunities secured by the Constitution and laws, shall be liable to the party injured in an action at law, suit in equity, or other proper proceeding for redress."

The legislative history of § 1983 * * * demonstrates that it was intended to "[create] a species of tort liability" in favor of persons who are deprived of "rights, privileges, or immunities secured" to them by the Constitution. * * *

* * *

Insofar as petitioners contend that the basic purpose of a § 1983 damages award should be to compensate persons for injuries caused by the deprivation of constitutional rights, they have the better of the argument. Rights, constitutional and otherwise, do not exist in a vacuum. Their purpose is to protect persons from injuries to particular interests, and their contours are shaped by the interests they protect.

Our legal system's concept of damages reflects this view of legal rights. "The cardinal principal of damages in Anglo-American law is that of *compensation* for the injury caused to plaintiff by defendant's breach of duty." * * * The Court implicitly has recognized the applicability of this principle to actions under § 1983 by stating that damages are available under that section for actions "found . . . to have been violative of . . . constitutional rights *and to have caused compensable injury. . . .*" *Wood* v. *Strickland*, 420 U.S., at 319 (emphasis supplied). * * *

The Members of the Congress that enacted § 1983 did not address directly the question of damages, but the principle that damages are designed to compensate persons for injuries caused by the deprivation of rights hardly could have been foreign to the many lawyers in Congress in 1871. Two other sections of the Civil Rights Act of 1871 appear to incorporate this principle, and no reason suggests itself for reading § 1983 differently. To the extent that Congress intended that awards under § 1983 should deter the deprivation of constitutional rights, there is no evidence that it meant to establish a deterrent more formidable than that inherent in the award of compensatory damages. * * *

It is less difficult to conclude that damages awards under § 1983 should be governed by the principle of compensation than it is to apply this principle to concrete cases. But over the centuries the common law of torts has developed a set of rules to implement the principle that a person should be compensated fairly for injuries caused by the violation of his legal rights. These rules, defining the elements of damages and the prerequisites for their recovery, provide the appropriate starting point for the inquiry under § 1983 as well.

It is not clear, however, that common-law tort rules of damages will provide a complete solution to the damages issue in every § 1983 case. In some cases, the interests protected by a particular branch of the common law of torts may parallel closely the interests protected by a particular constitutional right. In such cases, it may be appropriate to apply the tort rules of damages directly to the § 1983 action. * * * In other cases, the interests protected by a particular constitutional right may not also be protected by an analogous branch of the common law of torts. * * * In those cases, the task will be the more difficult one of adapting common-law rules of damages to provide fair compensation for injuries caused by the deprivation of a constitutional right.

Although this task of adaptation will be one of some delicacy—as this case demonstrates—it must be undertaken. The purpose of § 1983 would be defeated if injuries caused by the deprivation of constitutional rights went uncompensated simply because the common law does not recognize an analogous cause of action. * * * In order to further the purpose of § 1983, the rules governing compensation for injuries caused by the deprivation of constitutional rights should be tailored to the interests protected by the particular right in question—just as the common-law rules of damages themselves were defined by the interests protected in the various branches of tort law. * * *

* * *

Even if respondents' suspensions were justified, and even if they did not suffer any other actual injury, the fact remains that they were deprived of their right to procedural due process. "It is enough to invoke the procedural safeguards of the Fourteenth Amendment that a significant property interest is at stake, whatever the ultimate outcome of a hearing. . . ." * * *

Common-law courts traditionally have vindicated deprivations of certain "absolute" rights that are not shown to have caused actual injury through the award of a nominal sum of money. By making the deprivation of such rights actionable for nominal damages without proof of actual injury, the law recognizes the importance to organized society that those rights be scrupulously observed; but at the same time, it remains true to the principle that substantial damages should be awarded only to compensate actual injury or, in the case of exemplary or punitive damages, to deter or punish malicious deprivations of rights.

Because the right to procedural due process is "absolute" in the sense that it does not depend upon the merits of a claimant's substantive assertions, and because of the importance to organized society that procedural due process be observed, * * * we believe that the denial of procedural due process should be actionable for nominal damages without proof of actual injury. We therefore hold that if, upon remand, the District Court determines that respondents' suspensions were justified, respondents nevertheless will be entitled to recover nominal damages not to exceed one dollar from petitioners.

The judgment of the Court of Appeals is reversed, and the case is remanded for further proceedings consistent with this opinion.

It is so ordered.

II. Educator Liability

A. Intentional Torts

The most common intentional torts with which educators become involved are assault and battery. Battery is the unpermitted and unprivileged contact with another's person, such as striking someone. Actual harm is not necessary in order to bring suit. However, ordinary contact allowed by social usage is not actionable. Assault is the placing of someone in apprehension of immediate harmful or offensive contact. Shaking a fist at someone or holding a weapon in a hostile manner are examples of an assault. Although courts have allowed wide latitude, a teacher may be charged with assault and battery as a result of disciplining a student. A teacher could be held liable if he or she administered punishment while angry or in a brutal, cruel, or excessive manner. Other factors taken into consideration to determine liability would be where on the body the child was struck, the child's age, the child's mental capacity, and the nature of the child's offense. A teacher may use only sufficient force for self-protection when in an altercation with a student or when attempting to restrain a student.

B. Negligence

An educator may be liable if an injury to a student, for instance, can be shown to have resulted from the educator's negligence. Liability for negligence may accrue if it can be shown that the alleged negligent party should have anticipated the possible harmful results of his or her actions or inactions. It differs from the intentional torts in the sense that there is no conscious desire to injure someone. A commonly employed test to determine negligence in a particular factual situation is whether a reasonable and prudent degree of care has been exercised. When this test is used, the question often asked is whether the person accused of negligence acted as a reasonable and prudent person would have acted in a similar situation under similar circumstances.

Several elements must be present to have a valid cause of action for negligence: (1) a legal duty to conform to a standard of conduct for the protection of others, (2) a failure to exercise an appropriate standard of care, (3) a causal connection often referred to as "proximate cause" between the conduct and the resultant injury, and (4) actual loss or damage as a result of the injury.

1. Duty of Care

There is a duty of care not to harm or injure another person with whom a common-law or statutory relationship exists. The common law, for instance, has established a teacher-student relationship that imposes a duty of care on the part of the teacher. The common-law liability may be reduced by statutory provision, as has been done in Illinois. There liability is imposed only for willful or wanton misconduct. A state's "Good Samaritan" law may be applicable to educators, and if so, may reduce liability.

2. Standard of Care

For the most part the standard of care a teacher must exercise to avoid liability is defined as that of the "reasonable and prudent" person. It is that degree of care a reasonable and prudent teacher, charged with like duties, would exercise under similar circumstances. This standard is not absolute, and many factors are taken into consideration when determining liability. The standard of care varies according to such factors as the age of the student, the child's mental capacity, and the environment and circumstances under which an injury took place. The amount of care due school children increases with the immaturity of the child; therefore, it is expected that greater care will be given while supervising extremely young children.

A higher degree of care should also be exercised in such potentially dangerous classroom situations as a "shop" class or a chemistry laboratory than in an English class or a library. Particular circumstances surrounding an injury must also be taken into consideration. If a teacher suffered a disability prior to a student's injury, for instance, the disability would have to be taken into consideration. A teacher is not necessarily liable for all injuries sustained by students, since it would be impossible for a teacher to foresee every possible situation where student injury could result. However, whenever a school-related injury occurs, the question of whether it could have been foreseen will be raised. Because many factors impinge on liability for alleged negligence, dissimilar court judgments are often rendered regarding seemingly similar factual situations.

3. Proximate Cause

A causal connection must exist between a teacher's conduct and the resultant injury for an action in negligence to prevail. The teacher's negligence must be a substantial cause of the injury to a student. Liability may be mitigated, however, if it can be shown that the cause of injury was the result of an intervening act or if responsibility can be legitimately shifted. Misconduct by a student, for instance, could be advanced as an intervening act. Alleging failure to maintain a safe playground could be an example of a legitimate shift of responsibility from a teacher to those responsible for properly maintaining the playground.

4. Actual Loss or Injury

Proof of damage is an essential element in a negligence action. Damages to assuage one's feelings generally cannot be recovered in a negligence action where there has been no actual loss. Damages may be apportioned if more than one person has been adjudged to have been negligent.

C. Defenses for Negligence

In seeking to avoid liability for an allegedly negligent act, a teacher may attempt to demonstrate that the elements necessary to establish negligence discussed above were not present. However, other defenses may be applicable. The more common defenses include contributory negligence and assumption of risk.

Contributory negligence may be available as a defense if it can be demonstrated that the injured party failed to exercise the required degree of care necessary to ensure safety. This defense is not always available to teachers since courts generally consider children unable to act with the same standard of care as adults. Because of their youth students are often careless and do not act in a responsible manner; therefore, it may be difficult to convince a court that they were contributorially negligent.

Assumption of risk may be available as a defense when the injured party knew of the possible danger and either by agreement or actions voluntarily accepted the possibility of harm. Participants in athletic contests or spectators assume the normal risks associated with these activities by voluntarily placing themselves in a potentially harmful environment.

III. Duties of Supervision

Variations in the required common-law, statutory, or constitutional standard of duty and care among the states make it difficult to generalize about the extent of educators' tort liability in certain situations. Further compounding the difficulty in generalizing about tort liability is that seemingly similar factual situations giving rise to an alleged tort may contain sufficient nuance to produce different court holdings. The following brief descriptions of court decisions are offered as illustrations. Caution should be exercised in generalizing from them since only a partial description of the factual situation is provided, and since the duty and standard of care varies among the jurisdictions.

A. Before and after School

In the absence of statutory requirements, courts generally do not find a duty on the part of schools to supervise students on their way to and from school except when they are on school buses. There is no duty, for instance, in the absence of legislation, to provide a school safety patrol. In a case where a seven-year-old child was killed while crossing a road in front of his school, a Louisiana appellate court, *Johnson* v. *Ouachita Parish Police Jury*, 377 So. 2d 397 (La. Ct. App. 1979), held that the public school did not have a legal duty to provide safety patrols or adult school-crossing guards.

A duty of care on the part of the school may not be established if parents do not follow school rules which have been communicated to them. This issue was raised by a case in which a first-grade student, having missed his bus, rode his bicycle to school and was injured while riding home that afternoon. School rules stated that riding a bicycle was a privilege given to students in grades four through six and that students who did not plan to ride the bus on a particular day should bring notification from home to the school. Although the case was remanded on the question of the school district's duty of care, the Colorado Supreme Court held that, as a matter of law, the school did not have a duty to prevent the student from riding his bicycle home. See *Jefferson County School District R-1* v. *Justus*, 725 P.2d 767 (Colo. 1986).

Adequate supervision must be afforded students for a reasonable time as they congregate and wait for school to begin in the morning. In a New Jersey decision, *Titus* v. *Lindberg,* 49 N.J. 66, 228 A.2d 65 (1967), a principal was held liable for an injury to a student that occurred before school. In this instance the injury resulted from a paper clip that was propelled by a student waiting for transportation to another school. It was customary for students to arrive at school about 8:00 A.M., although classrooms did not officially open until 8:15 A.M. This incident occurred at approximately 8:05 A.M. The court offered several reasons for its holding that the principal's negligent supervision was a proximate cause of the injury: his failure to announce rules concerning playground supervision before school, to assign teachers to supervision, and personally to provide adequate supervision.

In another Louisiana decision, *Richard* v. *St. Landry Parish School Board,* 344 So. 2d 1116 (La. Ct. App. 1977), a teacher was not held liable for an injury to a third grade student that occurred while unsupervised students were cleaning the classroom after school. While engaged at this task, one of the students went through the teacher's desk and found a knife, which subsequently was used to inflict injury. In its opinion, the court emphasized that the students had been forbidden to go near the desk and, furthermore, the teacher had not placed the knife in the student's hand.

In a California decision, *Bartell* v. *Palos Verdes Peninsula School District,* 83 Cal. App.3d 492, 147 Cal. Rptr. 898 (1978), the school district was not held liable for an injury occuring after school hours. In this instance a twelve-year-old boy was fatally injured while playing a skateboard version of crack-the-whip after school hours. The court maintained that school districts and their employees are placed under a general duty to supervise the conduct of children on school grounds during school sessions, school activities, recesses, and lunch periods. Furthermore, the court stated:

> To require virtual round-the-clock supervision or prison-tight security for school premises, as plaintiffs suggest, would impose a financial burden which manifestly would impinge on the very educational purpose for which the school exists. While it is common knowledge that children often heedlessly engage in games or activities which are dangerous or harmful to their health, at some point the obligation of the public entity to answer for the malfeasance or misfeasance of others, whether children or parents, reaches its outer limits. Public entities labor under budgetary constraints which peculiarly affect their obligation of care. * * * (P. 500)

B. During School Hours

Generally, the standard of care owed to pupils by a teacher during school hours is that care which a reasonable and prudent teacher would observe in comparable circumstances.

A court in Louisiana ruled that a school board was not liable for injuries to a student by a rock thrown on school property. The court held that adequate supervision had been provided for the students and that reasonable supervision did not require constant supervision of every child on the playground. See *Hampton* v. *Orleans Parish School Board*, 422 So. 2d 202 (La. Ct. App. 1982).

Although a state statute may require a teacher to "keep good order" in the classroom, this implies the use of reasonable force and does not authorize the teacher's use of excessive force. Additionally, state statutes may provide that a teacher or principal shall not be liable in a civil lawsuit for the use of reasonable force on a pupil for the purpose of maintaining discipline at school, except in cases of gross disregard for the health and safety of the pupil. A Michigan court, in *Willoughby* v. *Lehrbass*, 150 Mich. App. 319, 388 N.W.2d 688 (1986), concluded that a teacher had used reasonable force when in an attempt to take the student to the principal's office, he grabbed the student in a "full nelson"—with his arms underneath the student's armpits and his palms on the back of the student's neck—and pulled the student into the hall and up a stairway.

Schools must provide proper supervision during times when students are out of class, such as recess, passing through the halls, or lunch hour. The California Supreme Court, in *Dailey* v. *Los Angeles Unified School District*, 2 Cal.3d 741, 470 P.2d 360 (1970), contended that school authorities were negligent in the supervision provided at a noon recess. In this case two high school students engaged in "slap fighting," a form of boxing employing open hands, which resulted in the death of one of the students. The court maintained that since adolescent high school students are not adults, they should not be expected to exhibit the degree of discretion and judgment associated with mature adults. Therefore, the court contended it was negligent not to have a comprehensive schedule of supervising assignments and proper instructions for subordinates as to what was expected of them while they were supervising.

A physical education teacher was found to have a duty of properly instructing students before a vertical jumping exercise was attempted. After she failed to provide sufficient instruction, a child suffered injury when she ran into a wall while performing the exercise. Although the court felt that the facts of the case should be ascertained in a jury trial, it was noted that proper instruction could have prevented the injury. See *Dibortolo* v. *Metropolitan School District of Washington Township*, 440 N.E.2d 506 (Ind. App. 1982).

Schools may be liable for injury to a student who leaves school without school or parental permission. In one such case, *Hoyem* v. *Manhattan Beach City School District*, 22 Cal.3d 508, 585 P.2d 851 (1978), the

California Supreme Court held that the school district could be held liable for injuries suffered by a ten-year-old truant student who was hit by a motorcycle. The court contended that the school district would not be liable for injury sustained by a truant under all circumstances; however, the school district would be legally responsible if the district's supervisory procedures to thwart truancy fell below that degree of care which reasonably prudent persons would exercise.

A Florida appellate court upheld a jury verdict in favor of a high school student who was attacked and beaten by three other students while he waited in the school cafeteria for transportation to his home. The court ruled that the school had a duty to provide some form of security to prevent such incidents from occurring. The student misbehavior in this case could reasonably have been foreseen, especially since the school was entrusted with the care of students and had a legal duty to supervise them. See *Broward County School Board* v. *Ruiz*, 493 So. 2d 474 (Fla. App. 1986).

C. Off-Campus Activities

Required participation in off-campus activities, such as a field trip or excursion, or interscholastic activities, such as athletics or debate, places the school in the same position of duty to use care to prevent injury as if students were on campus.

In Florida, for instance, a teacher and principal were found to be negligent in failing to supervise school club activities. When a student was injured during a hazing incident, the court ruled that the school had violated a duty of supervision that had been established by school board policy when the club advisor was appointed. The court felt that the incident would not have occurred if the advisor had been present. See *Rupp* v. *Bryant*, 417 So. 2d 658 (Fla. 1982).

A school district was found negligent in failing to provide adequate supervision at a required attendance by students of a downtown showing of a controversial movie entitled *King*. Students were bused to the theater accompanied by chaperones. Obscene racial comments were made by both white and black students during the showing. Upon leaving the balcony for the lobby, a student was pushed, her wrist slashed, and her purse taken. The Minnesota Supreme Court in *Raleigh* v. *Independent School District No. 625*, 275 N.W.2d 572 (Minn. 1979), upheld the awarding of damages against the school for failure to provide sufficient precautions in the light of having knowledge about racial tensions.

IV. Parental Consent

Written parental consent for participation in extracurricular activities, such as athletic competition or travel related to a school activity, is often required by school district policy. The importance of having parental consent for travel to an off-campus activity is obvious. One can only imagine the difficulty, and increased legal complications, in having to inform parents of an off-campus injury to their child when those parents had no knowledge of an away-from-school activity or had not given consent for their child to participate. Parental consent forms may contain language purporting to release the school from liability in the event of an injury. It is questionable whether such a signed form would offer those supervising the school activity any immunity from suit in the event of negligence. Parental consent not only would be a surrendering of the independent claim of the child but would also be considered by many courts to be counter to public policy because it was the intentional waiving of a suit to recover damages for subsequent negligent supervision.

V. Malpractice

Suits alleging "educational malpractice" have been brought in several states. Plaintiffs in these suits generally allege that the school district has been negligent because it has issued a certificate or diploma, yet the student does not have the basic academic skills necessary for such tasks as understanding and completing a job application. In one of the first suits of this kind, *Peter W. v. San Francisco Unified School District*, 60 Cal. App.3d 814, 131 Cal Rptr. 854 (1976), plaintiff's position was not upheld. The California court contended that failure of educational achievement is not an injury within the meaning of tort law. Additionally, the court stated:

> . . . Few of our institutions, if any, have aroused the controversies, or incurred the public dissatisfaction, which have attended the operation of the public schools during the last few decades. Rightly or wrongly, but widely, they are charged with outright failure in the achievement of their educational objectives; according to some critics, they bear responsibility for many of the social and moral problems of our society at large. Their public plight in these respects is attested in the daily media, in bitter governing board elections, in wholesale rejections of school bond proposals, and in survey upon survey. To hold them to an actionable "duty of care," in the discharge of their academic functions, would expose them to the tort claims—real or imagined—of disaffected students and parents in countless numbers. They are already beset by social and financial problems which have gone to major litigation, but for which no permanent solution has . yet appeared. . . . The ultimate consequences, in terms of public time and money, would burden them—and society—beyond calculation. (P. 825)

In another decision, *Donohue v. Copiague Union Free School District*, 47 N.Y.2d 440, 391 N.E.2d 1352 (1979), New York's Court of Appeals also disallowed a cause of action against a school district that sought monetary damages for educational malpractice. The plaintiff alleged that notwithstanding his receipt of a certificate of graduation, he lacked "the rudimentary ability to comprehend written English on a level sufficient to enable him to complete applications for employment." In its decision the court held that

> the Constitution places the obligation of *maintaining and supporting* a system of public schools upon the *Legislature.* To be sure, this general directive was never intended to impose a duty flowing directly from a local school district to individual pupils to ensure that each pupil receives a minimum level of education, the breach of which duty would entitle a pupil to compensatory damages. . . . (P. 443)

Recent educational-malpractice litigation has addressed claims for monetary damages resulting from misdiagnoses of learning abilities or of special educational needs. In 1982 the Maryland Supreme Court considered a claim based on a complaint that a school system had negligently evaluated a first-grade student and had consequently caused him to be taught first-grade materials for a second year while he was physically placed in second grade. Charges were also made that certain educators had furnished false information concerning the child's learning problems, had altered school records to cover their actions, and had demeaned the child. In reviewing earlier malpractice claims, the court concluded that an award of monetary damages represents an inappropriate remedy for errors in the educational process. It noted, however, that the parents could take later legal action against the educators who had demonstrated alleged outrageous conduct. See *Hunter* v. *Board of Education of Montgomery County,* 292 Md. 481, 439 A.2d 582 (1982).

A Michigan appellate court also considered monetary claims resulting from misdiagnosis of a language impairment. Although the child had been treated for a period of time based on the diagnosis, the court held the speech therapist and the school system to be immune from liability. Since the evaluation and treatment of speech problems were a part of the regular functions of a school system, the court ruled that school personnel should not be held liable in tort for honest mistakes. See *Brosnan* v. *Livonia Public Schools,* 123 Mich. App. 377, 333 N.W.2d 288 (1983). A Montana decision, however, supported the monetary claims of foster parents of a child who had been improperly placed in a program for the educable mentally retarded. Since the child had been placed in the program despite scores showing that the placement was inappropriate, the court ruled that this case was not like other educational-malpractice claims. This situation involved misplacement despite accurate knowledge of ability scores, not misdiagnosis of a handicap. See *B.M.* v. *Montana,* 649 P.2d 425 (Mont. 1982).

VI. Insurance

Although it is important for educators to be aware of their potential liability for failure to act in a reasonable and prudent manner in preventing injury, the fear of significant monetary loss has been lessened by the availability of liability insurance. Many educators have such coverage as a part of their membership in a professional organization. Individual liability-insurance policies are also available. Although a strong case for liability may be made against them, impecunious and uninsured educators are often unlikely candidates for suit.

Questions

What is the status of school district immunity in your state? What are the advantages and disadvantages of school district immunity?

What is the common law or statutory duty and standard of care in your state for tortious liability of individual school board members? administrators? teachers?

appendix a

analyzing
a court decision

Significant information may be extracted from court decisions by employing an orderly process such as a case analysis, sometimes referred to as "briefing" a case. General categories of information included in a case analysis are the title and citation of the case, the level or type of court hearing the case, the relevant facts involved in the case, the disputed issue or issues in the case, the holding or holdings of the court, the legal doctrine(s) or legal principle(s) underlying the decision, and the significance of the decision regarding future actions of individuals or institutions.

Title and Citation

The title of the decision contains the name of the litigants. A judicial citation contains the volume number and page number of the reporter system(s) in which the decision appears as well as the year in which the decision was issued. A complete citation includes reference to all reporter systems, official or unofficial, in which the decision appears. These are referred to as parallel citations. See appendix B for a fuller explanation of the citation process.

Level or Type of Court

Noting the level or type of court hearing the case is important because it indicates the federal or state jurisdiction immediately affected by the decision. For example, decisions by the United States Supreme Court or states' highest courts represent the final authority on issues within the courts' respective jurisdictions.

Facts

Facts include the actual circumstances, events, or occurrences involved in the case. Disputed facts must be resolved at the trial level. Appellate courts do not decide questions of fact. Their decision is based on the facts given. If these are insufficient, the case may be remanded to the lower court for further proceedings to determine additional facts.

Issue

An issue is a disputed point or question of law upon which a legal action is based. One or more issues may be present in a single case. Issues are of two types, procedural and substantive. Procedural issues involve specific disputed questions of law, and these issues are the basis for an appeal to a higher court. They may include whether a particular legal motion should have been granted or denied, whether certain information was admissible, or whether injunctive relief should have been granted. Substantive issues, on the other hand, involve broader questions of legal rights and principles, such as liberty and property interests. Substantive issues are generally of greater importance to the nonlawyer/student of school law.

Holding

The court's decision consists of a holding or holdings in regard to the question or questions before it and usually includes an opinion stating the reasons for the particular holding(s). Written opinions normally include an analysis of the arguments and supporting legal precedent presented by each side and the court's examination of the arguments, precedents, statutes, and facts applicable to the decision.

Concurring or dissenting opinions written by individual judges are frequently included in court decisions. In these opinions judges may discuss reasons for agreeing or disagreeing with the action of the court, elaborate on the issues considered by the court, or introduce additional principles or concepts not considered in the majority opinion. Concurring and dissenting opinions are often quite beneficial in analyzing the decision of the court.

In addition, decisions often include dicta, additional statements of opinion by the court or an individual judge concerning a question or point of law that arises during the hearing of a case. Since these comments may not be vital to the formulation of the holding, they are not binding as precedent. However, dicta may indicate the persuasion of a particular court or judge.

In some instances, if specific legal relief is required or if the appellate court wishes the trial court to reexamine the case in the light of the appellate court's legal reasoning, a case may be remanded to the trial court.

Legal Doctrine

Court decisions generally are based on a particular legal doctrine or principle. Analysis of a decision includes identifying the doctrine or principle and determining how it is affected by the decision. For example, a student should attempt to ascertain whether a decision may establish, distinguish, extend, affirm, modify, overturn, or reverse a legal doctrine.

Significance

A concise statement of the implications of the decision with regard to future actions by individuals and institutions completes the analysis. Naturally, certain decisions possess greater significance for educational practices than do others.

A court decision's significance is determined to a large degree by its generalizability to a particular judicial jurisdiction. For example, courts in different jurisdictions may disagree on particular issues when no precedent has been established by a higher court. Consequently, an authoritative decision in one jurisdiction may not be applicable to actions within other jurisdictions. In fact, courts in other jurisdictions may reach opposite decisions.

appendix b

an introduction to research in school law

There are several sources with which an educator may begin legal research. These may be divided into three broad categories—primary sources, secondary sources, and finding aids. Primary sources of law represent some form of binding or highly persuasive authority. State and federal statutes and constitutional provisions, along with court decisions interpreting them, are the most important primary sources of law. Secondary-source materials provide interpretive references regarding primary sources of law. Textbooks and casebooks, periodicals and law reviews, dissertations, legal encyclopedias, and legal dictionaries are examples of secondary materials. In addition, finding aids facilitate the location of primary sources of law related to a particular topic of interest. These include digests of the case law, citators, and various indexing materials.

Thorough legal research involves a systematic examination of an appropriate portion of the voluminous legal literature. This examination may be facilitated by the use of numerous research aids. While the aids are quite effective in locating relevant materials, a word of caution may be appropriate. A limitation to most legal research aids is the perspective of an aid's publisher. Many publications in the legal field are prepared primarily for use by attorneys and may not necessarily address the needs of the educational researcher.

Legal issues may be divided into substantive and procedural ones. Procedural issues address the various rules of form in legal proceedings, whereas substantive issues are concerned with legal rights and principles. Procedural questions are generally of greater interest to attorneys than to educators; therefore, the location of substantive legal information is emphasized in this discussion of legal research.

Elements of School Law Research

Primary Sources of Law

Statutes
Federal statutes are officially compiled according to topic in the *United States Code* (U.S.C.). Unofficial annotated editions of the federal statutes are available in the *United States Code Annotated* (U.S.C.A.) and *United States Code Service* (U.S.C.S.). Annotated versions include supplemental historical notes, editorial comments, and a digest of interpretive court decisions related to each provision. Statutes are popularly known by reference to their enactment rather than to their place in the *Code*. Congressional acts in their chronological order of passage are compiled in the *United States Statutes at Large (Stat.)* by public law number (P.L. 94–142, for instance, was the 142nd law passed during the 94th Congressional session). A citation to the *Statutes* does not reflect subsequent changes to the law; since the *Code* is continuously modified to reflect amendments and deletions, it should be cited when referring to current law. When applicable, rules and regulations designed to assist in the implementation of federal statutes are published in the *Federal Register* (Fed. Reg.), the *Code of Federal Regulations* (C.F.R.), and *A Compilation of Federal Education Laws*, which is prepared for the use of the House Committee on Education and Labor and the Senate Committee of Human Resources.

Official state codes and unofficial annotated versions generally group related statutes into chapters, which are indexed to facilitate search within the volumes. Laws related to the schools are often included in chapters entitled "Education" or "Schools and School Districts." Both official codes and related annotated publications are kept up to date by the use of paperback pocket supplements. Unofficial annotated codes often provide faster and more convenient supplementation as well as additional analytical and interpretive material. Local ordinances are not generally compiled in a standardized code; however, some counties and larger cities may publish local ordinances.

Constitutions

Provisions of federal and state constitutions may be located in several sources. The *United States Code* contains the official text of the Constitution of the United States. Annotated versions appear in the *United States Code Annotated* and *United States Code Service.* Similarly, state constitutions are generally set forth in official state codes. Annotated state constitutions are available for many states.

Court Decisions

Disputes between parties and the interpretation of statutory and constitutional provisions are resolved in court decisions. Lawsuits are initiated in trial courts, which examine the formal written statements of the parties and hear the parties' oral arguments as well as the testimony of witnesses. Trial court decisions may be appealed to higher courts. These appellate courts do not repeat the trial proceedings; rather, the courts review the written record of lower courts' decisions. They may affirm, reverse, vacate, or modify the judgment of the lower courts or order that a case be tried again.

Most trial-court decisions are not reported for general distribution. Therefore, copies of trial-court decisions usually must be obtained from the court issuing the decision. However, decisions of most appellate courts and certain trial courts are available in official and unofficial reporters. Reporters are published in a series of numbered bound volumes. Preliminary paperback booklets containing the most recent decisions available, referred to as advance sheets, are issued periodically as supplements to the bound volumes. These advance sheets are compiled to form the subsequent bound volumes of the reporters. Unofficial reporters are useful because of greater speed of publication through more extensive use of advance sheets. In addition, they include special research aids as well as other supplementary materials.

United States Supreme Court   Decisions of the United States Supreme Court are officially reported in the *United States Reports* (U.S.). Supreme Court decisions also appear in two privately published unofficial reporters called the *Supreme Court Reporter* (S. Ct.) and the *United States Supreme Court Reports, Lawyers' Edition* (L.Ed.). Although unofficial reporters include features unique to their particular series, text of the Court's decisions is identical in these reporters.

Each decision of the Supreme Court is reported by the Court in a separate pamphlet shortly after the decision is announced. These slip opinions are the first official text of the Court's decisions. Slip opinions are later paginated and compiled into advance sheets.

Supreme Court decisions also appear in two unofficial looseleaf publications. *United States Law Week* (U.S.L.W.) and the *Supreme Court Bulletin* (S. Ct. Bull.) report Supreme Court decisions immediately after they are issued by the Court. These publications provide the researcher timely access to reported decisions of the Supreme Court.

Lower Federal Courts   Decisions of the lower federal courts may be found in two publications. Decisions of the United States Courts of Appeals are published in the *Federal Reporter* (F.), now in its second series, *Federal Reporter, Second Series* (F.2d). Selected decisions of the United States District Courts are contained in the *Federal Supplement* (F.Supp.). *Federal Rules Decisions* (F.R.D.) includes various lower-federal-court decisions addressing procedural issues. In addition to these publications, a selection of annotated federal court decisions addressing particular areas of legal questions is offered in *American Law Reports—Federal* (A.L.R.).

State Courts   Decisions of state courts are published in two main sources. In many states official reporters are published by the courts. Where such reporters are available, they provide the authoritative texts of the reported decisions. Generally, only decisions of the state's highest court are officially reported; however, several states also report decisions of lower appellate courts. Slip opinions and advance sheets are not always incorporated within state courts' reporting systems.

The National Reporter System provides the most comprehensive system of unofficial reports of state court decisions. Within the National Reporter System, which also includes the *Supreme Court Reporter, Federal Reporter,* and *Federal Supplement,* the nation is divided into geographic regions for the purpose of reporting state court decisions. Reporters for each of the seven regions are published periodically containing state supreme court decisions and many state appellate court decisions within the region.* These regional reporters are supplemented by the *California Reporter* (Cal. Rptr.) and *New York Supplement* (N.Y.S.), including selected decisions of the lower courts in those two states. Some states have ceased

---

* The seven regions and their states are: *Atlantic* (A. or A.2d)—Conn., Del., Me., Md., N.H., N.J., Pa., R.I., Vt.; *Northeastern* (N.E. or N.E.2d)—Ill., Ind., Mass., N.Y., Ohio; *Southeastern*—(S.E. or S.E.2d)—Ga., N.C., S.C., Va., W. Va; *Southern* (So. or So.2d)—Ala., Fla., La., Miss.; *Southwestern* (S.W. or S.W.2d)—Ark., Ky., Mo., Tenn., Tex.; *Northwestern* (N.W. or N.W.2d)—Iowa, Mich., Minn., Neb., N.D., S.D., Wis.; *Pacific* (P. or P.2d)—Alaska, Ariz., Cal., Colo., Hawaii, Idaho, Kan., Mont., Nev., N.M., Okla., Or., Utah, Wash., Wyo.

official publication of court decisions and have adopted the appropriate regional reporter as the state's official reporter.

West's Education Law Reporter includes the full text of all reported cases dealing with education from the United States Supreme Court, the United States Courts of Appeals, the United States District Courts, and all state appellate courts. Additionally, the *Reporter* includes commentaries on court opinions and legislation that promise to have a significant impact on education, along with reports of empirical research on school law topics.

Selected significant state court decisions are also published in *American Law Reports* (A.L.R.). These unofficial reports include analytical annotations to each decision, which discuss the various points of law presented in the case.

Judicial Citation   In order to locate reported court decisions contained in the diverse official and unofficial reporters, a shorthand method of reference is provided by a system of judicial citation. A citation of a reported court decision reveals specific information regarding where the decision is reported. For example, a researcher investigating the subject of academic freedom may determine that the decision in *Fowler* v. *Board of Education of Lincoln County,* 819 F.2d 657 (1987), *cert. denied,* 484 U.S. 986 (1987), is applicable. In this instance the title of the case, *Fowler* v. *Board of Education of Lincoln County,* indicates that Fowler and the Board of Education of Lincoln County are the parties involved in the action. In case titles *versus* is abbreviated by a lowercase *v.* When legal action is initiated in the court of original jurisdiction, the plaintiff's name is listed first. However, upon appeal of the case, the names of the parties may switch positions or be altered should the parties to the action change. Following the case title is a reference to the volume number, the title of the reporter, and the page number at which the decision appears. *Fowler* v. *Board of Education of Lincoln County,* for instance, is reported in volume number 819 of the *Federal Reporter, Second Series,* (F.2d), beginning on page 657. This particular format is consistent throughout all case citations. The initial number designates the volume number of the reporter; then the title of the reporter and the series are indicated, followed by the page number on which the text of the decision begins. Within parentheses following the information regarding the reporter is the year in which the decision was issued and in some instances the court issuing the decision. In 1987 the United States Court of Appeals for the Sixth Circuit issued the decision in *Fowler* v. *Board of Education of Lincoln County.* Explanatory words or phrases often appear in citations in explanation of the prior or subsequent history of a decision. In this instance, the United States

Supreme Court denied certiorari (declined to review the case). This action by the Court in 1987 is reported on page 986 of volume 484 of the *United States Reports.*

As a second example, consider *Ponton* v. *Newport News School Board,* 632 F.Supp. 1056 (E.D.Va. 1986). Here the decision in the case of *Ponton* v. *Newport News School Board* is reported in volume 632 of the *Federal Supplement* at page 1056. A federal district court for the eastern district of Virginia rendered the decision in 1986.

When decisions appear in more than one reporter, parallel, also known as dual, citations are often used to indicate other sources in which the decision is reported. When parallel citations are used, the official reporter, or authoritative text of the decision, is cited first. For example, the citation to the well-known Bible reading and prayer decision of the United States Supreme Court may appear as *Abington School District* v. *Schempp,* 374 U.S. 203, 83 S. Ct. 1560, 10 L.Ed.2d 844 (1963). This parallel citation reveals that the decision is officially reported in volume 374 of the *United States Reports* at page 203, and also appears in volume 83 of the *Supreme Court Reporter* at page 1560, and in the second series of the *United States Supreme Court Reports, Lawyers' Edition,* at page 844 of volume 10. The decision was issued by the Court in 1963.

Consider a decision of the California Supreme Court, cited as *Hartzell* v. *Connell,* 35 Cal.3d 899, 679 P.2d 35, 201 Cal. Rptr. 601 (1984). In 1984, the California Supreme Court issued a decision in the case, which was officially reported by the court in volume 35 of the *California Reports, Third Series,* at page 899. Two unofficial reporters of the National Reporter System contain the decision as well: volume 679 of the *Pacific Reporter, Second Series* at page 35 and volume 201 of the *California Reporter* at page 601.

In addition to court decisions, many other sources of legal literature are subject to similar uniform rules of citation. However, a treatment of all of these areas is beyond the scope of this discussion. For a generally accepted reference to rules of citation for all forms of legal literature, the researcher is directed to *A Uniform System of Citation,* published by the Harvard Law Review Association.

Board of Education Policies and Regulations

At the state and local levels the educational system is subject to policies and procedures implemented by the appropriate boards of education. State board of education policies are generally arranged according to subject matter and available in a form providing convenient access and rapid updating. While local board policies are most likely available in printed form, access to them may be somewhat less convenient for the researcher.

Attorney General Opinions

States' legal counsels are frequently requested to issue advisory opinions concerning proposed legislative or administrative action or questions related to present constitutional and statutory provisions. While these opinions are only advisory, they are often helpful in the study of legal topics. Reports of attorneys general are published by many states.

Secondary Sources of Legal Literature

Textbooks and Casebooks

Available textbooks in the field of school law vary from general texts to brief monographs presenting discussion of a specific area of school law. While some textbooks offer in-depth analysis of legal issues, others contain no endeavors at such scholarly analysis, but provide convenient manuals to introduce the reader to particular issues in school law. Many textbooks contain tables of cases, bibliographies, or other reference materials that may serve as useful research aids. Casebooks contain edited versions of decisions with particular significance. These works often provide supplementary, explanatory, and interpretive material. Although textbooks and casebooks provide valuable information, they are somewhat limited in that they may become dated as the law changes and interpretive court decisions are rendered.

Periodical and Law Review Articles

Expositive articles of interest may be found in the legal and educational literature. Law reviews and bar journals are indexed in the *Index to Legal Periodicals. Shephard's Law Review Citations,* a compilation of citations to articles in over one hundred law reviews and legal periodicals, enables the researcher to determine where articles appearing in these publications in recent decades have been cited in subsequent articles and in federal or state court decisions. *The Journal of Law and Education* is a specialized journal containing articles related to school law issues. Educational periodical articles related to legal topics may be located by utilizing the *Education Index, Current Index to Journals in Education,* and *Educational Administration Abstracts.*

Dissertations

Unpublished doctoral research often provides comprehensive treatment of particular topics regarding education and the law. Pertinent dissertations may be identified by examining *Dissertation Abstracts International* and the *Comprehensive Dissertation Index, 1861–1972, 1973–1982,* and subsequent yearly editions.

Encyclopedias

Corpus Juris Secundum and *American Jurisprudence 2d,* the two major legal encyclopedias of national scope, include narrative discussion of a wide variety of legal topics. Each series of encyclopedias includes volumes providing a general index and topical indexes (such as Schools and School Districts) of the subject matter. In addition, several state encyclopedias are published following the same basic format as the national publications.

Since the copious extended footnotes contain numerous case references, these encyclopedias are often quite helpful in locating pertinent court decisions. However, the encyclopedias may not always be as helpful as they might first appear. Although periodic supplements are published, it is difficult for works of this nature to reflect accurately the rapidly changing law. Suffering from the same limitations as many other encyclopedic efforts, the works are often criticized for a lack of scholarly analysis and a tendency toward oversimplification and generalization regarding complex legal issues.

Legally significant words and phrases are listed alphabetically in an encyclopedic collection entitled *Words and Phrases.* Each word or phrase is followed by brief summaries of judicial decisions in which it has been interpreted or defined, as well as citations to the decisions. Annual supplements are issued to keep *Words and Phrases* up to date.

Other Secondary Materials

Additional aids may be helpful in employing the various research procedures. For example, *A Uniform Code of Citation,* commonly referred to as the Bluebook, provides a generally accepted standard for the rules of citation and style. This reference enables the researcher to report research effectively and may answer questions related to the shorthand system of legal citation. Legal terms and abbreviations may be clarified by the use of a reputable legal dictionary, such as *Black's Law Dictionary, Revised Fifth Edition.*

Finding Aids

Various methods may be employed to locate pertinent court decisions. Each of the various sources possesses particular strengths and limitations, but may be used effectively in reviewing the existing case law. It is not likely that a particular method of case finding will prove most effective in all situations. Consideration of the individual research problem, the tools available, and the researcher's personal preference will probably determine which sources are employed in the search for applicable case law.

Case Digests

The *American Digest System* provides an exhaustive compilation of case references, appearing under alphabetically arranged topic headings (such as Schools and School Districts). The system is divided into decennial digests, each addressing a ten-year period. The *Ninth Decennial Digest* deals with the years 1976–1986. Cases reported since 1986 are included in the *General Digest, Seventh Series*. The system's current component is kept up to date by the use of paperback supplements issued monthly.

In addition to the *American Digest System*, digests devoted to the geographic regions covered by most of the regional reporters and many of the individual states are available. There are also digests dealing solely with federal court decisions, as well as a digest covering decisions of the United States Supreme Court.

Looseleaf Services

Several looseleaf services are published that aid in locating pertinent court decisions. A bimonthly publication of the National Organization on Legal Problems of Education, the *NOLPE School Law Reporter,* contains brief summaries and citations to judicial decisions related to school law. Among the looseleaf services available, the *School Law Reporter* provides the most comprehensive source of school law cases. Decisions addressing school law issues are also cited and summarized in the *School Law Bulletin.* *United States Law Week* and the *Supreme Court Reporter* provide rapid access to recent United States Supreme Court decisions. Both of these publications also include information concerning Court proceedings, calendars, cases docketed, and general Court news. In addition, *United States Law Week* includes a section entitled *General Law,* summarizing significant weekly developments in all legal areas, including judicial, legislative, and administrative actions at both the state and federal levels.

Annotated Codes and Reporters

Annotated constitutions and statutory codes are useful sources for ascertaining applicable case law. Citations and summaries of interpretive court decisions are usually included in the analytical annotations to the particular provisions.

American Law Reports and *American Law Reports—Federal* report a small selection of significant cases, each annotated by an editorial discussion of the point of law dealt with in the case. Appropriate tables of cases, word indexes, and digests are published in conjunction with these, facilitating the location of decisions and annotations. Related cases are cited within the analytical annotations.

Secondary Materials

Secondary materials previously discussed may be helpful as sources of case citations. Textbooks, periodical and law review articles, dissertations, and encyclopedias often include numerous references to court decisions within their text and footnotes. In addition, summaries of recent school law cases are published in issues of the *Journal of Law and Education*. The *School Law Yearbook*, published annually by the National Organization of Legal Problems of Education, also contains numerous references to decisions addressing a diverse selection of school law issues.

Shephard's Citations

A court decision's current status may be determined by using an appropriate volume of *Shephard's Citations*. It is possible to ascertain whether a decision has been affirmed, reversed, overruled, vacated, distinguished, or otherwise modified by subsequent court action through the use of this comprehensive system of case citators. A series of bound volumes, paperback supplements, and advance sheets covers state and federal decisions reported in an official or unofficial reporter. Volumes are devoted to United States Supreme Court decisions, United States Courts of Appeals decisions, United States District Court decisions, the various regional reporters in the National Reporter System, and the individual states. Every volume of *Shephard's Citations* follows a similar format utilizing a system of symbols, which is described in the preliminary pages of each volume.

Besides verifying the current status of court decisions, *Shephard's Citations* provides a method by which parallel citations may be determined, the judicial history of a case may be traced, and citations to all subsequent proceedings in a case located. In addition, the citators indicate all subsequent decisions in which a case in question is cited and reveal other research leads, such as periodical and law review articles, attorney general opinions, and annotated reports in which the case is cited.

A system of *Shephard's Citations*, similar to the case citators, is also available to verify the current status of constitutional and statutory provisions. Volumes are devoted to the federal Constitution and statutes and to similar provisions of the individual states, with limited reference to local ordinances contained in the various state volumes. Though use of these citators is considerably more complex than the case citators, similar information is revealed. Subsequent legislative action or court interpretation regarding particular provisions is cited. The legislative and judicial history of a provision may be ascertained to determine whether it has been altered or otherwise affected by such action or interpretation.

Computer-Assisted Services

There are several commercially available, computer-assisted systems for legal research. Presently, these services include *Lexis, Westlaw,* and *Auto-Cite.* Primary advantages of using these services include: eliminating the need for direct access to a law library; availability of a wider selection of law materials than most law libraries contain; availability of decisions from most reporter systems; up-to-date shepardizing; access to major law reviews; capability of parallel citations; and specific topic or subject matter search.

A Final Note

A legal researcher may be confident of the fruits of his or her labors when a systematic use of research tools continues to reveal references which have previously been identified. Depending upon the particular problem or issue being examined, it may not be necessary or practical to employ all of the available research procedures that have been discussed.

appendix c

the constitution of the united states of america—edited

Preamble

We the People of the United States, in Order to form a more perfect Union, establish Justice, insure domestic Tranquility, provide for the common defence, promote the general Welfare, and secure the Blessings of Liberty to ourselves and our Posterity, do ordain and establish this Constitution for the United States of America.

Article I

Section 1. All legislative Powers herein granted shall be vested in a Congress of the United States, which shall consist of a Senate and House of Representatives.

* * *

Section 8. The Congress shall have Power To lay and collect Taxes, Duties, Imposts and Excises, to pay the Debts and provide for the common Defence and general Welfare of the United States; * * * To constitute Tribunals inferior to the supreme Court; * * *

* * *

Section 10. No state shall * * * pass any * * * Law impairing the Obligation of Contracts, * * *

* * *

Article II

Section 1. The executive Power shall be vested in a President of the United States of America. * * *

* * *

Article III

Section 1. The judicial Power of the United States, shall be vested in one supreme Court, and in such inferior Courts as the Congress may from time to time ordain and establish. The Judges, both of the supreme and inferior Courts, shall hold their Offices during good Behavior, and shall, at stated Times, receive for their Services a Compensation, which shall not be diminished during their Continuance in Office.

Section 2. The judicial Power shall extend to all Cases, in Law and Equity, arising under this Constitution, the Laws of the United States, * * * In all Cases affecting Ambassadors, other public Ministers and Consuls, and those in which a State shall be a Party, the supreme Court shall have original Jurisdiction. In all the other Cases before mentioned, the supreme Court shall have appellate Jurisdiction, both as to Law and Fact, with such Exceptions, and under such Regulations as the Congress shall make.

* * *

Article IV

Section 1. Full Faith and Credit shall be given in each State to the public Acts, Records, and judicial Proceedings of every other State. And the Congress may by general Laws prescribe the Manner in which such Acts, Records and Proceedings shall be proved, and the Effect thereof.

Section 2. The Citizens of each State shall be entitled to all Privileges and Immunities of Citizens in the several States. * * *

* * *

Article V

The Congress, whenever two-thirds of both Houses shall deem it necessary, shall propose Amendments to this Constitution, or, on the Application of the Legislatures of two-thirds of the several States, shall call a Convention for proposing Amendments, which, in either Case, shall be valid to all Intents and Purposes, as part of this Constitution, when ratified by the Legislatures of three-fourths of the several States, or by Conventions in three-fourths thereof, as the one or the other Mode of Ratification may be proposed by Congress; Provided that no Amendment which may be made prior to the Year One thousand eight hundred and eight shall in any Manner affect the first and fourth Clauses in the Ninth Section of the first Article; and that no State, without its Consent, shall be deprived of its equal Suffrage in the Senate.

Article VI

* * *

This Constitution, and the Laws of the United States which shall be made in Pursuance thereof; and all Treaties made, or which shall be made, under the Authority of the United States, shall be the supreme Law of the Land; and the Judges in every State shall be bound thereby, any Thing in the Constitution or Laws of any State to the Contrary notwithstanding.

The Senators and Representatives before mentioned, and the Members of the several State Legislatures, and all executive and judicial Officers, both of the United States and of the several States, shall be bound by Oath or Affirmation, to support this Constitution; but no religious Test shall ever be required as a Qualification to any Office or public Trust under the United States.

* * *

Amendment I [1791]

Congress shall make no law respecting an establishment of religion, or prohibiting the free exercise thereof; or abridging the freedom of speech, or of the press; or the right of the people peaceably to assemble, and to petition the Government for a redress of grievances.

* * *

Amendment IV [1791]

The right of the people to be secure in their persons, houses, papers, and effects, against unreasonable searches and seizures, shall not be violated, and no Warrants shall issue, but upon probable cause, supported by Oath or affirmation, and particularly describing the place to be searched, and the persons or things to be seized.

Amendment V [1791]

No person shall * * * be subject for the same offense to be twice put in jeopardy of life or limb; nor shall be compelled in any criminal case to be a witness against himself, nor be deprived of life, liberty, or property, without due process of law; nor shall private property be taken for public use without just compensation.

Amendment VI [1791]

In all criminal prosecutions, the accused shall enjoy the right to a speedy and public trial, by an impartial jury of the State and district wherein the crime shall have been committed, which district shall have been previously ascertained by law, and to be informed of the nature and cause of the accusation: to be confronted with the witnesses against him; to have compulsory process for obtaining witnesses in his favor, and to have the Assistance of Counsel for his defence.

Amendment VII [1791]

In Suits at common law, where the value in controversy shall exceed twenty dollars, the right of trial by jury shall be preserved, and no fact tried by a jury, shall be otherwise reexamined in any Court of the United States, than according to the rules of the common law.

Amendment VIII [1791]

Excessive bail shall not be required, nor excessive fines imposed, nor cruel and unusual punishments inflicted.

Amendment IX [1791]

The enumeration in the Constitution, of certain rights, shall not be construed to deny or disparage others retained by the people.

Amendment X [1791]

The powers not delegated to the United States by the Constitution, nor prohibited by it to the States, are reserved to the States respectively, or to the people.

Amendment XI [1798]

The Judicial power of the United States shall not be construed to extend to any suit in law or equity, commenced or prosecuted against one of the United States by Citizens of another State, or by Citizens or Subjects of any Foreign State.

* * *

Amendment XIII [1865]

Section 1. Neither slavery nor involuntary servitude, except as a punishment for crime whereof the party shall have been duly convicted, shall exist within the United States, or any place subject to their jurisdiction.

Section 2. Congress shall have power to enforce this article by appropriate legislation.

Amendment XIV [1868]

Section 1. All persons born or naturalized in the United States, and subject to the jurisdiction thereof, are citizens of the United States and of the State wherein they reside. No State shall make or enforce any law which shall abridge the privileges or immunities of citizens of the United States; nor shall any State deprive any person of life, liberty, or property, without due process of law; nor deny to any person within its jurisdiction the equal protection of the laws.

* * *

Amendment XV [1870]

Section 1. The right of citizens of the United States to vote shall not be denied or abridged by the United States or by any State on account of race, color, or previous condition of servitude.

Section 2. The Congress shall have power to enforce this article by appropriate legislation.

Amendment XVI [1913]

The Congress shall have power to lay and collect taxes on incomes, from whatever source derived, without apportionment among the several States, and without regard to any census or enumeration.

* * *

Amendment XIX [1920]

Section 1. The right of citizens of the United States to vote shall not be denied or abridged by the United States or by any State on account of sex.

Section 2. Congress shall have power to enforce this article by appropriate legislation.

* * *

Amendment XXIV [1964]

Section 1. The right of citizens of the United States to vote in any primary or other election for President or Vice President, for electors for President or Vice President, or for Senator or Representative in

Congress, shall not be denied or abridged by the United States or any State by reason of failure to pay any poll tax or other tax.

Section 2. The Congress shall have power to enforce this article by appropriate legislation.

* * *

Amendment XXVI [1971]

Section 1. The right of citizens of the United States, who are eighteen years of age or older, to vote shall not be denied or abridged by the United States or by any State on account of age.

Section 2. The Congress shall have power to enforce this article by appropriate legislation.

appendix d

statutory material*

Title VII of the Civil Rights Act of 1964—P.L. 88–352

Discrimination Because of Race, Color, Religion, Sex, or National Origin

SEC. 703. (a) It shall be an unlawful employment practice for an employer—

(1) to fail or refuse to hire or to discharge any individual, or otherwise to discriminate against any individual with respect to his compensation, terms, conditions, or privileges of employment, because of such individual's race, color, religion, sex, or national origin; or

* Statutory material appearing in this appendix is edited. Complete versions may be found in *United States Statutes at Large.* Students requiring the latest text of the law, as amended, are directed to the *United States Code.* Regulations pertaining to these statutes may be found in the *Code of Federal Regulations.*

(2) to limit, segregate, or classify his employees in any way which would deprive or tend to deprive any individual of employment opportunities or otherwise adversely affect his status as an employee, because of such individual's race, color, religion, sex, or national origin.

* * *

(e) * * * (1) it shall not be an unlawful employment practice to hire and employ employees, * * * on the basis of his religion, sex, or national origin in those certain instances where religion, sex, or national origin is a bona fide occupational qualification reasonably necessary to the normal operation of that particular business or enterprise, and (2) it shall not be an unlawful employment practice for a school, college, university, or other educational institution or institution of learning to hire and employ employees of a particular religion if such school, college, university, or other educational institution or institution of learning is, in whole or in substantial part, owned, supported, controlled, or managed by a particular religion or by a particular religious corporation, association, or society, or if the curriculum of such school, college, university, or other educational institution or institution of learning is directed toward the propagation of a particular religion.

* * *

(h) Notwithstanding any other provision of this time, it shall not be an unlawful employment practice for an employer to apply different standards of compensation, or different terms, conditions, or privileges of employment pursuant to a bona fide seniority or merit system, or a system which measures earnings by quantity or quality of production or to employees who work in different locations, provided that such differences are not the result of an intention to discriminate because of race, color, religion, sex, or national origin, nor shall it be an unlawful employment practice for an employer to give and to act upon the results of any professionally developed ability test provided that such test, its administration or action upon the results is not designed, intended or used to discriminate because of race, color, religion, sex or national origin.

(j) Nothing contained in this title shall be interpreted to require * * * preferential treatment to any individual or to any group because of the race, color, religion, sex, or national origin of such individual or group on account of an imbalance which may exist with respect to the total number or percentage of persons of any race, color, religion, sex, or national origin employed by any employer, referred or classified for employment * * * in comparison with the total number or percentage of persons of such race, color, religion, sex, or national origin in any community, State, section, or other area, or in the available work force in any community, State, section, or other area.

* * *

Prevention of Unlawful Employment Practices

SEC. 706.

* * *

(g) If the court finds that the respondent has intentionally engaged in or is intentionally engaging in an unlawful employment practice charged in the complaint, the court may enjoin the respondent from engaging in such unlawful employment practice, and order such affirmative action as may be appropriate, which may include reinstatement or hiring of employees, with or without back pay.

* * *

Effect on State Laws

SEC. 708. Nothing in this title shall be deemed to exempt or relieve any person from any liability, duty, penalty, or punishment provided by any present or future law of any State or political subdivision of a State, other than any such law which purports to require or permit the doing of any act which would be an unlawful employment practice under this title.

* * *

Notices to Be Posted

SEC. 711. (a) Every employer, * * * shall post and keep posted in conspicuous places upon its premises where notices to employees, applicants for employment, and members are customarily posted a notice to be prepared or approved by the Commission setting forth excerpts from or, summaries of, the pertinent provisions of this title and information pertinent to the filing of a complaint.

(b) A willful violation of this section shall be punishable by a fine of not more than $100 for each separate offense.

* * *

Pregnancy Discrimination Act of 1978—P.L. 95–555

Be it enacted by the Senate and House of Representatives of the United States of American in Congress assembled, That section 701 of the Civil Rights Act of 1964 is amended by adding at the end thereof the following new subsection:

"(k) The Terms 'because of sex' or 'on the basis of sex' include, but are not limited to, because of or on the basis of pregnancy, childbirth, or related medical conditions; and women affected by pregnancy, childbirth, or related medical conditions shall be treated the same for all employment-related purposes, including the receipt of benefits under fringe benefit programs, as other persons not so affected but similar in their ability or inability to work, and nothing in section 703(h) of this title shall be interpreted to permit otherwise. This subsection shall not require an employer to pay for health insurance benefits for abortion, except where the life of the mother would be endangered if the fetus were carried to term, or except where medical complications have arisen from an abortion: *Provided,* That nothing herein shall preclude an employer from providing abortion benefits or otherwise affect bargaining agreements in regard to abortion."

* * *

Age Discrimination in Employment Act of 1967—P.L. 90–202

Statement of Findings and Purpose

SEC. 2 (a) The Congress hereby finds and declares that—

(1) in the face of rising productivity and affluence, older workers find themselves disadvantaged in their efforts to retain employment, and especially to regain employment when displaced from jobs;

(2) the setting of arbitrary age limits regardless of potential for job performance has become a common practice, and certain otherwise desirable practices may work to the disadvantage of older persons;

(3) the incidence of unemployment, especially long-term unemployment with resultant deterioration of skill, morale, and employer acceptability is, relative to the younger ages, high among older workers; their numbers are great and growing; and their employment problems grave;

* * *

(b) It is therefore the purpose of this Act to promote employment of older persons based on their ability rather than age; to prohibit arbitrary age discrimination in employment; to help employers and workers find ways of meeting problems arising from the impact of age on employment.

* * *

Prohibition of Age Discrimination

SEC. 4. (a) It shall be unlawful for an employer—

(1) to fail or refuse to hire or to discharge any individual or otherwise discriminate against any individual with respect to his compensation, terms, conditions, or privileges of employment, because of such individual's age;

(2) to limit, segregate, or classify his employees in any way which would deprive or tend to deprive any individual of employment opportunities or otherwise adversely affect his status as an employee, because of such individual's age; or

(3) to reduce the wage rate of any employee in order to comply with this Act.

* * *

(f) It shall not be unlawful for an employer, employment agency, or labor organization—

(1) to take any action otherwise prohibited * * * where age is a bona fide occupational qualification reasonably necessary to the normal operation of the particular business, or where the differentiation is based on reasonable factors other than age;

(2) to observe the terms of a bona fide seniority system or any bona fide employee benefit plan such as a retirement, pension, or insurance plan, which is not a subterfuge to evade the purposes of this Act, except that no such employee benefit plan shall excuse the failure to hire any individual; or

(3) to discharge or otherwise discipline an individual for good cause.

* * *

Age Discrimination in Employment Act Amendments of 1978— P.L. 95–256

Seniority Systems and Employee Benefit Plans

SEC. 2. (a) Section 4(f) (2) of the Age Discrimination in Employment Act of 1967 * * * is amended by inserting after "individual" a comma and the following: "and no such seniority system or employee benefit plan shall require or permit the involuntary retirement of any individual specified * * * because of the age of such individual".

* * *

SEC. 3 (a) Section 12 of the Age Discrimination in Employment Act of 1967 (29 U.S.C. 631) is amended to read as follows:

* * *

"SEC. 12. (a) The prohibitions in this Act shall be limited to individuals who are at least 40 years of age but less than 70 years of age.

* * *

"(d) Nothing in this Act shall be construed to prohibit compulsory retirement of any employee who has attained 65 years of age but not 70 years of age, and who is serving under a contract of unlimited tenure * * * at an institution of higher education."

* * *

Age Discrimination in Employment Act Amendments of 1986— P.L. 99–592

* * *

SEC. 6. Special Rule for Tenured Faculty.

(a) SPECIAL RULE.—Section 12 of the Age Discrimination in Employment Act of 1967 (29 U.S.C. 631) is amended by adding at the end thereof the following new subsection:

"(d) Nothing in this Act shall be construed to prohibit compulsory retirement of any employee who has attained 70 years of age, and who is serving under a contract of unlimited tenure (or similar arrangement providing for unlimited tenure) at an institution of higher education (as defined by section 1201(a) of the Higher Education Act of 1965)."

(b) TERMINATION PROVISION.—The amendment made by subsection (a) of this section is repealed December 31, 1993.

* * *

Title IX of the Education Amendments of 1972—P.L. 92–318

Sex Discrimination Prohibited

SEC. 901. (a) No person in the United States shall, on the basis of sex, be excluded from participation in, be denied the benefits of, or be subjected to discrimination under any education program or activity receiving Federal financial assistance, except that:

(1) in regard to admissions to educational institutions, this section shall apply only to institutions of vocational education, professional education, and graduate higher education, and to public institutions of undergraduate higher education;

* * *

(3) this section shall not apply to an educational institution which is controlled by a religious organization if the application of this subsection would not be consistent with the religious tenets of such organization;

(4) this section shall not apply to an educational institution whose primary purpose is the training of individuals for the military services of the United States, or the merchant marine; and

(5) in regard to admissions this section shall not apply to any public institution of undergraduate higher education which is an institution that traditionally and continually from its establishment has had a policy of admitting only students of one sex.

(b) Nothing contained in subsection (a) of this section shall be interpreted to require any educational institution to grant preferential or disparate treatment to the members of one sex on account of an imbalance which may exist with respect to the total number or percentage of persons of that sex participating in or receiving the benefits of any federally supported program or activity, in comparison with the total number or percentage of persons of that sex in any community, State, section, or other area: *Provided,* That this subsection shall not be construed to prevent the consideration in any hearing or proceeding under this title of statistical evidence tending to show that such an imbalance exists with respect to the participation in, or receipt of the benefits of, any such program or activity by the members of one sex.

(c) For purposes of this title an educational institution means any public or private preschool, elementary, or secondary school, or any institution of vocational, professional, or higher education, except that in the case of an educational institution composed of more than one school, college, or department which are administratively separate units, such term means each such school, college, or department.

* * *

Section 504 of the Rehabilitation Act of 1973—P.L. 93–112

Nondiscrimination under Federal Grants

SEC. 504 No otherwise qualified handicapped individual in the United States, as defined in section 7(6), shall, solely by reason of his handicap, be excluded from the participation in, be denied the benefits of, or be subjected to discrimination under any program or activity receiving Federal financial assistance.

Family Educational Rights and Privacy Act of 1974—P.L. 93-380

Protection of the Rights and Privacy of Parents and Students

SEC. 438 (a) (1) No funds shall be made available under any applicable program to any State or local educational agency, any institution of higher education, any community college, any school, agency offering a preschool program, or any other educational institution which has a policy of denying, or which effectively prevents, the parents of students attending any school of such agency, or attending such institution of higher education, community college, school, preschool, or other educational institution, the right to inspect and review any and all official records, files, and data directly related to their children, including all material that is incorporated into each student's cumulative record folder, and intended for school use or to be available to parties outside the school or school system, and specifically including, but not necessarily limited to, identifying data, academic work completed, level of achievement (grades, standardized achievement test scores), attendance data, scores on standardized intelligence, aptitude, and psychological tests, interest inventory results, health data, family background information, teacher or counselor ratings and observations, and verified reports of serious or recurrent behavior patterns. Where such records or data include information on more than one student, the parents of any student shall be entitled to receive, or be informed of, that part of such record or data as pertains to their child. Each recipient shall establish appropriate procedures for the granting of a request by parents for access to their child's school records within a reasonable period of time, but in no case more than forty-five days after the request has been made.

(2) Parents shall have an opportunity for a hearing to challenge the content of their child's school records, to insure that the records are not inaccurate, misleading, or otherwise in violation of the privacy or other rights of students, and to provide an opportunity for the correction or deletion of any such inaccurate, misleading, or otherwise inappropriate data contained therein.

(b)(1) No funds shall be made available under any applicable program to any State or local educational agency, any institution of higher education, any community college, any school, agency offering a preschool program, or any other educational institution which has a policy of permitting the release of personally identifiable records or files (or personal information contained therein) of students without the written consent of their parents to any individual, agency, or organization, other than to the following—

(A) other school officials, including teachers within the educational institutional or local educational agency who have legitimate educational interests;

(B) officials of other schools or school systems in which the student intends to enroll, upon condition that the student's parents be notified of the transfer, receive a copy of the record if desired, and have an opportunity for a hearing to challenge the content of the record;

(C) authorized representatives of (i) the Comptroller General of the United States, (ii) the Secretary, (iii) an administrative head of an education agency (as defined in section 409 of this Act), or (iv) State educational authorities, under the conditions set forth in paragraph (3) of this subsection; and

(D) in connection with a student's application for, or receipt of, financial aid.

(2) No funds shall be made available under any applicable program to any State or local educational agency, any institution of higher education, any community college, any school, agency offering a preschool program, or any other educational institution which has a policy or practice of furnishing, in any form, any personally identifiable information contained in personal school records, to any persons other than those listed in subsection (b)(1) unless—

(A) there is written consent from the student's parents specifying records to be released, the reasons for such release, and to whom, and with a copy of the records to be released to the student's parents and the student if desired by the parents, or

(B) such information is furnished in compliance with judicial order, or pursuant to any lawfully issued subpoena, upon condition that parents and the students are notified of all such orders or subpoenas in advance of the compliance therewith by the educational institution or agency.

* * *

(4)(A) * * * all persons, agencies, or organizations desiring access to the records of a student shall be required to sign a written form which shall be kept permanently with the file of the student, but only for inspection by the parents or student, indicating specifically the legitimate educational or other interest that each person, agency, or organization has in seeking this information. Such form shall be available to parents and to the school official responsible for record maintenance as a means of auditing the operation of the system.

(B) * * * personal information shall only be transferred to a third party on the condition that such party will not permit any other party to have access to such information without the written consent of the parents of the student.

* * *

(d) For the purposes of this section, whenever a student has attained eighteen years of age, or is attending an institution of postsecondary education the permission or consent required of and the rights accorded to the parents of the student shall thereafter only be required of and accorded to the student.

(e) No funds shall be made available under any applicable program unless the recipient of such funds informs the parents of students, or the students, if they are eighteen years of age or older, or are attending an institution of postsecondary education, of the rights accorded them by this section.

* * *

Note: An amendment (P.L. 93–568) defined "directory information" to include the following: student's name, address, telephone listing, date and place of birth, major field of study, participation in officially recognized activities and sports, weight and height of members of athletic teams, dates of attendance, degrees and awards of attendance, degrees and awards received, and the most recent previous educational agency or institution attended by the student.

Equal Access Act of 1984—P.L. 98–377

Denial of Equal Access Prohibited

SEC. 802. (a) It shall be unlawful for any public secondary school which receives Federal financial assistance and which has a limited open forum to deny equal access or a fair opportunity to, or discriminate against, any students who wish to conduct a meeting within that limited open forum on the basis of the religious, political, philosophical, or other content of the speech at such meetings.

(b) A public secondary school has a limited open forum whenever such school grants an offering to or opportunity for one or more noncurriculum related students groups to meet on school premises during noninstructional time.

(c) Schools shall be deemed to offer a fair opportunity to students who wish to conduct a meeting within its limited open forum if such school uniformly provides that—

(1) the meeting is voluntary and student-initiated;

(2) there is no sponsorship of the meeting by the school, the government, or its agents or employees;

(3) employees or agents of the school or government are present at religious meetings only in a nonparticipatory capacity;

(4) the meeting does not materially and substantially interfere with the orderly conduct of educational activities within the school; and

(5) nonschool persons may not direct, conduct, control, or regularly attend activities of student groups.

(d) Nothing in this title shall be construed to authorize the United States or any State or political subdivision thereof—

(1) to influence the form or content of any prayer or other religious activity;

(2) to require any person to participate in prayer or other religious activity;

(3) to expend public funds beyond the incidental cost of providing the space for student-initiated meetings;

(4) to compel any school agent or employee to attend a school meeting if the content of the speech at the meeting is contrary to the beliefs of the agent or employee;

(5) to sanction meetings that are otherwise unlawful;

(6) to limit the rights of groups of students which are not of a specified numerical size; or

(7) to abridge the constitutional rights of any person.

(e) Notwithstanding the availability of any other remedy under the Constitution or the laws of the United States, nothing in this title shall be construed to authorize the United States to deny or withhold Federal financial assistance to any school.

(f) Nothing in this title shall be construed to limit the authority of the school, its agents or employees, to maintain order and discipline on school premises, to protect the well-being of students and faculty, and to assure that attendance of students at meetings is voluntary.

Definitions

SEC. 803. As used in this title—

(1) The term "secondary school" means a public school which provides secondary education as determined by State law.

(2) The term "sponsorship" includes the act of promoting, leading, or participating in a meeting. The assignment of a teacher, administrator,

or other school employee to a meeting for custodial purposes does not constitute sponsorship of the meeting.

(3) The term "meeting" includes those activities of student groups which are permitted under a school's limited open forum and are not directly related to the school curriculum.

(4) The term "noninstructional time" means time set aside by the school before actual classroom instruction begins or after actual classroom instruction ends.

* * *

Civil Rights—42 U.S.C. § 1981–1983*

§ 1981. Equal Rights under the Law

All persons within the jurisdiction of the United States shall have the right in every State and Territory to make and enforce contracts, to sue, be parties, give evidence, and to full and equal benefit of all laws and proceedings for the security of persons and property as is enjoyed by white citizens, and shall be subject to like punishment, pains, penalties, taxes, licenses, and exactions of every kind, and to no other.

§ 1982. Property Rights of Citizens

All citizens of the United States shall have the same right, in every State and Territory, as is enjoyed by white citizens thereof to inherit, purchase, lease, sell, hold, and convey real and personal property.

§ 1983. Civil Action for Deprivation of Rights

Every person who, under color of any statute, ordinance, regulation, custom or usage, of any State or Territory or the District of Columbia, subjects, or causes to be subjected, any citizen of the United States or other person within the jurisdiction thereof to the deprivation of any rights, privileges, or immunities secured by the Constitution and laws, shall be liable to the party injured in an action at law, suit in equity, or other proper proceeding for redress. * * *

* Original versions of these statutes were enacted shortly after the Civil War.

glossary

Action A proceeding in a court of law, often referred to as a suit or lawsuit.

Ad litem A guardian ad litem is one appointed to prosecute or defend a suit on behalf of a party incapacitated by infancy or otherwise.

Advisory opinion An opinion rendered by a court when no actual case is before it. Although some state courts render advisory opinions, the United States Supreme Court and lower federal courts do not.

Affirm To approve or uphold a lower court's judgment.

Amicus curiae A friend of the court. Generally, one who has an indirect interest in a case and offers or is requested to provide information to the court in order to clarify particular matters before the court.

Appeal An application to a higher court to amend a lower court's ruling.

Appellant One who takes an appeal to a higher court. The appellant may have been the plaintiff or defendant in the lower court proceeding.

Appellee The party in an action against whom an appeal has been sought. Sometimes also called the respondent.

Bill A formal written statement or complaint filed in a court.

Case law A body of law created by judicial decisions. By establishing precedents upon which courts rely, the case law provides a primary source of legal authority.

Certiorari A judicial process whereby a case is removed from a lower court to a higher court for review. The record of the proceedings is transmitted to the higher court.

Civil action A court action brought to gain or to recover individual or civil rights or to obtain redress for an alleged noncriminal injustice.

Class action A court action brought by one or more individuals on behalf of themselves and all others who have a similar interest in a particular issue.

Code A systematic compilation of statutes, usually incorporating an indexing procedure to facilitate location of pertinent provisions.

Collateral attack An attempt to challenge the credibility or validity of a judicial proceeding based on related or incidental issues.

Common law A system of law in which authority is not derived expressly from statutes. Rather, traditional legal principles are derived from usage and custom as enunciated by court decisions.

Compensatory damages Damages awarded to reimburse the injured party only for the actual loss incurred. Punitive or exemplary damages are not considered compensatory.

Complaint A formal pleading to a court demanding relief as well as informing the defendant of the grounds of the suit.

Concurring opinion An opinion written by a judge expressing agreement with the majority's holding. However, the concurring judge may disagree with the majority's reasoning or discuss additional principles or points of law.

Conflict of laws An area of law dealing with the clarification of inconsistencies and differences in laws or jurisdictions as they apply to the rights of individuals in particular actions.

Consent decree An agreement by parties to a dispute, and although not properly a judicial sentence, it is in effect an admission by them that the decree is a just determination of their rights based upon the facts of the case.

Constitution The supreme fundamental law of a nation or state. Provisions are included to establish and organize the government and to distribute, limit, and prescribe the manner of the exercise of sovereign powers. In addition, basic principles and rights of the citizenry are enumerated.

Court of record A court whose actions are recorded, possessing the authority to levy sanctions.

Criminal action A court action, brought by the state, against one charged with an offense against the state. This type of action may result in a fine or incarceration of the defendant.

Damages The compensation or indemnity claimed by the plaintiff or allowed by the court for injuries sustained as a result of a wrongful act or negligence of another.

De facto In fact. A state of affairs that must be accepted for all practical purposes, but does not have the sanction of laws behind it. As distinguished from de jure.

De jure By right. A legitimate state of affairs that has the force of law behind it.

De minimis Trifling or insignificant matters, with which a court will not concern itself.

De novo Anew, afresh, a second time. A second trial of a case that has been sent back from a higher court for a new trial.

Decision A conclusion or judgment of a court, as opposed to the reasoning or opinion of the court.

Declaratory judgment Without issuing an order for anything to be done, a court clarifies questions of law, recognizes the rights of the parties, or expresses an opinion.

Decree A court order issued in an equity suit.

Defendant The party against whom an action is brought.

Demurrer An allegation by a defendant admitting that although the facts are correct, a suit is not justified nor do they require an answer by the defendant.

Dictum (obiter dictum) An opinion expressed by a judge in a proceeding that is not necessary in formulating the court's decision. Therefore, it does not establish binding precedent. However, it may indicate the judge's persuasion.

Dismissal A final disposition of a suit by a court by sending it out of court without a trial of the issues.

Dissenting opinion An opinion written by a judge in disagreement with the rationale and/or decision of the majority of judges hearing the case.

Due process of law Implies that the powers of the government are exercised similarly in similar situations in order to protect individual's rights. Denial of this right is prohibited by the Fifth and Fourteenth Amendments when life, liberty, or property are involved.

En banc A proceeding in which all judges of a court participate in the decision.

Enjoin An individual or institution is required by a court of equity to cease or abstain from a particular action. See Injunction.

Equal protection of the law A guarantee that no person or class of persons shall be denied the same protection of the laws that is enjoyed by other persons or classes in similar circumstances. Denial of this right is prohibited by the Fourteenth Amendment.

Equity law A particular branch of law that differs from the common law. Primarily concerned with providing justice and fair treatment, equity law addresses issues the common law is unable to consider.

Et al. And others. Indicates that unnamed parties are involved in the proceedings.

Ex parte A proceeding for the benefit of one party only.

Ex post facto After the fact, often thought of in terms of a law making an act illegal after someone has committed the act.

Ex rel. Designates a private individual on whose behalf the state is acting in a legal proceeding.

Exclusionary rule A procedure in search-and-seizure cases seeking to suppress the use of evidence which has been improperly obtained.

Finding A conclusion of a court or jury regarding a question of fact.

Governmental immunity (See Sovereign immunity).

Hearing Judicial examination of factual or legal issues.

In loco parentis In place of the parent. Possessing a portion of the parent's rights, duties, and responsibilities.

In re In the matter of. A method of entitling a judicial proceeding in which there are no adversaries.

Injunction An order issued by a court of equity prohibiting a person from committing a threatened act or continuing to do some act that is injurious to the plaintiff.

Inter alia Among other things.

Ipso facto By the fact itself. As a necessary consequence.

Judgment A decision rendered by a court.

Liability A legal responsibility.

Litigation The formal contesting of a dispute in a court, a lawsuit.

Majority opinion The statement expressing the views of the majority of judges in a court decision.

Malfeasance Commission of an unlawful act.

Mandamus A court order compelling a public official or institution to perform a particular nondiscretionary duty.

Mandate A judicial command, order, or direction.

Minority opinion A statement expressing the views of a judge or a minority of judges in a court decision. This may take the form of separate minority opinions.

Misfeasance Improper performance of a lawful act.

Negligence Failure to exercise ordinary prudence and foresight when such failure results in an injury to another.

Nolens volens Whether willing or unwilling.

Nonfeasance Failure to perform a required duty.

Nuisance Continuous private or public use of property that results in injury, inconvenience, or damage.

Original jurisdiction The jurisdiction of a court to entertain a case at its inception, as contrasted with appellate jurisdiction.

Parens patriae The state as a sovereign—referring to the sovereign power of guardianship over persons such as minors.

Per curiam An opinion rendered by an entire court, as opposed to an opinion of any one of several justices.

Petition A written application to a court for the redress of a wrong or the grant of a privilege or license.

Petitioner One who presents a petition to a court.

Plaintiff One who brings an action or files a complaint in a court.

Plea A formal allegation filed by a defendant in an action in reply to the plaintiff's complaint or charges.

Pleadings Formal documents filed in a court action. They include the plaintiff's complaint and the defendant's reply, indicating that which is alleged by one party and denied or conceded by the other party.

Plenary Full, entire, complete.

Prayer A request by the plaintiff that the court of equity grant the particular relief sought.

Precedent Previously decided authoritative court decisions addressing identical or similar questions of law.

Prima facie At first view, before investigation. A fact presumed to be true unless disproved by some evidence to the contrary.

Pro se In person, in their own behalf.

Quasi As if. Almost as it were, analogous to.

Quid pro quo   A consideration, giving one valuable thing for another.

Relief   Legal redress or assistance sought in court by the complainant.

Remand   To send back. Following an appellate decision a case may be sent back to the court from which it came for further proceedings.

Remedy   A court's enforcement of a right or the prevention of the violation of a right.

Res ipsa loquitur   The thing speaks for itself.

Res judicata   A matter judicially decided.

Respondent   The party against whom an appeal is taken in a higher court.

Restrain   To enjoin or prohibit.

Sovereign immunity   A doctrine providing that a governmental body is immune to suit without the expressed permission of the body itself.

Standing   The right to raise an issue in a lawsuit.

Stare decisis   To stand by decided cases. The doctrine whereby precedent assumes the authority of established law.

Status quo   The existing state of affairs.

Statute   An act of the state or federal legislature, a law.

Sub nom.   A different case name in subsequent judicial history.

Sui generis   Of its own kind or class, unique.

Suit   A proceeding in a court of law brought by a plaintiff.

Summary judgment   A court's decision to settle a controversy or dispose of a case promptly without conducting full legal proceedings.

Tort   A private or civil wrong or injury.

Trial   The examination of a civil or criminal case by a competent tribunal. It may be made by a judge or judges, with or without a jury.

Ultra vires   Exceeding the power or authority.

Vacate   To cancel or rescind a court decision.

Void   Without force or binding effect. Absolutely null.

Waive   To forego, renounce, or abandon a legal right. By waiver, the right is lost.

Writ   A written court order requiring performance of a specific act, such as a writ of injunction or mandamus.

index

Academic freedom, 207, 213, 219
Affirmative action, 252, 259, 312
Age discrimination acts, 428–30
AIDS, 154, 275
Appearance, 135, 139, 220, 266
Attorney general opinions, 12, 14–15, 275, 413

Baccalaureate services, 48
Benedictions, 49
Bible reading, 5, 12, 30, 36
Board of education, state, 14, 412
"Briefing," 404
Buckley amendment, 432

Catheterization, clean intermittent, 152
Censorship. *See* Freedom of expression.
Chief state school officer, 14
Church and State, separation of. *See* Religion and education.
Civil Rights Act of 1871, 383, 436
Civil Rights Act of 1964, Title VII, 251, 265, 425
Classification, suspect, 10, 354, 370
Collective bargaining, 13, 275
Communicable diseases, 72, 154, 274–75
Compulsory education, 22, 64
Constitution, federal, 418
Corporal punishment, 116, 381
"Corporate due process," 189
Courts of appeals, U.S., 18
Court systems, 16, 17, 410
Creationism, 50
Criminal activities, teachers', 241

Department of education, state, 14
Desegregation, 288
Directory information, 434
Discrimination
  age, 266, 428–30
  employment, 251
  handicapped, 143, 273. *See also Rehabilitation Act of 1973, Section 504.*
  racial, 252, 288. *See also* Civil Rights Act of 1964, Title VII.
  religious. *See* Religion and education.
  sex, 142, 169, 254. *See also* Educational Amendments of 1972, Title IX; Pregnancy Discrimination Act of 1978.
Dismissal, teacher. *See* Teachers, dismissal
District courts, U.S., 18
Dress, 135, 220, 266
Drug testing, 134, 219
Due process, 4, 6, 12, 13, 16, 77, 102, 111, 116, 122, 123, 153, 160, 179, 183, 251, 259

Education Amendments of 1972, Title IX, 11, 142, 251, 430
Education and religion. *See* Religion and education.
Education for All Handicapped Children Act of 1975, 144, 153, 154, 178. *See also* Handicapped students.
Equal Access Act, 49, 434
Equality of educational opportunity, 351, 369
Equal protection, 4, 6, 9, 12, 16, 59, 72, 92, 159, 166, 170, 251, 252, 253, 299, 303, 351, 369, 371, 377
Evolution, 50
Expulsion, 112, 153
Extra-curricular participation, 160, 176

Facilities, use of, 59, 266
Family Educational Rights and Privacy Act of 1974 (Buckley amendment), 432
Fees, 68, 72
Finance, school, 351
Flag salute, 99–100. *See also* Freedom of expression.
Fourteenth Amendment, 4, 6, 86, 123, 159, 166, 170, 251, 259, 303, 369, 377
Free appropriate education, 145
Freedom of choice, 27, 307
Freedom of expression
  students, 77, 92, 99
  teachers, 189, 197, 285
  users of facilities, 59
Fundamental interest, 10, 354

"Gangs," 92
General Welfare Clause, 10, 419
Grooming, 139

Handicapped students, 143
  clean intermittent catheterization, 152
  Education for All Handicapped Children Act of 1975, 144, 153, 154, 178
  expulsion and suspension, 153
  extracurricular activities, 176
  free appropriate education, 145
  individual educational program (IEP), 153
  "mainstreaming," 144, 152
  placement, 153
  "stay put" provision, 153
Hobbes, Thomas, 8
Home instruction, 28
Homosexuality, 226

Immunity, governmental, 382
Immunization, 72
Individual educational program (IEP), 153
Invocations, 49

Law, sources of, 3
Liability, 381
Libraries, removal of books from, 213
Literature, religious, 57
Locke, John, 8
Locker search, 123

"Mainstreaming," 144, 152
Malpractice, educational, 401
Marriage, student, 142
Maternity leave, teacher, 265
Meditation, 40

Negligence, 395
Newspapers, school, 92
Nonpublic schools, 22, 27, 28, 65, 66, 86,
    289, 307
"No pass, no play" rules, 166

Parenthood, student, 142. See also
    Pregnancy, student.
Patriotic exercises, 99
"Pickering balance," 196
Plays, school, 98, 99
Prayer, 5, 12, 30, 36, 40, 47, 49, 72
Pregnancy
    student, 9, 11, 142, 251
    teacher, 11, 251, 259, 265, 427
Pregnancy Discrimination Act of 1978,
    11, 251, 259, 427
Private schools. See Nonpublic schools.
Punishment for out-of-school offenses, 178

Rehabilitation Act of 1973, Section 504,
    11, 144, 154, 159, 178, 251, 431
Released time, 57
Religion and education, 30
    baccalaureate services, 48
    beneditions, 49
    Bible reading, 5, 12, 30, 36
    creationism, 50
    discrimination against teachers, 265
    dress, 266
    Equal Access Act, 49, 434
    evolution, 50
    holidays, 48
    immunization, 72
    invocations, 49
    literature, distribution of, 57
    meditation, 40
    meetings on school property, 266
    nonpublic schools, aid to, 65
    prayer, 5, 12, 30, 36, 40, 47, 49, 72
    released time, 57
    shared time, 57
    Ten Commandments display, 47
    textbooks, parents' objections to, 56
Rousseau, Jean Jacques, 8
Rules of Conduct for Teachers, 225

School system, dual, 288, 312, 336, 348
Searches, 123, 219
Segregation
    de facto, 303, 323, 336
    de jure, 5, 252, 288, 298, 303, 323,
        336, 348, 350
"Separate but equal," 288, 323
Shared time, 57
Social contract theory, 8
Socratic method, xxiv
States right theory, 6
"Stay put" provision, 153
Strict-scrutiny test, 10, 72, 371
Strikes by teachers, 276
Students
    appearance, 135, 139
    extra-curricular participation, 160
    expulsion, 112
    fees, 68
    "gangs," 92
    handicapped. See Handicapped students.
    marriage, 142
    parenthood, 142. See also Pregnancy,
        student.
    punishment for out-of-school offenses,
        178
    search of, 123
    suspension, 102
    transfer, disciplinary, 116
Suspension, 102, 153

Teachers
    appearance, 220, 266
    collective bargaining, 13, 275
    competency tests, 253–54
    criminal activities, 241
    discrimination, religious, 265
    dismissal, 13, 183, 196, 225, 240, 250,
        276
    exemplar, 225
    homosexual, 226
    immoral conduct, 246
    impropriety with students, 246
    maternity leave, 265
    meetings, religious, 266
    political activities, 285
    pregnancy, 11, 251, 259, 265, 427
    Rules of Conduct for, 225
    search of, 219
    strikes, 276
    union dues, 281
Ten Commandments display, 47
Tests, teacher competency, 253–54
Textbooks, parents' objections to, 56
"Time-out" box, use of, 111
Title VII of the Civil Rights Act of 1964,
    251, 265, 425
Title IX of the Education Amendments
    of 1972, 11, 142, 251, 430
Torts, 381
Transfer, disciplinary, 116

"Unitary status," 348, 349, 350
Union dues, 281